MW01716632

Using Application Software in Business

Using the IBM PC
VP-Planner Plus
dBASE III PLUS
WordPerfect 4.2

Kathleen A. Dolan

Keiko M. Pitter

Mitchell McGRAW-HILL
New York St. Louis San Francisco Auckland Bogotá Caracas
Hamburg Lisbon London Madrid Mexico Milan Montreal
New Delhi Oklahoma City Paris San Juan São Paulo Singapore
Sydney Tokyo Toronto Watsonville

Using Application Software in Business

1 2 3 4 5 6 7 8 9 0 VH VH 9 5 4 3 2 1 0

P/N: 050262-5

ORDER INFORMATION*
ISBN 0-07-909777-4: Text with 3½" Data Disk
ISBN 0-07-909776-6: Text with 5¼" Data Disk
ISBN 0-07-836098-6: Text with 3½" Data Disk and BUSINESS COMPUTER SYSTEMS, 4/e, Kroenke and Dolan
ISBN 0-07-836099-4: Text with 5¼" Data Disk and BUSINESS COMPUTER SYSTEMS, 4/e, Kroenke and Dolan

*The McGraw-Hill Software Pack, featuring the educational versions of VP-Planner Plus, dBASE III PLUS, and WordPerfect 4.2, is available with any of the options listed above: ISBN 0-07-835745-4 for 5¼"; ISBN 0-07-835771-3 for 3½". Ask your McGraw-Hill representative for details.

The sponsoring editor was Erika Berg.
The production manager was Betty Drury.
The cover design was by John Edeen.
The production was supervised by Greg Hubit.
Graphics West was the typesetter.
Von Hoffmann Press was the printer and binder.

Library of Congress Card Catalog No.: 89-62691

Brief Contents

Module 4 WordPerfect 343

Detailed Contents

Module 4 WordPerfect 343

Preface

Introductory computer courses have changed over the years, adjusting to the changing needs of the students. Ten years ago students were either data processing majors—in need of much technical training—or future business users of large mainframe systems, dependent on technicians and sheltered from much contact with computer "stuff." Today's students are very different from those two groups.

Today's students need to learn how to use information systems to enhance their job performance. They need to know what tools are available to help them be more productive. They need to learn how to use a computer as a piece of business equipment. They need to become conversant with today's technology. They need to be smart shoppers, savvy consumers of both hardware and software.

In conjunction with the fourth edition of *Business Computer Systems* by Kroenke and Dolan, *Using Application Software in Business* helps address many of the needs of today's students. Throughout this tutorial, students learn how to use MS-DOS, VP-Planner PLUS (a Lotus 1-2-3- "clone"), dBASE III PLUS, and WordPerfect 4.2.

This tutorial follows the highly praised methodology used by Keiko Pitter in her series of personal software tutorials: step-by-step instructions, brief but lucid explanations, reinforcement through practice sessions, and end-of-lesson exercises to help students pull together their new knowledge.

In addition, *Using Application Software in Business* includes illustrations, examples, practice sessions, and exercises related directly to *Business Computer Systems.* Thus, students have a unique opportunity to experience hands-on what they have read about in the text, or seen illustrated in figures and screen displays. Using this tutorial to supplement the text is like watching a moving picture rather than a set of still photographs. It helps the text come alive.

This tutorial is presented in four modules. The first module introduces the student to the IBM PC and to DOS. The remaining three modules parallel Chapters 5, 6, and 7 in *Business Computer Systems.* Module 2 presents VP-Planner PLUS; Module 3 presents dBASE III PLUS; and Module 4 presents WordPerfect 4.2

SOFTWARE REQUIREMENTS

Available with this tutorial are several diskettes which contain the educational versions of the software packages presented. The BCS Data Diskette contains examples and illustrations taken directly from *Business Computer Systems.* The student also will need a DOS disk or access to DOS through a network, and a scratch disk. (A scratch disk contains information no longer needed.)

HARDWARE REQUIREMENTS

The student will need an IBM PC (or PC compatible) with 256K bytes of RAM (384K if you are using dBASE III PLUS with DOS version 3.0 or higher). A monochrome or color monitor, two floppy drives, and a printer also are required.

ACKNOWLEDGMENTS

I extend much gratitude to the staff at Mitchell Publishing, Inc.: Erika Berg, Raleigh Wilson, and especially Roger Howell. I thank Greg Hubit of Bookworks for his great patience and understanding. Ralph Moore of Modesto Junior College, Jane Ewing of Independence Community College, and Les Hayes of Pima Community College reviewed the first edition of *Using Application Software* and gave me suggestions for changes. Don Myers of Vincennes University, Raj Gill of Anne Arundel Community College, and Claudia Duncan of Heald Business College reviewed the manuscript and made many thoughtful suggestions. I thank you all very much. Moreover, I extend much gratitude to all those instructors from across the country who were in my classes at the National Computer Educator's Institute at James Madison University in the summer of 1988 and at Central State University in the summer of 1989, for giving me ideas on ways to improve the manual. Last but not least, I'd like to thank Marianne Taflinger, the Marketing Director at Mitchell Publishing, for keeping me straight on user expectations and giving me support and friendship.

As always, I thank my children Greg and Jackie for understanding Mom and somehow growing up and maturing without much help from me.

Keiko Pitter

Keiko Pitter's understanding of personal productivity software is inspirational. What a pleasure to work with a text that so many have used to learn about these wonderful tools we call microcomputers. I am grateful to Keiko for generously allowing her work to be adapted to *Business Computer Systems.* The result of this endeavor is a complete system that students can use to gain a firm foundation in computer technology.

Finally, my acknowledgments would be incomplete without expressing my gratitude to Erika Berg of Mitchell Publishing for keeping me on schedule, and for doling out the "way-to-gos" just when they were needed. Thanks, Erika.

Kathleen A. Dolan

MODULE 1

Using the IBM PC

1

Introduction

You walk into a computer store and the salesperson says, "Sit down and try it." You wave your hand and walk away. You are at a computer demonstration and you are asked to come up and press some keys. You shake your head. You are envious as you watch other people work with the computer. You know that computers are here to stay. You know that one of these days you have to learn how to use one. Yet, you won't even try.

Your introduction to using computers may seem to be a combination of fascination and horror. You have read about all that a computer can do. At the same time, you have seen movies in which computers subdue mankind and rule the world, or a computer with a mind of its own ruin the credit rating for someone it didn't like. However, the fantasy of the computer doing something on its own is rapidly disappearing. Many people today understand that a computer is a tool which *people* use to accomplish *their* objectives. The computer will do what people tell it to do. People understand that, for the most part, there is no such thing as "computer error," just "people error." That is why the greatest fears many beginners have are damaging the computer or disks, or not knowing what to do next (which key to press).

This first module will help you to understand what a computer is, and how to treat the computer and disks to avoid damage. By learning these things, you will also avoid many problems related to not knowing what to do. The module also covers the disk operating system (DOS)—the commands you use to access and manage information on the computer. It provides easy ways for you to find the content of a floppy disk or copy data from one disk to another. If you are planning to use computers in any serious way at all, you need to learn DOS.

To study this module, you will need a DOS disk and a scratch disk. The DOS disk should be MS-DOS or PC-DOS. A scratch disk is a blank disk or one whose content you no longer need. The instructions on how to use DOS are given within this module.

Lesson 1
Components of the IBM PC

Objectives

Upon completion of the material presented in this lesson, you should understand the following features and processes:

- Know the function of a computer.
- Be able to identify and state the function of various components of a computer.
- Know how to turn the computer on and off.
- Be familiar with a computer keyboard.

Supplies Needed

For this part of the manual you need

- The DOS disk: A DOS disk is the one that accompanies the computer at the time of purchase.

FUNCTION OF A COMPUTER

The function of a computer is to process data and produce a result. Data includes any raw facts you enter into the computer for processing. The result of processing is the processed data, or **information**, presented in a format (or medium) that people, computers, or other machines can use.

This means a computer system not only processes data but also must provide ways for data to be entered (**input**) and for the results to be produced (**output**).

IBM PC with two disk drives

The components discussed here are as follows:

Processing Components
- Microprocessor (MPU)
- Random Access Memory (RAM)
- Read Only Memory (ROM)
- Peripheral Interfaces and Expansion Boards

Output Components
- Printer
- Monitor
- Disk Drive(s)
- Modem

Input Components
- Keyboard
- Mouse
- Disk Drive(s)
- Modem

PROCESSING COMPONENTS

The inside of the computer contains circuit boards much like those in the accompanying photograph. A number of options are available for the IBM PC, so the way your computer is configured may be slightly different from the configuration of the system illustrated here.

MPU

Inside the computer are little black rectangular boxes arranged over several boards. The large board on the bottom is the **motherboard**, which connects all the individual pieces electronically. The black rectangular boxes are called **integrated circuits**, or **chips**.

One of the larger chips on the motherboard is the **microprocessing unit**, or the **MPU**. Inside the MPU is the circuitry needed to do addition, subtraction, and comparison—functions that a computer performs. In the IBM PC this is an Intel 8088, 80286, or 80386 chip. The number refers to the design of a specific model of chip. Other microcomputers use different chips: for example, Apple IIGS uses 65C816 and Apple Macintosh uses a Motorola 68000.

The Intel 80286 and 80386 are newer generations of the 8088 chip. A machine with an 80286 chip can process information faster than a machine with an 8088 chip, and an 80386 machine can process information much faster than on an 80286 machine.

Inside of IBM PC

Main Memory

A computer also must store information while data is being processed. That storage place is called **main memory**. The main memory is on the chips. There are two types of main memory—**Random Access Memory (RAM)** and **Read Only Memory (ROM)**.

Random Access Memory (RAM). The Random Access Memory, or RAM, stores what you enter into the computer as well as the intermediate results from the computer's calculations. What you enter may be a program or data.

Information on RAM is **volatile**, meaning its contents are erased when the power is interrupted, or turned off. Thus it is important when you are using the computer to make sure to save the data on another medium from time to time. Otherwise, you can lose all the data you have just entered or processed.

The IBM PC RAM holds from approximately 128,000 characters, or 128K **bytes**, to 640K bytes or more. A **character** is a single letter, digit, or special symbol. This amount is **expandable**, or can be increased to several **megabytes** (million bytes).

NOTE ■ A byte is a computer-system format for encoding characters.

As mentioned earlier, for a program to be used on a computer—that is, for its instructions to be carried out—it must first be brought into the RAM. That means the computer must have enough RAM capacity to hold that program. In addition, RAM has to hold the data being processed.

WordPerfect 5.0 requires 384K of RAM. Version 4.2 requires only 205K of RAM. LOTUS 1-2-3 Release 2 requires 215K of memory. dBASE III Plus (for a single user) requires a minimum of 256K of memory (although more memory is recommended). You can see that you need a computer with 512K of memory or more to be able to run all of this software.

BUYING TIP ■ Before purchasing software, check the memory requirement and make sure you have enough RAM on your computer to support it. You will find that some software requires RAM capacity of 1 Mb (megabyte) or more.

Read Only Memory (ROM). The Read Only Memory, or ROM, comes already loaded with the information that the computer needs to understand what you enter. The information on ROM is not volatile. You can use the information, but you cannot erase or change it. The information that comes on ROM is called **firmware**.

Expansion Slots. At the back, left of the motherboard, are expansion slots. Your monitor and your printer, if you have one, may be connected to a board in one of these slots. These boards are called **interface boards** or **adaptor cards**. They allow the IBM PC to be connected, or interfaced, to **peripherals** (devices that perform support functions). Sometimes also in the expansion slots are **memory boards** that let you expand the RAM of the computer.

BUYING TIP ■ In the past the number of available slots dictated how much peripheral equipment could be attached to a computer. Although it is still true to some extent, many of today's micros already have various connectors (such as one to connect the printer) built-in, thus eliminating the need for you to purchase interface boards.

PRACTICE TIME

Enter the following information on your computer. You may need to consult your instructor to find these answers.

My computer is a(n) ______________________.

My computer has an 80286 or 80386 chip (Y/N) ______________.

If Yes, which? ______________________

The RAM capacity of my computer is ______________________.

OUTPUT COMPONENTS

The information a computer produces (output) must be in a form (medium) that a person, a computer, or other machines can use. The media that can be used by noncomputer machines will not be discussed here.

Monitor and Printer

When a person uses the output, it must be in a readable format. The output can be printed on screen or on paper by using a monitor or printer.

Monitor. The monitor has a screen that can display either 80 or 40 columns by 24 lines. Most programs use the 80 column display. Those monitors that produce two tones (green and black, amber and black, or white and black) are called **monochrome**. Monochrome monitors, in general, will not display graphics unless a special graphics card (such as the Hercules graphics card) is installed. However, they are easy to read for text displays.

There are three kinds of color monitors: CGA, EGA, and VGA. Technical differences between the three types are not discussed here. The clarity and crispness of output, by which these can be compared, are referred to as **resolution. CGA (Color Graphics Adaptor)** monitors are excellent for presenting graphics or playing games. They are mediocre for working with text processing because of their low resolution. **EGA (Enhanced Graphics Adaptor)** monitors have higher resolution than CGA monitors. They are capable of showing 64 or more different colors. The problem is that some equipment (such as monitor projection devices) that work with CGA signals will not work with EGA signals, and vice versa. The newest, **VGA (Video Graphics Array)** monitors, can receive both CGA and EGA signals, and, in addition, have higher resolution and more colors.

BUYING TIP ■ The type of monitor you purchase depends on the use. In the past if your usage was primarily text processing (such as word processing and spreadsheet), a monochrome monitor was recommended. This was because the low resolution on a CGA monitor could cause eye strain. Today much software takes advantage of color display to distinguish commands, and the use of graphics (again, in various colors) is increasing. Thus the high-resolution EGA and VGA monitors are easy to read and make software easy to use because of the use of color. You will have to weigh these factors (colors and resolution) against the cost to make your selection.

PRACTICE TIME

Enter the following information on your computer. You may need to consult with your instructor to find the answer.

My monitor is a (monochrome, CGA, EGA, VGA)
______________ monitor.

Printers. In general three types of printers are used today. They are dot matrix, letter quality, and laser printers. **Dot matrix** printers form characters as a combination of dots. The number of dots used to form characters determines how good the resolution of the output is. Some of the better dot matrix printers use 24 dots, or pins. Dot matrix printers can print characters in different styles or sizes, and are controlled by special codes. They can also print graphics.

Letter quality printers are like typewriters. They produce documents of legal quality. They cannot produce graphics. They are slower than the dot matrix printer and generally cost a little more. To change the character style or size in most, the print head must be changed, as in an electric typewriter.

Laser printers produce high-resolution output using the laser technology. The result is almost of publication quality. They can also produce graphics that are smooth. Their popularity of use with microcomputers is increasing (although they are not always easy to use with software). They are the most expensive of the three and are slow in producing output.

There is one additional item to note on printers. That is, all printers are either **parallel** or **serial printers**. Again the technical discussion on the difference is not given here. A parallel printer is connected to a **parallel** port at the back of the computer, and a serial printer is connected to a **serial port** at the back of the computer. (They use different interface boards.) A parallel port on a computer is referred to as LPT1 (a second parallel port is called LPT2; the third, LPT3; and so on). A serial port on a computer is referred to as COM1 (then COM2, COM3, and so on). This information is needed because some software is written to work with parallel printers, while others are written to work with serial printers. In most cases you need to specify the port where the printer is connected (so the program knows where to send the output).

BUYING TIP ■ For most general-purpose printing a dot matrix printer is adequate. Today's better dot matrix printers have near-letter quality resolution, and their output is very difficult to distinguish from that of a letter quality printer (at least to the naked eye).

A laser printer is nice to have if you require a high-quality output. The price has dropped to the level that most businesses can afford them. You will have to weigh cost, software compatibility, speed, resolution, and ease of use in making your selection.

PRACTICE TIME

Enter the following information on your computer. You may need to consult your instructor to find these answers.

The printer attached to my computer is a ____________.

(give brand name and model)

It is a ____________ (dot matrix, letter quality, laser) printer and is connected to ________________
(LPT1 or COM1).

Disk Drive and Modem

When output is to be used by a computer, data must be in computer-readable format. The medium most commonly used to store information to be passed on to another computer is a disk, either a floppy diskette or a hard disk. Disks are discussed in more detail in the next lesson.

If the output is sent directly to another computer, a **modem** might be used. A modem (*mo*dulator-*dem*odulator) is a device that connects the computer to another by a communication line, such as a telephone, through which information can be transmitted.

INPUT COMPONENTS

Input is the data the computer receives. There must be a way to input data.

Keyboard

Data is normally entered by typing on the keyboard. As you type, the corresponding characters are echoed (displayed) on the monitor. After entering certain kinds of information, you must press the ENTER (or RETURN) key before the computer can process the typed data. In other cases the typed information is processed directly. The entry method depends on the software you are using.

The two types of keyboard being used with IBM PCs will be discussed later.

Mouse

A mouse is a small, handheld device with a roller ball on the bottom. It allows you to send instructions to the computer by moving the mouse about on the desk, causing the cursor on the screen to move likewise, pointing at the options displayed on the screen. A mouse

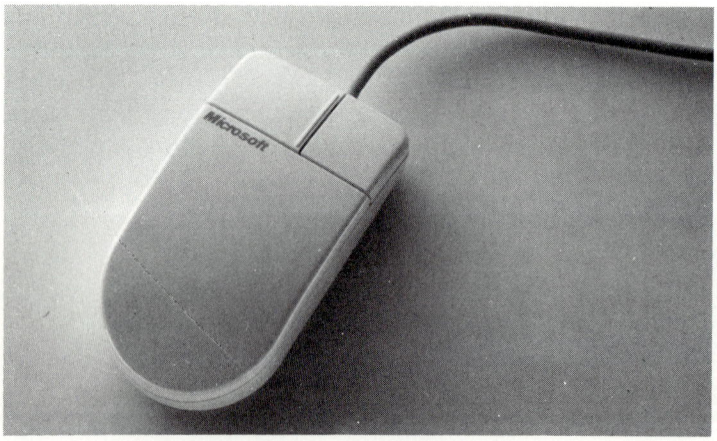

A mouse for the IBM PC

can be used with a program only if the application program recognizes its use. The usage of a mouse with IBM software is increasing.

Disk Drive and Modem

If the information you want to process is on a disk, you use a disk drive as an input device. The use of disks and disk drives is explained in the next lesson. If the information is coming from another computer via a communication line, you may use a modem.

STARTING THE COMPUTER

So you can see how the keyboard works, you will now turn your IBM PC on. This way you can see that the characters you type on the keyboard are displayed on the screen.

NOTE ■ If you are working on a computer with a hard disk, all you have to do to start a computer is to turn it on. All the information that a computer needs is on the hard disk. For practice, however, you will go through the procedure given here.

Make sure that you have a DOS disk, and just follow these steps. A DOS disk is either the IBM Disk Operating System disk (DOS System disk) or a disk that has DOS placed on it. Your DOS disk may be a 5¼-inch disk or a 3½-inch disk. A 3½-inch disk is in a solid metal-and-plastic casing, whereas the 5¼-inch disk is in an envelope. Other differences between the two are discussed in a later section.

- Turn the monitor switch ON. On some models the monitor is turned on with the computer.
- Make sure the computer is OFF.
- Lift the door for drive A (the drive on your left or on top). If there is a disk in the slot, remove it carefully.

If you are using a 5¼-inch disk

- Remove the DOS disk from its envelope and insert it into drive A, oval cutout end first, label side up. Be careful not to bend or force the disk. If you feel any resistance, pull the disk back out slowly and try again.
- Close the door to the disk drive.

If you are using a 3½-inch disk

- Insert the DOS disk into drive A, metal end first, label side up. When inserted properly, the disk will lock into place.

To continue with the rest of start-up

- Turn the computer switch ON.

> It takes 15 seconds or more for anything to happen. The IBM PC goes through a diagnostic routine each time it is turned on. Be patient.

> The red light on the disk drive lights up and the disk drive starts to operate.

> The following message appears on the screen:

```
Current data is Tue 1-01-1980
Enter new date (mm-dd-yy):
```

The computer offers you a chance to reset its internal calendar, which begins at 1-01-80 when the computer is booted up. Your computer may be equipped with a clock, or a battery-run device that keeps track of date and time even when the computer is turned off. Once you activate this clock, the correct date and time will be displayed when you turn the computer on. If that is the case, there is really no need to change the time or date, unless that is what you specifically want to do. (To activate the clock, see the instruction for the clock installed on your machine.)

The calendar format is month-day-year, with the numbers separated by hyphens. On September 29, 1989, for example, you can enter 9-29-89.

- Enter the date as shown above. Then press the ENTER key. The ENTER key is the left arrow key between the main keyboard and the numeric keyboard on the right. The ENTER key is referred to as the RETURN key in some software.

> A message similar to the following appears on the screen:

```
Current time is 0:00:41.24
Enter new time:
```

> The computer offers you a chance to reset its internal time, which started when it was booted up. The format, using a 24-hour clock, is hours:minutes:seconds, with the numbers separated by colons. If you want to enter 2:35 p.m., you enter 14:35.

- Enter the time as shown above. Then press the ENTER key.

> The screen displays a message similar to the following:

```
The IBM Personal Computer DOS
Version 3.30(C)Copyright International Business
         Machines Corp 1981, 1987
         (C)Copyright Microsoft Corp 1981, 1986

  A>
```

You may have a slightly different message, depending on the version of DOS you are using.

This is the IBM PC DOS copyright notice. A> is the DOS prompt. A **prompt** is a message from the computer to an operator that requests a response or entry. This prompt indicates that drive A is the default drive. More information about disk drives is presented later in this module.

> The flashing underscore character to the right of the prompt is the cursor. The cursor shows the position on the screen where your entries are made.

- Remove the disk from the drive and store it.

You have just completed a **cold start** of the computer. A cold start involves turning the computer ON to start it automatically.

You can restart the computer when it is ON without turning the power switch off. This is done by simultaneously holding down keys marked CTRL and ALT while you press the key marked DEL. This is called a **warm start**, since the computer is already on and warmed up.

THE KEYBOARD

The IBM PC you are using has one of two different types of keyboards, depending on when it was purchased. It may have the standard keyboard found on the earlier models, or an enhanced keyboard that comes with the newer models. Although they both have the

Keyboard for an IBM PC

IBM PS/2 keyboard

same keys, they are not in the same locations on the keyboard, the most obvious being the location and number of function keys and the presence of a second set of arrow keys. If you are using one of the IBM compatibles, your keyboard may also be slightly different.

This manual describes a standard keyboard. If you have one of the others, you may have to look around for placement of some keys.

KEYBOARD FEATURES

You might notice how similar it is to a typewriter keyboard. The purpose of the keyboard is to send characters to the computer. Which of these characters are recognized or what each is used for depends on the software that is being used at the time.

As different features of the keyboard are explained in this section, take time to try the features yourself. As you type the keys, the computer might respond with

```
Bad command or file name
```

The computer is indicating that DOS, the software that is running in the computer right now, does not recognize what you typed. Ignore this message for the time being.

Characters

The keyboard can generate 256 characters. Not all of them are visible, and many have special meanings. The character set of an IBM PC includes 26 lowercase letters, 26 uppercase letters, 10 numerals, and 34 special characters. The uppercase letters can be obtained by holding down one of the keys with the broad up arrows (a SHIFT key) while you press the key or by pressing the key marked Caps Lock (the CAPS LOCK key) once and then pressing the keys.

Some of the special characters require that you hold down the SHIFT key even if the CAPS LOCK key has been pressed. These are the characters that appear on the upper half of a key. For example, the key with a semicolon (;) has a colon (:) on the upper half. To type a semicolon, you just press the key; but to type a colon, you must hold the SHIFT key down while you press the key. The CAPS LOCK key is a toggle key. The first time you press it, it shifts the keyboard into uppercase mode. The second time, all letters are lowercase (unless the SHIFT key is pressed).

SPACE BAR

The long bar at the bottom of the keyboard is the space bar. Press it to generate blank spaces between characters. Unlike a blank space on a typed sheet, pressing the space bar actually inserts a space character into the data being typed.

ENTER

The ENTER key is the down left arrow key between the main keyboard and the numeric keyboard. It does not necessarily have the same function as on the typewriter keyboard. Its use depends on the software.

- Pressing ENTER might cause the cursor to move to the beginning of the next line. In that case the ENTER is being used to indicate the end of a line or is being used as a cursor movement key. This use is similar to the use of a carriage return on a typewriter.
- Pressing ENTER might indicate the end of a command (or instruction). In this role ENTER signals the computer to accept the line just typed. Until ENTER is pressed, the computer does not recognize the line.

Some software does not require that the ENTER key be pressed after a command. In fact much software allows you to press either the ENTER key, a function key, or a single keystroke indicating the first letter of a command. Please pay particular attention to these rules as you study this manual.

Control Characters

You can enter 32 control characters into the computer. These are generated by holding down the key marked Ctrl (the CTRL key) and pressing a character key. This sequence is indicated in the text as CTRL/character. Such a sequence of keypresses may or may not cause characters or message to appear on the screen. These keypresses have variable functions as defined by each software package.

Function Keys

To the left of the main keyboard are 10 function keys, marked F1 to F10. (On the enhanced keyboard, there are 12 function keys, found across the top of the keyboard.) Some software uses the function keys as shortcuts for entering certain commands.

ALT

The key marked Alt, located to the left of the space bar, is the ALTERNATE key. It, too, has variable functions depending on the software.

Numeric Keyboard

To the right of the main keyboard is the numeric keyboard. You need to know several important things about it. Before you can enter numerals or the period from the keypad, you must either hold down the SHIFT key or press the NUM LOCK key. Like CAPS LOCK, NUM LOCK is a toggle key. After pressing NUM LOCK once, you can generate the characters that appear on the upper half of the keys in the keypad. Press it again to generate the cursor moves on the bottom half of the keys. NUM LOCK has no effect on the number keys of the main keyboard, just on the keys in the numeric keypad.

On the lower half of the 8, 6, 4, and 2 keys are short arrows. In lowercase mode these may be used for cursor movement if the software in use supports these functions. That is, when you press one of the arrow keys, the cursor moves one position in the direction of the arrow.

On the lower half of the 7 key is Home. The HOME key also may be a cursor movement key. When you use certain software, pressing the HOME key causes the cursor to move to the top left corner of the screen.

The 1, 3, and 9 keys have the labels END, PgDn, and PgUp, respectively. These keys may have special cursor movements defined in the software.

NOTE ■ The enhanced keyboard has a second set of cursor movement keys between the main keyboard and the numeric keyboard. This way, you can leave the numeric keyboard in numeric mode all the time.

ESC

At the upper left corner of the main keyboard is the ESCAPE key, marked Esc (the ESC key). Its function, again, depends on the software.

TAB

The TAB key has two arrows pointing in opposite directions. It is just below the ESC key. In some word processing software the TAB key has a function very similar to that of a typewriter Tab key. That is, pressing this key sends the cursor to the next tab setting.

PRTSC

The key marked PrtSc (PRINT SCREEN) on the upper half is found just below the ENTER key. (There is a second PrtSc key on the enhanced keyboard.) Of course, you must have a printer attached to your computer. In some software, however, the SHIFT/PrtSc feature is disabled.

BACKSPACE

The key with the arrow pointing left, found just above the ENTER key, is the BACKSPACE key. It may be used to move the cursor to the left one position, or to erase the character to the left of the cursor.

INS and DEL

Two wide keys found below the numeric keyboard are the INS and DEL keys. INS, or INSERT, is a toggle key. Sometimes, as you insert characters in the middle of a pretyped line, the characters to the right of the cursor move over to let you insert the new characters. If you press the INS key, the characters you type then replace the characters already there. If you press the INS key for the second time, the characters you type are inserted once more. The third time, they overstrike, and so on.

The DEL key is used by some software to DELETE the character at the cursor position.

NOTE ■ The SCROLL LOCK key at the top right corner of the keyboard is not discussed.

Keys to Keep Distinct

Some characters must be used carefully. On a typewriter you can use one character for another if they look similar as typed; on a computer you must type the exact key, since each key generates a unique signal to the computer. The following two pairs of keys are often confused by users, but never by computers:

- Lowercase letter L and number 1
- Letter O (oh) and number 0 (zero)

Wraparound

On an ordinary typewriter you must press the carriage return at the end of each line. On a computer if you continue typing past the right edge of the screen, the next character will appear on the next line down. This feature is called **wraparound**. It allows you to enter lines that are longer than the width of the screen.

Auto-Repeat

When you hold down a key on the keyboard, the character will repeat itself.

LEARN TO USE THE SOFTWARE

Each key generates a unique signal to the computer. The function of each key and its recognition by the computer depend on the software being used. Even the method used to correct your typing errors depends on the software being used. You should be getting the idea that, beyond turning it on, learning how to use a computer means learning how to use specific software.

Don't be frustrated or intimidated. If you type a command for the wrong software, the computer usually just responds with an error message indicating that it doesn't recognize what you typed. These errors do not harm the computer. And, most often, they do not affect whatever it is you are trying to accomplish by using the computer. The worst that can happen is that you might have to turn the computer off and start all over again.

FUNCTION OF A DISK

A disk is an external storage medium. It is used to store information that is needed at a later time. It has the RAM internal storage feature of allowing information to be written on it, plus the ROM internal storage feature of retaining the information when the computer is turned off or power is interrupted. External storage is permanent storage where you can read and write information.

When information is written onto a disk, each grouping of information is stored as a file. That is, if you prepare a letter using a word processor, the letter is stored on a disk as a file with a filename to identify it. A computer program is stored on a disk as a file, again with a proper filename to identify it. Most application software has commands to let you store and retrieve files from a disk.

CHARACTERISTICS OF DISKS

Two types of disks are used with a PC: **floppy disks** and **hard disks**. Although they operate in a similar manner, floppy disks are flexible and portable, whereas hard disks are rigid, metallic platters. Floppy disks are used with floppy disk drives (referred to simply as disk drives in this manual) and hard disks are housed in a hard disk drive unit. Hard disks are explained in a little more detail at the end of this section.

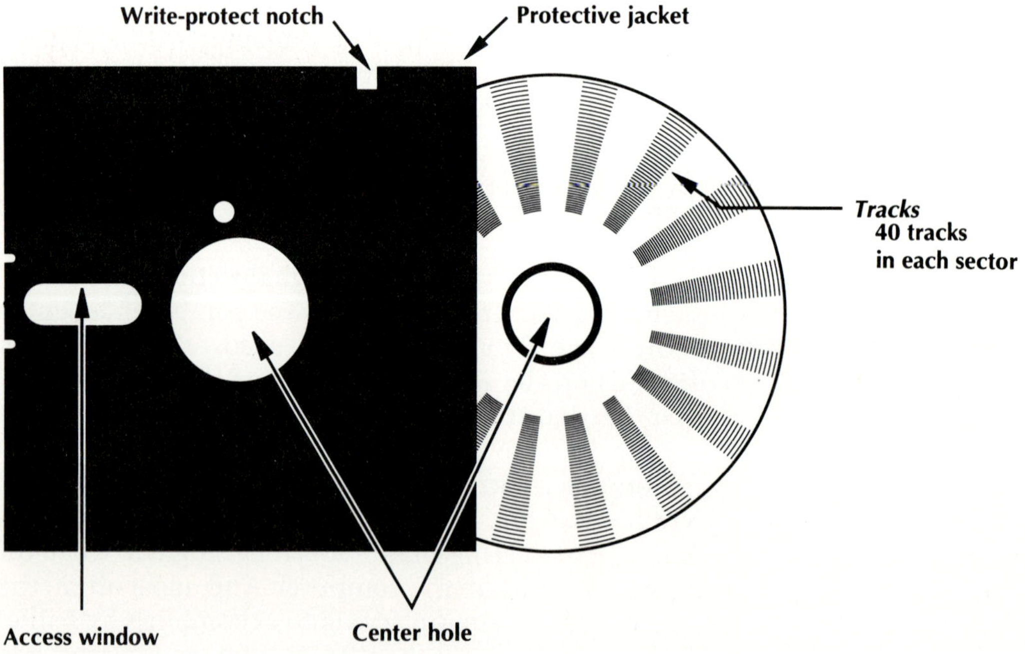

143K, 5.25 inch disk

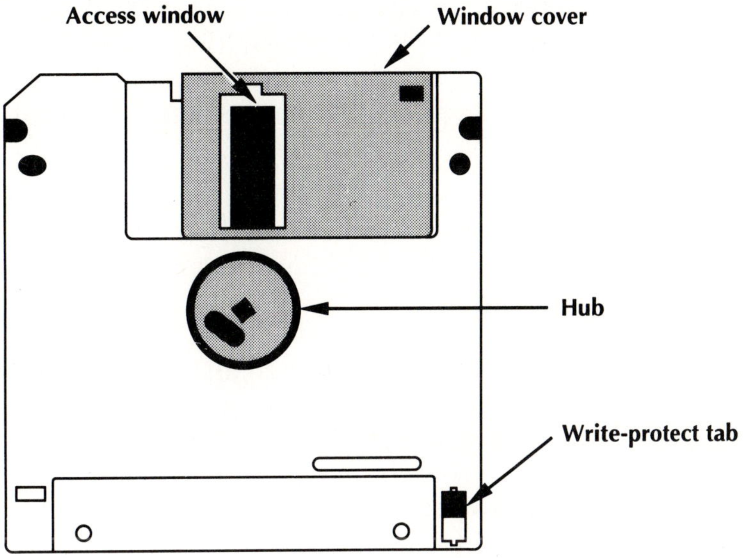

800K, 3.5 inch disk

The disks used on the IBM PCs are either 5¼-inch floppy disks or 3½-inch disks, and either double density or high density. All these disks are referred to simply as disks in this manual. These disks are very similar in function and operation, with some subtle differences.

A disk stores data as magnetic spots on a circular piece of Mylar that has an oxide coating. The disk is inside a protective jacket (for 5¼-inch disks) or plastic cartridge (for 3½-inch disks). The larger ones are called floppy disks because the Mylar material is pliant, and in the protective jackets, 5¼-inch disks can "flop" (flex) back and forth. The 3½-inch disks come in rigid, plastic cartridges, so the term does not apply to them. The cartridge on a 3½-inch disk protects the diskette inside much better than the jacket on a 5¼-inch disk.

The information on a disk is stored along concentric recording positions on the side, known as **tracks** or **cylinders**. Information may be stored on both sides of the disk. A double-density disk has 40 tracks per side on each 5¼-inch disk and 80 per side on each 3½-inch disk. A high-density disk has 80 tracks per side on each 5¼-inch and 160 per side on each 3½-inch disk. The storage capacity on a 5¼-inch disk is approximately 360K for double density and 1.2 Mb for high density, and on a 3½-inch disk it is approximately 720K for double density and 1.44 Mb for high density.

NOTE ■ If you have a high-density disk drive, you use high-density disks. If you have a 360K or 720K disk drive, you use double-density disks. You can use double-density disks in a high-density disk drive, although the capacity is limited to 360K or 720K—consult the DOS manual.

The information is written onto and read from the disk through an opening in the jacket or cartridge. The circular Mylar disk inside spins like a phonograph record, and a **read-write head** accesses information.

In the case of 5¼-inch disks the opening is visible and is called the **access window**. A 3½-inch disk has a mechanical shutter that opens automatically to reveal the access window when the disk is inserted into the disk drive and closes automatically when taken out.

Most 5¼-inch disks have a small notch on the side. This is the **write-protect notch**. If you cover the write-protect notch, the disk is protected from being written over or changed. When you purchase disks, gummed tabs are provided for this purpose.

NOTE ■ If you have covered the write-protect notch with a gummed tab, check periodically to make sure that it is securely in place. Many disk drive problems occur from gummed tabs coming off and getting stuck inside the drive. This is also true of labels you might have attached on the disk.

A 3½-inch disk can be write-protected by using the write-protect tab. It is write-protected (cannot change information) when the tab is moved to reveal the hollow opening. When the opening is closed, the disk is not write-protected (and you can read or write information).

When you purchase a disk, it does not contain any information. The disk must be prepared so that it is able to store and retrieve data. The process of preparing a disk to accept data is called **formatting** a disk; this is explained in the next lesson.

NOTE ■ A high-density disk drive will read information written by a double-density disk drive. However, a double-density disk drive will not read information written by a high-density disk drive.

CARE AND HANDLING OF 5¼-INCH DISKS

You must use proper care in handling 5¼-inch disks. They are very fragile. Here are some suggestions for their care and handling.

- Always handle a disk by its plastic jacket only.
- Insert the disk into the disk drive, access window end first, label side up.
- Always keep the disk in its envelope when not in use.

- Do not touch the surface of the disk or wipe the surface with rags or tissue paper.
- Do not let disks collect dust.
- Keep disks out of the sun and away from other sources of heat, which can cause them to warp or lose data.
- Keep disks at least two feet way from magnetic fields, such as those generated by electrical motors, radios, televisions, tape recorders, and other devices. A strong magnetic field will erase information on a disk.
- When writing on a disk label already attached to the disk, use only a felt-tipped pen. Never use any sort of instrument with a sharp point. Also, never use an eraser. Eraser dust is abrasive and may get on the Mylar surface.
- Store disks in a vertical position. Never bend them or attach paper clips to them.
- Never open the drive door or remove a disk while the drive is running—that is, while the red IN USE light on the front of the disk drive is on. If you do, you can damage the data on your disk.
- Check to make sure that gummed tab and external labels are on securely.

CARE AND HANDLING OF 3½-INCH DISKS

A 3½-inch disk is well protected and is quite sturdy. However, there are some general rules you should follow in handling the disk.

- Insert the disk in the disk drive, metal end first, label side up.
- Never open the mechanical shutter while a disk is out of the drive. Doing this exposes the surface to dirt, dust, fingerprints, and other contaminants.
- Do not let disks collect dust.
- Keep disks out of the sun and away from other sources of heat, which can cause them to warp or lose data.
- Keep disks at least two feet away from magnetic fields, such as those generated by electrical motors, radios, televisions, tape recorders, and other devices. A strong magnetic field will erase information on a disk.
- When writing on a disk label already attached to the disk, use only a felt-tipped pen. Also, never use an eraser. Eraser dust is abrasive and may get on the Mylar surface.
- Never remove a disk while the drive is running—that is, while the red IN USE light on the front of the disk drive is on. If you do, you can damage the data on your disk.
- Check to make sure that the external labels are on securely.

HARD DISKS

A hard disk unit is a sealed enclosure containing one or more rigid metallic platters (usually an aluminum platter covered with a thin iron-oxide coating). This enclosure may be installed in the same cabinet as the processing unit (internal hard disk) or in a separate cabinet (external hard disk). A hard disk is sometimes called a **fixed disk** or **Winchester drive**.

NOTE ■ Hard disks available on interface boards to be inserted in unused expansion slots in the computer are called **hard cards**.

Hard and floppy disks use similar principles. Both record data in tracks. The advantage of a hard disk is greater storage capacity and speed. You can install 20-, 40-, or even 200-megabyte hard disks on the computer. The access speed of a hard drive is two to ten times faster than that of a floppy disk.

CARE OF DISK DRIVES

A disk drive is a sensitive mechanical device and should be treated as such. Because it has moving parts, it is even more sensitive than the computer. You should not drop it, jar it sharply, or plug it in or unplug it when the computer is on.

The read-write head on the disk drive should be cleaned periodically. A minute amount of dust, dirt, oils, or magnetic oxide particles on the disk drive head can cause problems.

When you transport the disk drive, insert the cardboard packing disk (that accompanied the drive when it was purchased) or a blank disk to protect the drive's internal mechanism.

A hard disk is even more susceptible to physical damage because of its design. You must be very careful not to move the unit without first properly positioning (parking) its read-write head. You must also use extreme caution when shutting down the system to avoid turning off power when the hard disk is writing data.

IDENTIFYING DISK DRIVES

The IBM PC comes with one or more installed floppy disk drives. Some have a hard disk drive installed. Each disk drive must be connected to a disk interface board, or **disk controller card**. The disk controller card, in turn, is inserted into one of the expansion slots in the computer. If there is only one drive, it is known as drive A. If there are two drives, they are drives A and B. If there is a hard drive, it is usually drive C.

PRACTICE TIME

Enter the following information on your computer. You may need to consult your instructor to find these answers.

There are ____ (how many) 3½-inch disk drives on my computer.
There are ____ (how many) 5¼-inch disk drives on my computer.
There is a hard disk on my computer. ____ (Y/N)

Visually identify which drive is drive A.

END OF LESSON 1

At this time you will end your lesson.

- If you have not already done so, remove the disk from the drive.
- Turn OFF two switches: one for the computer and one for the monitor. The order in which you turn off the computer and monitor is not important.

SUMMARY

In this lesson various components of a computer are presented.

- The function of a computer is to process data and produce a result.
- The microprocessor unit (MPU) is the brain of the computer.
- The Random Access Memory (RAM) is where both the program and data are stored. It is a volatile memory.
- The Read Only Memory (ROM) contains firmware.
- Expansion slots are where peripheral devices are connected.
- Two-tone monitors are called monochrome monitors.
- There are three kinds of color monitors: Color Graphics Adaptor (CGA), Enhanced Graphics Adaptor (EGA), and Video Graphics Array (VGA).
- Computer output can be passed onto a computer via disk or modem.
- Input components include keyboard, mouse, disk drive, and modem.
- In general there are two types of disks: floppy and hard. There are two types of floppy disks: 3½-inch and 5¼-inch.
- Information on a disk is accessed through an access window. On a 3½-inch disk the access window is protected by a mechanical shutter.
- A disk can be write-protected.

REVIEW QUESTIONS

1. What is the function of a computer?
2. Why do different computers have different microprocessor chips?
3. What does *volatile* mean?
4. Is a blank space a byte? Explain.
5. Name three types of printers and list an advantage and a disadvantage of each.
6. Why is a disk drive both an input and an output component?
7. Why do you need an external storage device?
8. How is information stored on a disk?
9. What does it mean when a disk is write-protected? How is it done?
10. What are the advantages of having a hard disk on a computer?

CONFIGURATION OF MY COMPUTER

Transfer the information you entered in PRACTICE TIME to this page for future reference.

My computer is a(n) ______________________________.
My computer has an 80286 or 80386 chip (Y/N) ____.
If Yes, which? ____

The RAM capacity of my computer is __________.

The printer attached to my computer is a ____________________.

(give brand name and model)

It is a ______________ (dot matrix, letter quality, laser) printer and is connected to ____________ (LPT1 OR COM1).

My monitor is a (monochrome, CGA, EGA, VGA) __________ monitor.

There are ____ (how many) 3½-inch disk drives on my computer.

There are ____ (how many) 5¼-inch disk drives on my computer.

There is a hard disk on my computer. ____ (Y/N)

Lesson 2
Disk Operating System

Objectives

Upon completion of the material presented in this lesson, you should understand the following:

- What a default drive is and how to change it.
- The purpose of the Disk Operating System (DOS).
- The difference between internal and external DOS commands.
- How to format a disk.
- How to manage files on a disk.

Supplies Needed

For this part of the manual you need

- The DOS disk: A DOS disk is the one that accompanied the computer at the time of purchase.
- A scratch disk: A scratch disk is a blank disk or one whose content you no longer need.

ORIENTATION

The **disk operating system**, or **DOS**, is a computer program that controls the information transfer between the computer and the disk drives. It allows files of information to be easily saved, copied, listed, and deleted. Anyone who wishes to make serious use of a microcomputer should become familiar with the DOS commands.

The IBM PC version of DOS is available on a disk that is provided with the IBM PC. Some software provides its own set of DOS instructions; thus there is no need for you to know the IBM PC DOS. Still, much of the software for the IBM PC uses some of the DOS commands.

STARTING UP

Start up the IBM PC, using the DOS disk. You did this in the first lesson.

DEFAULT DISK DRIVE

The **prompt** on the screen consists of two characters. Right now, the first character is an **A**. The second character is always >. The purpose of the first character is to indicate the default disk drive—the drive the computer will use unless instructed otherwise. When you give a command, it may require the computer to get a file from the disk. If you want the computer to get a file from a disk in a drive other than the default drive, you must indicate the drive to be used. This will become clearer in the next section.

CHANGING THE DEFAULT DRIVE

To change the default drive, you simply type the drive name, **A** or **B**, followed by the colon (:). That is, if your default is currently drive A and you want to change to B, you type **B:** and press ENTER. The prompt will then read **B**>. To change it back to A, you type **A:** and press ENTER.

One word of warning: there must be a disk in the new drive before you can change the default. If you try to change the default without a disk in the new drive, you get the message

```
Abort, Retry, or Ignore?
```

If that happens, you can insert a disk in the new drive and type **R** for Retry and press ENTER. If you changed your mind about changing the default, type **I** for Ignore and press ENTER. You will get the message

```
Current drive is no longer valid >
```

Then enter the drive you would like to have as the default.

DOS COMMANDS

As mentioned earlier, you should become familiar with DOS commands, as they give an efficient way to manage your data. There are times when you want to prepare a disk to store data, examine the contents of a disk, or transfer files (for creating backup, for example), without going into any application software.

Some DOS commands are **internal** and others are **external** (sometimes called **resident** and **transient** commands). Internal commands are transferred to memory when the computer is started. This means that, once you load DOS by starting up the computer, you do not need to have the DOS disk in a drive to carry out these commands.

External commands are on a disk as files. Therefore the disk containing the command files (generally the DOS disk) must be in a disk drive for the command to be carried out.

An internal (resident) command can be issued by simply typing the proper entry. For an external command you must specify which drive contains the DOS disk. If the drive that contains the DOS disk is the default drive, you may omit the drive specification. For example, you can use the (internal) DIR command simply by typing **DIR**. However, if the DOS disk is in drive B and the default drive is A, you must type **B:FORMAT** to issue the (external) FORMAT command.

The following commands are discussed briefly in this manual. You should consult the DOS manual for detail.

VER	Displays the DOS version under which you are operating.

Commands Used with Disks:

FORMAT	Formats a disk.
CHKDSK	Checks the status of a disk.

Commands for Using and Moving Files:

DIR	Displays the names of all files on the disk in the disk drive.
COPY	Copies a file.
RENAME	Renames the file.
ERASE	Erases the specified filename.
TYPE	Displays the contents of a file on the screen.

Commands Used to Safeguard Your Files:

COMP	Compares the contents of two files.
DISKCOPY	Creates a copy of one disk on another. Formats the target disk, if necessary.
DISKCOMP	Compares the contents of two disks.

Commands Most Often Used with Hard Disk:

MKDIR	Creates a new subdirectory.
CHDIR	Changes the current directory on a specified drive.
RMDIR	Deletes a specified subdirectory.
TREE	Displays all the directory paths on a specified drive.

When a DOS command is entered, the command may or may not be preceded by the drive where the disk containing the command file is found, depending on whether the command is internal or external and which drive is set as the default. The command may also require that you specify one or more drives or a drive and filename. In addition the command may allow for a number of options. Options are usually a slash followed by a character, such as /S. These options expand the versatility of DOS commands, allowing you to have a command do things a certain way.

VER

This internal command displays the DOS version number that you are working with. There are many versions of DOS. Sometimes you need to know the version since certain software is supported by a particular version of DOS. Just type VER and press ENTER and see what is displayed.

FORMAT

Next you need to know how to prepare a disk for use. When you buy blank disks, there is nothing on them. A disk must be formatted before you can put information on it. This applies to a hard disk as well. To format a disk means to prepare it to store information.

Some software provides instructions on how to format a disk from within the command set for that package. Other software packages require that your data disk already be formatted. A hard disk must be formatted with DOS, not from an application package.

The following is the procedure of formatting a disk in DOS with the FORMAT command.

- Insert the DOS disk in drive A. Make sure that the default drive is A.

The FORMAT command is an external command. You must specify the drive on which the file that contains FORMAT command can be found. Since the DOS disk is in drive A and the default drive is A, you can just type **FORMAT**. Had the DOS disk been in drive B (with default still being A), you would have had to type **B:FORMAT**. On the other hand, if the default was B and the DOS disk was A, you would have had to type **A:FORMAT**.

As part of the FORMAT command you also have to specify the disk drive in which you intend to insert the disk to be formatted. If it is to be in drive A, you type **FORMAT A:**, and if it is to be found in drive B, you type **FORMAT B:**. If you do not specify this, the computer assumes that the new disk is in the default drive.

- Type FORMAT B: and press the ENTER (or RETURN) key. The command can be typed in uppercase or lowercase, but *there must be a space before the B.*

  > The screen displays the message

```
Insert new diskette for drive B
and strike ENTER when ready
```

Insert a scratch disk in drive B. A scratch disk is either a blank disk or one whose contents you no longer need. You can reformat a disk that already contains information. However, when you do, the existing information is lost. Therefore you must make sure that you no longer need the information on a disk before you reformat it.

- Press ENTER to begin formatting.

  > When the formatting is complete, the screen message shown may look as follows:

  ```
  Formatting..Format complete

  362496 bytes total disk space
  362496 bytes available on disk
  Format another (Y/N)?
  ```

DOS specifies that the disk is formatted for a total of 362,496 bytes, or characters, and that all 362,496 bytes are available for storing information. The program is ready to format another disk, if instructed to do so. You are to enter **Y** or **N**, depending on whether you want another disk formatted.

- Enter N if you do not want to format any more disks and press ENTER.
- Leave the newly formatted disk in drive B.

The disk in drive B is now formatted and ready for use. That is, it is ready to hold your data. However, it cannot be used to start the computer.

For a disk to be a system disk (the one with which to start the computer), it must contain three files: IBMBIO.COM, IBMDOS.COM, and COMMAND.COM. That is, aside from being formatted, these three files must be transferred (from the DOS disk in drive A, in this case, to the formatted disk in drive B).

You might note that two of these files (IBMBIO.COM and IBMDOS.COM) are "hidden" files. This will be explained later. To create a disk that can be used to start the computer, you include an option, or a system parameter, (/S), with the format command. That is, you type **FORMAT B: /S**.

Do not confuse the "system" disk formatted with /S option with the "DOS" disk used to start up the computer at the beginning of the lesson. A system disk will let you start up the computer. A DOS disk not only lets you start up the computer, but it contains all the external DOS commands. Consult the DOS manual for detail.

CHKDSK

CHKDSK command is used to analyze the directories and the way files are stored on a disk found in a designated drive or individual file on the disk specified. It can also optionally correct damage (/F). Here you will use the command to check the status of the recently formatted disk.

- Enter **B:** and press ENTER to change the logged disk drive from A to B.

  > The prompt now reads **B>**.

You will now use CHKDSK command to check the disk in drive B. However, CHKDSK is an external command, and the DOS disk is in drive A. Since drive A is not the default drive, you need to specify that the DOS disk is in drive A and that the disk to be checked is in drive B.

- Enter **A:CHKDSK B:** and press ENTER.

  > The screen message shown may look as follows:

```
362496 bytes total disk space
362496 bytes available on disk

655360 bytes total memory
618496 bytes free
```

Had there been files on the disk, CHKDSK would have reported the number of files and how much space they take up on the disk. The second set of numbers tells the status of memory on the computer you are using.

PRACTICE TIME

Try the CHKDSK command on the DOS disk in drive A.

DIR

To see what files are on a disk, use the DIR command. DIR is an internal command. You can issue it at any time after you have started the computer. Again you can specify the drive in which the disk to be examined is located. If none is specified, the default is assumed.

- With drive A as the default, type **DIR** and press ENTER.

  > The directory for the disk in drive A is displayed, scrolling by rather quickly. **Scrolling** means after the screen fills up, as each new line appears at the bottom, the line at the top disappears.

Let's try this again, using the /P option.

- Type **DIR /P** and press ENTER.

  > A screen similar to the one shown in Screen Display 1 should appear on your monitor.

```
COMMAND   COM    23210  3-07-85   1:43p
ANSI      SYS     1651  3-07-85   1:43p
ASSIGN    COM     1509  3-07-85   1:43p
ATTRIB    EXE    15091  3-07-85   1:43p
BACKUP    COM     5577  3-07-85   1:43p
BASIC     COM    17792  3-07-85   1:43p
BASICA    COM    27520  3-07-85   1:43p
CHKDSK    COM     9435  3-07-85   1:43p
COMP      COM     3664  3-07-85   1:43p
DISKCOMP  COM     4073  3-07-85   1:43p
DISKCOPY  COM     4329  3-07-85   1:43p
EDLIN     COM     7261  3-07-85   1:43p
FDISK     COM     8173  3-07-85   1:43p
FIND      EXE     6403  3-07-85   1:43p
FORMAT    COM     9398  3-07-85   1:43p
GRAFTABL  COM     1169  3-07-85   1:43p
GRAPHICS  COM     3111  3-07-85   1:43p
JOIN      EXE    15971  3-07-85   1:43p
KEYBFR    COM     2473  4-12-85   4:22p
KEYBGR    COM     2418  4-12-85   4:23p
KEYBIT    COM     2361  4-12-85   4:24p
KEYBSP    COM     2451  4-12-85   4:25p
KEYBUK    COM     2348  4-12-85   4:26p
Strike a key when ready . . .
```

Screen Display 1-1

This display is not explained in detail in this manual. The things to note are that **filenames** appear in the first column and their **extensions** appear in the second column. The third column displays the **file size** and the fourth column displays the **date** the file was created.

The name in the first column often is the one used to store or retrieve a file for use by an application program. The extension in the second column often is assigned by the application program to distinguish the data file according to its use. When a complete filename is requested, you must give both the filename and extension, separated by a period (.). For example, if the filename is **MYFILE** and extension is **DAT**, the complete filename is **MYFILE.DAT**. A filename is from one to eight characters in length, and an extension is from one to three characters in length. Almost any characters can be used in a filename and extension, except the following set of characters:

. , " / \ [ ] : ; | < > + = * ?

At this point you are probably still pretty hazy about terms like *file* and *filename.* Don't worry for the time being. These will become clearer to you as you go through the rest of this manual.

- Press any key to see the rest of the directory. Repeat as needed to finish.

You can look at the directory of a disk that is in another drive (nondefault).

- Type **DIR B:** (or **DIR B: /P**) and press ENTER.

  > You see the directory of the disk in drive B, which should be pretty empty.

If you want to look at just those files on drive A with say, **EXE** as extension, you can use the **wild card** character to specify this. This special wild card character is the asterisk (*). When it is used, it is the place holder for any possible characters.

- Type **DIR A:*.EXE** and press ENTER.

  > Only those files with extension **EXE** are listed.

PRACTICE TIME

Try **DIR A:*.*** What do you think happened?

Earlier it was mentioned that IBMBIO.COM and IBMDOS.COM are hidden files. That means they do not appear on any directory. Hence the only way those files can be transferred is by using the /S option with the FORMAT command.

COPY

To copy some files that are on one disk onto another, you use the COPY command, which is another internal command. Although there are many options in copying files, only the procedures needed for making backup copies of a file are discussed here. That is, you will learn how to (1) copy a file from one disk to another and to use either the same name or a different name, and (2) copy all files from one disk to another.

The idea is that you have a disk that contains data files from which you want to make backup copies. You want to copy these data files onto the disk you formatted earlier. Since you do not yet have any data files, you will copy a command file on the DOS disk in drive A onto your disk in drive B. Since you do not want to accidentally erase a file on the DOS disk, it is suggested that you copy protect the DOS disk before you start. (See Lesson 1.)

The file you will copy is FORMAT.COM. Here, you have to use the complete name (both the filename and the extenson).

- Type COPY A:FORMAT.COM B: and press ENTER.

  > The message

  ```
  1 File(s) copied
  ```

  appears on the screen.

DOS created a file by the same name on the disk in drive B and copied the contents to it. The original file stays intact. If there had been a file by the same name on the disk in drive B, it would have been overwritten; that is, new information replaces the old.

PRACTICE TIME

Use DIR to check the content of the disk in drive B.

If you want to copy a file on a disk in drive A (*filenamel*) onto a file with a different name (*filename2*) on drive B, type **COPY A:*filenamel* B:*filename2*** and press ENTER. If a *filename2* is specified, the file from drive A is copied to the file *filename2* on drive B. If it is not specified, then the same name as used in drive A is assumed.

PRACTICE TIME

Copy the file FORMAT.COM from drive A again, this time onto a file named MYOWN.COM in drive B. Use DIR to make sure that the file MYOWN.COM exists in drive B.

If you want to copy all the files from the disk in drive A to the disk in drive B, you can use the wild card. That is, enter **COPY A:*.* B:** and press ENTER.

RENAME

The RENAME command is used to rename a file on a disk. It is an internal command, and its format is **RENAME *filename1 filename2*,** where *filename1* is the old name and *filename2* is the new name. Again these names must be complete names and may include the drive specification (for *filename1*). Otherwise, the file is assumed to be on the disk in the default drive.

It is best not to depend on the default drive setting. Get into the habit of specifying the drive with the filename. This will reduce accidental erasure of files and may eliminate many hours of frustration.

- Type RENAME B:MYOWN.COM YOURS.COM and press ENTER.
  > The light in front of drive B goes on for a while. When it goes out, the file has been renamed.

- Use the DIR command to verify.

ERASE

To remove an unwanted file from a disk, you use the ERASE command (internal). The format is **ERASE *filename***, where *filename* is the complete name of the file to be removed. As part of the filename you also can specify the drive that holds the source file. You will remove the file YOURS.COM in drive B.

- Type ERASE B:YOURS.COM and press ENTER.
  > The light in front of drive B goes on for a while. When it goes off, the file YOURS.COM has been erased.

- Use the DIR command to verify.

NOTE ■ Care must be taken when you issue the ERASE command so that you don't inadvertently remove a file you want to keep.

TYPE

The TYPE command (internal) is used to display the contents of a file on the screen. Certain types of files can be displayed in a legible format. Other files, however, may appear unreadable. This command will be explained in the next lesson when discussing the AUTOEXEC.BAT file.

COMP

The COMP command (external) is used to compare the contents of two specified files. You will compare the FORMAT.COM file in drive A with the FORMAT.COM file in drive B. Remember, this is an external command. You have to be sure that the disk containing the command file either is the default or is specified.

- Type A:COMP A:FORMAT.COM B:FORMAT.COM and press ENTER.

  > A message similar to the following is displayed:

```
Files compare OK
Compare more files (Y/N)?
```

If there were a mismatch, a message indicating the nature of the mismatch would be displayed. For specific messages see the DOS manual.

DISKCOPY

The DISKCOPY command (external) creates a track-by-track copy of one disk on another disk. If necessary, it formats the target disk. Its format is DISKCOPY d1: d2:, where d1 is the drive where the source disk is found and d2 is the drive where the target disk is found. If the same disk is specified for both d1 and d2, you will have to do disk swapping to accomplish the process.

You will copy the DOS disk in drive A onto the disk in drive B.

- With A as the default drive, type DISKCOPY A: B: and press ENTER.

  > The following message appears:

```
Insert SOURCE diskette in drive A:
Insert TARGET diskette in drive B:
Press any key when ready
```

At this point verify that the DOS disk is in drive A and your formatted (scratch) disk is in drive B. When satisfied, press any key.

> Drives A and B go on intermittently as messages appear on the screen indicating sectors and tracks being copied.

> The message

```
Copy another diskette (Y/N)?
```

appears on the screen.

- Type N and press ENTER since you do not want to copy any more disks.
- Use the DIR command on both disks to check the contents.

DISKCOMP

This external command lets you compare the contents of two disks, sector by sector. You will compare the two disks from the DISKCOPY operation.

- Type A:DISKCOMP A: B: and press ENTER.
  > The following message appears on the screen:

```
Insert FIRST diskette in drive A:
Insert SECOND diskette in drive B:
Press any key when ready . . .
```

The first disk is the original. In your case it is the DOS disk in drive A. The second disk is the one you are comparing with the first to see if it is the same. In your case the one in drive B is the second disk.

- Verify the disks in drives A and B and press any key.
  > Messages appear on the screen indicating the tracks being compared.
  > After a while the following message appears on the screen:

```
Compares OK
Compare another diskette (Y/N)?
```

If some other message appears on the screen, see the DOS manual.

- Type N and press ENTER, since you do not want to compare any more disks at this time.

PRACTICE TIME

Erase all files in the disk drive B. First remove the DOS disk in drive A so that you don't accidentally erase its information. You can now find out names of all files in the disk (using DIR) and erase them individually, or you can use the wild card, or *, symbol. Simply type **ERASE B:*.*** and press ENTER.

MKDIR

As the number of files on each disk increases, so does the need to have the disk well organized. This is specially true of a hard disk with its large capacity. DOS allows you to create tree-structured directories. The original directory, or the **root directory**, can have a number of subdivisions, or **subdirectories**, each containing files with a common subject matter. The subdirectories, in turn, can have more specific subdirectories of their own.

Let's say, for example, that you still had all kinds of files in the disk in drive B. If you were to add data files from an application, such as WordPerfect, onto the disk, it would be very difficult to identify

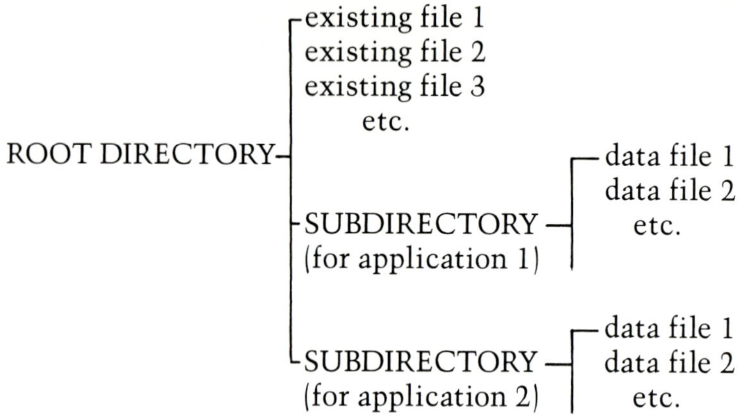

these data files selectively at a later time. If you were to create a subdirectory and place all your data files in the subdirectory, they would be easier to access.

To create a subdirectory, you use the MKDIR command (internal). MKDIR stands for MAKE DIRECTORY. Its format is MKDIR d:*name*, where d: is the drive on which a subdirectory is to be created and *name* is the name you want to call this subdirectory. The subdirectory name follows the same rules as the filename.

- Type **MKDIR B:MYSUB** and press ENTER. If B was already the default drive, there is no need to specify. MKDIR can be abbreviated as MD.

- Now type **DIR B:** to look at the directory for the disk in drive B.

  > You see the entry

  MYSUB <DIR>

  You have created a subdirectory.

CHDIR

You are still in the root directory. That is, if you were to copy a file onto the disk in drive B, it would be placed in the root directory along with other existing files. It is like having a little pointer. The location of the pointer tells which directory or subdirectory is currently being utilized. To move the pointer to the newly created subdirectory, you use the CHDIR command (internal), which stands for CHANGE DIRECTORY.

- With B as the default drive, type **CHDIR MYSUB** and press ENTER. You can type **CD** as abbreviation for CHDIR.
- Use DIR on drive B again.

  > The message

  `Directory of B:\MYSUB`

  indicates that you are now in MYSUB subdirectory.

You can create another level of subdirectory within MYSUB. At this point if you were to copy a file onto the disk in drive B, that file would be placed in MYSUB subdirectory.

You can get back to the root directory, no matter where you are, by typing **CD**. If you want to get back to the subdirectory just above the current one, you type **CD..** (two periods).

PRACTICE TIME

1. Create another subdirectory NEXTSUB within MYSUB.
2. Create subdirectory YOURSUB in the root directory (the same level as MYSUB).
3. Try moving from one subdirectory to another.

Once you create subdirectories on a disk, it is very important that you keep track of which subdirectory contains a particular file. The complete name of a file will now include the subdirectory, or the path, it is placed in. The name now starts with the root directory, which is the drive name, such as B:, followed by a backslash (\) and the subdirectory name. The backslash with subdirectory name is repeated as many times as needed to go down different levels of subdirectory. When the subdirectory where the file is located is reached, place a backslash followed by the filename. For example, to refer to the data file called ADATA.DAT in subdirectory MYSUB, you use B:\MYSUB\ADATA.DAT. To refer to the data file called BDATA.DAT in subdirectory NEXTSUB, you use B:\MYSUB\NEXTSUB\BDATA.DAT.

TREE

If you wonder what your tree structure looks like right now, you can use the external command TREE.

- Make sure that you are in the root directory of drive B by entering **CD**.
- Insert the DOS disk in drive A (remember, TREE is an external command), and type **A:TREE B:** and press ENTER.

  > You will see the following:

```
DIRECTORY PATH LISTING FOR VOLUME XXXXX
Path: \MYSUB
Sub-directories: NEXTSUB

Path: \MYSUB\NEXTSUB
Sub-directories: None

Path: \YOURSUB
Sub-directories: None
```

Remember, path is the same as the subdirectory name. If you were to use the /F option with the TREE command – TREE B:/F, for example – the files in each subdirectory would be listed as well.

RMDIR

The REMOVE DIRECTORY command, RMDIR, is an internal command that lets you remove a subdirectory. Before a subdirectory can be removed, it must be empty; the subdirectory must not contain any files or other subdirectories. Once it is empty, place yourself in the subdirectory just above the one you want to remove, then issue the command.

- Make sure that the subdirectory NEXTSUB is empty.
- Change directory to the subdirectory above NEXTSUB, which would be MYSUB.
- Type **RMDIR NEXTSUB** and press ENTER. You can abbreviate RMDIR as RD.
- Use DIR on MYSUB **(DIR:\MYSUB)** to verify.

PRACTICE TIME Remove MYSUB subdirectory.

Executing Programs

Usually when an application program is to be executed, you start up the machine with a disk containing DOS, replace the DOS disk with the program disk, and type the program name. You can find the program name in the user manual. The names used to start the software in this manual are given in each module.

END OF LESSON 2

- Remove disks from the disk drives and store them.
- Turn OFF the computer and monitor.

SUMMARY

In this lesson various DOS commands are presented.

- The default drive is the drive the computer will use unless instructed otherwise.
- To change the default drive, simply press the drive name, A or B, followed by a colon (:).
- Some DOS commands are internal and others are external. To use external commands, the DOS disk must be in the computer.
- Directories are used to organize files kept on a disk.
- The following commands are discussed:

VER	Displays the DOS version under which you are operating.

Commands Used with Disks:

FORMAT	Formats a disk.
CHKDSK	Checks the status of a disk.

Commands for Using and Moving Files:

DIR	Displays the names of all files on the disk in the disk drive.
COPY	Copies a file.
RENAME	Renames the file.
ERASE	Erases the specified filename.
TYPE	Displays the contents of a file on the screen.

Commands Used to Safeguard Your Files:

COMP	Compares the contents of two files.
DISKCOPY	Creates a copy of one disk on another. Formats the target disk, if necessary.
DISKCOMP	Compares the contents of two disks.

Commands Most Often Used with Hard Disk:

MKDIR	Creates a new subdirectory.
CHDIR	Changes the current directory on a specified drive.

RMDIR	Deletes a specified subdirectory.
TREE	Displays all the directory paths on a specified drive.

REVIEW QUESTIONS

1. Explain what is meant by the default disk drive. How do you know what it is at any time, and how do you change it? ______

2. What does the FORMAT command do? ______

3. When you have 30 or more files on a disk, how do you get a listing of the filenames on screen without some scrolling off the top before they can be read? ______

4. What is a wild card character? How do you use it?

5. How does DISKCOPY A: B: differ from COPY A:*.* B:?

6. How do you move to a subdirectory named SUBA? How do you move back to the root directory? ______

7. How do you verify that a file, once copied, is an exact duplicate of the original file? ______

8. If you've created a maze of subdirectories on a disk over time, how can you locate the path to one particular subdirectory? ____________________

9. Why might a disk be organized with several subdirectories? __________

Lesson 3
Some Advanced DOS Features

Objectives

Upon completion of material presented in this lesson, you should understand the following:

- How to create and execute batch files.
- Purpose of the AUTOEXEC.BAT file.
- Purpose of the CONFIG.SYS FILE.

Supplies Needed

For this part of the manual you need

- The DOS disk.
- A scratch disk.

ORIENTATION

There are many things to learn in using DOS. In the previous section the basic commands of DOS were mentioned so that you might make use of them while working with various types of software in this manual. In this section some advanced features and commands are presented. These commands and features are advanced only in terms of the extra capabilities they provide.

STARTING UP

Start up your computer, using the DOS disk. You will make a **system disk** (not a DOS disk), that is, a data disk with which you can start the computer.

PRACTICE TIME

Format a disk in drive B (it can be the disk you used during the previous lesson) with the systems option (/S).

BATCH FILES

Most of the time you enter DOS commands one by one from the keyboard. Sometimes, however, it is necessary to enter the same sequence of DOS commands repeatedly. For example, let's say that at the end of the computer session every day, you have to copy four data files in different subdirectories onto a backup disk. You may have to type the following four commands:

```
COPY A:\MYSUB\ADATA.DAT B:
COPY A:\MYSUB\NEXTSUB\BDATA.DAT B:
COPY A:\YOURSUB\CDATA.DAT B:
COPY A:\YOURSUB\ANSUB\DDATA.DAT
```

With the names being so long, it is very easy to make typing errors. There is a much better way to do this chore, and that is to use a batch file.

A **batch file** is a disk file consisting of a list of DOS COMMANDS. That is, a series of DOS commands are stored in a text file. It is given a filename with the extension .BAT. You can create it by using the COPY command.

Earlier the COPY command was discussed in terms of making backup copies of a file. The COPY command can be used to create a text file from keyboard input as well. Two things need to be specified with a COPY command: where to copy from (**source**) and where to copy to (**target**). To create a batch file, the source is keyboard input, or CON:, and the target is the batch file.

- Make sure that your formatted disk is still in drive B.
- Type COPY CON: B:MY.BAT and press ENTER.

  > The cursor moves to the next line down.

- Type the four lines shown below, making sure to press ENTER after each line except the last line. After you finish typing the fourth line, wait. Be sure to verify what you type on each line before you press ENTER. You must not make any typing errors. (If you do, you need to start over.)

```
COPY A:\MYSUB\ADATA.DAT B:
COPY A:\MYSUB\NEXTSUB\BDATA.DAT B:
COPY A:\YOURSUB\CDATA.DAT B:
COPY A:\YOURSUB\ANSUB\DDATA.DAT B:
```

- Press the F6 function key and then press ENTER.

  > The message

  ```
  1 file(s) copied
  ```

  appears on the screen.

The batch file MY.BAT has been created. To make sure that you did not make any typing errors, you will look at the contents of the MY.BAT file, using the TYPE command.

- Type TYPE B:MY.BAT and press ENTER.

  > The contents of B:MY.BAT are displayed.

To have the computer carry out the series of DOS commands in the batch file, you just type the batch filename, in this case **MY** (leave out the extension). DOS will then search the default drive, find the batch file, and carry out the various commands in the order specified. Since you used some nonexistent filenames in this batch file, you cannot test it right now.

PRACTICE TIME

1. Create a batch file, B:TEST.BAT, that contains the following DOS commands:

   ```
   DIR A:
   DIR B:
   ```

2. Test the batch file by entering TEST.
3. From the root directory, create a subdirectory named TESTSUB.
4. Copy the batch file, TEST.BAT, to the subdirectory TESTSUB. That is, you give the command

   ```
   COPY  B:TEST.BAT  B:\TESTSUB\TEST.BAT
   ```

5. Erase the batch file TEST.BAT from the root directory.
6. With the DOS disk in drive A, enter the TREE command. That is, type `A:TREE  B:  /F` and press ENTER.

PATH COMMAND

When the execution of a batch file was mentioned above, it was noted that DOS searched for the batch file in the current directory. What if the batch file was not there? In your case the TEST.BAT file is in TESTSUB subdirectory. What happens if you try to execute it from the root directory?

- Make sure you are at the root directory.
- Execute the batch file TEST.

  > You get an error message

  ```
  Bad command or file name
  ```

  That means the batch file was not found in the current directory.

The PATH command (internal) defines the search sequence for batch files and DOS commands. The format for the PATH command is **PATH d:*path*;d:*path*; . . . ,** where d: is the drive and *path* is the subdirectory name. You can specify as many drive and subdirectory names as you wish, separated by semicolons (;). When you enter a command that is not found in the current directory of the default drive, DOS searches the named paths in the sequence you specified.

Typing **PATH** with no parameters displays the current path, or what you specified the last time you entered PATH. If you were to type **PATH** and press ENTER right now, you would get the message

```
No Path
```

since you haven't entered any yet.

When you create a lot of batch files, you may want to place all these batch files in one subdirectory (for organization). Then each time you use the computer, you would enter the PATH command, specifying that subdirectory. Then you could use the batch files from any directory.

- Type PATH B:\;B:\TESTSUB and press ENTER.
- Now execute the batch file TEST.

  > The batch file commands are executed.

First the computer searched the root directory for the batch file TEST. When it could not be found, the computer searched B:\TESTSUB subdirectory and carried out the commands.

AUTOEXEC.BAT FILE

The AUTOEXEC.BAT file is a special batch file that is automatically executed whenever the computer is started up. If your startup disk contains a file with the name AUTOEXEC.BAT, then it is executed on DOS startup without any action on your part.

This means that the PATH command mentioned in the previous section can be placed in the AUTOEXEC.BAT file. That way, every time you start the computer, AUTOEXEC.BAT file is executed and hence the PATH command is executed.

If you do include an AUTOEXEC.BAT file, when the computer is started, only the commands that are in AUTOEXEC.BAT file are executed. Two commands that you see when you start the computer from the DOS disk are DATE and TIME commands. These are the commands that let you specify date and time. You can include these in your AUTOEXEC.BAT as well. If you have a clock/calendar installed in your system, you would place the command to activate the clock in the AUTOEXEC.BAT file instead.

Let's say that you want to create an AUTOEXEC.BAT file that contains the TIME, DATE, and PATH commands.

- Remove the DOS disk from drive A.
- Move the disk in drive B to drive A.

You will create an AUTOEXEC.BAT file in the system disk.

- Enter **COPY CON: AUTOEXEC.BAT**.
- Enter the following commands in the AUTOEXEC.BAT file.

```
TIME
DATE
PATH A:\;A:\TESTSUB\    PATH B:
```

- Press the F6 function key followed by ENTER.
- Now warm start the computer. Do you remember how? Hold down the keys marked CTRL and ALT, and press the key marked DEL.

  > The computer starts up, asking for the time and date, then the PATH is set.

A batch file might contain several other commands. However, the use of these commands is not limited to batch files. That is, these commands can be issued at any time that you are in DOS mode.

One is ECHO OFF. It prevents the screen display of DOS commands executed from a batch file. Usually as commands are executed from a batch file, they are displayed, or echoed, on the screen. Once ECHO OFF is executed, these commands are not echoed. ECHO ON command will reactivate echoing. A reason for including an ECHO OFF command might be to keep the screen from getting cluttered.

- Type **ECHO OFF** and press ENTER.

  > The prompt disappears from the screen.

- Type **ECHO ON** and press ENTER.

  > The prompt reappears.

Another command that "cleans up" the screen is the CLS command. This command clears the screen and sends the cursor to **home**, which is the top left corner of the screen.

- Type **CLS** and press ENTER.

  > The screen clears and the cursor goes home.

A useful command to include in a batch file, particularly in an AUTOEXEC.BAT file, is the PROMPT command; this lets you set a new DOS prompt. Right now your prompt is the default drive, followed by >. When you have many subdirectories, it is helpful to see which subdirectory you are located in.

- Type **PROMPT pg** and press ENTER.
- Change to the TESTSUB subdirectory by using CD TESTSUB.

  > The prompt now reads **B:\TESTSUB>**.

The pg that followed the word PROMPT are special options. These options are each in the form of $c, where c can be one of many options. $p means you want to show the current directory as the prompt. $g means you want to show the symbol >. Consult your DOS manual for other options. You can even set the color of your screen's background and lettering through the PROMPT command.

- Type **PROMPT** and press ENTER to get back to the way it was.

If you want a message displayed on the screen, you can create a file containing text by using the COPY CON: (copy from keyboard to a specified file) and by using TYPE.

- Enter **COPY CON: MESSAGE** to create a text file named MESSAGE.
- Type the following. At end, press the F6 function key, followed by ENTER.

```
This disk was prepared for your use.
```

- Enter **TYPE MESSAGE**.

You will now re-create the AUTOEXEC.BAT file utilizing all the above-mentioned commands.

- Enter the following in the AUTOEXEC.BAT file. (When you COPY CON: to AUTOEXEC.BAT file, it will replace the previous one.)

```
ECHO OFF
PATH A:\;A:\TESTSUB\
PROMPT $p$g
CLS
TYPE MESSAGE
DIR A:
```

- Check to make sure that your AUTOEXEC.BAT file is correct.
- Warm start the computer.

You can change the content of MESSAGE file to display whatever other message you want to see.

PRACTICE TIME

1. Experiment with the AUTOEXEC.BAT file by taking out some commands or inserting other commands.
2. Create other batch files in TESTSUB subdirectory that do the following:
   a. Clear the screen, change directory to TESTSUB, then display the content of the current directory (DIR).
   b. Clear the screen, change directory to the root directory, then display the content of the current directory.
   c. Turn off echoing, clear the screen, and execute the TEST batch file.

The MODE command is often included in the AUTOEXEC.BAT file, but its use requires some knowledge of the peripheral units that you are using, and hence will not be discussed in detail here. In general the MODE command is used to set the way that a printer, a monitor, or a communication port operates. For example, most software is designed to be used with a parallel printer. If you have a serial printer, then you can use the MODE command to redirect all output intended for a parallel port (where a parallel printer is connected) to a serial port (where a serial printer is connected) instead. This allows you to use the serial printer.

CONFIG.SYS

One feature that is worth mentioning is the CONFIG.SYS file. Whenever you start up your computer, DOS files are loaded and the computer searches for an AUTOEXEC.BAT file in the root directory (and if it's there, its commands are carried out). One other step that is carried out is that DOS searches for a file called CONFIG.SYS. If it is found, its commands are executed just like the AUTOEXEC.BAT file. The difference between these two files is that CONFIG.SYS contains a very limited set of commands that can be executed only from the CONFIG.SYS file. These commands are BREAK, BUFFERS, COUNTRY, DEVICES, FCBS, FILES, LASTDRIVE, and SHELL. Some software requires that some of these be set to certain values. Consult your software manual for specific requirements. CONFIG.SYS can be created by using COPY CON: CONFIG.SYS.

END OF LESSON 3

- Remove disks from the disk drives and store them.
- Turn OFF the computer and monitor.

SUMMARY

In this lesson various advanced DOS commands are presented.

- A batch file is a file containing a list of DOS commands.
- An AUTOEXEC.BAT file is a special batch file that is automatically executed when the computer is started up.
- The CONFIG.SYS file contains other commands that some software needs to set specific parameters.
- The following commands are discussed:

PATH	Defines the search sequence for batch files and DOS commands.
ECHO OFF	Disables the screen display of DOS commands.
ECHO ON	Enables the screen display of DOS commands.
CLS	Clears the screen and sends the cursor to the top left corner of the screen.
PROMPT	Changes the prompt on the screen.

REVIEW QUESTIONS

1. What does the PATH command do? ______________________________

   ____

2. What is a batch file? ______________________________

   ____

3. How is a batch file caused to execute? ______________________________

   ____

4. How do you create a batch file? How do you terminate keyboard entry for a batch file? ______________________________________

____

5. What is special about the file AUTOEXEC.BAT?

____

____

____

MODULE 2

VP-Planner Plus

Introduction

Worksheets (also known as spreadsheets) with rows and columns have been used in business for over a century. A lot of information used in running a business is kept on a worksheet. Information is entered with pen or pencil, and calculations are done with calculators. This work, however, usually takes many hours of tedious calculations and recalculations – precisely the kind of job best done with a computer.

This is where an **electronic spreadsheet** comes in. It lets the computer be the pencil, the worksheet, and the calculator. The main memory of the computer is the worksheet, and the monitor (the screen) is the window through which you view your work. The keyboard is the pencil. You store the formulas and values used in the calculations in the computer's memory, and you instruct the computer to do the calculations as needed. If you need to recalculate, you need only to enter the changes.

Because the computer can calculate and recalculate rapidly, the electronic spreadsheet is the best tool to answer the "what if" questions that arise in business. What if we increase the interest rate? What if we increase the markup percentage? What if we give our employees a 10% wage increase? Spreadsheets can be used for financial forecasting, budgeting, stock portfolio analysis, cost analysis, and more.

Impressed? Maybe not. You might wonder what good it would do you to learn how to use a spreadsheet program. After all, you might not work for a business. Well, you can use spreadsheets for other chores as well.

- With a spreadsheet, teachers can keep track of students' grades on exams and homework. The computer can be instructed to figure out the class average for a test, each student's total score and average for several tests, and so on.
- An electronic spreadsheet can be used to do the household budget, too. Did you ever wonder if you could afford to buy a new car? If you save $20 a month this year and increase the amount by 5 percent each year, how much can you save in five years? What if you increase the amount by 8 percent instead? Using the spreadsheet program, you can answer these questions very, very quickly.

What an electronic spreadsheet does is to give flexibility and convenience to the person working with numbers. Without an electronic spreadsheet, one can get bogged down on the mechanical process of doing the calculations and not make the proper analysis of the results.

It was the introduction of spreadsheets that led businesspeople to view the microcomputer as a potentially useful business tool rather than as a toy for hobbyists. Today, there are many spreadsheet software packages on the market, such as VP-Planner Plus, LOTUS 1-2-3, SuperCalc, Quattro, MultiPlan, and Excel. They all perform basic spreadsheet functions in a similar manner. In fact, if you can use one, adapting to another is not difficult.

The spreadsheet program used here is VP-Planner Plus. VP-Planner Plus is an integrated software. That is, in addition to spreadsheet (the ability to manipulate rows and columns of numbers), it also features capabilities for data management and graphics without leaving the program (thus the term "integrated"). The data management part of VP-Planner Plus allows you to arrange the data and extract a certain portion of the spreadsheet. The graphics part of VP-Planner Plus allows you to create graphs out of data on the spreadsheet.

VP-Planner Plus offers many options. Only some of these are covered in this manual. You will learn enough to get started. It is up to you to explore the rest.

NOTE ■ The features mentioned above are not unique to VP-Planner Plus. Most spreadsheet software includes these features. The principal difference between various brands of spreadsheet software is the extent of these options. Some offer better graphics than the others, while others let you manipulate data more conveniently, or offer better use of colors on the screen or an easier way to enter commands.

STARTING VP-PLANNER PLUS

To use this module, you need a DOS disk (to start the computer), a VP-Planner Plus program disk, the **BCS data disk**, and a **formatted data disk**.

1. Insert the DOS disk into drive A (the one on the left), close the door, and start up the computer. Enter the date and time as requested.
2. Remove the DOS disk from drive A.
3. Insert the VP-Planner Plus system disk into drive A and close the door.
4. Type **VPP** and press ENTER.

   > A worksheet with the copyright message is displayed on the screen.

5. Press ENTER.

   > A blank worksheet appears.

USING A PRINTER

You will need a printer to do the lessons in this manual. Furthermore, if you plan to print graphics, you will need access to a printer that is capable of printing graphics. The manual assumes that the correct printer has been installed.

Lesson 1
Creating a Simple Spreadsheet

Objectives

Upon completion of the material presented in this lesson, you should be able to understand and do the following:

- Understand the terminology used with spreadsheets.
- Move the cursor around in a spreadsheet.
- Enter spreadsheet commands.
- Enter data into a spreadsheet file.
- Understand the difference between labels and values.
- Enter simple formulas.
- Save a file on a disk.
- Print a spreadsheet.

STARTING OFF

First, start VP-Planner Plus on the computer by following instructions given in the introduction to this module so that a blank worksheet is displayed, as seen in Screen Display 1-1.

WORKSHEET

The top 21 lines make up the **worksheet display**, and the bottom 4 lines make up the **control panel**. The worksheet has top and left borders, which are highlighted. The top border has letters that label the columns displayed, while the left border has the numbers that label the rows displayed. Initially, 8 columns and 20 rows are displayed. Each intersection of a row and a column contains a **cell** in the

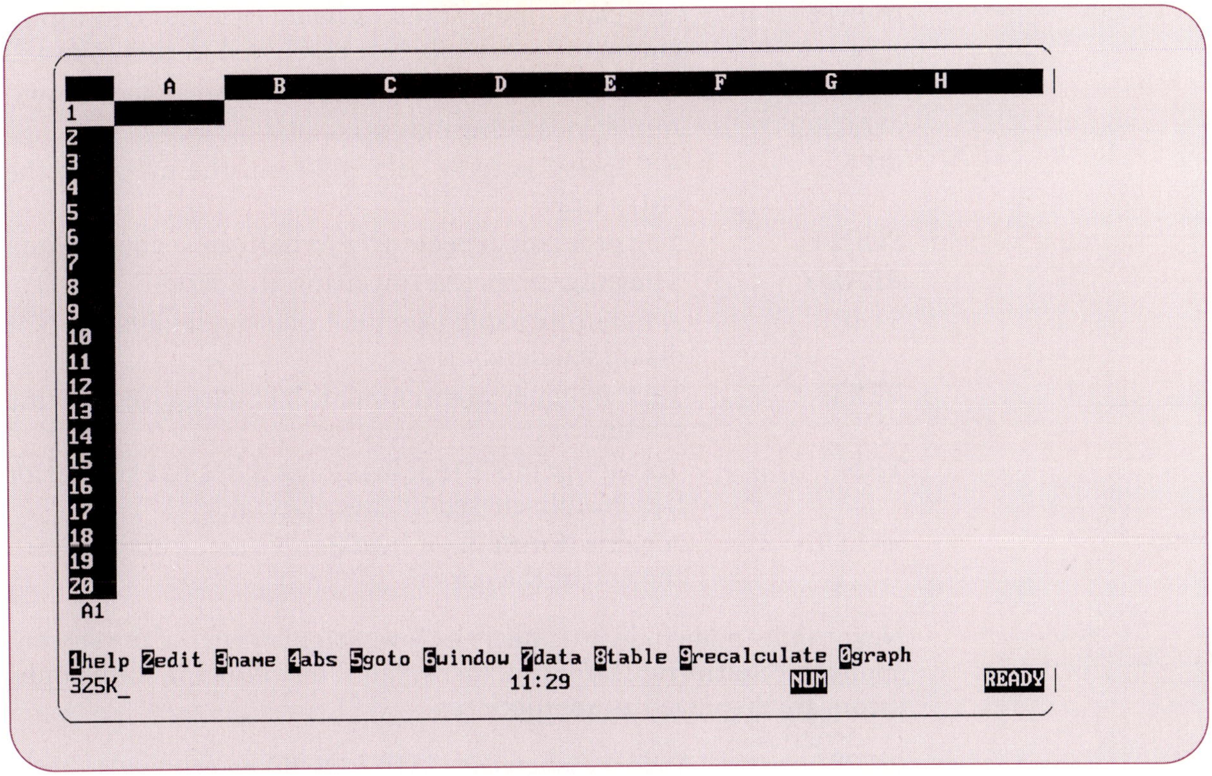

Screen Display 1-1

worksheet. Each cell is identified by specifying the letter and number combination of its column and row, such as A1 or G8. This identification is referred to as the **address** of the cell (cell address).

CONTROL PANEL

The bottom four lines make up the control panel. The top line of the panel is the **status line**, displaying information on data entered. The second line is the **input line**. It shows what you are typing as you enter or edit data. In Screen Display 1-1 this line is blank since nothing has been input. The third line displays the **functions keys usage options**. The bottom line displays **available memory and time**. It also displays the current worksheet mode, using the **mode indicator**. The program can be in one of the following modes:

EDIT	You are to edit an entry or complete a formula by using the keyboard.
FIND	The program is in the data search mode.
HELP	The Help facility has been invoked.

INPUT	/DI (Data Input) or /DEDI (Data External DBF Input) command is issued. Not discussed in this manual.
LABEL	A label is being entered into the cell at the cursor.
MACRO	A macro is being executed.
MENU	An option is to be selected from the menu on the entry line.
POINT	The program expects you to indicate a coordinate.
READY	The program is idle, awaiting an entry.
STEP	A macro is being executed one step at a time. Not discussed here.
TEXT	Text is being manipulated. Not discussed in this manual.
TRN	Transcript mode that logs keystrokes to a transcript file. Not discussed in this manual.
VALUE	A value (formula, or function) is being entered into the cell at the cursor.

Next to the mode indicator, near the lower right corner of the screen, applicable **status indicators** are displayed. The following status indicators are displayed as appropriate:

CAPS	Appears when the CAPS LOCK key is on. All letters are entered in uppercase.
CIRC	Appears when a circular reference has been created. Not discussed in this manual.
END	Appears when the END key is pressed in READY mode.
ERROR	Appears when an error condition has occurred. Press the ESC key to continue.
NUM	Appears when the NUM LOCK key is on. The numeric keypad produces numbers, rather than cursor movement.
SCROLL	Appears when the SCROLL LOCK key is on. Arrow keys move the worksheet under the cursor. (Cursor stays at the current cell.)
WAIT	Appears when you must wait for the program to perform an operation.

Some of the terms are not familiar to you yet. They will be explained to you as the lesson progresses.

CURSOR MOVEMENT

The **reverse video** rectangle (a bright, solid bar) you see at cell A1 (column A, row 1) is the **cell cursor**. You can enter data on the spreadsheet at the cell where the cell cursor is located. This cell is referred to as the **current cell**. If you want to enter data elsewhere (in this case, other than A1), you must move the cell cursor to the desired entry position. You can move the cell cursor around by using the arrow keys to the right of the main keyboard. The four arrow keys move the cell cursor one cell in the indicated direction. Also, the HOME key moves the cell cursor to cell A1.

PRACTICE TIME

Move the cell cursor around the worksheet by using the keys just described. Press the **RIGHT ARROW** key at least 10 times, then the **DOWN ARROW** key at least 25 times. As you do so, notice the status line and also the column and row headings.

WORKSHEET SIZE

As you pressed the arrow keys, you saw the column and row headings change. The worksheet cursor can move to the right beyond column H, and it can move down beyond row 20. Altogether, the worksheet contains 64 columns, labeled A through Z, AA through AZ, and BA through BL. The worksheet also contains 256 rows. Because of the space limitation imposed by your screen size, however, you can see only as many rows and columns as your screen can display at any one time. The screen display, referred to as the **window**, always has twenty rows; the number of columns displayed depends on the column width. (On the regular version of VP-Planner Plus, there are 256 columns—A through IV—and 9999 rows.)

As you continue pressing the RIGHT ARROW key, new columns appear to the right, and the leftmost columns disappear. You are **scrolling** to the right. That is, you are moving the window to the right. As you continue pressing the DOWN ARROW key, new rows appear on the bottom, and the top rows disappear; you are scrolling down, or moving the window down. It is as though you are looking at a map with a magnifying glass. You see just one portion of the map at a time, but you can move the magnifying glass around to look at the whole map.

If you want to move the cell cursor around a little faster, just hold the arrow key down and it will keep repeating. If you want to move the cell cursor around even faster, you can use the PgUp and PgDn (PG UP and PG DN) keys to move the cell cursor 20 rows, or one page, up or down at a time. You can move the cell cursor fast to the left or right, too. Depressing the TAB key moves the cell cursor right to the next screen of columns, and depressing SHIFT/TAB (pressing the TAB key while holding down the SHIFT key) moves the cell cursor one screen to the left.

One more key to note is the SCROLL LOCK key. When you press the SCROLL LOCK key, the status indicator, SCROLL, appears at the bottom of the screen. When you press the LEFT and RIGHT ARROW keys, the cell cursor stays on the same cell, but the screen scrolls under it. Depress the SCROLL LOCK key the second time; then the arrow keys go back to their normal function.

Try these.

GOTO KEY (F5)

Sometimes you want to move your worksheet cursor to a particular cell without having to press the key a certain number of times or hold it down; there is a way. Use the GOTO command (the F5 function key) by following the instruction below.

If you press a wrong key, press the ESC key to back out. If you make an error in typing a cell address, you can press the BACKSPACE key (BKSP key—left arrow key located above the ENTER key) to go back up and retype.

- Press the **F5** function key.

  > The message

  ```
  Enter destination cell
  ```

  appears on the status line, followed by the address of the current cell and a blinking underline character.

  > The mode indicator shows that you are in the POINT mode.

The blinking underline character is the **insert cursor** (which is different from the cell cursor). It shows where your response to the prompts will appear. The insert cursor will be referred to simply as a **cursor** in this manual. The current cell is the **default address**. That is, if you were to press ENTER without entering an address, the cell cursor would not move. You are to point to the cell to which you want to move the cell cursor.

- Enter the address of the cell to which you want to move the cell cursor. If you want to move the cell cursor to cell L56, then type **L56** and press ENTER.

> The cell cursor has moved to the specified cell.

> VP-Planner Plus is in the READY mode.

PRACTICE TIME

1. Move the cell cursor to cell C115 by using the GOTO command.
2. Move the cell cursor to cell F23 by using the GOTO command.
3. Move the cell cursor to other cells.
4. When you are satisfied that you can move the cell cursor to any location you choose, move it to cell A1.

LOADING A SPREADSHEET FILE

Now that you have learned how to load the spreadsheet program and how to move the cursor, you should try using a spreadsheet, just to see how it works. Recall the opening scene from Chapter 5 of *Business Computer Systems.* Tom was using a spreadsheet to plan his home-building costs. The following instructions will enable you to load part of Tom's spreadsheet file from a data diskette (the BCS data diskette you received with this tutorial). Once the worksheet is loaded you can manipulate the figures on it and observe the results. You will learn the details of the following commands in later lessons. For now, just type what is written here, and see what an electronic spreadsheet looks like.

Type only what is printed in boldface. For example, **/F**ile means you type **/F**. (The entire word is printed so you can learn the command names.)

- Place the BCS data diskette in drive A.
- Type **/F**ile **R**etrieve.

  > VP-Planner Plus displays for you a list of filenames. These are the files stored on the disk in drive A.

- Use the DOWN ARROW key to highlight the filename TOM1.WKS.
- Press **ENTER**.

  > The screen looks like the one in Screen Display 1-2.

You have loaded a spreadsheet file. Now you can work with the figures on the screen. The original copy of this file still is stored on disk. Thus, even if you change some of the figures on the worksheet, as long as you don't erase the file called TOM1.WKS you will be able to retrieve it in its original form.

```
      A          B            C            D           E          F
1                       TOM'S BUILDING COSTS
2                         Text Figure 5-1
3
4   MATERIALS
5
6   LUMBER
7
8              Board feet          Type       Cost/ft        Total
9
10                    6000 2 X 4                 1.25      7500.00
11                    4000 2 X 6                 2.30      9200.00
12                   15000 3/4" ext plywood       .70     10500.00
13
14   INSULATION
15
16                  Unit               Type      Cost/unit      Total
17
18                     180 Roll 16" R23 Kraft   12.00      2160.00
19                      50 Roll 16" R16          8.50       425.00
20                     200 Lb. loose fibergl      .28        56.00
 C2     ^Text Figure 5-1

1help 2edit 3name 4abs 5goto 6window 7data 8table 9recalculate 0graph
300K                     16:17                                READY
```

Screen Display 1-2

CHANGING SPREADSHEET FIGURES

You will recall from the text that Tom had carefully recorded the costs of his new home on a spreadsheet. This is part of his spreadsheet. You can see the rest of this spreadsheet by moving the cursor around. Press the DOWN ARROW key enough times so the grand total of $30,874.70 comes into view. (Notice that the top rows have scrolled off the screen.) Now press HOME.

When Tom discovered that some material prices were going up, he modified his spreadsheet to see the results of the changes. With Tom's spreadsheet loaded, enter the changes that Tom did, and observe the results.

PRACTICE TIME

1. Change the price of 2 × 4 lumber from 1.25 to 1.65.

Type	*Results*
F5 D10 ENTER	Positions cursor at cell D10.
1.65 ENTER	Changes 2 × 4 cost to 1.65.
	Changes 2 × 4 total to 9900.00.

2. Change the price of 2 × 6 lumber from 2.30 to 2.45.

DOWN ARROW	Positions the cursor at cell D11.
2.45 ENTER	Changes 2 × 6 cost to 2.45. Changes 2 × 6 total to 9800.00.

3. Change the price of ¾″ ext. plywood from .70 to .95.

DOWN ARROW	Positions cursor at cell D12.
.95 ENTER	Changes plywood cost to .95. Changes plywood total to 14250.00.

4. Change the price of #10d common from 3.40 to 3.57.

Press **DOWN ARROW** 14 times	Positions cursor at cell D26.
3.57 ENTER	Changes #10d common cost to 3.57. Changes #10d common total to 357.00.

5. Change the price of #8d finish from 4.20 to 4.41.

DOWN ARROW	Positions cursor at cell D27.
4.41 ENTER	Changes #8d finish cost to 4.41. Changes #8d finish to 88.20.

6. Change the price of #6d roofing from 6.15 to 6.45.

DOWN ARROW	Positions cursor at cell D28.
6.45 ENTER	Changes #6d roofing to 6.45. Changes #6d roofing total to 307.50.

7. Observe the new building cost total.

Press **DOWN ARROW** 5 times.	Positions cursor at cell D33. Read the figure in cell E33. It should be $37,660.90. If it is not, go back and correct any entries in error.

Now press **HOME** in preparation for the next practice session.

PRACTICE TIME

Tom's brother-in-law just told Tom he had 20 rolls of 16″ R16 insulation and 50 pounds of loose fiberglass insulation that Tom can have. Now Tom won't have to buy so much insulation. Make the appropriate changes to Tom's spreadsheet and answer the following questions:

1. How much will 16″ R16 insulation cost Tom now?
2. How much will loose fiberglass insulation cost Tom now?
3. What is Tom's total material cost now?

ERASING THE WHOLE WORKSHEET (/WEY)

You will now clear the entire worksheet by using the Worksheet Erase command, which will be explained in the next lesson. Note that when you clear an entire worksheet, VP-Planner Plus beeps after you enter /WE and asks for confirmation before it carries out the command. This is to make sure you know what you are doing. If you inadvertently erase an entire worksheet without saving it, then it is gone forever.

- Type **/WE**.

  > The following message is displayed:

  ```
    You have asked that the worksheet be ERASED. Are
  you sure? (Y/N)
  ```

- Press **Y** to confirm.

COMMAND STRUCTURE

When you work with a spreadsheet, you are either inserting data to be processed or giving a command for the VP-Planner Plus to carry out immediately. When you make entries at the current cell, you are *inserting data*. When you give an instruction for VP-Planner Plus to carry out, such as moving data or printing the spreadsheet on a printer, you are *giving a command*. A command in VP-Planner Plus is invoked with a / (slash). Hence, they also are referred to as **slash commands**. The / key is just to the right of the . (period) key on the main keyboard.

When you press the / (slash) key, two **pop-up windows** appear. A pop-up window is a rectangle that appears, or pops up, on the screen, temporarily overwriting any text behind it. It displays information or menu options. After you select an option from the window, additional pop-up windows may appear or all the pop-up windows disappear, revealing whatever was previously displayed in that position on the screen.

- Press **/** (no ENTER).

  > Two pop-up windows appear.

The pop-up window on the left displays the command menu. It provides the means by which all commands are accessed. The following first-level-command options are displayed:

2 Worksheet	Commands that affect the entire worksheet.
3 Range	Commands that affect part of the worksheet.
4 Copy	A command that lets you copy any part of a worksheet to another area.
5 Move	A command that lets you pick up and relocate any part of the worksheet.
6 File	Commands that let you access disk storage to save, retrieve, or combine worksheets.
7 Print	Commands that let you print any part of your worksheet.
8 Graph	Commands that let you create and print graphic screens from data in your worksheet.
9 Data	Commands that let you sort or retrieve data in your worksheet.
0 Tools	Commands that let you use word-processing and graphics features.
System	A command that allows you to leave VP-Planner Plus temporarily to run some DOS commands.
Quit	A command to end the VP-Planner session and return to DOS.

You can make selections from the command menu by any one of the following ways:

1. Type the first character of the command you want.
2. Use the UP and DOWN ARROW keys to highlight your selection, and press ENTER.
3. Press the function key with the same number.

If you make a mistake and select an option or command that you do not want to pursue, you can exit from that command by pressing the ESC key.

You will notice on the command menu that the Worksheet option is already highlighted. That option is called the **default option**. It is the option the VP-Planner Plus program preselected. To select this option, you simply press the ENTER key.

The pop-up window on the right displays either second-level options for, or the explanation of, the highlighted first-level option.

(Notice the double line on the perimeter of this pop-up window.) Second-level options are further options you have within the highlighted first-level option.

PRACTICE TIME

1. Press the **DOWN ARROW** key once. Notice that the Range command is now highlighted, and the second-level menu displays the Range command's options.
2. Continue to press the **DOWN** and **UP ARROW** keys to highlight all the options in the first-level menu. Do not press ENTER, but notice the second-level menu for each.

ERASING AN ENTRY (/RE)

Let's try a slash command. You will make an incorrect entry in a cell, and then erase that entry by using a Range command.

- Press **ESC** key repeatedly if needed, until pop-up windows disappear.
- Move the cursor to cell H1.
- Type MISTAKE and press **ENTER**.

Range commands are those commands that affect specific cells or a set of adjacent cells. In this case you want to erase the entry at a specific cell.

- Press **/R** to select the Range commands option.

> The second-level option window moves in front of the first-level option window. The following second-level options are displayed.

2 Format	Sets display format for a cell or a range of cells.
3 Label	Modifies the alignment of a label or a range of labels (Left, Right, or Center).
4 Erase	Erases the contents of a cell or a range of cells.
5 Name	Assigns a name to a cell or range of cells.
6 Justify	Reformats a column of label cells.
7 Protect	Disallows changes to a range.
8 Unprot	Allows changes to a range.
9 Input	Restricts worksheet cursor movement to unprotected cells only, within a specified range.
0 Col	Sets or resets column width for a specified range of adjacent columns.
Value	Copies formulas in the source range and converts them to values in the target range.

Transpose	Moves the source range to the target range, transposing the contents of rows into columns, and columns into rows.

The third-level pop-up window displays either the description of, or suboptions for, the highlighted second-level command. Again, notice the double-lined perimeter.

- Press E for Erase.

  > A message
  > `Select Range of Cells to be blanked: H1..H1`
  >
  > appears on the input line (since H1 is the current cell).

A range is rectangular. You have to specify the top left and bottom right corners of the range. In this case, since there is only one cell in the range, both corners are the same. You will be specifying larger ranges in later lessons.

- Press ENTER to erase only the entry at the cell cursor.

  > The cell at the cell cursor becomes blank.

If you wanted to erase an entry at a cell other than the current cell, you would type the cell address. When you are either responding to a menu or following through on a command by entering a range, the location of the cell cursor is not affected.

As you become more familiar with the VP-Planner Plus commands, you will not need to pause to look at the menu options after entering each character of a command. For example, you will be able to erase an entry in the current cell by entering /RE and pressing ENTER.

Now clear the entire worksheet.

- Type /WE (do not press ENTER).

  > The following message is displayed:
  > `You have asked that the worksheet be ERASED. Are you sure? (Y/N)`

- Press Y to confirm.

LABELS AND VALUES

The use of a spreadsheet requires more than just entering the numbers, called **values**, needed for calculations. It is necessary to enter various headings or texts, called **labels**, so you can later identify just what the numbers stand for. Thus at each cell in the worksheet you have the option of entering either a label or a value. A label is any word or words you enter in the cell, while a value is either a numeric value or an expression which, when evaluated, yields the number to be displayed at that cell.

The program distinguishes an entry as a value or a label by the first character typed.

Characters Designating Values

Values begin with digits or one of the following special characters: + (plus), – (minus), . (period), @, #, $, or ((left parenthesis).

Characters Designating Labels

Labels begin with letters of the alphabet or any special characters other than / (slash), >, or the ones indicating values.

You will see examples of both values and labels as the lesson progresses. As soon as the first character of an entry is typed, the mode indicator displays whether a label or a value is being entered. Always check to be sure of your entry.

ENTERING LABELS

Labels are entered by positioning the cell cursor at the appropriate cell, typing the characters, and pressing either ENTER or a cursor movement key. If you want a label to begin with a digit or another character indicative of a value, such as + or $, the label needs to be preceded by a **label-prefix character**. The label-prefix characters are also used to position the entry within the cell. The four label-prefix characters are these:

- ' (apostrophe) The entry is displayed aligned with the left edge of the cell.
- " (quotes) The entry is displayed aligned with the right edge of the cell.
- ^ (caret) The entry is displayed centered within the cell.
- \ (backslash) Repeating label—to be discussed later.

If no label-prefix character is entered, the program assumes left alignment.

UPPERCASE

To enter uppercase characters in your label entry, hold the SHIFT key down while you press the character, just as you would do on a typewriter. The SHIFT keys are the wide up arrow keys located at either end of the main keyboard. If you want to type the whole entry in uppercase, press the CAPS LOCK key. To get out of all uppercase, simply press the CAPS LOCK key again. When entering special characters (nonalphabetic shifted characters), you need to hold the SHIFT key down even if the CAPS LOCK has been pressed.

CORRECTING ERRORS

Occasionally, you make a typing error. It is important to know how to correct errors, either during typing or after you have pressed ENTER or a cursor movement key.

If you notice a typing error during an entry, you can erase characters in the entry by pressing the BKSP key. The BKSP key is the long left arrow located above the ENTER key, and is not to be confused with the LEFT ARROW key.

If you notice an error after an entry, you can retype the entire entry by moving the cell cursor to the cell with the error and then entering the correct data.

ENTERING VALUES

Entering values means you want numbers (such as 150, 2, and −37) to appear in cells. You won't necessarily be entering the values that will appear at those positions, however. As you will see later, you can enter a **formula** (an expression) that will be used to calculate the value that is to be displayed in the corresponding cell.

To enter a numeric value, you position the cell cursor at the appropriate cell, type in the value, and then press either a cursor movement key or the ENTER key. Again, if you make a typing error, you can correct it the same way as you would when entering labels.

PREPARING THE WORKSHEET

The various features of VP-Planner Plus will be illustrated through several examples. In the first you will help Susan, who started a new business and wants to keep track of her income and expenses by using a spreadsheet. She wants to find out what her profit is each day.

You will start by setting up the worksheet for just the first day. In the next two lessons you will add more entries and expand and modify the worksheet.

She will use the heading "Income" for income, "Expense" for expenses, and "Profit" for profit.

- Move the cell cursor to cell A1.
- Type in the word ^Income. (Do not press ENTER.) If you mistype a letter, press the **BKSP** key to back up and make corrections.

  > The input line displays **^Income**.

  > The mode indicator displays LABEL.
- Press the **DOWN ARROW** key.

  > The word **Income** is centered on cell A1, and the cell cursor has moved to A2.

- Type ^Expense and press the **DOWN ARROW** key.

  > The word **Expense** is centered in A2, and the cell cursor has moved to A3.

Are you getting the hang of it yet? When you press the ^ key, you are setting the label-prefix that specifies that the label is to be centered in the cell. When you press the DOWN ARROW key, it is equivalent to pressing ENTER followed by the DOWN ARROW key. The entry is terminated and the cell cursor is moved in the direction of the arrow.

- Enter the label Profit centered in cell A3.

Susan earns $600 the first day, and she spends $400 in advertising. Enter these values in the worksheet.

- With the cell cursor on cell B1, type 600 and press the **DOWN ARROW** key.

  > Notice that as you type the numbers, the mode indicator reads VALUE.

- Enter the value 400 in cell B2.

ENTERING FORMULAS (Expressions)

Instead of entering a value at cell B3, you will enter a formula (an expression) that will cause the computer to calculate the profit. The formula is "income minus expense." That is, the formula is to determine the value at B1 minus the value at B2, or B1 minus B2. The result is to be displayed as the profit.

When a formula is entered, the formula itself will appear on the status line as the content of that cell. At the cell, however, the result of evaluating the formula appears.

In a formula, + is the operator used to indicate addition, − is for subtraction, * is for multiplication, and / is for division. These operators are evaluated from left to right. As in ordinary mathematics, multiplication and division take precedence over addition and subtraction unless the latter operations are enclosed in parentheses. Example: 6 + 4/2 will result in 8, whereas (6 + 4)/2 will result in 5.

Let's go on with Susan's business:

- The formula for profit is B1 − B2. With the cell cursor at cell B3, type B1 − B2. (Do not press ENTER.)

Do you see a problem? Look at the mode indicator; it displays LABEL, not a value as you intended.

Because the first character of this formula is "B," a letter of the alphabet, the VP-Planner Plus program assumes that you are entering a label. When a formula starts with a cell address, type the special character + first. That is, instead of simply typing in B1, type +B1. Thus the formula to use is +B1 – B2.

- Use the **BKSP** key to erase what you've typed already, or press the **ESC** key.
- Type +B1 – B2 and press **ENTER**.
  > The status line shows the content of cell B3 as the expression +B1 – B2.

  > Cell B3 shows the number **200**, which is the result of the formula (600 – 400).
- At cell B2 enter any number other than 400, say 250. Did you notice what happened to the number at B3? If you missed it, type in another number.
  > The number at B3 changes. The computer saves the formula for the value at B3. This cell always will display the result of the expression +B1 – B2. The computer recalculates B3 every time you change the values at B1 or B2.

Are you beginning to see the power of an electronic spreadsheet?

As you wrote this formula, you may have had to check on which cell contained the number for income and which cell contained the expense. If this had been a large spreadsheet, you may have had trouble remembering which cell contained which value. If the cells you wanted had scrolled off the window, you would have had to move the cell cursor to find them; when you found them, you would have had to note their positions, move the cell cursor back to the cell where you wanted to make the entry, and then enter the formula. The VP-Planner Plus program can make this process a little easier.

- Put the cell cursor at B3 and enter /RE, followed by **ENTER**, to clear the entry at cell B3.
- Press the + key. (Do not press ENTER.)
  > The mode indicator shows that a value is being entered.

  > The input line shows + followed by the cursor.

- Use the **UP ARROW** key to move the cell cursor to the cell where the value for income appears.

  > Look on the input line. It now reads **+B1.**

  > The mode indicator shows POINT. That is, you are in the process of entering a cell address.

- Press the – key.

  > The cell cursor jumps back to B3, the cell where you are entering the formula.

- Enter the second part of the formula by pointing to it with the cell cursor. Press the **UP ARROW** key once to place the cell cursor at the cell containing the value for the expense.

  > The input line now reads **+B1–B2**.

- To enter the formula as it is shown on the input line, press the **ENTER** key.

  > The cell B3 displays the appropriate value.

You can see that the results of pointing to cells with the worksheet cursor, known as the POINT mode, is the same as for typing those cell numbers in directly from the keyboard.

- Enter the value 400 at B2.

PRACTICE TIME

1. Susan decides that 25% of her profit should go toward purchasing new equipment. Enter the label Equipment at cell A4 and the formula for evaluating the amount for equipment in cell B4. The formula is .25 multiplied by the value in cell B3.
2. Susan wants to know her net profit after purchasing equipment. Enter in row 5 the label -Net- centered and the formula used to calculate it. The formula for net is profit minus equipment, or +B3–B4. Your screen should now look like the one in Screen Display 1-3.

FILE COMMANDS (/F)

The spreadsheet you see in front of you is in the main memory of the computer. When you turn the computer off, all the information will be gone. Most of the time a worksheet is developed in one or more sessions, and then used over and over again in subsequent sessions. Thus it is important to be able to save the worksheet by some

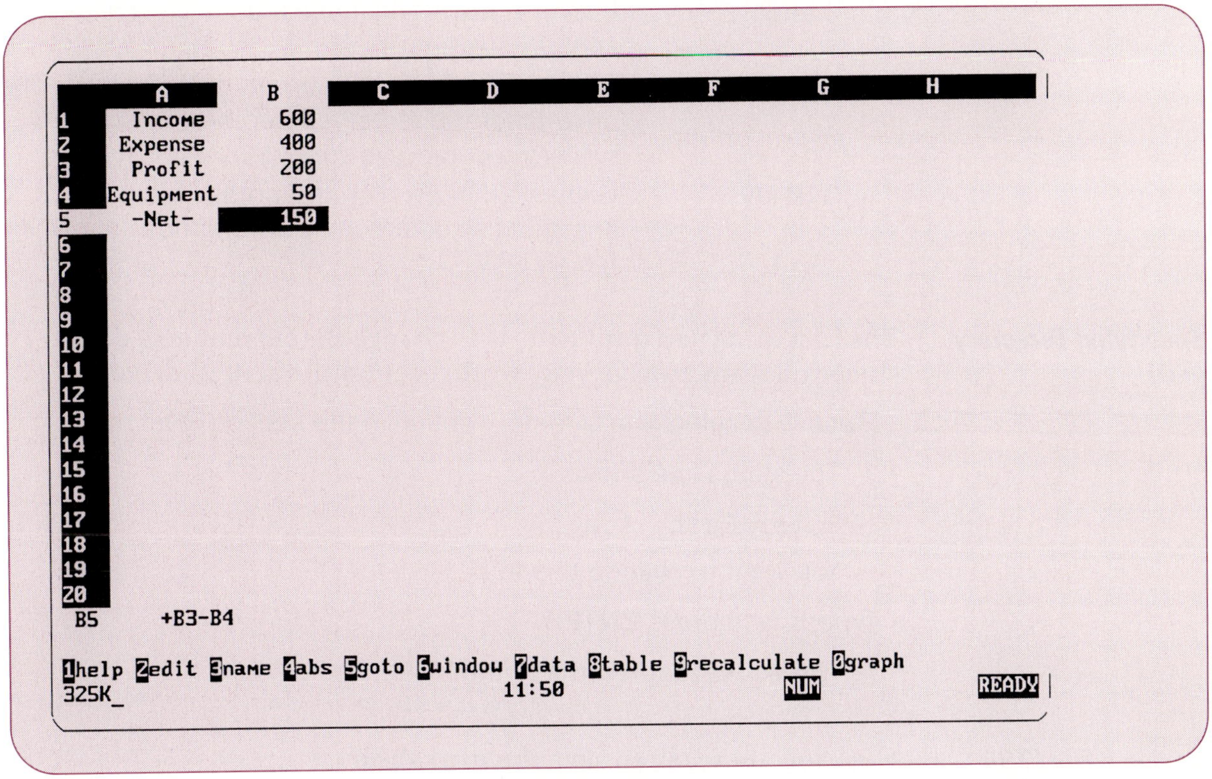

Screen Display 1-3

convenient means. You will insert a formatted data disk into drive B to save the contents of the worksheet.

- Insert the data disk (*not* the BCS data disk) into drive B.
- Press /F to select the File option in the command menu:

> The following options are available in the File second-level menu:

2 Retrieve	Retrieves a specified file from disk.
3 Save	Saves the current worksheet to disk.
4 Combine	Combines values from a specified file with the values on the current worksheet. Values can be copied onto the worksheet or added to or subtracted from the values on the worksheet.
5 Xtract	Saves a range from the current worksheet to a file on disk.
6 Erase	Erases a specified disk file.
7 List	Lists filenames from the disk.

8 Import	Imports into VP-Planner Plus a file created on another system.
9 Directory	Displays or resets the current disk directory. The drive (and/or directory) listed here is where you will store or retrieve your files.
0 Utility	Copies a file on disk to another filename or to another disk or directory, or renames an existing file on disk.

Specifying Directory (/FD)

The first thing you want to do is to change the current disk directory, since you want to save your worksheet on the disk in drive B.

- Press D to select the Directory option in the second-level menu.

  > The status line shows

  `Enter Path: A:\`

  You want to change this to B:.

- Type B: and press **ENTER**.

  > The worksheet returns to the READY mode.

Saving a File (/FS)

Now you are ready to save the worksheet.

- Press /FS for File Save.

  > The input line displays
  `Enter file name: B:\`

Since you can save more than one spreadsheet on a disk, each spreadsheet on the same disk must have a unique name. The saved information is called a **disk file**, and the name that identifies the file is called a **filename**.

A valid filename can be from one to eight characters in length and must be letters, numbers, or the underscore character (—). When you enter the filename, the extension .WKS is added by the VP-Planner Plus program. For example, if you were to call the file MYFILE, it is stored as MYFILE.WKS. Letters may be entered in upper- or lowercase, but are converted to uppercase.

To continue, use the filename VPP1.

- Type VPP1 and press **ENTER**.

  > The red light on disk drive B goes on and the worksheet is stored on disk.

PRINTING FILES (/PP)

Now let's print the spreadsheet.

- Make sure you are working with an IBM-PC that is connected to a printer. Also, make sure that the printer is turned ON and is ready for use. If you are using a continuous sheet of paper, make sure that the perforation is at the print head.
- Send the cell cursor to A1.
- Type /P for Print.

  > There are two options in the second-level menu:

2 Printer	Prints on the printer.
3 File	Stores the print images as a file on disk.

You want to send it to the printer to be printed.

- Type P to select Printer.

  > The following options are displayed in the third-level menu:

2 Range	Specifies a range to print.
3 Line	Advances one line.
4 Page	Advances to top-of-page as calculated by VP-Planner Plus.
5 Options	Header, Footer, Margins, Borders, Setup, Page-Length, Others.
6 Clear	Resets some or all print settings.
7 Align	Resets to top of page (after adjusting paper).
8 Go	Prints the specified range.
9 Quit	Exits the Print command.
0 Status	Displays the current status of print settings.
Eject	Ejects paper to the top of the next physical page based on the printer top-of-page.

First, you have to specify which rectangular portion, or range, of the worksheet you want printed. Obviously, you cannot always print the whole worksheet on a little piece of paper. On 8-1/2-by-11-inch paper, the most that will fit on a sheet is 8 columns (of 9-character width).

- Type R to select Range.

  > The input line shows the following message:

  ```
  Select range of cells for printing: A1
  ```

You specify the top left and bottom right corners of the rectangle you want printed. In the present example, which is a very small spreadsheet, you can print the whole thing. The range is A1 for the top left corner and B5 for the bottom right corner.

- Type A1.B5 and press ENTER.

  > The PRINT Printer third-level menu is displayed again.

NOTE ■ If you do not specify the range, the entire worksheet is printed. That is, the range is set from A1 to the address composed of the leftmost column with an entry and the bottommost row with an entry.

You are now ready to print the worksheet. First, however, you must **align** the paper. VP-Planner Plus keeps track of the number of lines printed, and after the appropriate number are printed (taking top and bottom spacing into account), it leaves several blank lines at the bottom and top margins. Hence you need to tell VP-Planner Plus that the printer is, indeed, at the top of the paper.

- Select Align.
- Select Go.

  > The worksheet is printed.

- Select Page to advance the paper to the top of next page.
- Select Quit to exit the Print command.

END OF LESSON 1

This is the end of the first VP-Planner Plus lesson.

- Type /Q, then Y, to exit VP-Planner Plus and return to DOS.
- Remove and store your disks in their envelopes.
- Turn OFF the monitor, computer, and printer.

SUMMARY

In this lesson many of the terms and concepts that are necessary to use spreadsheets effectively are introduced.

- The control panel consists of status, input, and command lines.
- The mode indicator and status indicators tell you what the program is doing.
- The cell cursor highlights the cell where the entries are being made. You can move it around the spreadsheet by using the following keys:

arrow keys	move cell cursor in the direction of the arrow.
TAB	moves cursor to the next screen of columns.
SHIFT/TAB	moves the cell cursor one screen to the left.
HOME	moves the cell cursor to cell A1.
PGUP, PGDN	move the cell cursor 20 lines up or down.
the F5 function key	moves the cell cursor to the coordinate specified.

- Uppercase letters are entered by using either the SHIFT key or the CAPS LOCK key. To enter special characters that appear on the upper half of a key, the SHIFT key must be held down even if the CAPS LOCK key has been pressed.
- Errors can be corrected by using the BACKSPACE key or by reentering the information for a cell. You can also cancel a command by pressing the ESC key.
- A cell may contain either a label or a value. A label is used to identify the information; a value is numerical information.
- Values can be arithmetic expressions, such as formulas. The cell address in a formula can be entered by pointing to the cell with the cell cursor.
- A label-prefix character is used to position a label entry in a cell.
- A range is rectangular. It is referred to by specifying the addresses of the top left and bottom right corner cells, separated by a period.
- Commands in VP-Planner Plus are invoked with a / (slash) key.
- The following commands are discussed:

/FD	File Directory—specifies the directory (disk drive) to use.
/FS	File Save—saves the spreadsheet file to disk.
/RE	Range Erase—erases contents of a range of cells.
/WEY	Worksheet Erase Yes—erases the entire worksheet.
/PP	Prints spreadsheet to printer.

REVIEW QUESTIONS

1. How do you send the cell cursor to a particular cell without using the arrow keys? ____________________

____

2. What information do you see on the status line? ______________________

____

____

3. How do you invoke commands in VP-Planner Plus? ______________

____

4. How does VP-Planner Plus distinguish a label entry from a value entry?

____

____

____

5. What is a label-prefix character and when is it used? ____________

____

____

6. How do you enter a value that starts with a cell address? __________

____

7. How do you move the cell cursor one screen down at a time? ______

____

____

8. How do you correct a data entry error in a cell? ________________

____

____

9. How do you blank (erase) an entry in a cell? __________________

____

____

10. Give the commands needed to print a spreadsheet. ______________

____

____

____

EXERCISES

1. a. Design and create a telephone directory, that is, a spreadsheet that holds names and phone numbers. Phone numbers are entered without area codes. Think very carefully whether a phone number is a value or label.
   b. Enter names and phone numbers of your ten best friends.

   c. Save the file as EX1__1 (it is needed in a later exercise).
   d. Print the entire spreadsheet.

2. a. Design and create a spreadsheet that holds scores of ten students on three exams.
   b. Enter names of 10 students and scores (1 to 100).
   c. Save the file on disk as EX1__2 (it is needed in a later exercise).
   d. Print the entire spreadsheet.

Lesson 2
Enhancing the Simple Spreadsheet

Objectives

Upon completion of the material presented in this lesson, you should be able to understand and do the following:

- Retrieve a spreadsheet file from a disk.
- Insert a row.
- Copy cell contents.
- Enter repeated labels.
- Change the width of a column.
- Use a simple function.
- Change the display format of numeric entries.
- Save a file using a different filename.
- Assign range names.
- Print a spreadsheet by sections.

STARTING OFF

Start VP-Planner Plus so that a blank spreadsheet is displayed. Insert your data disk into drive B. In this lesson you will retrieve the spreadsheet file you prepared in the first lesson and will learn new commands to extend the basic principles.

RETRIEVING A FILE (/FR)

You will retrieve the file from the disk, but before you can do so, you have to tell the computer where your data disk is.

- Type /FD for File Directory.
- Type B: and press **ENTER** to indicate that your data disk is in drive B.

Now you are ready to retrieve the file.

- Type **/FR** for File Retrieve.

  > The input line reads

  ```
  Enter file name:B:\*.WK?
  ```

  > A pop-up window appears at the top left corner of the spreadsheet, displaying the names of files on the disk in drive B. VPP1.WKS should be one of the files displayed.

To specify the file you want retrieved, you can simply type whatever filename you gave at the end of the previous lesson and press the ENTER key or move the highlight in the usual manner and press ENTER when the filename you want is highlighted.

- With VPP1 highlighted, press **ENTER**.

  > The selected file is loaded into the worksheet as shown in Screen Display 2-1.

INSERTING ROWS (/WIR)

Right now your worksheet shows values for one day. You will now extend these entries to show ten days of business activity. You will enter the figures for the second day in column C, for the third day in column D, and so on. To identify the values easily, you give these columns headings.

Column headings should go on row 1. Do you see a problem? Row 1 already has some entries. You could erase the whole spreadsheet and start over again, putting income in row 2, expense in row 3, profit in row 4, and so on. However, there is an easier way. You can insert a row.

- Place cell cursor on row 1, say cell A1.
- Type /W for Worksheet.

  > The following Worksheet second-level options are displayed:

2 Global	Commands that affect the entire worksheet.
3 Insert	Inserts blank row(s) or column(s).
4 Delete	Deletes entire column(s) or row(s).

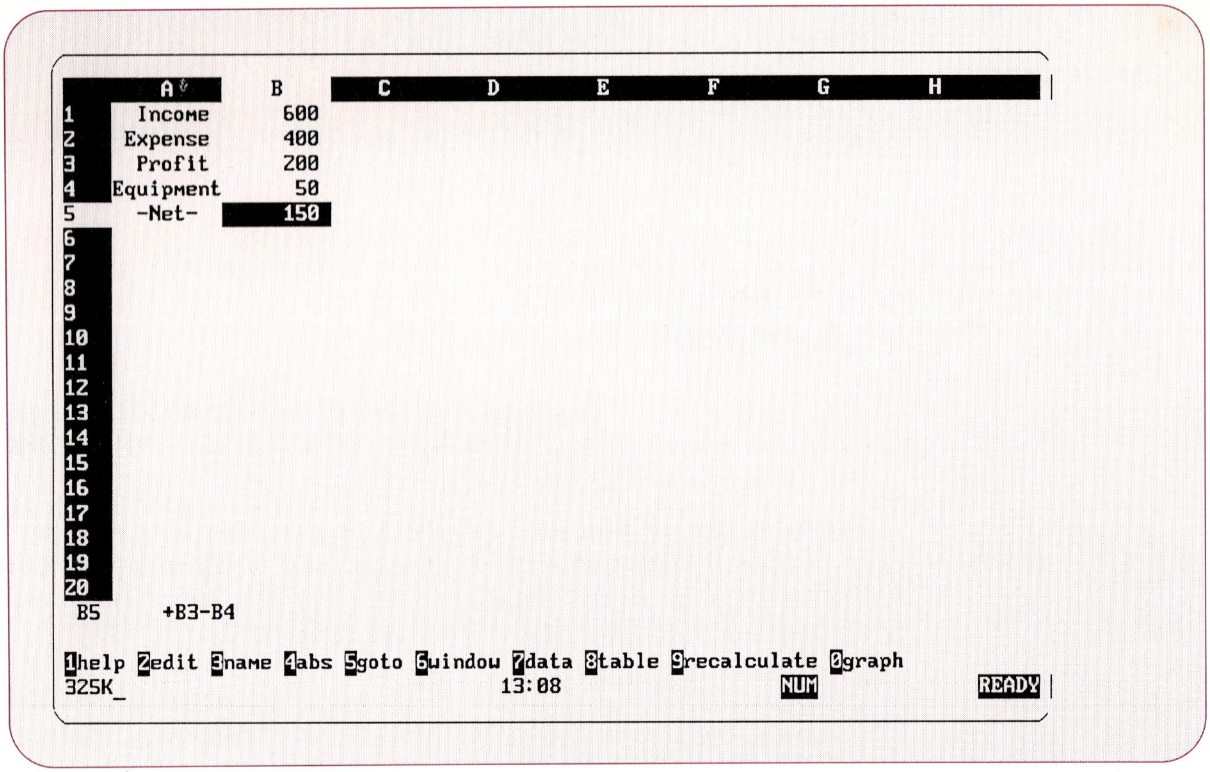

Screen Display 2-1

5 Col-width	Sets display width of current column.
6 Erase	Erases entire worksheet.
7 Titles	Sets horizontal or vertical titles.
8 Window	Sets split screen and synchronized scrolling.
9 Status	Displays format, column-width, and recalculation settings, and memory available.
0 Autokey	Records "macros."
Page	Inserts a page break flag into the worksheet.

- Select **I**nsert.

  > The third-level menu displays two options:

2 Row	Inserts row(s)
3 Column	Inserts column(s)

- Select **R**ow since you want to insert a row.

  > The input line displays

  ```
  Select range of rows to insert: A1..A1
  ```

Since you just want to insert a row at 1, you need only press ENTER.

- Press **ENTER**.

  > All the information on the spreadsheet moves down one row, and row 1 is now blank.

Now put headings on the columns. First, you will label row 1.

- Enter ^Day at cell A1.
- Enter 1 (numeric) at cell B1 as a column heading.

Now you are going to enter 2 at C1, 3 at D1, . . ., 10 at K1. To do this, you could press the RIGHT ARROW key, make an entry, press the RIGHT ARROW key, make an entry, and so on. But try another way. Each entry is one greater than the previous entry. The entry at C1 is the entry at B1 plus 1; the entry at D1 is the entry at C1 plus 1; and so on. So you could enter the formula +B1+1 at C1, +C1+1 at D1, and so on.

- With cell cursor on cell C1, type +B1+1 and press **ENTER**.

  > The cell C1 shows the value **2**.

Now think for a moment. You will have to enter the formula +C1+1 at cell D1, +D1+1 at cell E1, and so on up to +J1+1 at K1. How tedious to enter a similar formula over and over. It's a lot of work. Yet you need to do this only nine times. What if you were setting up the worksheet for a month or a year?

COPY COMMAND (/C)

There is an easier way; use the Copy command. This command can be used to make copies of formulas, texts, numbers, blank entries, and so on across columns, down rows, and wherever you want.

- With the cell cursor at C1, type /C for copy.

  > The input line reads

  ```
  Source cell range: C1..C1
  ```

The VP-Planner Plus program wants to know what to copy. You want to copy the formula at C1, that is, the range is one cell, C1. All you have to do is press ENTER.

- Press **ENTER**.

  > Another message appears on the input line.

  ```
  Destination cell range: C1
  ```

So far you've told the VP-Planner Plus program to copy the formula at C1. Now it wants to know where to copy to. You are entering headings for 10 days (columns B to K). Since you've already inserted headings for columns B and C, the target range is D1 to K1. You could type in the range D1.K1, but this time you will point to the cell with the cell cursor. This method was discussed in Lesson 1.

- Move the cell cursor to cell D1, the first cell where you want to copy the information.

  > Destination range now reads **D1**.

If you were copying the formula to just one cell, you would press ENTER at this point. However, you want to copy the formula to more than one cell: to the range of cells whose upper left corner is D1 and bottom right corner is K1. Therefore you press the period (.) key. This anchors, or marks, the start of the range to the computer.

- Type a period (.).

  > Destination range now reads **D1..D1**.

- Use the cursor movement keys to highlight cells D1 through K1. As you do this, the screen will scroll to the left. If you move too far to the right with the RIGHT ARROW key, you can move back with the LEFT ARROW key.
- Press **ENTER**.

  > The cell cursor appears at C1 and numbers appear in columns D to K as partially shown in Screen Display 2-2.

- Move the cell cursor along row 1 and notice the content of each cell as displayed on the status line.

You will notice that VP-Planner Plus inserted the relative formula in each cell. That is, rather than copying the formula +B1+1 in each cell, it copied a formula that says content of the cell to the left plus one. So, at cell F1, it wrote +E1+1. If you really wanted the absolute formula +B1+1 copied onto all the cells in the target range, you

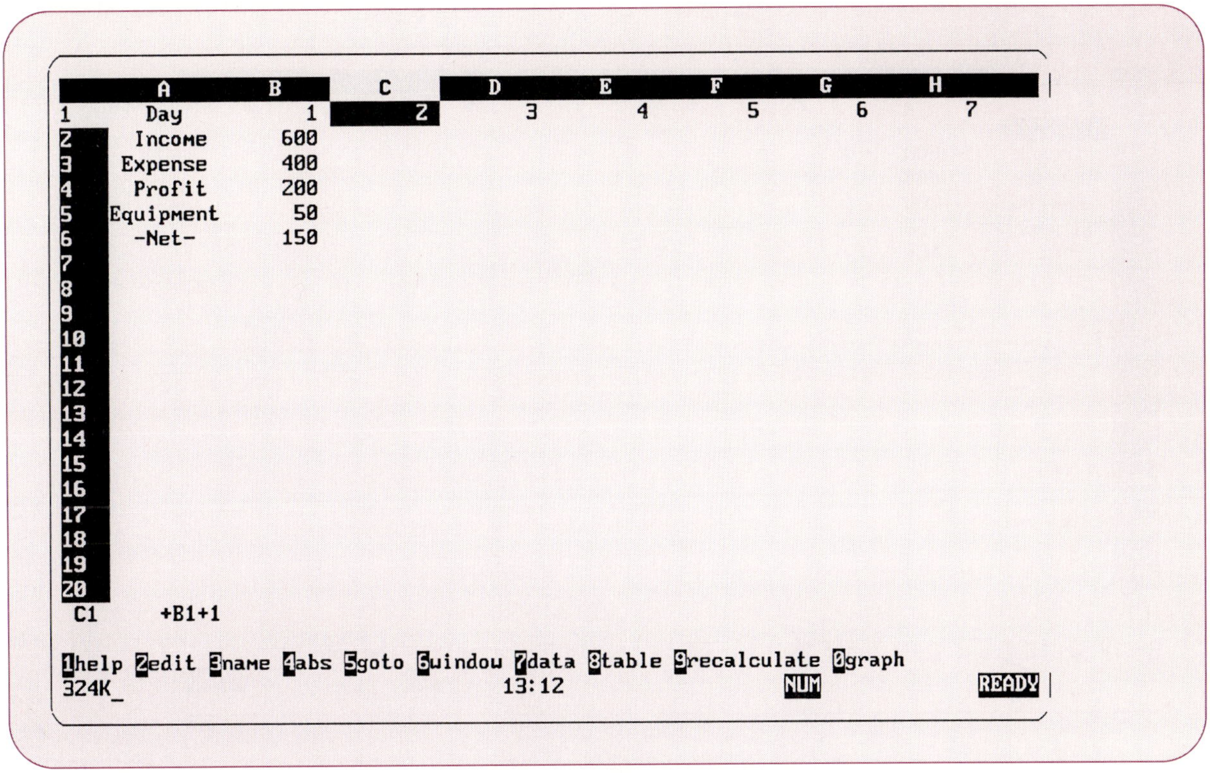

Screen Display 2-2

would have had to enter the formula in C1 originally with $ (dollar) signs preceding the cell's column label and row number. That is, the formula would have been +B1+1. This will be discussed in more detail later.

PRACTICE TIME

Insert a blank line at row 2, producing the screen shown in Screen Display 2-3.

REPEATING LABELS (\)

Now you want to make the spreadsheet look good. You will put hyphens across the spreadsheet at row 2, columns A through K, to separate the headings from the values.

- With the cell cursor at A2, type \ (backslash).

  > The mode indicator shows that you are entering a LABEL.

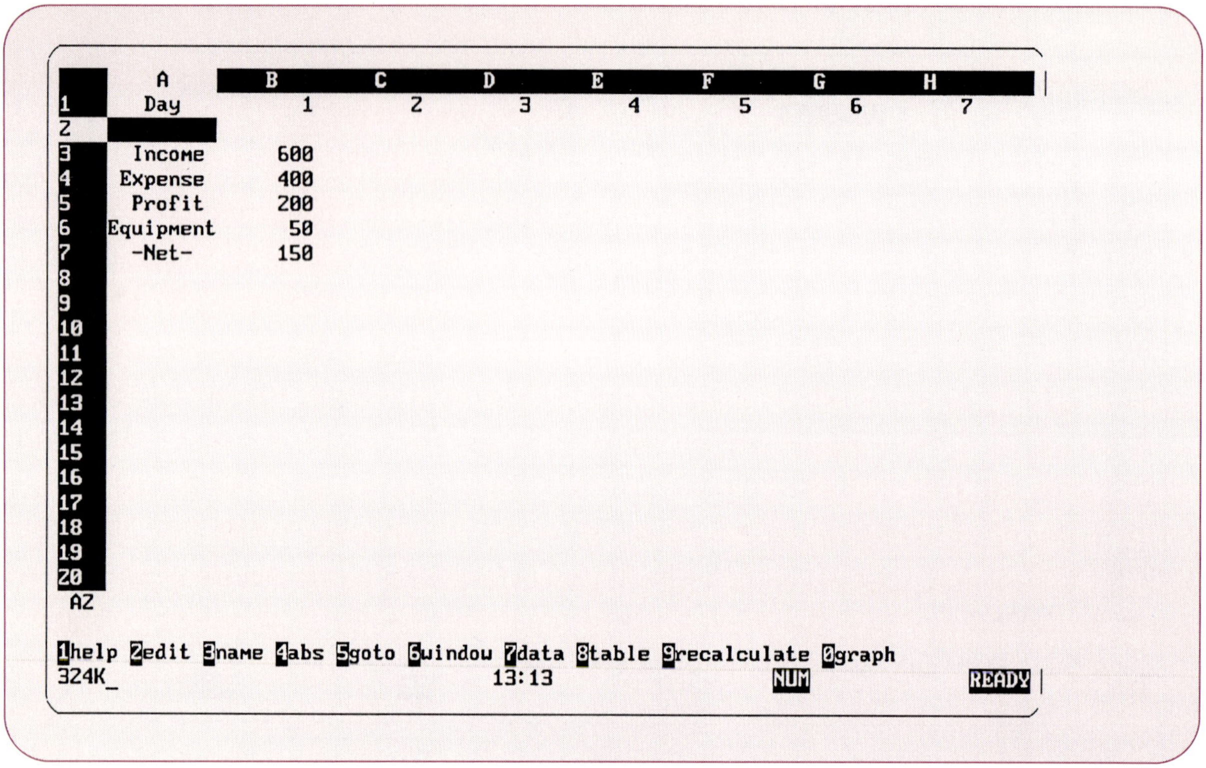

Screen Display 2-3

You are to enter the character you want repeated across a cell.

- Type **–** and press **ENTER**.

  > Cell A2 is filled with hyphens. In fact, cell A2 is filled with hyphens regardless of its column width as you will see in the next section.

You will now have to copy this entry through the range B2 through K2 by using the Copy command.

- With the cell cursor on cell A2, type **/C** for copy.
- Source range is just A2, so press **ENTER**.
- Destination range is cell B2 on top left corner and cell K2 on bottom right, type **B2.K2** and press **ENTER**.

  > Row 2 has hyphens from A2 through K2.

SETTING WIDTH OF A COLUMN (/WC)

Initially, every column in the spreadsheet is nine characters wide; that is, nine characters can be displayed at each cell. You can change the width of a particular column, several adjacent columns, or the entire worksheet. Right now you will change the width of column A to see if it is still being filled with hyphens. This can be accomplished by using either the Worksheet command or the Range command. The Worksheet command is used when you want to change the column width of either just one column or the entire spreadsheet. The Range command lets you specify column(s) you want affected. You will use the Worksheet command.

- With the cell cursor on any cell in column A, type /W for Worksheet command.

  > The Worksheet second-level options are displayed.

- Select **Col-width**.

  > The third-level options are now displayed.

2 Set	Specifies a new column width.
3 Reset	Changes the setting back to the initial, or default, setting.

- Select **Set**.

  > The input line displays the following message:

  ```
  Enter desired column width (0-240): 9
  ```

The default, or preset value, is 9. Suppose you want to change it to 12.

- Type 12 and press **ENTER**.

  > The width of column A changed to 12. Notice that even though the column width changed from 9 to 12, cell A2 is still filled with hyphens.

NOTE ■ If a label is too long to be displayed, the excessive characters are displayed on the consecutive cell(s) to the right, provided that these cells do not contain data. If a value is too large to be displayed in a cell, the cell fills with asterisks (*). *In either case it is only the display that is affected. The correct data is entered into the cell.*

PRACTICE TIME

1. Change the width of column A back to 9.
2. Enter the following values for days 2 through 5.

DAY	2	3	4	5
INCOME	300	950	1000	692.50
EXPENSES	275	500	500	600.34

3. Copy the formulas for profit, equipment, and net, as entered in cells B5, B6, and B7, onto the range C5 through K5, C6 through K6, and C7 through K7, respectively. Your screen should now look like the one in Screen Display 2-4.

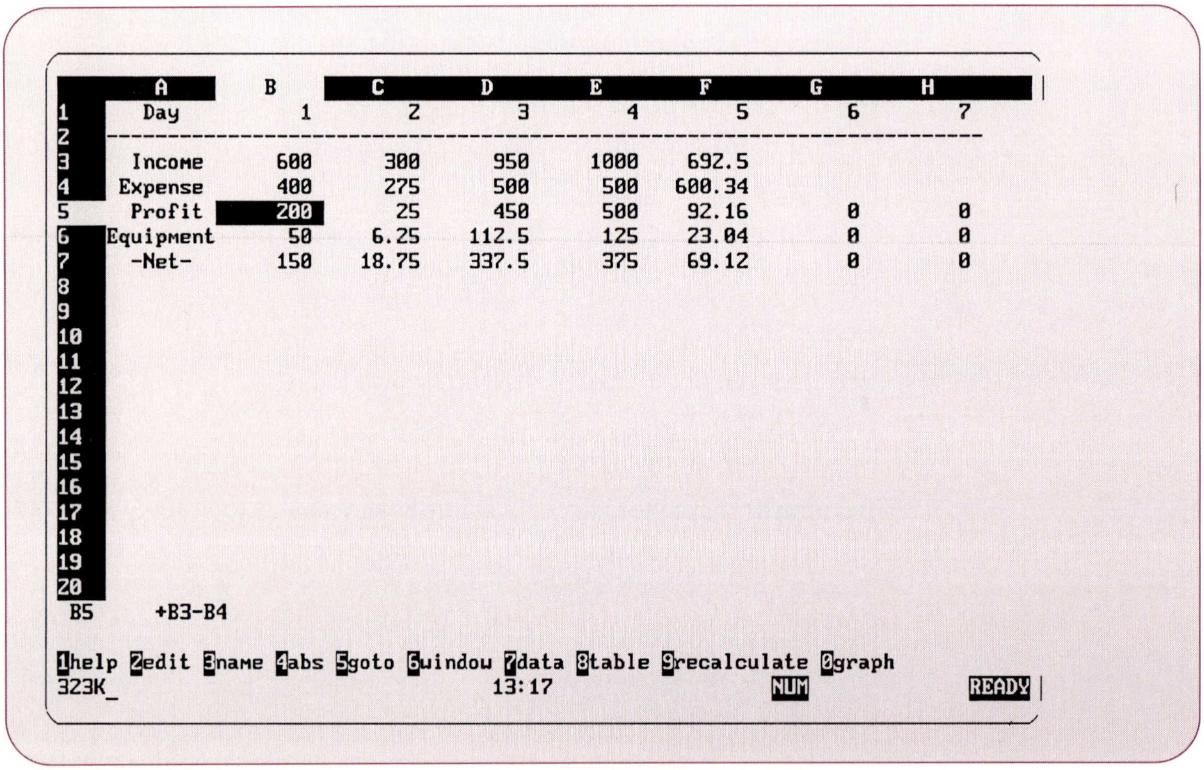

Screen Display 2-4

Now Susan can see the profitability of the business at a glance. Columns G through K are blank for "income" and "expense" rows and show 0 (zero) for the rest. These columns are already set up so that as Susan enters values for income and expense on days 6 through 10, profit, equipment, and net will be calculated and displayed automatically.

NOTE ■ It is possible to set up an entire spreadsheet without data. It can contain all the headings and formulas needed, have all columns set to proper width, and have the display format specified. Such a spreadsheet is called a **template**. A template is a prewritten spreadsheet that is ready to accept data. All one has to do to utilize a template is to retrieve it and enter data into the proper cells.

It occurs to Susan at this point that she had a certain amount of cash she started the business with. Call it Cash-on-Hand. She would like to see the change in that value from day to day. She decides that she would like to see this figure on row 3.

PRACTICE TIME

1. Insert a blank row at row 3.
2. Place the row heading "Cash-on-Hand" in cell A3. You will notice that the characters that did not fit in cell A3 appear in cell B3. If a label is too long to fit in one cell, VP-Planner Plus automatically displays each section in adjacent cells, unless the adjacent cells are occupied.
3. Adjust the width of column A so that the heading will fit.
4. Insert the value 750 in cell B3 as the starting figure. This should make your screen like the one in Screen Display 2-5.

Think about this for a minute. The value for cash-on-hand changes daily, depending on the net profit. On the second day the cash-on-hand is cash-on-hand for the first day plus net profit for the first day. So the formula used for cash-on-hand for the second day is the value at cell B3 plus the value at cell B8.

PRACTICE TIME

1. In cell C3 enter the formula for cash-on-hand for the second day.
2. Copy this formula to the range D3 through K3.

As Screen Display 2-6 shows, the Cash-on-Hand values for Days 6 through 10 remain constant since net values are zeros for those days.

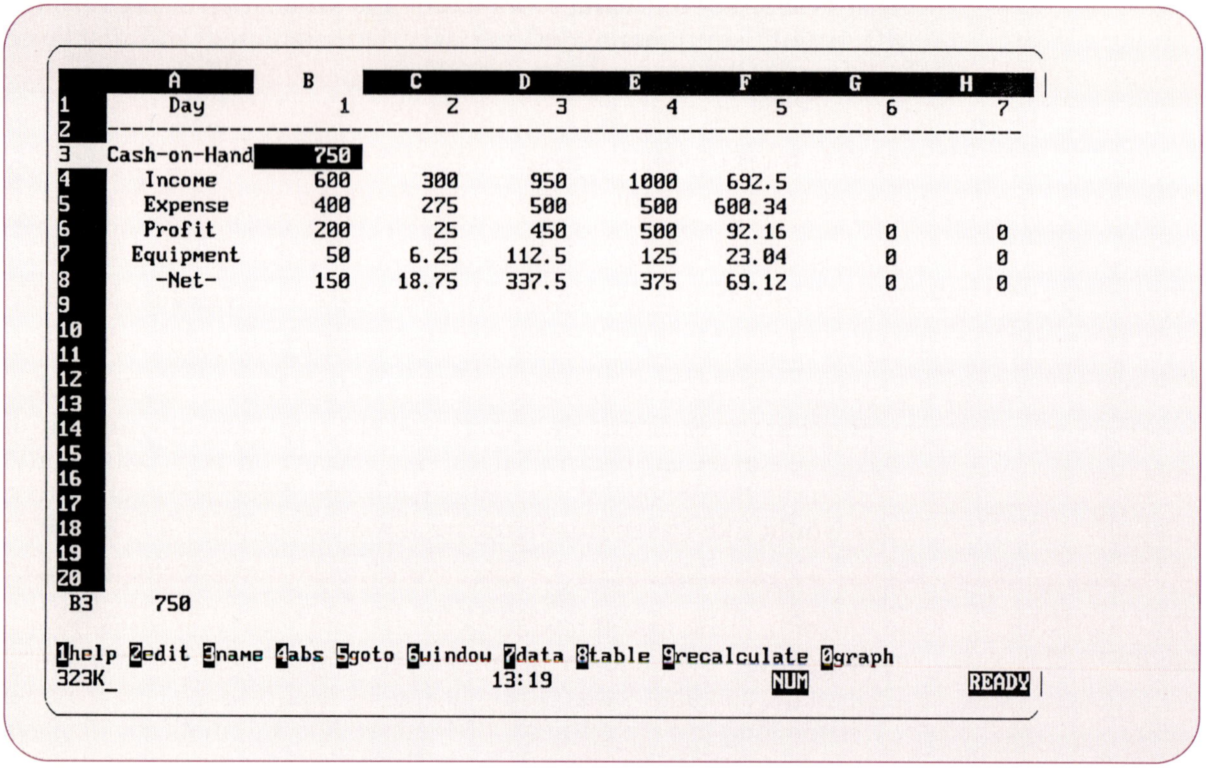

Screen Display 2-5

SUM FUNCTION (@SUM)

For column L Susan decides that she would like to see totals for income, expense, profit, equipment, and net for the ten-day period. To enter the total income at L4, for instance, you can enter the formula

+B4+C4+D4+E4+F4+G4+H4+I4+J4+K4

That's a long formula. Suppose you had to find the total income for 60 days? As you might have guessed, there is an easier way to total numbers. You can use the @SUM function.

· With the cell cursor at L4, type @SUM, but do not press ENTER yet.

You are to indicate what values you want totaled. These values are known as the **arguments**, and are entered within parentheses. The arguments you enter can be any of the following:

- A range of cells, such as row 3, column B to E. This is entered as (B3.E3). A period serves as a **delimiter**, or separator, that separates the beginning of the range from the end.

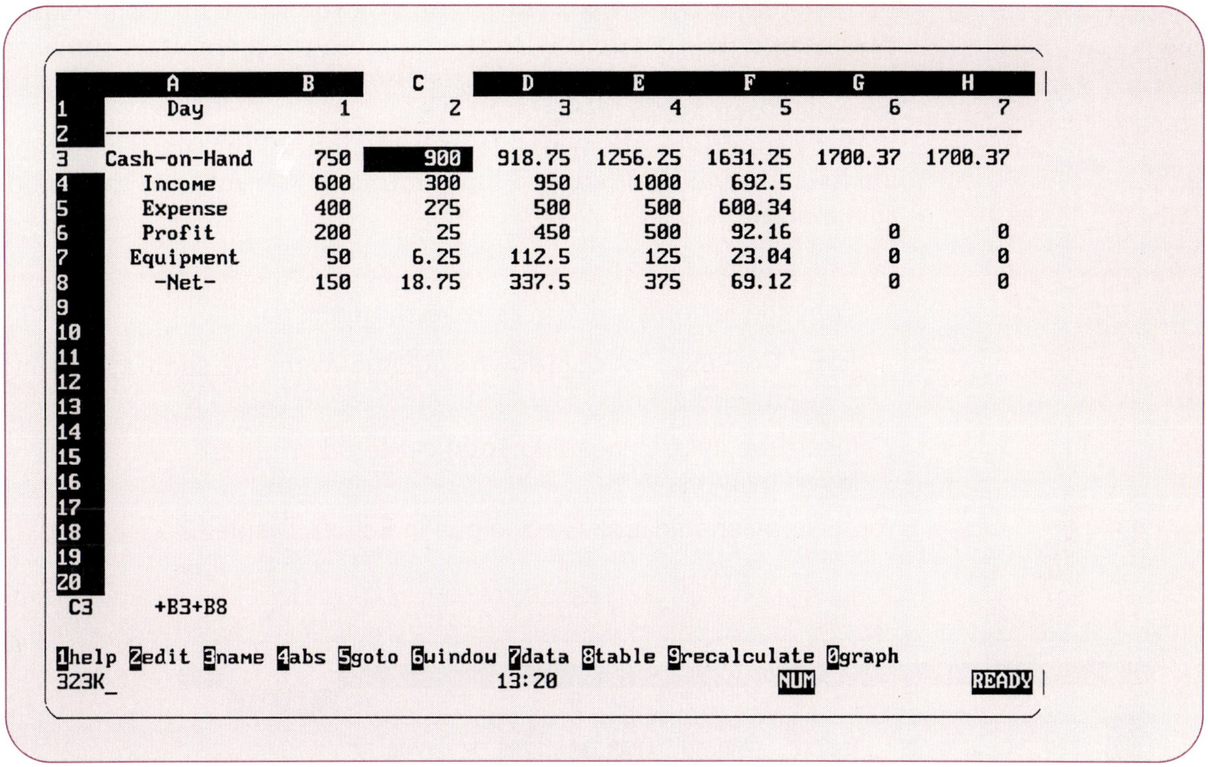

Screen Display 2-6

- A list of specific cells separated by commas, such as (B3, C3, D3).
- A combination of range of cells, list of cells, numbers, and formulas, such as (B3.B7,B9,4,7*C9).

In your case you want to enter a range of cells. You want to total the values on row 4, columns B to K.

- Type (B4.K4) and press **ENTER**.

  > The status line shows **@SUM(B4..K4)**.

  > At cell L4 the value **3542.5** appears.

The range could have been specified by using the POINT mode. To enter in POINT mode, you type @SUM(, then use the arrow key to point to the first cell of the range, type . (period), point to the last cell of the range, type), and press ENTER. You can try this on your own.

All functions start with the @ character. When you enter @, the VP-Planner Plus program recognizes the entry as a value and knows that the characters between @ and (are the name of the function.

Each function performs a calculation on the value or list of values (its arguments) specified with it, and produces a result. A function can be used as a value entry by itself or it can be used as part of a formula, such as .25*@SUM(A1.A6).

Many functions are available in VP-Planner Plus, some of which are listed in the VP-Planner Plus Command Summary at the end of this module.

PRACTICE TIME

1. Copy the formula at L4 to cells L5 through L8.

   Hint: Copying a formula down a column works the same as copying it across a row. The destination range is L5.L8.

2. Insert the column heading **Total** centered in cell L1.
3. Insert hyphens in cell L2.

Your screen should look like the one in Screen Display 2-7.

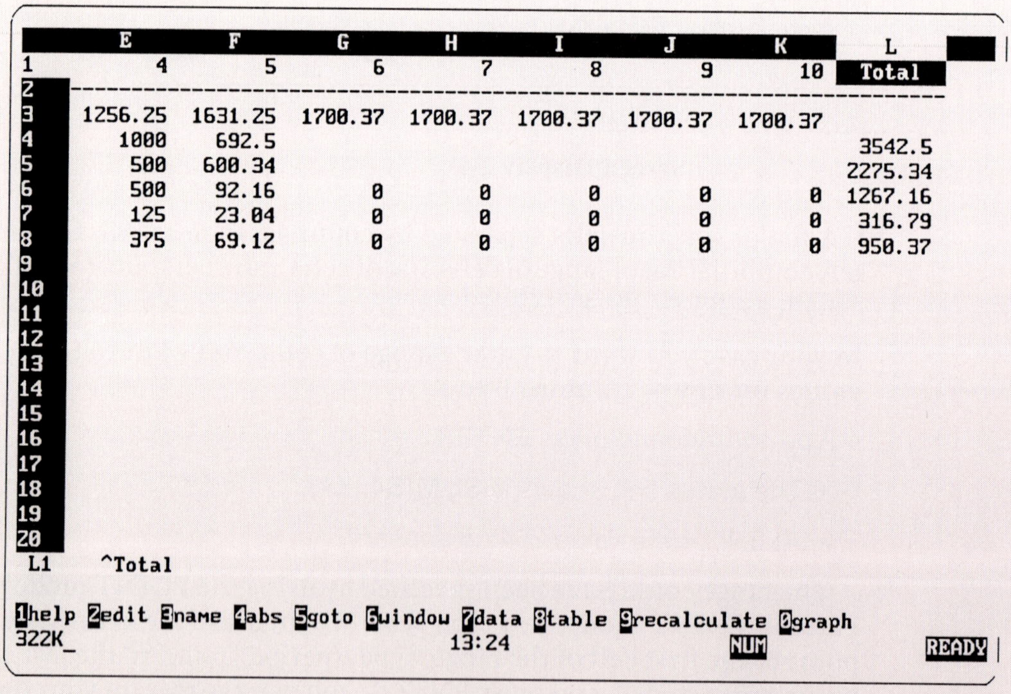

Screen Display 2-7

GLOBAL DISPLAY FORMAT (/WGF)

Consider the ways by which you can change the display format. The methods for changing the column width have been covered. Now you will learn how to change a format in which values are displayed in each cell. You can use a Worksheet command to change the whole worksheet (a global change) to, say, an integer format (whole numbers only). Note that the values on columns F through L have decimals.

- Enter /W for Worksheet.

  > The Worksheet second-level options are displayed.

- Select **G**lobal, meaning that you want to affect the entire worksheet.

  > The Global third-level options are displayed:

2 Format	Sets global format.
3 Label-prefix	Sets global label alignment prefix.
4 Col-width	Sets global column width.
5 Recalculation	Sets conditions of recalculation of worksheet.
6 Protection	Turns protection on or off.
7 Default	Defines default disk and printer settings.
8 Zero-suppress	Turns zero suppression on or off.

The Format option allows you to specify how values or labels should appear within their cells.

- Select **F**ormat.

  > The following fourth-level options are now displayed:

2 Fixed	Fixed number of decimal places (0–15).
3 Sci	(Scientific) Exponential notation (x.xxE+xx).
4 Currency	Shows dollar sign, commas, and decimal point (with specified number of decimal places, 0–15). Negative values set in parentheses.
5 , (comma)	The same as currency, but without dollar sign.
6 General	No nonsignificant zeros after the decimal point.
7 +/−	For horizontal bar graph: shows +'s for positive values, −'s for negative values.
8 Percent	Percent value (value × 100) shown with percent sign (%).
9 Date	Date format.
0 Text	Formulas displayed as they are entered.

1	Custom format.
2	Custom format.

You want to change the entire spreadsheet to integer format (whole numbers only—no decimal).

- Select **F**ixed.

> The input line shows the following message:

```
Enter default decimal position: 2
```

The computer prompts you to enter the number of decimal places. If you press ENTER without typing any number, it will be set to 2.

- Type 0 and press **ENTER**.

> Notice that in column F, the decimal portions of the values were dropped.

NOTE ■ Display format changes affect the way numbers are displayed on the screen only. They do not change the way numbers are stored in the computer's memory.

Since you are dealing with money in this spreadsheet, you probably want your values to show two places to the right of the decimal point. You can use the Currency format, but let's say that you don't want to see the $ signs. You can use the , (comma) format.

PRACTICE TIME

Make the global change to set the format to , (comma) with 2 decimal positions.

RANGE DISPLAY FORMAT (/RF)

All values on the screen are displayed with two places to the right of the decimal. Do you see a problem? Even the column headings show two places to the right of the decimal, and they are supposed to be day numbers (integers).

You can change the format of a particular row, column, or entry by using the Range command (instead of Worksheet).

- Type /R for Range.

> The Range second-level options are displayed.

- Select **F**ormat.

> The screen displays a list of third-level options similar to the one displayed when you changed the format through the Worksheet Global command.

- Select **F**ixed with 0 decimal places.

You need to specify the range that should be affected. In this case the range is B1 through K1.

- Type B1.K1 and press **ENTER**.

> The format of the numerical values in row 1 is changed to integer. The value displayed at cell B1, for example, is 1 instead of 1.00.

- Place the cell cursor on cell B1.

> The status line shows **(F0)** indicating that the value is displayed as Fixed with 0 decimal places.

The value display format is indicated on the status line only when it is different from what is done globally, that is, only when the display format was set by using the Range option.

SAVING A FILE FOR THE SECOND TIME

You need to save your spreadsheet for use during the next lesson. When you are saving the spreadsheet, however, you have to be careful in choosing the filename.

If you use the same filename you used at the end of the first lesson, the current spreadsheet will replace the existing contents of the disk file. This may be acceptable in some situations. By using a different filename, both the old and new spreadsheets will be stored on the disk.

The VP-Planner Plus program makes sure that you don't accidentally replace an existing disk file. If you enter a filename that already exists on the disk, a pop-up window appears with the following:

2 Cancel	Cancels the command and does not save.
3 Replace	Replaces the existing file.
4 Backup	The existing file is made into a backup file, and the spreadsheet is saved (replaced).

PRACTICE TIME

Save your spreadsheet, using the filename VPP2.

PRINTING THE SPREADSHEET IN SECTIONS

As noted in Lesson 1, the most that will fit on a sheet 8½ by 11 inches is 8 columns (of 9-character width). Since this spreadsheet contains 12 columns (A to L) and column A is wider than 9 characters, it must be printed in two sections: The first section will contain seven columns (A through G), and the second section will contain five columns (H through L).

Rather than remembering (or pointing) the top left and bottom right corners of each section range, you will *name* these.

- Position the cell cursor on cell A1.
- Type /RN for Range Name.

> The following Range Name third-level options are displayed:

2 Create	Creates a range name.
3 Delete	Deletes a range name.
4 Labels	Names a cell or range of cells with their adjacent labels.
5 Reset	Deletes all range names in the worksheet.
6 Show	Displays all the name ranges associated with the current spreadsheet along with the range addresses.
7 Table	Creates a table showing a list of range names and their range.

- Select **C**reate.

> The input line prompts you to enter the name to use.

A range name can be up to 16 characters in length. Make range names simple and easy to remember. You will use the name FIRST for the first section, and SECOND for the second section.

- Type FIRST; then press **ENTER**.

> The input line displays a message prompting you to enter the range of cells that will be named FIRST.

You can assign a name to a single cell or a range of cells. As always, you enter the addresses of the top left and bottom right cells of the range. Rather than typing these addresses separated by a period, you will point with the arrow keys.

- Press the **RIGHT ARROW** key until cells A1 through G1 are highlighted.
- Press the **DOWN ARROW** key until the range A1 through G8 is highlighted.

- Press **ENTER**.

  > The specified range has been named.

PRACTICE TIME

1. Move the cell cursor to cell H1.
2. Assign the name SECOND to the range H1 through L8.

NOTE ■ Assigning range names makes it easy to refer to often used cells and ranges. However, you do have to keep track of these names. You can see all the range names for the current spreadsheet with the Range Name Show command.

Now you are ready to print.

- Type /PP to print to the printer.
- Select **Range**.

At this point you would ordinarily enter the corner addresses of the range.

- Type FIRST and press **ENTER**.

  > The third-level menu is displayed again.

- Select **Align**, then **Go**.

  > The first section is printed.

- Select **Page** to advance printer to the top of the next page.
- Select **Range** again to specify the range of the second section.
- Type SECOND and press **ENTER**.
- Select **Go**.

  > The second section is printed.

- Select **Page**, then **Quit**.

NOTE ■ Range names are not mentioned in the remainder of this manual. However, you may use them if you feel comfortable with the concept.

- Save the worksheet as **VPP2** again to preserve the range names.

END OF LESSON 2

As you did at the end of Lesson 1:

- Type /**QY** to exit to DOS.

- Remove the disks from the disk drives.
- Turn OFF the monitor, computer, and printer.

SUMMARY

In this lesson many of the terms and concepts that are necessary to use spreadsheets effectively are introduced.

- Repeated labels can be entered by typing \ (backslash), followed by the character(s) you want repeated across the cell. Even if the column width is changed, the cell is still filled with the specified character(s).
- Functions are introduced with the @SUM function.
- If you save a file to disk for a second time, the current contents write over those of the original file. If you want to keep the original file, the file must be saved with a different name.
- A cell or a range of cells can be named so that it can be referred to by using a meaningful name instead of cell addresses.
- If a spreadsheet is too large to be printed on a single sheet of paper, it must be printed in sections.
- The following commands are discussed:

/C	Copy—copies cell content to another cell or range of cells.
/FR	File Retrieve—reads in a spreadsheet file on a disk.
/FD	File Directory—specifies the directory (disk drive) to use.
/RF	Range Format—specifies the display format for a range of cells.
/RN	Range Name—assigns a name to a cell or a range of cells.
/WCS	Worksheet Column Set-width—changes the width of a column.
/WGF	Worksheet Global Format—specifies the display format of the entire worksheet.
/WIR	Worksheet Insert Row—inserts row(s).

REVIEW QUESTIONS

1. A cell is to contain the formula +B1+C1+C2+C3. What formula can you use instead? ______________________________

____

2. After you copy the formula 1 + B1 in cell C1 to cell D1 by using the /C command, what formula is stored in cell D1? ____________________

____

3. After you copy the formula 1 + B1 in cell C1 to cell D1 by using the /C command, what formula is stored in cell D1? ____________________

____

4. Which command lets you change the width of a column? ____________

____

5. What do source range and destination range mean in a Copy command?

____

____

6. What does "repeated label" mean? How do you enter it? ____________

____

7. What is an argument in a function? ____________________

____

8. What is the difference between setting the display format by using the Range command and by using the Worksheet Global command? ______

____

9. What is the purpose of naming a cell or a range of cells? ____________

____

____

10. What happens when you save a file the second time, using the same filename? ____________________

____

____

EXERCISES

1. Retrieve the spreadsheet EX1__1 prepared in Lesson 1. It occurred to you that your ten best friends have been borrowing considerable amounts of money from you.
   a. Expand the spreadsheet by adding four columns for four weeks (each column for a week). Insert the amount each friend borrowed each week.
   b. Calculate and display the total amount each friend borrowed from you in the four-week period (row totals).

c. Calculate and display the total amount you lent each week (column totals).
d. Make sure to insert proper headings.
e. Change to appropriate display format.
f. Save the spreadsheet as EX2_1.
g. Print the spreadsheet.

2. Retrieve the spreadsheet EX1_2 prepared in Lesson 1. You, as a teacher, would like to expand the spreadsheet to calculate students' total points and averages.
   a. Calculate and display total points for each student after three exams.
   b. Calculate and display average score for each student after three exams. Average is total divided by number of exams.
   c. Calculate and display class average for each exam.
   d. Insert appropriate headings.
   e. Change to appropriate display format. Average should show one place to the right of the decimal.
   f. Save the apreadsheet as EX2_2.
   g. Print the spreadsheet.

3. From the BCS data diskette you received with this tutorial, retrieve the file called LUMBER.WKS. This spreadsheet was discussed in the text (*Business Computer Systems* Figures 5-4 and 5-5). Notice that this spreadsheet does not start at cell A1. Spreadsheets can begin at any cell.
   This is a partial invoice that contains formulas that calculate the discount, discounted price, sales tax, and item total for one item.
   a. Copy the formulas for the other items.
   b. Place the formula for calculating the invoice total in cell G57. Write the invoice total here: ___________
   c. Save the lumberyard invoice as LUMBER2. You will need it for the next exercise.

4. Retrieve the spreadsheet called LUMBER2.
   In the text the authors said that although the current lumberyard policy is to give each contractor a 5 percent discount, the owner could change that policy any time he wanted to. Suppose the boss recognizes a customer to be an old school chum and tells the clerk to give him a higher discount.
   a. Change the discount in the invoice in LUMBER2 to 12 percent.
   b. What are the new item totals?
   c. What is the new invoice total?
   d. Save the spreadsheet as LUMBER3.
   e. Print the spreadsheet.

Lesson 3
Modifying the Display Format

Objectives

Upon completion of the material presented in this lesson, you should be able to understand and do the following:

- Set (freeze) titles.
- Split the screen into multiple windows and move the cell cursor to any window.
- Move information within the worksheet.
- Suppress the column display.
- Delete columns.
- Edit cell content.
- Display formulas that were entered in the worksheet.
- Get a printout of formulas entered in the worksheet.

STARTING OFF

Start VP-Planner Plus so that the blank spreadsheet is displayed. Insert your own data disk into drive B.

PRACTICE TIME

1. Change the file directory to drive B.
2. Retrieve spreadsheet file VPP2 from the previous lesson.

FREEZE TITLE COMMAND

Scroll your screen so that column L appears. At this point you cannot see column A, the row headings. Without the headings, can you tell which value is which? Since this is a small spreadsheet, you may not have any trouble identifying the values. But if you were working with a large spreadsheet containing many rows of data, you might find it difficult to remember which row contains what data. To eliminate this problem, you can **freeze** the row headings, known as **titles**, on the screen so that they will not scroll off.

- Make sure that cell A1 appears on the screen.
- Move the cursor to column B, to cell B1.
- Type /WT for Worksheet Title.

  > The third-level options are as follows:

2 Both	Freezes columns to the left and rows above the cell cursor.
3 Horizontal	Freezes rows above the cell cursor.
4 Vertical	Freezes columns to the left of the cell cursor.
5 Clear	Clears previous title settings and restores full-screen scrolling.

You want to freeze titles on column A, which is the column to the left of the cell cursor.

- Select Vertical.

Press the RIGHT ARROW key at least 10 times. As the screen scrolls to the left (look at the column labels at the top), column A stays on the screen. These headings are "frozen" on the screen.

- Press the **LEFT ARROW** key repeatedly until the computer beeps.

  > The cell cursor will not go beyond column B.

If you need to access cells that are frozen, use the GOTO (F5) command.

- Press the **F5** function key and specify cell **A1**.

  > A second column A appears on the screen, and the cell cursor is on cell A1 as shown in Screen Display 3-1.

If you change the content of cell A1 where the cursor is currently located, you will also change the content of cell A1 that is frozen.

- Type   to clear the title setting. That is, this command unfreezes the title.

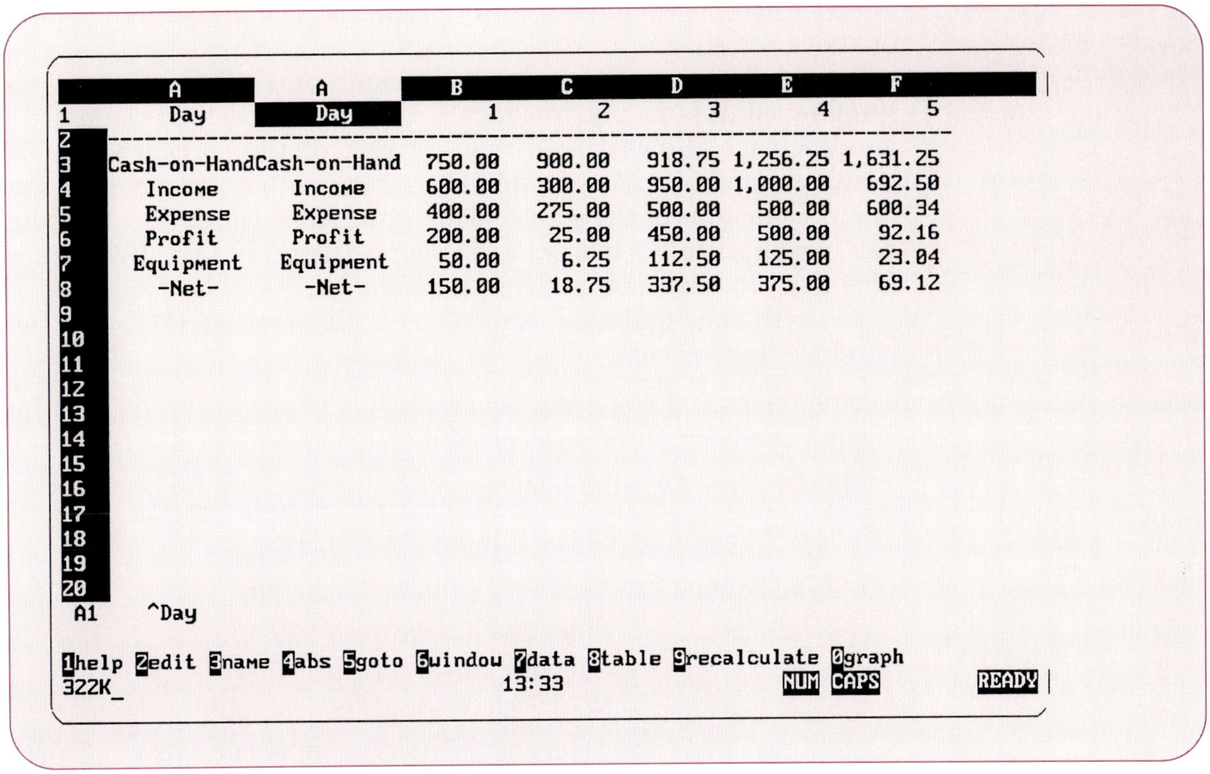

Screen Display 3-1

- Move the cell cursor around and verify that the titles are not frozen.
- With the cell cursor at A3, type /WTH for horizontal freeze.

Press the DOWN ARROW key at least 21 times. As the screen scrolls up, notice that rows 1 and 2 stay on the screen.

- Type /WTC to unfreeze the title.
- With the cell cursor at B3, type /WTB. This command freezes both the columns to the left and the rows above the cell cursor.

Press the arrow keys in all directions. Notice that both column headings and row headings are frozen.

- Unfreeze the titles.

MULTIPLE WINDOWS (/WW)

There are times when it is convenient to see two different sections of the spreadsheet at the same time. One way to do so is to freeze the title. But when you give the Title command, the same set of information stays in view all the time (as titles). Also, the Title command allows you to freeze rows or columns only to the left of the cell cursor or above it.

Another way to see multiple sections of a spreadsheet is the Window command. As you recall, the monitor screen is only the window that allows you to view a part of the spreadsheet. The Window command lets you split the screen so that you can view two or more portions of the spreadsheet at the same time. That is, it lets you have multiple windows to the spreadsheet. In fact, VP-Planner Plus lets you have as many as six windows.

You will now split the screen vertically so that there are two windows side by side.

- Place the cell cursor in the column that is to be the left edge of the right-hand window. You will place it on column E, say cell E1.
- Type /WW for Worksheet Window command.

  > The following third-level options are displayed:

2 Horizontal	Splits the screen horizontally.
3 Vertical	Splits the screen vertically.
4 Sync	Synchronously scrolls all the windows.
5 Unsync	Scrolls all windows separately.
6 Clear	Clears all previous window settings.

- Select **V**ertical.

  > The cell cursor moves to the rightmost column of the window on the left (the same row). The screen is split as shown in Screen Display 3-2.

- Press arrow keys to scroll the left window.

  > As the window on the left scrolls, the window on the right remains stationary.

JUMPING BETWEEN WINDOWS (F6)

You can move the cell cursor to the other window by using the F6 function key.

- Press the **F6** function key.

  > The cursor jumps to the right-hand window.

The F6 function key moves the cursor to its last position on the other window.

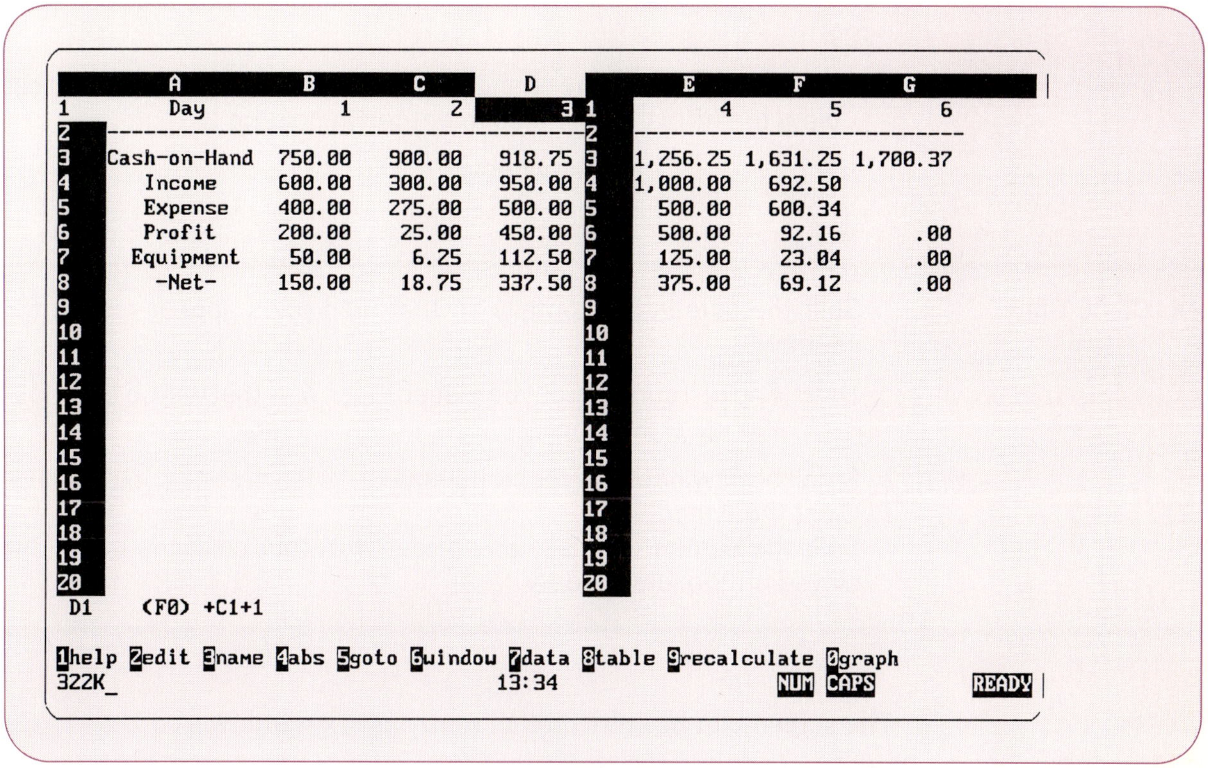

Screen Display 3-2

- Press the arrow keys to scroll the right-hand window.

  > As the screen on the right scrolls, the screen on the left remains stationary.

PRACTICE TIME

Scroll both windows (individually) so that the window on the left displays columns A through D, rows 1 to 20, and the window on the right shows columns J through L, rows 1 to 20.

- With the cell cursor in either window, type /WWS for Synchronous scroll.
- Press the **DOWN ARROW** key at least 20 times.

  > Both screens scroll up at the same time.

If you split the screen horizontally, the Synchronous scroll command will cause the two screens to scroll together sideways.

- With the cell cursor on the left window, change the value at cell B5 to 100.

  > Values affected by the change in entry B5 are recalculated. You can view the effect of changes in entries in column L.

- Type /WWC to clear the windows.

PRACTICE TIME

1. Split the screen horizontally so that nine rows appear on the top window.

   Hint: The cell cursor must be placed in the row that will be the top of the lower window.

2. Scroll both windows synchronously.
3. Clear the windows.
4. Split the screen vertically as before, with four columns being displayed on the left window.

The screen can be split into as many as six windows.

- Place the cell cursor on the left window, row 10.
- Type /WWH to split horizontally within the left window.

  > The screen appears as shown in Screen Display 3-3.

You can still jump from window to window by using the F6 function key.

When the screen is split into more than two windows, the windows will scroll synchronously if their upper left corners line up horizontally and they contain the same number of rows (vertically synchronous) or if their upper left corners line up vertically and they contain the same number of columns (horizontally synchronous).

In Figure 3-1 windows D and E and windows G, H, and I are synchronized vertically, for up-and-down movement. The upper left corners are lined up horizontally, and the windows have the same number of rows. Windows A and B, C and F, and K and L are synchronized horizontally, for side-to-side movement. In each set of windows, the upper left corners are lined up vertically, and each set contains the same number of columns.

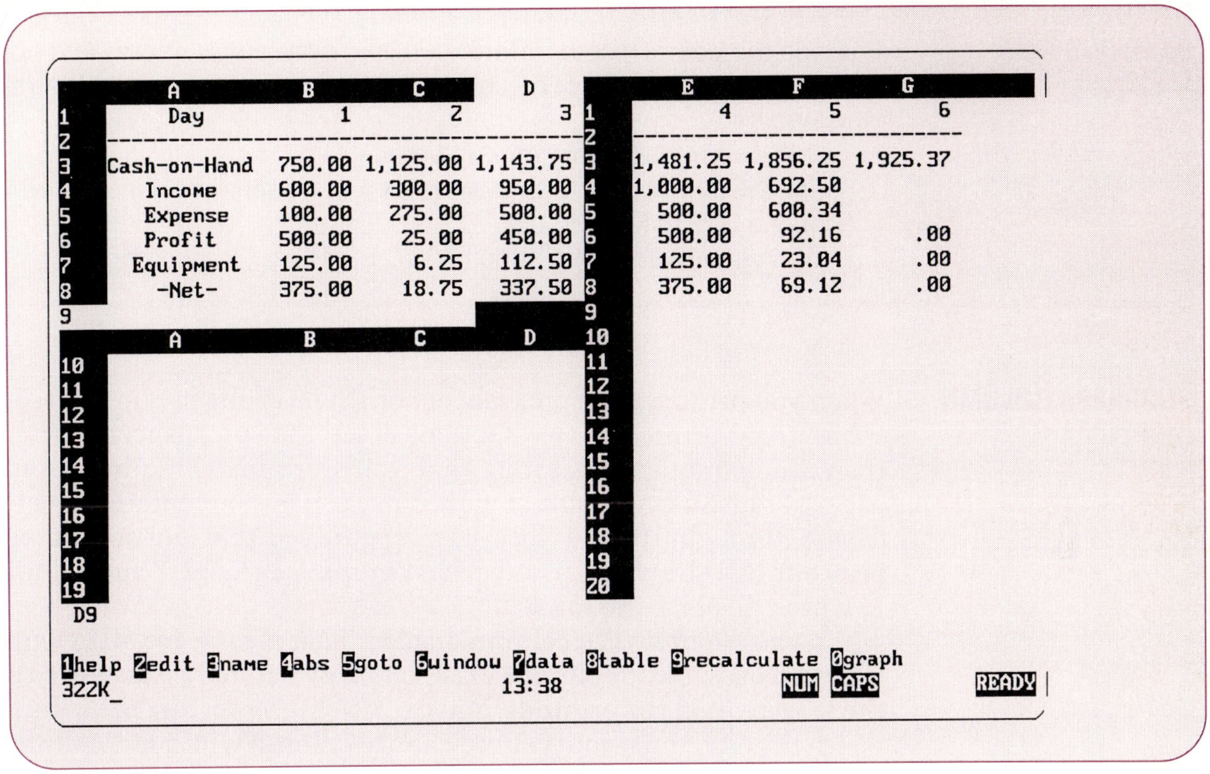

Screen Display 3-3

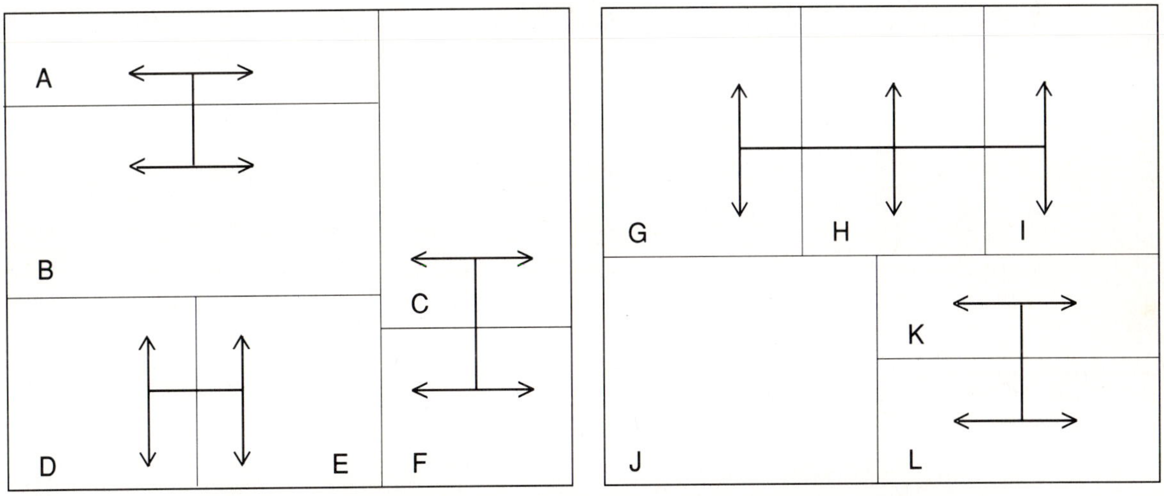

Figure 3-1 Effect of synchronous scroll on multiple windows

PRACTICE TIME

1. Place the cell cursor at different cells in different windows and split the screen. You will not be able to split the screen into more than six windows.
2. Set the screen to synchronous scroll.
3. Place the cursor in different windows and try scrolling. Find out what works and what doesn't.
4. When you are satisfied, type **/WWC** to return to one window.

SUPPRESS COLUMN DISPLAY

When you printed this spreadsheet at the end of the previous lesson, it had to be printed in two sections since the spreadsheet is wider than 80 characters (assuming that you were using 8½-by-11-inch paper). From Susan's point of view, since she has not entered data for days 6 through 10, she does not care to see that portion on the printout. All she wants printed is columns A through F and column L, which displays the totals.

You can suppress the column display. That means, for all calculation purposes, these columns exist, but they will not be displayed on the screen or on the printout. You can do this by setting the column width to zero. Since you want to change column width of 5 columns (G through K), you will use the Range command.

- With the cell cursor on column G (the first column you want to suppress), type /RC for Range Column.

  > As was the case in the /WC command, you have options of setting the column width or resetting the width to global format.

- Select **Set** since you want to set the column width.

  > The input line displays the following message:

  ```
  Select Range of Columns to be altered: G1..G1
  ```

- You can either type G1.K1 or press the **RIGHT ARROW** key until cells G1 through K1 are highlighted. Then press **ENTER**.

  > The following message appears on the input line:

  ```
  Enter desired column width (0-240): 9
  ```

- Type 0 (zero) and press **ENTER**.

  > The columns G through K disappear as shown in Screen Display 3-4.

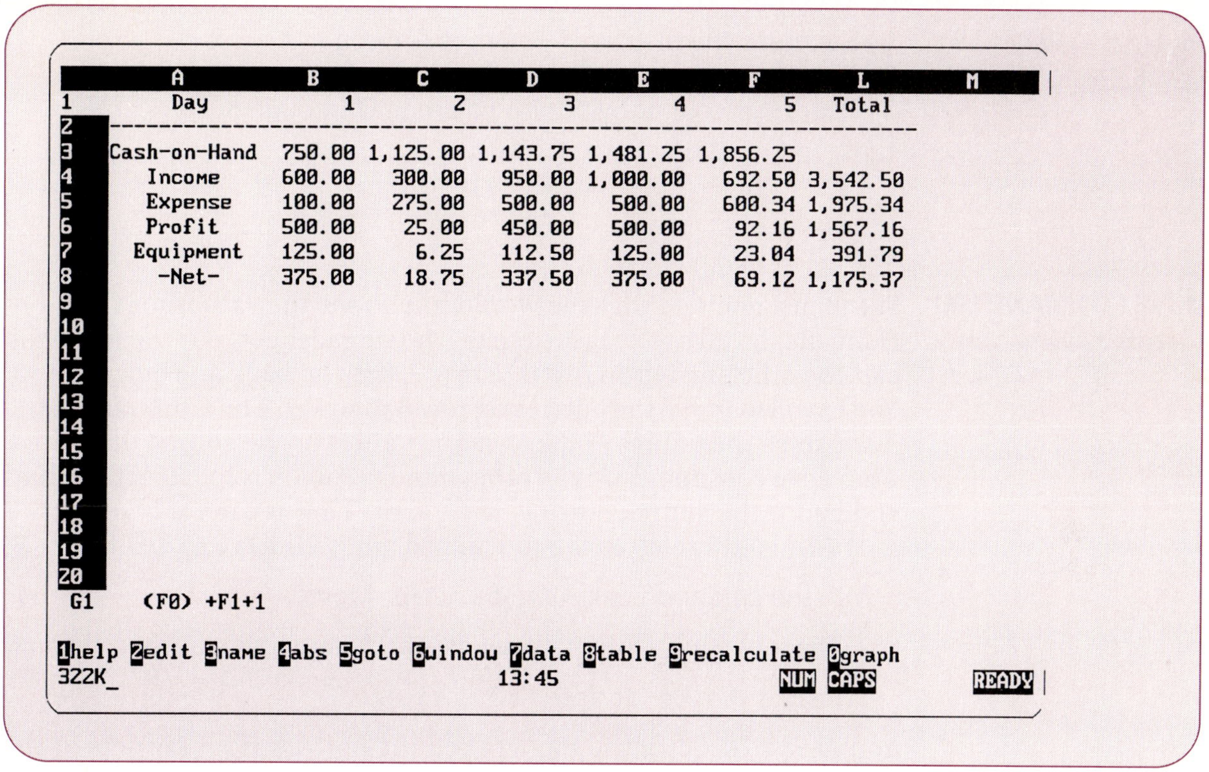

Screen Display 3-4

Now you can print the entire spreadsheet on one sheet of paper. Right now you will display the columns again. Columns will be displayed if you set the width to a number greater than zero. You will set these to global setting (9). That is, you will simply reset the column width.

- Type **/RC**, then select **Reset**.
  > The input line shows the following:

  `Select Range of Columns to be altered: G1..G1`

You are asked to specify columns to be altered.

- Type **G1.K1** (or point to the range with arrow keys).
- Press **ENTER**.
  > All columns appear on the display.

PRACTICE TIME

1. Suppress the display of columns G through K.
2. Print the entire spreadsheet.
3. Reset the column width for columns G through K.

MOVE COMMAND (/M)

Susan just decided that she would like to see the values for Cash-on-Hand displayed as the last item on the spreadsheet, not the first. You can *copy* the entries on row 3 to row 9, then go back and delete row 3. You can also *move* the entries on row 3 to row 9. The Copy command just copies the values and leaves the values at the source unaltered. The Move command, on the other hand, actually relocates the values and hence the source range is left blank. That means, a blank row 3 will still be there after the move, and you will have to delete row 3.

- With the cursor on cell A3, type /M for Move.

  > The input line prompts you with the following message:

  ```
  Range to be moved: A3..A3
  ```

You need to specify the top left and the bottom right corners of the range. Row 3 contains information on columns A through K.

- Specify the range A3.K3.

  > The input line now prompts you to enter the destination.

When you move the data, whatever is currently displayed in the destination range is overwritten.

You want to move the data to row 9. You can specify just the cell A9 as the destination. When the source range is larger than the destination range, the extra source cell contents will be placed in the cells to the right and below the destination range, overwriting the contents of any affected cell.

- Type A9 and press **ENTER**.

  > Cash-on-Hand values appear on row 9, and row 3 is now blank.

You will notice that the formula in cells C3 through K3 were changed automatically. That is, the formula at C9 (moved from C3), for example, is now +B9+B8 since the content of cell B3 was moved to B9.

DELETING ROWS (/WDR)

You will now delete row 3. The Delete command is very similar to the Insert command.

- Place the cell cursor on row 3, the row you want deleted.
- Type /WD for the Worksheet Delete command.

  > The third-level menu gives you the option of deleting rows or columns.
- Select **R**ow.

  > The status line asks for the range of rows to be deleted.
- Press **ENTER** since you want only row 3 deleted.

  > The blank row 3 is deleted, and hence all information on rows 4 through 9 moves up one row.

PRACTICE TIME

1. Move the contents of row 8 to row 9.
2. Fill row 8 with ='s to look like the screen in Screen Display 3-5.
3. Save the spreadsheet, using the filename VPP3.

DELETING A COLUMN (/WDC)

You might have wondered, when suppressing display of columns G through K earlier, what would have happened if you had deleted those columns instead. Before starting, note the value 3542.50 that appears as the total income in cell L3.

- Place the cell cursor on column G, say cell G1.
- Type /WDC for the Worksheet Delete command for Columns.

  > The input line reads

  ```
  Select range of columns to be deleted: G1..G1
  ```
- Press the **RIGHT ARROW** key until cells G1 through K1 are highlighted, and press **ENTER**.

  > Total now appears in column G.

Now note the total income in cell G3. It is now 7085.00.

- Place the cell cursor on cell G3 so that you can see the cell content on the status line.

  > The content still reads @SUM(B3..K3).

```
        A            B         C         D         E         F         G         H
1      Day           1         2         3         4         5         6         7
2 -----------------------------------------------------------------------------------
3     Income      600.00    300.00    950.00  1,000.00    692.50
4     Expense     100.00    275.00    500.00    500.00    600.34
5     Profit      500.00     25.00    450.00    500.00     92.16       .00       .00
6    Equipment    125.00      6.25    112.50    125.00     23.04       .00       .00
7      -Net-      375.00     18.75    337.50    375.00     69.12       .00       .00
8 ===================================================================================
9 Cash-on-Hand    750.00  1,125.00  1,143.75  1,481.25  1,856.25  1,925.37  1,925.37
10
11
12
13
14
15
16
17
18
19
20
 A8     \=

1help 2edit 3name 4abs 5goto 6window 7data 8table 9recalculate 0graph
322K_                          13:48                  NUM CAPS             READY
```

Screen Display 3-5

The VP-Planner Plus did not make adjustments for the deleted columns. Hence, it added the contents of columns A through K (H through K were blank) and placed the sum back into G, thus doubling the sum.

EDIT KEY (F2)

To make the spreadsheet correct, you need to change the formula used for totals. You need to enter the correct arguments for the SUM function. You will correct the entry by using the edit key, F2.

- Place the cell cursor on cell G3.
- Press the **F2** function key.

  > The input line displays @SUM(B3..K3) followed by a square cursor.

You can edit, or correct, what appears on the input line by using the RIGHT and LEFT ARROW keys, BACKSPACE key, and DELETE key.

- Press the **LEFT ARROW** key three times so that the square cursor is on K in K3.

- Press the **DEL** key once.

  > The character K disappears.

- Type F.

  > The character F is inserted so that the input line now reads @SUM(B3..F3), which is the desired formula.

- Press **ENTER**.

  > The total income, cell G3, now reads 3542.50.

PRACTICE TIME

Copy the formula at G3 to the range G4 through G7.

TEXT DISPLAY

It is very difficult for someone just looking at a spreadsheet to tell whether a value or a formula was entered into a cell (other than by moving the cell cursor to a particular cell and looking at the status line). You can change the display format so that the actual texts of the formulas that were entered are shown rather than the evaluated values.

- Type /WGF for Worksheet Global Format.
- Select **Text**.

  > The screen display changes to that shown in Screen Display 3-6.

One drawback to looking at cell entries this way is that, without adjusting the column widths, it may not be possible to see the entire text that was entered at a cell, and an entry can be very long.

NOTE ■ When you change the display format globally, the change will not affect those cells whose formats were set with the Range command.

PRACTICE TIME

Make the worksheet global format change to , (comma) with 2 decimal places.

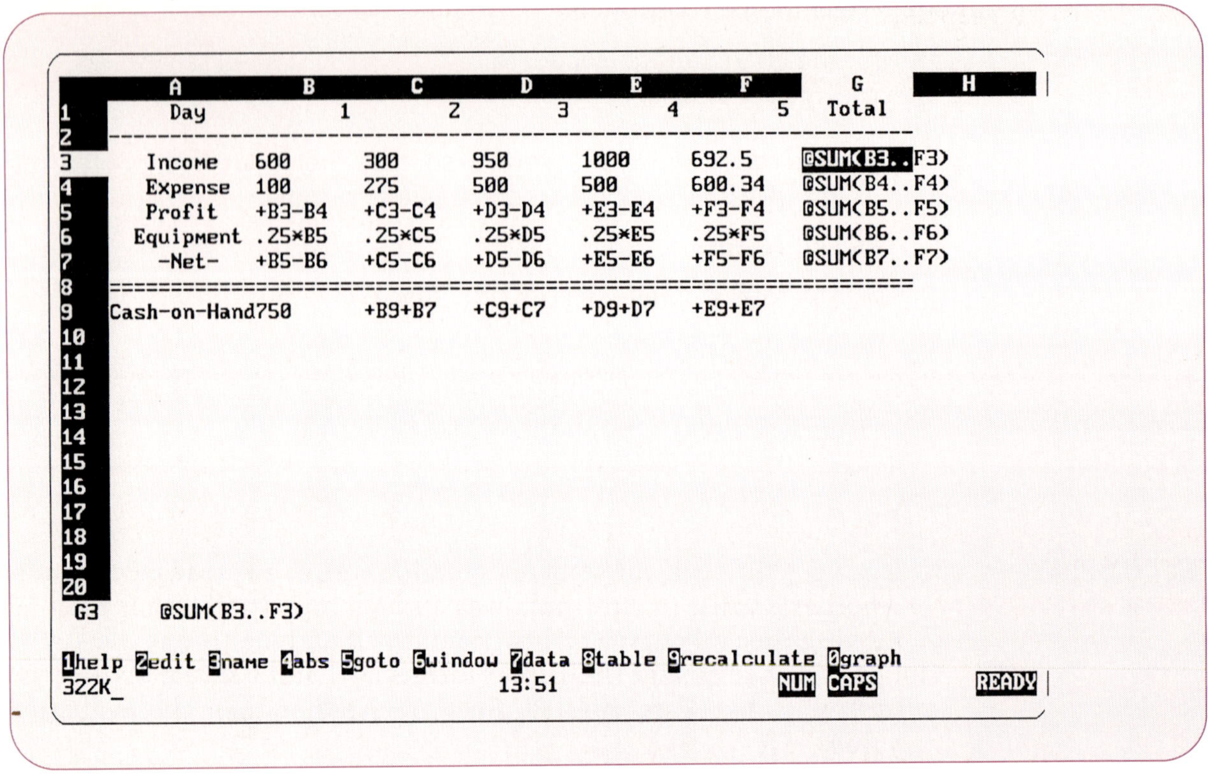

Screen Display 3-6

FORMULA PRINTOUT

When you make a printout of the worksheet, an image of what is displayed on the screen is printed on the paper. This is part of the power of an electronic spreadsheet. It is possible to print a spreadsheet with Text display format to obtain a paper copy of what was entered at each cell. However, there are restrictions (column width) as mentioned previously.

You can get a printout of the exact entries you made into this worksheet, one cell per line, called a **formula printout**. You do not need to adjust the column width or the size of the range to be printed when printing worksheet formulas.

- Make sure that you are working with an IBM-PC connected to a printer, and that the printer is turned on and is ready to use.
- Type /PP for printout to printer.
- Select Options.

 > The screen shown in Screen Display 3-7 is displayed.

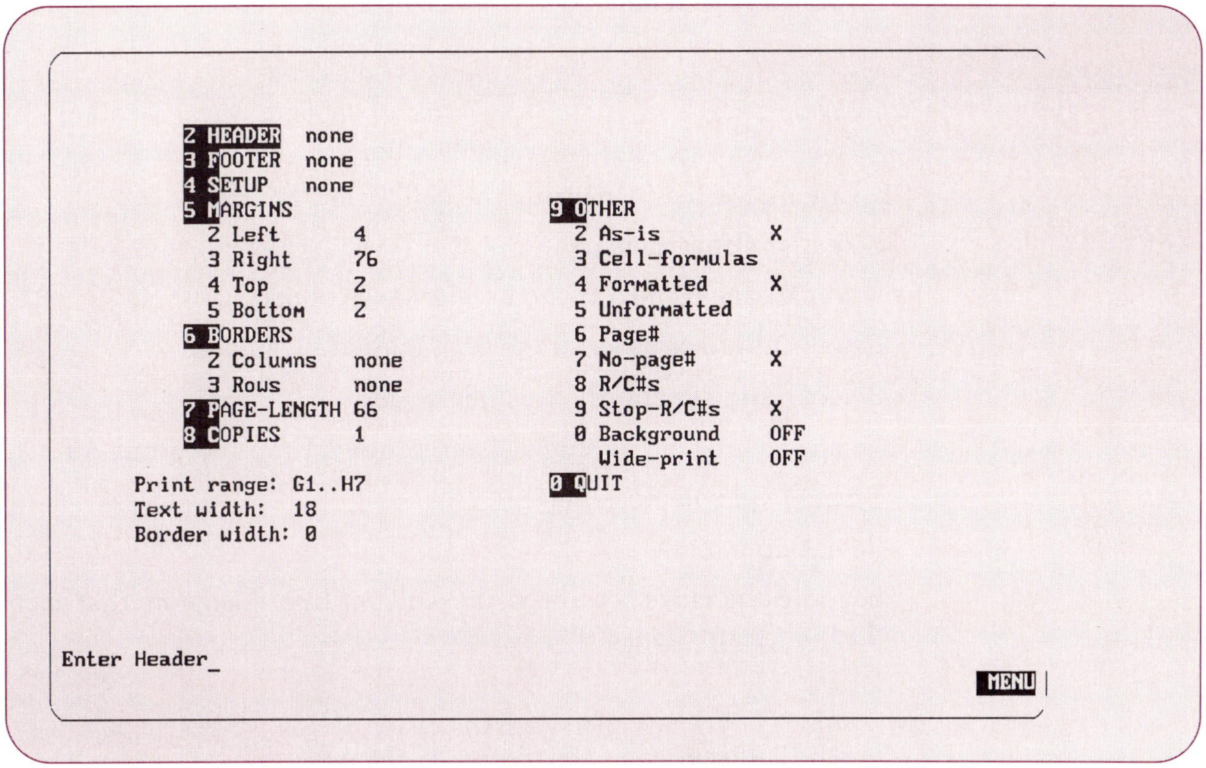

Screen Display 3-7

- Select **Other**.

> The options under Other are highlighted:

2 As-is	Prints the worksheet as displayed on the screen.
3 Cell-formulas	Prints worksheet formulas.
4 Formatted	Prints with page breaks, headers, footer, and printer setup strings.
5 Unformatted	Prints without page breaks, headers, footer, and printer setup strings.
6 Page#	Prints the page number on each page.
7 No page#	Turns page numbers off.
8 R\C#s	Prints row and column numbers on the top and side of each page.
9 Stop R/C#	Cancels row and column numbers.

0 Background Printing	Enables or disables background printing of worksheet or graphs. The default is "disabled."
Wide-print	Turns wide (sideways) printing On and Off.

You are interested in printing the cell formulas.

- Select **Cell-formulas**.

  > An **X** appears next to the Cell-formulas option.

- Select **Quit** to get back to the Print third-level options.
- Select **Range** to specify the print range.

The range is the entire spreadsheet, or rows 1 to 9, columns A to G.

- Type **A1.G9** and press **ENTER**.
- Select **Go** to print.

The indicated range is printed, one cell per line. Also note that each column is printed on a separate sheet.

```
A1^Day
A2\-
A3^Income
A4^Expense
A5^Profit
A6^Equipment
   .
   .
B5 +B3-B4
```

And so forth, to the end:

```
   .
   .
G4 @SUM(B4..F4)
G5 @SUM(B5..F5)
G6 @SUM(B6..F6)
G7 @SUM(B7..F7)
G8\=
G9
```

Each line of the entry printout begins with the cell address, followed by the entry as it was typed in, including label-prefix characters.

- Select **Quit** to exit the PRINT mode.

END OF LESSON 3

- Type /QY to exit to DOS.
- Remove the disks from the disk drive.
- Turn OFF the monitor, computer, and printer.

SUMMARY

In this lesson many of the terms and concepts that are necessary to change the display format of a spreadsheet are discussed.

- Column and row headings (labels) can be made to stay displayed on the screen (as the rest of the data scrolls) through the Worksheet Title command.
- Up to six sections of the spreadsheet can be displayed on the screen by using the Worksheet Window command. The cell cursor is moved between the windows by using the F6 function key.
- When column width(s) are set to zero, they are suppressed from screen display only. They still exist and can be used for all calculation purposes.
- An entry in a cell can be edited by using the F2 function key.
- The Text display format shows the actual text entered at a cell.
- A formula printout prints the exact entries you made into the worksheet, one cell per line.
- The following commands are discussed:

/M	Move—moves specified row(s) or column(s) to another location within the spreadsheet.
/PPOOC	Print Printer Options Other Cell-Formula—specifies printing of the cell content (instead of screen display). You then specify the range, then Go.
/RCS	Range Column Set—changes the column width of selected columns.
/RCR	Range Column Reset—sets the column width of selected columns to global value.
/WGF	Worksheet Global Format—changes the display format of the entire worksheet.
/WD	Worksheet Delete—deletes specified row(s) or column(s).
/WT	Worksheet Title—freezes titles to the left of and/or above the cell cursor.
/WW	Worksheet Window—divides the screen into multiple windows, either side by side or top and bottom. The windows can be either synchronized or unsynchronized for scrolling.

REVIEW QUESTIONS

1. What is the purpose of setting the spreadsheet row titles? ______

2. What is the purpose of splitting the spreadsheet windows? ______

3. What does it mean to say "both windows scroll synchronously"? ______

4. What key do you press to move the cursor from one window to another? ______

5. What effect does suppressing the display of a column have in calculations? Explain. ______

6. When you move the content of a cell, what happens to formula entries in other cells that depend on it? Explain. ______

7. When you move cell contents to another cell that already contains data, what happens to the data in the destination cell? ______

8. When you delete the content of a cell, what happens to formula entries in other cells that depend on it? Explain. ______

9. What is the purpose of the edit key (F2)? ______________________________

____

____

10. What is a formula printout? How do you obtain it? ______________________

____

____

EXERCISES

1. Retrieve spreadsheet EX2_1 prepared in Lesson 2.
   a. Hide the column containing telephone numbers.
   b. Save the spreadsheet as EX3_1.
   c. Get a formula printout of the spreadsheet.

2. Retrieve spreadsheet EX2_2 prepared in Lesson 2.
   a. Freeze both the column headings and students' names.
   b. Delete one of the students (delete a row).
   c. Save the spreadsheet as EX3_2.
   d. Get a formula printout of the spreadsheet.

3. Retrieve the spreadsheet LUMBER3 prepared in Lesson 3.
   a. Get a formula printout of the spreadsheet.
   b. Explain why a formula printout should be included in every spreadsheet's external documentation.

PROJECT 1

Objectives

Upon completion of this project, you should be able to do the following:

- Design a spreadsheet.
- Read a problem statement and develop a solution.
- Apply the fundamental concepts of an electronic spreadsheet program to several related business problems.

Whereas in previous lessons you have been learning spreadsheet facts and trying them out on spreadsheets of our design, in this project you will design and build your own spreadsheet. Before attempting this, review the material in Chapter 5 of *Business Computer Systems* on spreadsheet design. It will not be repeated here.

BACKGROUND

Wilhemina runs a small cottage industry making accessories for outdoor enthusiasts. Her four products (clip-on field guide pouch, belt pack, drawstring duffle bag, and padded camera bag) are sold by mail order and through a small number of retail outlets.

Her products are made by at-home seamers whom she pays the current state minimum wage, $4.80 per hour.

Wil has developed a bill of materials for each product. You can review the bills of material in Figure 1.

Bills of Material

Clip-on field guide pouch		
Goretex	1	yd
Velcro	.5	ft
Webbing	.33	yd
Nylon thread	10	yd
Label set	1	
Snap	2	
Belt pack		
Goretex	1	yd
12″ zipper	1	
Webbing	1	yd
Fastex clip	1	
Nylon thread	20	yd
Label set	1	
Drawstring duffle		
Ripstop nylon	2	yd
Parachute cord	2	ft
Nylon thread	5	yd
Label set	1	
Camera bag		
Goretex	3	yd
Ripstop nylon	2	yd
12″ zipper	2	
Velcro	1	ft
Webbing	3	yd
Nylon thread	100	yd
Neoprene	1	yd
Fastex clip	1	
Label set	1	

Figure 1 Bills of material

Over time, Wil has determined how long it takes (on average) to make each product. The labor times are listed in Figure 2.

Item	*Hours*
Clip-on field guide pouch	1.0
Belt pack	1.0
Drawstring duffle	.5
Camera bag	2.5

Figure 2 Labor

The prices of all the materials appear in Figure 3.

Item	*Price*
12″ zipper	$1.30 each
Fastex clip	1.30 each
Goretex	6.00 yd
Label set	.15 each
Neoprene	5.00 yd
Nylon thread	.02 yd. ($2.00/100 yd)
Parachute cord	.85 ft
Ripstop nylon	5.80 yd
Snap	.08 each
Velcro	1.00 ft
Webbing	2.40 yd

Figure 3 Material prices

The retail (selling) price for each item is listed in Figure 4.

Item	*Retail Price*
Clip-on field guide pouch	$ 22.95
Belt pack	27.95
Drawstring duffle	21.95
Camera bag	120.95

Figure 4 Retail prices

Unit sales for the previous four quarters are listed in the table in Figure 5.

Unit Sales Per Quarter	*1*	*2*	*3*	*4*
Item				
Clip-on field guide pouch	80	120	65	400
Belt pack	60	35	40	220
Drawstring duffle	150	100	90	180
Camera bag	55	40	60	110

Figure 5 Unit sales per quarter

SPREADSHEET DESIGN

When designing this spreadsheet you must include internal documentation, starting in cell A1, that includes the following items:

- Your first and last names.
- Your class number.
- The spreadsheet title.
- The spreadsheet filename.
- A map identifying each section of the spreadsheet and where it starts.
- A list of all formulas used, expressed in English.

You also must develop external documentation that contains the same items as the ones listed above, plus a formula printout for the entire spreadsheet.

PROBLEMS

A. Given the current materials, labor, and minimum wage, how much does it cost to produce each item?

B. How much will each item cost to produce if the price of Goretex goes from $6.00 to $7.50 per yard?

C. How much will each item cost to produce if the price of Goretex remains at $6.00 per yard, but the minimum wage goes up to $5.20 per hour?

D. What were Wilhemina's gross sales (expressed in whole dollars) for each item for each of the last four quarters and for the last year?

E. Based on your findings for Problem 4, how much pretax profit (gross sales minus production cost) did Wil make
   1. for each item each quarter?
   2. for each item for the year?
   3. for each quarter?

   Express your answers in whole dollars.

Lesson 4
Using a Spreadsheet as a Database

Objectives

Upon completion of the material presented in this lesson, you should be able to do the following:

- Understand the terminology used in the VP-Planner Plus database.
- Sort data on a spreadsheet.
- Query data in the VP-Planner Plus database.
- Enter a sequence of evenly spaced numbers by using the Data Fill command.
- Set up a data distribution table.

STARTING OFF

Start VP-Planner Plus so that the blank spreadsheet is displayed on the screen. Insert the data disk into drive B and change the file directory to B.

DATA MANAGEMENT

The first three lessons dealt with the fundamentals of setting up and using a VP-Planner Plus spreadsheet: entering labels, numbers, and formulas; copying; moving; column widths; formats; and inserting rows/columns. In this lesson the focus is on storing, sorting, and retrieving your data, or **data management**.

A file used as a **database** stores and manages useful historical data that needs to be referred to again and again. Examples of business databases include inventory files and records of customers, suppliers (vendors), and employees. In this lesson you will make and use a database to keep track of inventory.

A database is any collection of **records** about a particular topic. In a customer database each record is information about a customer; in an employee database each record is information about an employee; and in an inventory database each record is information about a product. In a VP-Planner Plus database *each row of a spreadsheet is a record.*

Each record is composed of a series of related **fields**. A field is the smallest unit of data in a database. A customer record may have fields for that customer's number, name, address, balance, and credit rating. An inventory record may have fields for item number, quantity, and description. In a VP-Planner Plus database *each column of a spreadsheet is a field.*

A database is only a part of the whole spreadsheet. It takes up only as many columns as there are fields and only as many rows as there are records plus 1. The first row in the database holds the **field names**, which are descriptive names of the contents of the corresponding columns. In the rows below the first, you can enter either numeric data (called **values** in previous lessons) or text data (called **labels** in previous lessons). **Numeric data** consists of numbers, expressions, functions, and anything else that can be used in mathematical calculations. **Text data**, also called **string data**, cannot be used in calculations, even if it consists of numeric characters.

AN INVENTORY APPLICATION

You manufacture and sell surge/spike suppressors (SSS) and uninterrupted power supplies (UPS), and you want to set up inventory, using VP-Planner Plus.

Each item in your inventory represents a record. Each record has these fields: Number, Type (SSS or UPS), Description (details), (shipping) Weight, Cost (to you), Price (cost to the buyer), Quantity (in stock), and Location (in your warehouse).

The following is the list of inventory items:

Number	*Type*	*Description*	*Weight*	*Cost*	*Price*	*Quantity*	*Location*
L1003	UPS	200 watt capacity	18.75	195.00	389.00	325	A-8
L1011	UPS	325 watt capacity	36	240.00	479.00	72	C-1
L1029	UPS	450 watt capacity	38.5	315.00	625.00	46	B-1
L1037	UPS	1000 watt capacity	80	625.00	1249.00	12	A-2
L0005	SSS	modem surge protector	1	30.00	59.90	880	A-6
L1045	UPS	200 watt capacity	15	185.00	369.00	470	C-8
L1052	UPS	325 watt capacity	32	230.00	459.00	112	B-3

L1060	UPS	450 watt capacity	33	300.00	599.00	35	A-3
L1078	UPS	675 watt capacity	68	450.00	899.00	60	B-6
L0013	SSS	1800 watt capacity	14	150.00	299.00	0	A-5
L0047	SSS	2-outlet box	1	25.00	49.95	1480	C-4
L0054	SSS	4-outlet strip	3	29.00	57.95	2257	A-7
L0062	SSS	6-outlet strip	3	33.00	65.95	1326	B-7
L0104	SSS	2-outlet box	5	33.00	64.95	775	C-7
L0112	SSS	6-outlet strip	5	38.00	75.95	1843	A-4
L4502	SSS	power controller	8.25	50.00	99.85	422	C-5
L4510	SSS	power controller	9.25	85.00	169.95	633	B-9

PRACTICE TIME

Set up the worksheet for the inventory application.

1. Enter field names in row 1. Enter them centered, left-justified, or right-justified, depending on what you think looks good.
2. Determine the appropriate field width for all columns. The field should be wide enough to accommodate the longest or largest possible data.
3. In *numeric* fields enter data in an appropriate data format type (integer, currency, etc.).
4. In *text* fields enter data left-justified or centered (use ' or ^ as the label-prefix character).
5. Enter the data in the order shown above.
6. Save the spreadsheet with filename VPP4.

Your spreadsheet may look like the one in Screen Display 4-1.

SORTING

VP-Planner Plus allows you to rearrange the records in a file in whatever order you want. You can arrange records in alphabetical order (A to Z or Z to A) or in numerical order (ascending or descending), based on any field you select. Such rearranging of records is called **sorting**.

Practice by sorting the file according to Number (first field) in ascending order.

- Type /D for the Data command.

> The following second-level options are displayed:

2 Fill	Enters a series of numbers into a range when the increment or decrement is fixed.
3 Table	Automatic "what if" feature.

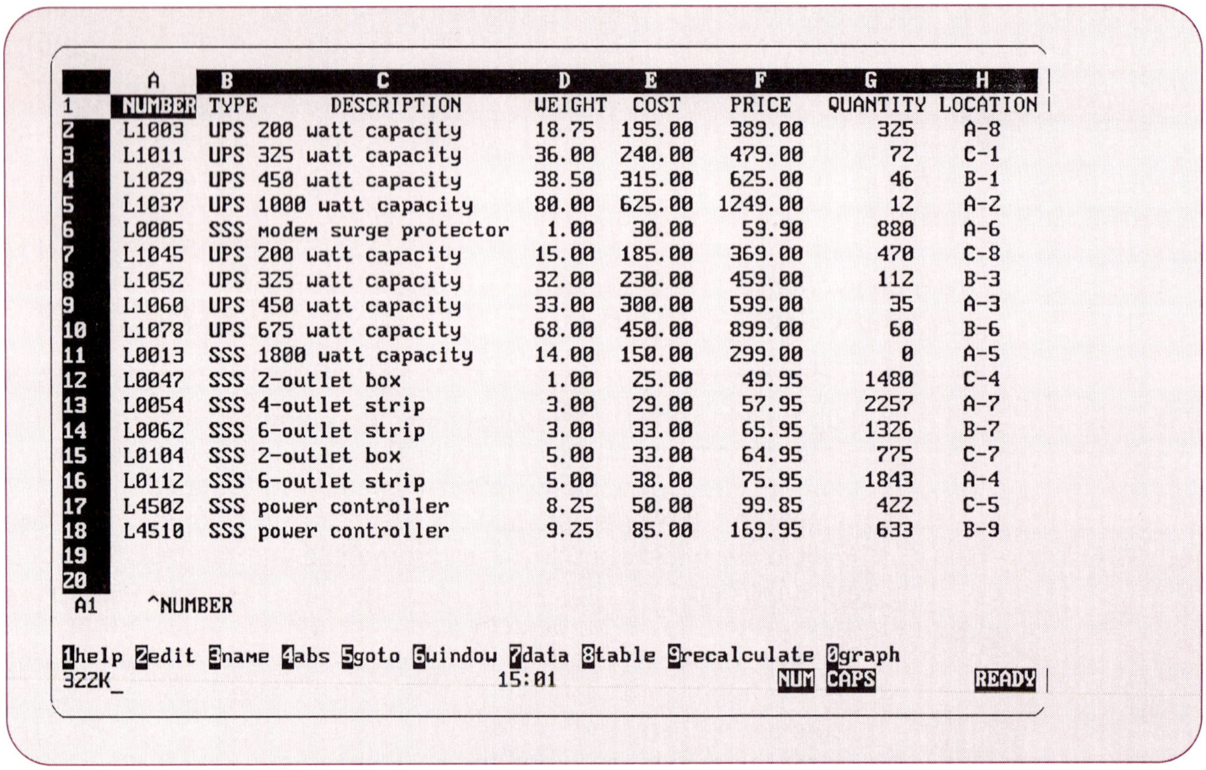

	A	B	C	D	E	F	G	H
1	NUMBER	TYPE	DESCRIPTION	WEIGHT	COST	PRICE	QUANTITY	LOCATION
2	L1003	UPS	200 watt capacity	18.75	195.00	389.00	325	A-8
3	L1011	UPS	325 watt capacity	36.00	240.00	479.00	72	C-1
4	L1029	UPS	450 watt capacity	38.50	315.00	625.00	46	B-1
5	L1037	UPS	1000 watt capacity	80.00	625.00	1249.00	12	A-2
6	L0005	SSS	modem surge protector	1.00	30.00	59.90	880	A-6
7	L1045	UPS	200 watt capacity	15.00	185.00	369.00	470	C-8
8	L1052	UPS	325 watt capacity	32.00	230.00	459.00	112	B-3
9	L1060	UPS	450 watt capacity	33.00	300.00	599.00	35	A-3
10	L1078	UPS	675 watt capacity	68.00	450.00	899.00	60	B-6
11	L0013	SSS	1800 watt capacity	14.00	150.00	299.00	0	A-5
12	L0047	SSS	2-outlet box	1.00	25.00	49.95	1480	C-4
13	L0054	SSS	4-outlet strip	3.00	29.00	57.95	2257	A-7
14	L0062	SSS	6-outlet strip	3.00	33.00	65.95	1326	B-7
15	L0104	SSS	2-outlet box	5.00	33.00	64.95	775	C-7
16	L0112	SSS	6-outlet strip	5.00	38.00	75.95	1843	A-4
17	L4502	SSS	power controller	8.25	50.00	99.85	422	C-5
18	L4510	SSS	power controller	9.25	85.00	169.95	633	B-9
19								
20								

A1 ^NUMBER

1help 2edit 3name 4abs 5goto 6window 7data 8table 9recalculate 0graph

322K_ 15:01 NUM CAPS READY

Screen Display 4-1

4 Sort	Sorts the records (rows) of a worksheet in ascending or descending order.
5 Query	Selects records from a worksheet according to specific conditions.
6 Distribution	Tabulates the frequency distribution of a specified range of values.
7 External	Allows transfer of data between the current worksheet and a database file (created by VP-Info and dBASE).
8 Input	Allows input to a worksheet using a full-screen data entry form.

- Select **Sort**.

> The Data Sort third-level options are displayed:

2 Data-range	Specifies the range containing the database to be sorted.

3 Primary-key	Specifies the field (column) on which to sort the records.
4 Secondary-key	Specifies a second field (column) to sort when there are identical primary key entries.
5 3rd-key	Specifies a third field (column) to sort when there are identical primary and secondary key entries.
6 4th-key	Specifies a fourth field (column) to sort when there are identical primary, secondary, and 3rd key entries.
7 Reset	Clears the settings for data range and all sort keys.
8 Go	Performs the sort.
9 Quit	Exits the Sort command.

Your first step is to specify the data range.

- Select **D**ata-range.

  > The input line reads

  `Enter Data Range: A1`

Just as for printing, you need to specify the top left corner and bottom right corner of cells to be sorted. Since you want to sort the entire database (except the headings on row 1), the data range is A2.H18.

- Type A2.H18 and press **ENTER**.

  > The third-level menu is displayed again.

- Select **P**rimary-key.

  > The input line reads

  `Enter Primary key address: A1`

Your primary key is the Number field, or column A.

- Place the cursor anywhere in the primary-key column (column A), and press **ENTER**.

  > The input line prompts **Enter Sort order (A or D): D**.

- Type A and press **ENTER** since you want to sort the records in ascending order.

The secondary key is used in case of a tie. For example, employees are often sorted in alphabetic order. The primary key is Last Name, and the secondary key is First Name. If two employees have the same last name, then the secondary key is used to break the tie. You do not have a secondary key since all items have unique item numbers. The same applies for 3rd-key and 4th-key. You are ready to sort.

- Select **G**o.

  > VP-Planner Plus sorts the worksheet as shown in Screen Display 4-2.

	A	B	C	D	E	F	G	H
1	NUMBER	TYPE	DESCRIPTION	WEIGHT	COST	PRICE	QUANTITY	LOCATION
2	L0005	SSS	modem surge protector	1.00	30.00	59.90	880	A-6
3	L0013	SSS	1800 watt capacity	14.00	150.00	299.00	0	A-5
4	L0047	SSS	2-outlet box	1.00	25.00	49.95	1480	C-4
5	L0054	SSS	4-outlet strip	3.00	29.00	57.95	2257	A-7
6	L0062	SSS	6-outlet strip	3.00	33.00	65.95	1326	B-7
7	L0104	SSS	2-outlet box	5.00	33.00	64.95	775	C-7
8	L0112	SSS	6-outlet strip	5.00	38.00	75.95	1843	A-4
9	L1003	UPS	200 watt capacity	18.75	195.00	389.00	325	A-8
10	L1011	UPS	325 watt capacity	36.00	240.00	479.00	72	C-1
11	L1029	UPS	450 watt capacity	38.50	315.00	625.00	46	B-1
12	L1037	UPS	1000 watt capacity	80.00	625.00	1249.00	12	A-2
13	L1045	UPS	200 watt capacity	15.00	185.00	369.00	470	C-8
14	L1052	UPS	325 watt capacity	32.00	230.00	459.00	112	B-3
15	L1060	UPS	450 watt capacity	33.00	300.00	599.00	35	A-3
16	L1078	UPS	675 watt capacity	68.00	450.00	899.00	60	B-6
17	L4502	SSS	power controller	8.25	50.00	99.85	422	C-5
18	L4510	SSS	power controller	9.25	85.00	169.95	633	B-9
19								
20								

```
A1     ^NUMBER

1help 2edit 3name 4abs 5goto 6window 7data 8table 9recalculate 0graph
322K_                        15:04                 NUM            READY
```

Screen Display 4-2

After sorting, each row is intact but has moved up or down according to the entry in the primary-key field.

PRACTICE TIME

1. Sort the spreadsheet in ascending order by Cost.
2. Re-sort the spreadsheet in ascending order by Number.

DATA QUERY (/DQ)

Suppose you had a very large database—say containing several hundred items—and you needed to find the data on one particular item. You could scan the data visually to find the item, but this takes time. As an alternative, you can use the Data Query command.

The Data Query command allows you to select all records that meet whatever criteria you specify. For example, you can find the item whose number is L0104, all UPSs that cost you under $500, or the item in warehouse location B-6.

Selected records can be highlighted, copied to another spreadsheet location, or deleted.

To use the Data Query command, you first need to do some preparation work. Specifically, you need to:

- Determine your selection criteria.
- Prepare a worksheet area to record the selection criteria (called the criterion range).
- Determine which spreadsheet area will be searched for records that meet the criteria (called the input range).
- Decide whether you want VP-Planner Plus to find (that is, to highlight one-by-one), extract, or delete the selected records. If you decide to extract them then:
- Determine where on the worksheet the extracted records will be copied (called the output range).

Let's say you want VP-Planner Plus to search the inventory data and highlight the record whose number is L0104. Following the guidelines listed above, you prepare for the data query as follows:

1. Determine your selection criteria.

   In this case, it is number equals L0104.
2. Prepare the criterion range.

   The criterion range is used to specify the conditions for selecting records from the database. The criterion range is an area on the spreadsheet that is outside the input range (the area that holds the records being searched). The criterion range must contain at least two rows. The first row contains the names of the fields to be tested. These names must match exactly the names used in the first row of the database. The second row contains the values or formulas used for matching. For this example, you will use rows 20 and 21 for the criterion range.

   You are selecting records just on the number field, so you only need to copy that label (uppercase and lowercase letters matter here) to cell A20. However, the easiest way to establish a versatile criterion range is to copy all the field names from the first row of the database to the first row of the criterion range. Use the copy command to do that now. Rows 1 and 20 should be identical.

In the second row of the criterion range, enter the value you are searching for under the appropriate field name. In this case, you are looking for the value L0104 in the number field. So in cell A21 type L0104.

Other criteria could be specified under other field names, but they are not needed here.

3. Determine which spreadsheet area will be searched, including the row of field names.

   In this case, the input range is A1.H18.

4. Determine whether you want the selected records found (highlighted), extracted, or deleted.

   In this case, you want selected records highlighted.

5. Determine the output range for extracted records.

   In this case you are not extracting records, so this step is unnecessary.

Now, let's do the data query.

· Type /DQ for Data Query.

> The following options are displayed:

2 Input	Prompts you to specify a range from which the program will select records.
3 Criterion	Prompts you to specify a range in which to enter the condition by which VP-Planner Plus will select records.
4 Output	Prompts you to specify a range to which selected data will be copied.
5 Find	Highlights selected records in the input range one at a time as you press the UP or DOWN ARROW keys.
6 Extract	Copies all selected records to the designated output range.
7 Unique	Copies selected records to the designated output range, but duplicate records are omitted.
8 Delete	Deletes selected records from the worksheet database (input range), and closes up empty space.
9 Reset	Cancels the range and option settings.
0 Quit	Exits the Data Query command.

- Select **Input**.

  > You are prompted to enter the input range.

- Type **A1.H18** and press **ENTER**.

  > The options are displayed again.

- Select **Criterion**.

  > The input line prompts you to enter the criterion range.

- Type **A20.H21** and press **ENTER**.

  > The options appear again. All of the factors are specified, so you can initiate the query process.

- Select **Find**.

  > Row 7, which contains the record for item number L0104, is highlighted, as shown in Screen Display 4-3. In this case, it is the only record that satisfies the criterion.

- Press **ENTER** to continue.

PRACTICE TIME

1. Search for and highlight the inventory records whose description is 200 watt capacity. Use the UP ARROW and DOWN ARROW to highlight them in the database. (Note: Use /RE to erase criteria you no longer need.) When done, press ENTER.
2. Search for and highlight inventory records stored in location B-6. When done, press ENTER.
3. Change the criteria back to the number L0104.

EXTRACTING SELECTED RECORDS

To extract records that meet the selection criteria, you need to set up an output range, which specifies a place on the spreadsheet where they can be copied. The output range contains one row of field names, followed by enough rows to hold the largest number of records that could be extracted (unused ones will contain blanks). You do not need to copy entire records; you can specify the names of only the fields you want copied.

For this example, let's say that the same criteria described above still are true: we want to extract whatever records have the number L0104. Thus the input range and criterion range are the same as above (change them back if you have not done so already). Select Quit to get out of the Data Query mode. You need to define the output range. Let's put it in A25.H45.

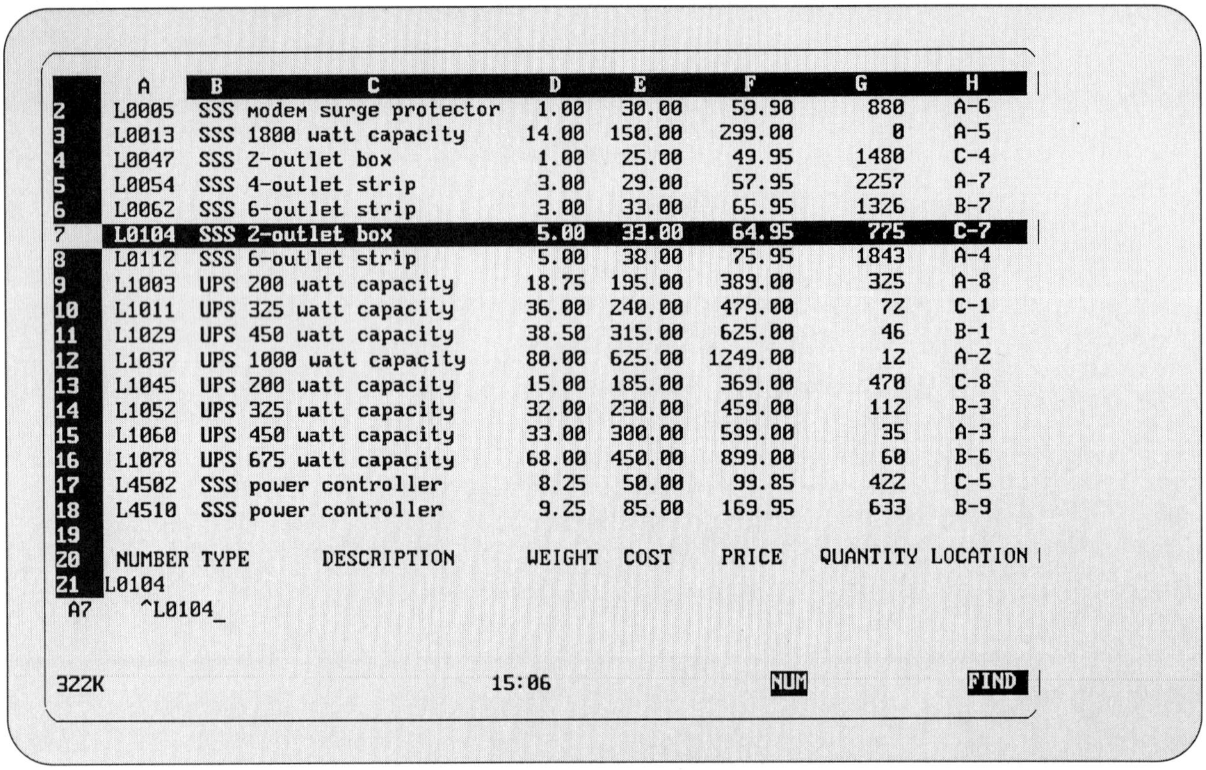

	A	B	C	D	E	F	G	H
2	L0005	SSS	modem surge protector	1.00	30.00	59.90	880	A-6
3	L0013	SSS	1800 watt capacity	14.00	150.00	299.00	0	A-5
4	L0047	SSS	2-outlet box	1.00	25.00	49.95	1480	C-4
5	L0054	SSS	4-outlet strip	3.00	29.00	57.95	2257	A-7
6	L0062	SSS	6-outlet strip	3.00	33.00	65.95	1326	B-7
7	L0104	SSS	2-outlet box	5.00	33.00	64.95	775	C-7
8	L0112	SSS	6-outlet strip	5.00	38.00	75.95	1843	A-4
9	L1003	UPS	200 watt capacity	18.75	195.00	389.00	325	A-8
10	L1011	UPS	325 watt capacity	36.00	240.00	479.00	72	C-1
11	L1029	UPS	450 watt capacity	38.50	315.00	625.00	46	B-1
12	L1037	UPS	1000 watt capacity	80.00	625.00	1249.00	12	A-2
13	L1045	UPS	200 watt capacity	15.00	185.00	369.00	470	C-8
14	L1052	UPS	325 watt capacity	32.00	230.00	459.00	112	B-3
15	L1060	UPS	450 watt capacity	33.00	300.00	599.00	35	A-3
16	L1078	UPS	675 watt capacity	68.00	450.00	899.00	60	B-6
17	L4502	SSS	power controller	8.25	50.00	99.85	422	C-5
18	L4510	SSS	power controller	9.25	85.00	169.95	633	B-9
19								
20	NUMBER	TYPE	DESCRIPTION	WEIGHT	COST	PRICE	QUANTITY	LOCATION
21	L0104							

A7 ^L0104_

322K 15:06 NUM FIND

Screen Display 4-3

When you define the first row of the output range you can copy the names from the first row of the input range. This ensures identical spelling of field names. The result will be that all the fields from all the selected records will be copied.

If you want only some of the fields to be copied to the output range, then you specify only those field names in row 1 of the output range. But be careful when you do this. Be sure that the column into which you are copying data is the proper width. For example, suppose you decided to extract only number and description from the inventory database. If you place those names in cells A25 and B25 you will have a problem: column B is not wide enough to hold a description. A better idea would be to locate the output range to the right of (rather than underneath) the database records. Then you can adjust column widths as you need to.

To extract records, do the following:

- Copy all the field names from row 1 to row 25 (same columns).
- Move the cell cursor so that rows 25-30 are visible on the screen.
- Type **/DQO** to specify the output range.
- Type **A25.H45** and press **ENTER**.
- Select **Extract**.

  > The third-level options appear again.

- Select **Quit** to exit the Data Query command.

  > The record for item L0104 appears on row 26 as shown in Screen Display 4-4.

- Save the spreadsheet, using the filename VPP5.

```
      A      B          C                D       E        F         G       H
9    L1003  UPS 200 watt capacity      18.75  195.00   389.00       325    A-8
10   L1011  UPS 325 watt capacity      36.00  240.00   479.00        72    C-1
11   L1029  UPS 450 watt capacity      38.50  315.00   625.00        46    B-1
12   L1037  UPS 1000 watt capacity     80.00  625.00  1249.00        12    A-2
13   L1045  UPS 200 watt capacity      15.00  185.00   369.00       470    C-8
14   L1052  UPS 325 watt capacity      32.00  230.00   459.00       112    B-3
15   L1060  UPS 450 watt capacity      33.00  300.00   599.00        35    A-3
16   L1078  UPS 675 watt capacity      68.00  450.00   899.00        60    B-6
17   L4502  SSS power controller        8.25   50.00    99.85       422    C-5
18   L4510  SSS power controller        9.25   85.00   169.95       633    B-9
19
20   NUMBER TYPE       DESCRIPTION     WEIGHT  COST     PRICE    QUANTITY LOCATION
21  L0104
22
23
24
25   NUMBER TYPE       DESCRIPTION     WEIGHT  COST     PRICE    QUANTITY LOCATION
26   L0104  SSS 2-outlet box            5.00   33.00    64.95       775    C-7
27
28
 A25    ^NUMBER

1help 2edit 3name 4abs 5goto 6window 7data 8table 9recalculate 0graph
322K_                          15:08                  NUM              READY
```

Screen Display 4-4

PRACTICE TIME

1. Erase the comparison value in cell A21, using /RE.
2. Set the selection criteria of Type = SSS (enter SSS in cell B21).
3. Give the Data Query command and select the Find option.

   > Only the first record with Type = SSS is highlighted. To see others, use the UP or DOWN ARROW keys. Other records are highlighted one at a time. If there are no more (above or below) satisfying the criterion, the computer beeps.

4. Press **ENTER** to continue.
5. Now extract records of Type = SSS by selecting the Extract option of the Data Query command. You have to exit the Data Query command before you can scroll the screen to look at the output range.
6. Try a multiple selection criteria, such as Type = SSS and Cost = 33.00.

OTHER TEXT SELECTION CRITERIA

So far all the selection criteria used were exact matches, or equal condition(s) to a specific value or label. When dealing with text (not numeric) entries, you can also use "wild card" symbols, like the ones used in DOS:

*	All items with any text after this symbol are selected.
?	All items with any letter in the position where ? appears are selected.
>	All items with text greater than (in terms of alphabetical order) what appears after > are selected.
<	All items with text less than (in terms of alphabetical order) what appears after < are selected.
$	All items that contain the character string that appears after $ (anywhere in the text) are selected.
~	Any text that is not the same as the text that follows the symbol is selected.

For example, if you want to find all items whose item number starts with the letter L, insert L* in the comparison value cell. If you want to find all items whose item numbers are L1202, L1212, L1222, . . . , L1292 (the first three characters are L12 and the last character is a 2, with any character in the fourth position), you use L12?2 in the comparison value cell. If you want to select all the items whose item number is greater than L1450, then use >L1450.

For practice extract all items whose Number field contains L00 in the first three positions.

- Make sure that input range, criterion range, and output range are still defined as before.
- Erase all entries on row 21, columns A to H.
- Enter **L00*** in cell A21 (comparison value for item number).
- Type **/DQE**, then quit the Data Query command.

Examine the output range shown in Screen Display 4-5. You will now extract all items of type = SSS whose item number is greater than L1000.

- Enter **>L1000** in cell A21.
- Enter **SSS** in cell B21 (comparison value for Type).
- Type **/DQE**, then exit the Data Query command.

  > The output range shows the records for L4502 and L4510.

```
      A      B          C                D       E        F        G        H
13   L1045  UPS 200 watt capacity      15.00   185.00   369.00     470     C-8
14   L1052  UPS 325 watt capacity      32.00   230.00   459.00     112     B-3
15   L1060  UPS 450 watt capacity      33.00   300.00   599.00      35     A-3
16   L1078  UPS 675 watt capacity      68.00   450.00   899.00      60     B-6
17   L4502  SSS power controller        8.25    50.00    99.85     422     C-5
18   L4510  SSS power controller        9.25    85.00   169.95     633     B-9
19
20   NUMBER TYPE       DESCRIPTION     WEIGHT  COST     PRICE    QUANTITY LOCATION
21   L00*
22
23
24
25   NUMBER TYPE       DESCRIPTION     WEIGHT  COST     PRICE    QUANTITY LOCATION
26   L0005  SSS modem surge protector   1.00    30.00    59.90     880     A-6
27   L0013  SSS 1800 watt capacity     14.00   150.00   299.00       0     A-5
28   L0047  SSS 2-outlet box            1.00    25.00    49.95    1480     C-4
29   L0054  SSS 4-outlet strip          3.00    29.00    57.95    2257     A-7
30   L0062  SSS 6-outlet strip          3.00    33.00    65.95    1326     B-7
31
32
 A21   'L00*

1help 2edit 3name 4abs 5goto 6window 7data 8table 9recalculate 0graph
320K_                     15:13                 NUM CAPS              READY
```

Screen Display 4-5

PRACTICE TIME

1. Extract all the records whose item number contains L in the first position, 0 in the third position, and 3 in the last position.

   Hint: Use ? in the second and fourth positions.

2. Try other wild card characters such as $78 for item number (any item that contains string 78 anywhere in the Number field).

FORMULA CONDITIONS

To select a record based on fields containing numeric data, you must use **formula conditions** as criteria. On the second line of the criterion range, you enter the formula to be used in testing the first record for selection. Then other records are tested by using a **relative** formula condition. That is, the cell address is replaced with the appropriate one as each record is evaluated. If the cell address used in the formula condition is to be an absolute one, you have to precede row and column numbers with $. This usually happens when the cell being referenced is outside the input range.

When the formula condition is evaluated, the result is a logical "true" or "false." That is, the formula contains a relational operator which, when evaluated, gives the result of "true" or "false." True yields the value 1, and a false result yields the value 0. When the result is true (value 1), the record is selected.

Relational operators include the following:

<	less than
>	greater than
=	equal to
<>	not equal to
<=	less than or equal to
>=	greater than or equal to

Practice by extracting the records of all items that cost you more than $100. You use the formula +E2>100 because E2 is the cell in the first record whose value is being compared to the value 100.

- Make sure that input range, criterion range, and output range are still defined as before.
- Erase all entries on row 21, columns A to H.

- With the cell cursor on cell E21 (cost comparison value), type **+E2>100** and press **ENTER**.

  > **0** (zero) appears in cell E21.

This means that in the first record, the value in cell E2 is *not* greater than 100, and that this record is not selected.

Rather than seeing the logical result 0 in cell E21, it would be more meaningful for you to see the selection criteria (that you typed in) displayed. This can be accomplished by changing the display format to Text.

- Type **/RF**, select **Text**, then press **ENTER**.

  > The text entered is displayed at cell E21.

- Type **/DQE**, then select **Quit**.

  > The output range contains the records of all items with values greater than 100 in the Cost field as shown in Screen Display 4-6.

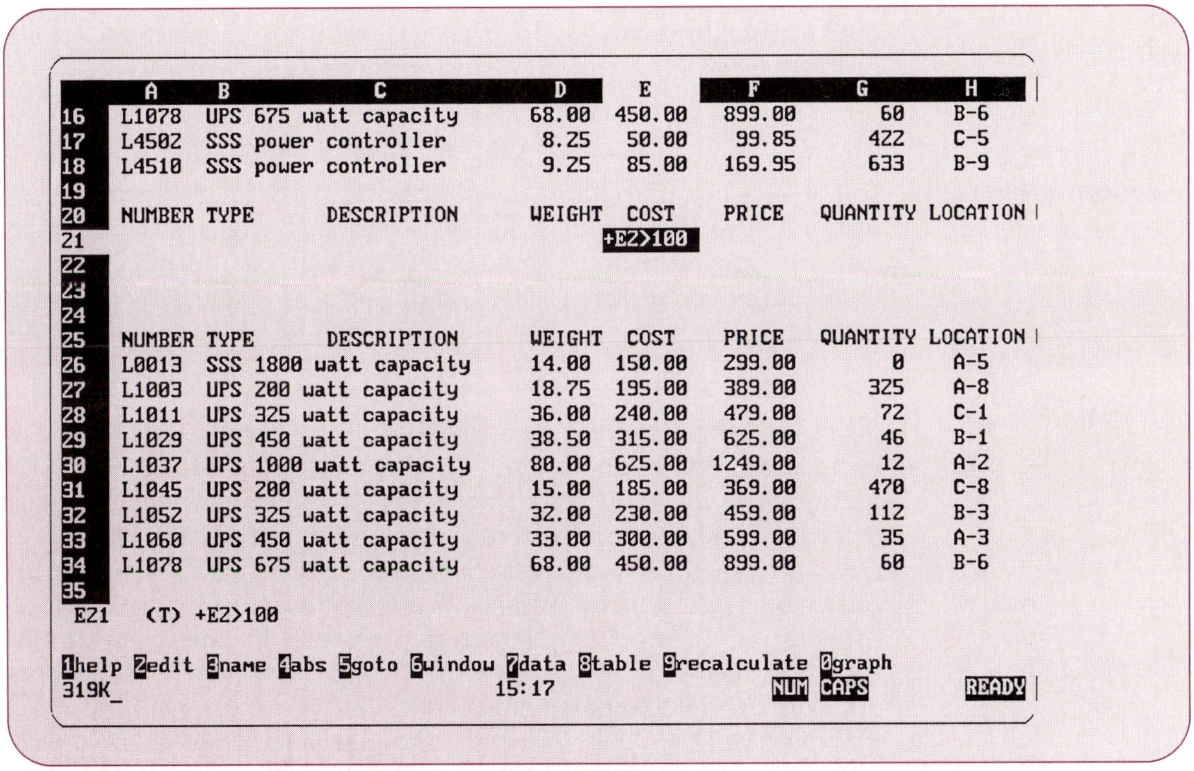

	A	B	C	D	E	F	G	H
16	L1078	UPS	675 watt capacity	68.00	450.00	899.00	60	B-6
17	L4502	SSS	power controller	8.25	50.00	99.85	422	C-5
18	L4510	SSS	power controller	9.25	85.00	169.95	633	B-9
19								
20	NUMBER	TYPE	DESCRIPTION	WEIGHT	COST	PRICE	QUANTITY	LOCATION
21					+E2>100			
22								
23								
24								
25	NUMBER	TYPE	DESCRIPTION	WEIGHT	COST	PRICE	QUANTITY	LOCATION
26	L0013	SSS	1800 watt capacity	14.00	150.00	299.00	0	A-5
27	L1003	UPS	200 watt capacity	18.75	195.00	389.00	325	A-8
28	L1011	UPS	325 watt capacity	36.00	240.00	479.00	72	C-1
29	L1029	UPS	450 watt capacity	38.50	315.00	625.00	46	B-1
30	L1037	UPS	1000 watt capacity	80.00	625.00	1249.00	12	A-2
31	L1045	UPS	200 watt capacity	15.00	185.00	369.00	470	C-8
32	L1052	UPS	325 watt capacity	32.00	230.00	459.00	112	B-3
33	L1060	UPS	450 watt capacity	33.00	300.00	599.00	35	A-3
34	L1078	UPS	675 watt capacity	68.00	450.00	899.00	60	B-6
35								

Screen Display 4-6

The Data Query command can be quite frustrating to use at first. Make sure that you've specified the input, output, and criterion ranges correctly. Also, avoid selection criteria that are overly complex.

PRACTICE TIME

1. Extract records of all items with values less than $500.00 in the Price field.
2. Extract all records of Type = UPS and Cost > $300. Get a printout of the output range.

Database files discussed here are two dimensional. That is, they have rows and columns. The VP-Planner Plus allows for database files with more than two (up to six) dimensions. To get an idea of what, for example, a three-dimensional file is, imagine that you have a database file containing sales data for a month. You can establish the months as the third dimension. There will be 12 such two-dimensional database files, one for each month. Since you cannot create multidimensional database files with the educational version of VP-Planner Plus, the subject is not discussed here.

DATA DISTRIBUTION

When working with a database containing many rows of data, it is sometimes useful to know the distribution of data. In this inventory example it would be nice to know how many items of a certain price category exist within the database. The Data Distribution command displays how values are divided among arbitrarily chosen categories, or **bins**.

- Retrieve spreadsheet VPP4

You will discover the cost distribution of items. Since the cost varies from $25 to $625, you will categorize items by cost in $100 increments. That is, you will find out how many items have a cost less than $100, how many items cost more than $100 and up to $200, how many over $200 and up to $300, and so on. This requires the use of two adjacent blank columns. You will use columns J and K.

In column J the cells will contain the values for the upper limit of each bin. That is, the first cell will contain the value 100, the second 200, the third 300, and so on to 700.

When the Data Distribution command is carried out, column K will show the distribution. That is, cell K1 will show the number of items in the cost range less than or equal to 100 (since the value 100 will be stored in cell J1), K2 will show the number of items in the cost range greater than 100 but less than or equal to 200 (since the value 200 will be stored in cell J2), and so on.

When you need to enter a sequence of evenly spaced numbers, as you will be doing in column J, you don't have to enter each value. Instead, you can fill a range (column or row) by giving the Data Fill command.

- Place the cursor on cell J1.
- Type /DF for Data Fill.

  > The input line prompts you with

  ```
  Enter data fill range: J1
  ```

The fill range specified can be larger than actually needed. VP-Planner Plus will use only the cells needed to carry out the instruction.

NOTE ■ If the fill range specified is too small, not all the numbers you require may be inserted.

- Type J1.J20 and press **ENTER**.

  > The input line prompts you for the start value.

- Type 100 and press **ENTER**.

  > It now prompts you for step, or increment, value.

- Type 100 and press **ENTER**.

  > It prompts you to enter the stop, or ending, value.

- Type 700 and press **ENTER**.

  > The appropriate values appear in column J, rows 1 to 7.

Now you can obtain the data distribution.

- Type /DD for Data Distribution.

  > The input line prompts

  ```
  Enter Values range: J1
  ```

You are to enter the range on which the distribution is based. In this case it is the COST, or cells E2 through E18.

- Type E2.E18 and press **ENTER**.

  > The input line prompts

  ```
  Enter Bin range: J1
  ```

Bin is the values on column J.

- Type J1.J7 and press ENTER.

  > Cells K1 through K8 display the distribution as shown in Screen Display 4-7.

As you can see, there are 8 items whose cost is below $100, 3 items that cost between $100 and $200, all the way to 1 item (shown in cell K8) that costs over $600. K8 displays the number of items whose values exceed the highest value entered in the bin range.

- Save the spreadsheet as VPP6.

PRACTICE TIME

Find the weight distribution of the items in your spreadsheet. The bins, or the categories, start at 20 pounds, incremented by 20 pounds, to 100 pounds.

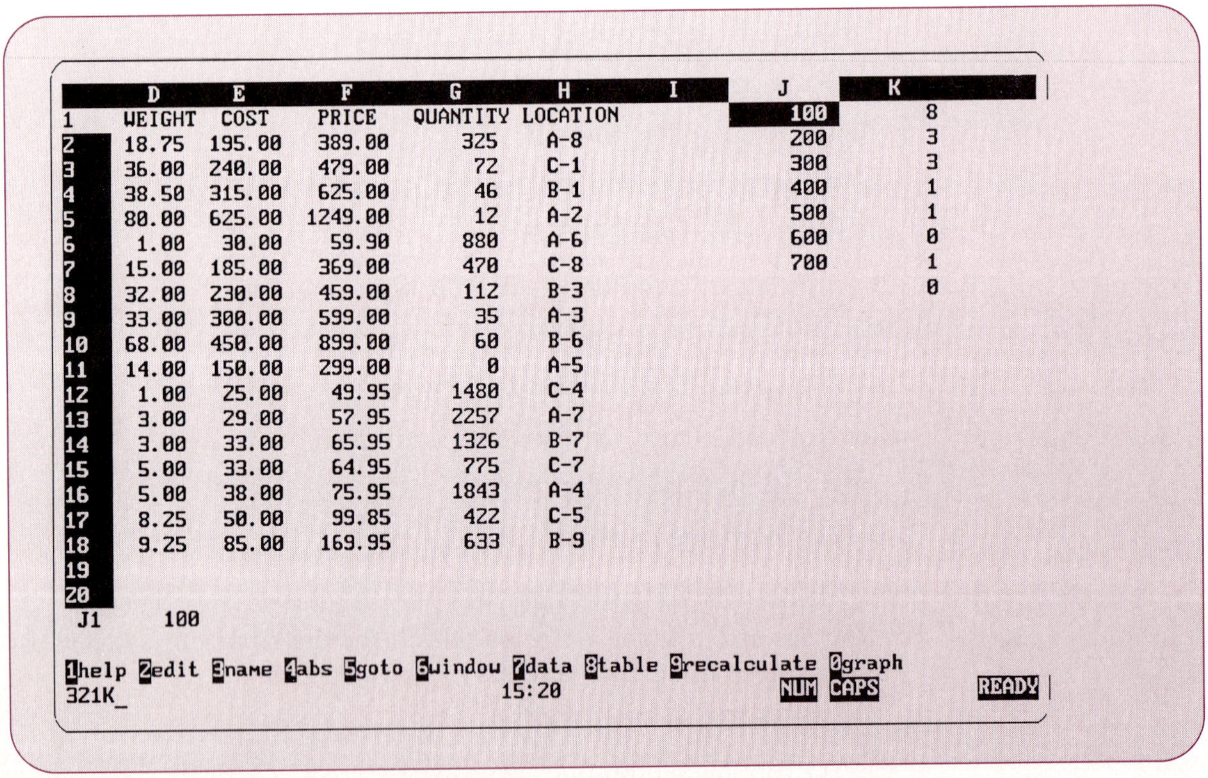

	D	E	F	G	H	I	J	K
1	WEIGHT	COST	PRICE	QUANTITY	LOCATION		100	8
2	18.75	195.00	389.00	325	A-8		200	3
3	36.00	240.00	479.00	72	C-1		300	3
4	38.50	315.00	625.00	46	B-1		400	1
5	80.00	625.00	1249.00	12	A-2		500	1
6	1.00	30.00	59.90	880	A-6		600	0
7	15.00	185.00	369.00	470	C-8		700	1
8	32.00	230.00	459.00	112	B-3			0
9	33.00	300.00	599.00	35	A-3			
10	68.00	450.00	899.00	60	B-6			
11	14.00	150.00	299.00	0	A-5			
12	1.00	25.00	49.95	1480	C-4			
13	3.00	29.00	57.95	2257	A-7			
14	3.00	33.00	65.95	1326	B-7			
15	5.00	33.00	64.95	775	C-7			
16	5.00	38.00	75.95	1843	A-4			
17	8.25	50.00	99.85	422	C-5			
18	9.25	85.00	169.95	633	B-9			
19								
20								

Screen Display 4-7

END OF LESSON 4

- Type /QY to exit to DOS.
- Remove the disks from the disk drive.
- Turn OFF the monitor, computer, and printer.

SUMMARY

In this lesson many of the terms and concepts that are necessary to use the spreadsheet file as database are discussed.

- A database file is a collection of records about a particular topic. Each record, in turn, is composed of a series of fields.
- When a spreadsheet is used as a database, each row is a record and each column is a field. Before a query can be made, the input range, criterion range, and output range (optional) must be specified.
- Data in a database may be numeric data (previously called values) or text data (previously called labels).
- Rows in a spreadsheet (or records in a database) may be sorted in whatever order specified.
- Records in a spreadsheet defined as a database can be selected, or queried, based on criteria you specify. Selected records can be highlighted, copied to another location, or deleted.
- When querying a database based on text entries, "wild card" symbols can be used.
- When querying a database based on numeric entries, formula conditions are used.
- The data distribution table shows how values are distributed among arbitrarily chosen categories, or bins.
- The following commands are discussed:

/DQ	Data Query—selects records from a worksheet (database) according to specific selection criteria.
/DS	Data Sort—arranges records (rows) of a worksheet in ascending or descending order.
/DF	Data Fill—enters a series of numbers into a range when the increment or decrement is fixed.
/DD	Data Distribution—tabulates the frequency distribution of a specified range of values.

REVIEW QUESTIONS

1. What is the purpose of Secondary-key in a sort? ____________________

____

____

2. What is a record in a database? a field? Relate them to a spreadsheet.

3. What is the minimum number of data management "pieces" (such as ranges) that have to be specified before a query can be made on a spreadsheet?

4. When do you have to specify the output range for the Data Query?

5. When entering field names in criterion range or output range, how important is it to match the names with those given in the input range?

6. Which records are selected when a field in the criterion range does not contain a value to be matched?

7. How are the wild card symbols used in a query? Explain.

8. Explain how formula conditions work in a query.

9. What is the purpose of the Data Fill command?

10. Explain what is meant by data distribution and how it is done.

EXERCISES

1. Retrieve the spreadsheet EX2_1 from Lesson 2.
   a. Delete any rows that separate field names from records.
   b. Sort the spreadsheet, based on the Name field.
   c. Query the spreadsheet to extract friends with the same three numbers as the first three digits of the phone number.
   d. Get a printout of the entire spreadsheet.
   e. Query the spreadsheet to extract those friends who owe you more than $10 (or another appropriate value) total.
   f. Get a printout of just the criterion and output ranges
   g. Find out the distribution based on money owed to you. Use whatever values are most appropriate.
   h. Insert appropriate headings and print the distribution table.
   i. Save the spreadsheet as EX4_1.
2. Retrieve the spreadsheet EX2_2 from Lesson 2.
   a. Set up proper field names. Also, delete rows that separate field names from records.
   b. Sort the spreadsheet on the Name field.
   c. Resort the spreadsheet in ascending order on Total Points.
   d. Query the spreadsheet to extract those students whose average is below 80.
   e. Get a printout of the entire spreadsheet.
   f. Query the spreadsheet to extract records of students who received more than 90 points on the first exam but whose average is lower than 90.
   g. Get a printout of just the criterion and output ranges.
   h. Find out the distribution of students based on average. Find out how many students have averages of 60 or below, 61 to 70, and so on.
   i. Insert appropriate headings and print the distribution table.
   j. Save the spreadsheet as EX4_2.

Lesson 5
Creating Business Graphics

Objectives

Upon completion of the material presented in this lesson, you should be able to do the following:

- Understand the terminology used in the VP-Planner Plus graphics.
- Identify various types of graphs.
- Create graphs from data in a spreadsheet.
- Insert titles and legends in a graph.
- Save parameters for a graph.
- Save a graph to a file.
- Print a graph.

STARTING OFF

Start VP-Planner Plus so that a blank worksheet is displayed on the screen. Insert a data disk into drive B and change the file directory to B. To print graphs, you must have access to a printer capable of printing graphics.

GRAPHICS

In this lesson you will learn about the various types of graphs that can be generated from the data on the worksheet. These graphs, also referred to as **presentation graphics**, can be displayed on the monitor or printed. Different types of graphs are useful for different purposes.

- A **pie chart** is used to show how the spreadsheet is divided. For example, it is used to show how income is generated or where the money goes (Figure 5-1).

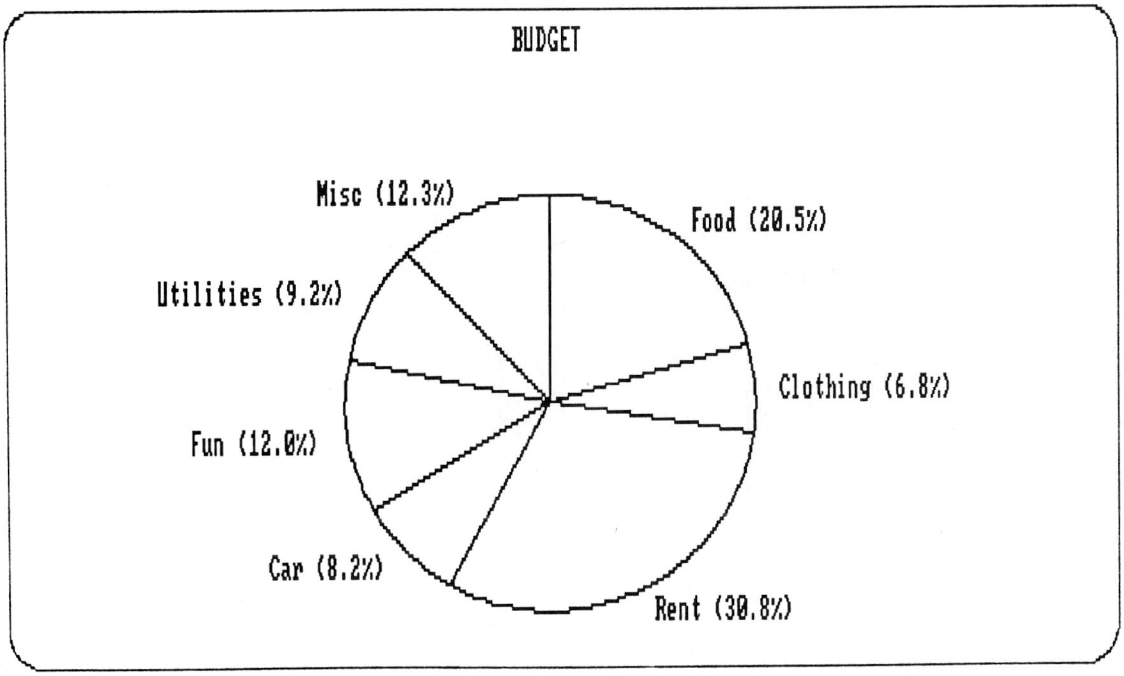

Figure 5-1 A Pie chart

- A **bar chart** is used to show how some quantity varies among different departments, or geographical regions, or with time. You may want to compare student enrollment for various departments (Figure 5-2).
- A **line chart** is used to show trends of one or more quantities over a period of time. You may want to compare the sales figures for two different brands of a product (Figure 5-3).

The first step in making a graph is to indicate the type of graph you want. Then you must specify where the data is located. Just as you must specify where the data ranges for copying and printing are, you must indicate the ranges for the various parts of the graph under construction. Finally, if appropriate, you may enter a title, label the horizontal and vertical ranges (X- and Y-axes), and add legends. At any stage of development, you can view the graph on the screen. When you are satisfied with the graph, you can print it or you can save it on your data disk, ready to be printed at a later time.

Graph development requires some planning. VP-Planner Plus is extremely flexible, however, and you can change your graph rather easily if you change your mind. In this lesson you will look at a few

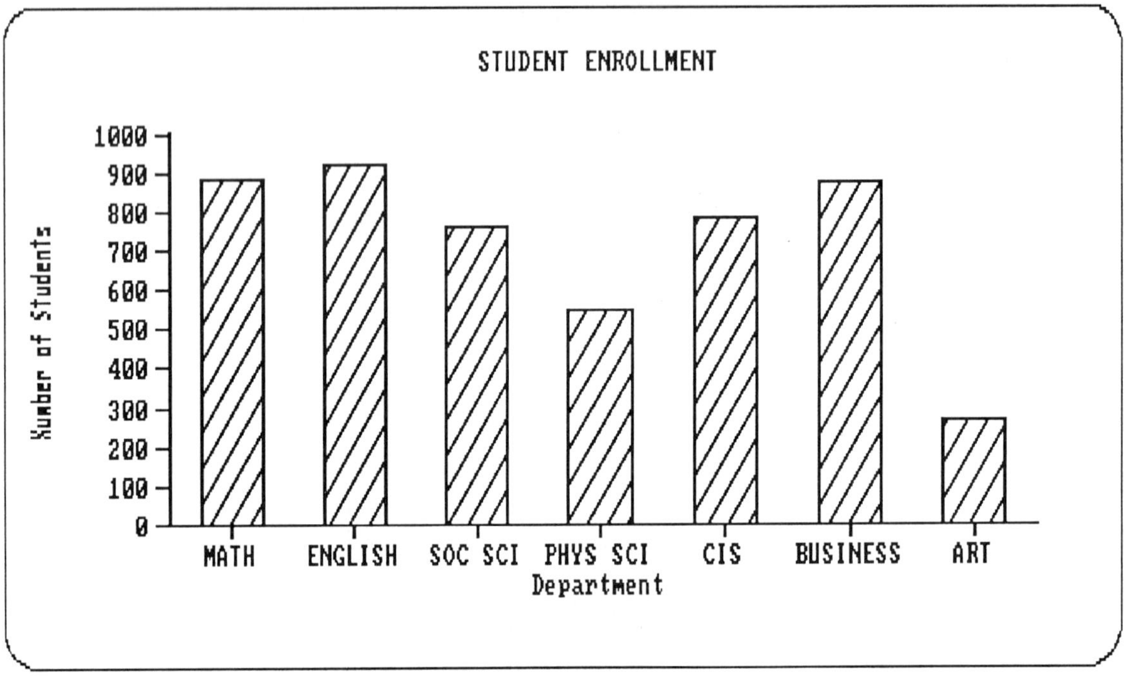

Figure 5-2 A bar chart

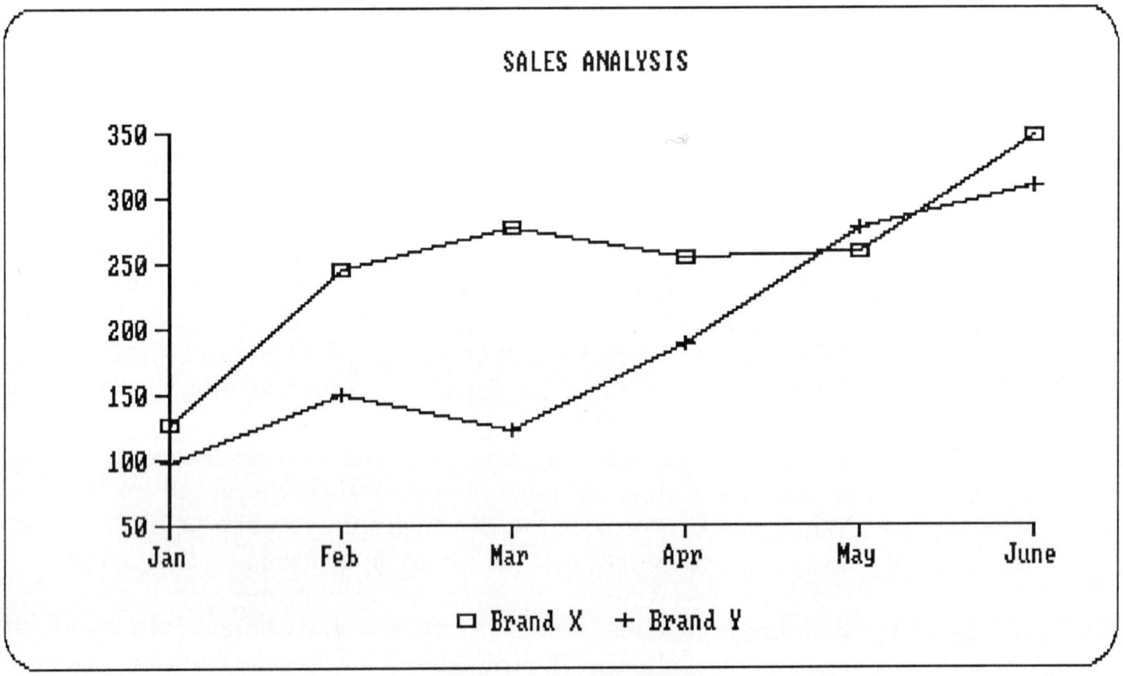

Figure 5-3 A line chart

very simple graphs to get an idea of what can be done, and what each type of graph looks like.

PIE CHARTS

A pie chart is a graph consisting of a circle divided into slices, much like a pie. Each section represents one item and shows what fraction it is of the whole. The best way to understand the various parameters of a pie chart is to go through the process of setting one up.

Suppose you are evaluating the budget for your business and you want to see a graphic representation of your expense categories.

- Set up a spreadsheet with the following data:

	A	B
1	Salaries	25125
2	Fringes	7595
3	Utilities	375
4	Rent	3450
5	Supplies	650
6	Equipment	1400
7	Travel	3535

After entering the data, do the following:

- Type **/G** for Graph.

> The following second-level options are displayed:

2 Type	Lets you select the type of graph.
3 Reset	Clears all graph settings.
4 View	Displays the current graph on the screen.
5 Print	Prints the current graph on a graphics printer.
6 Save	Saves the current graph as a file.
7 Options	Lets you refine the appearance of a graph.
8 Name	Lets you save a number of graph parameters with the current worksheet.
9 Quit	Exits the Graph command.
0 Look	Lets you view the saved graph on the screen.
X	Sets the range of cell labels for the horizontal axis for line, bar, and stacked-bar graphs, or for each "slice" of a pie graph.
A–F	Sets data ranges for the vertical axis for line, bar, XY, and stacked-bar graphs, and for each "slice" of a pie graph.

The meaning of these options, or the **parameters**, is best learned from examples. First, you must specify the graph type. You want Pie Chart.

- Select **Type**.

  > The third-level options are as follows:

  2 Line
  3 Bar
  4 XY
  5 Stacked Bar
  6 Pie

- Select **Pie**.

  > The Graph second-level options are displayed again.

Now you need to specify the range of cells to include in this pie chart. First, you specify the range of labels (X range). These are the categories into which the pie is divided. Then you specify the range of values (A range). These values determine the size of slice for each category. The X range is the labels in column A, and the A range is the values in column B.

- Select **X**.

  > You are prompted to enter the X-axis data range.

- Type **A1.A7** and press **ENTER**.
- Select **A**.

  > You are prompted to enter the first data range.

- Type **B1.B7** and press **ENTER**.

You will now look at the graph.

- Select **View**.

  > The pie chart shown in Figure 5-4 is displayed.

The graph looks good, but a title would improve it.

- Press any key to continue.

  > You are still in the Graph command.

- Select **Options**.

  > The screen shown in Screen Display 5-1 is displayed.

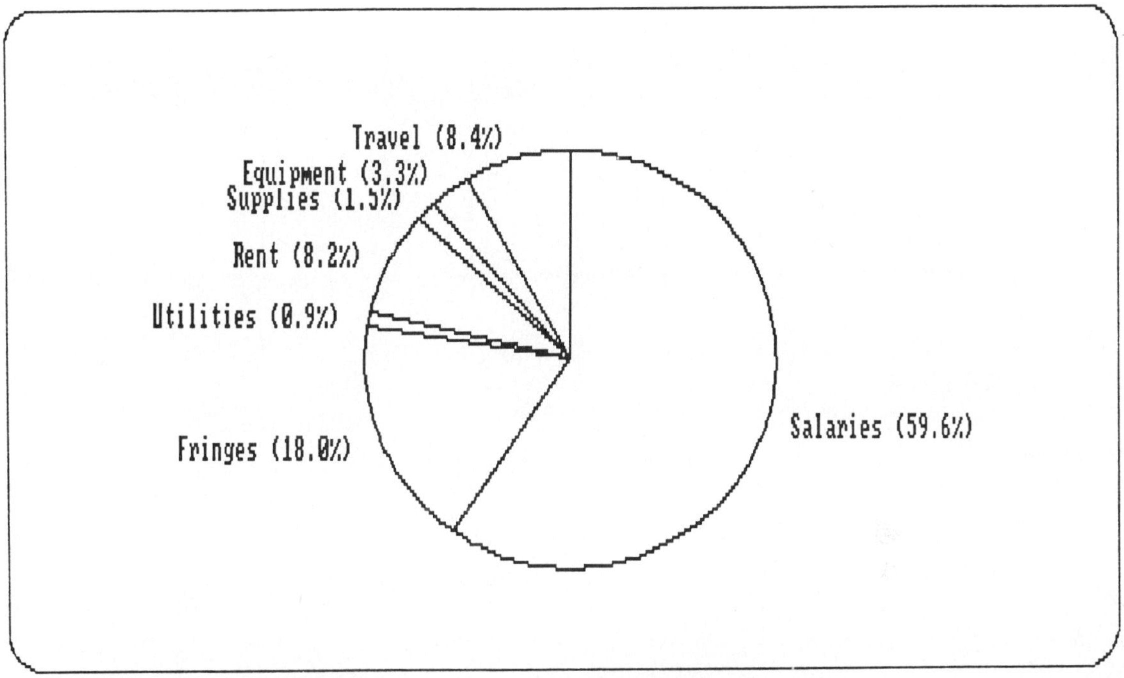

Figure 5-4 A pie chart of business expenses

where

2 Data-Labels	Uses worksheet labels as text in the graph.
3 Titles	Puts titles in the graph.
4 Legend	Puts descriptive text in the graph.
5 Scale	Sets upper and lower limits of graphs.
6 Format	Selects the format for displaying numbers.
7 Grid	Puts grid lines in the graph.
8 Color	Sets the graph for printing without cross-hatching.
9 B & W	Adds cross-hatching to the graph.
0 Quit	Exits the Options menu.

· Select **Titles**.

> The options below Titles are highlighted:

2 First	Centers text at the top of the graph.
3 Second	Adds a second line to the title.

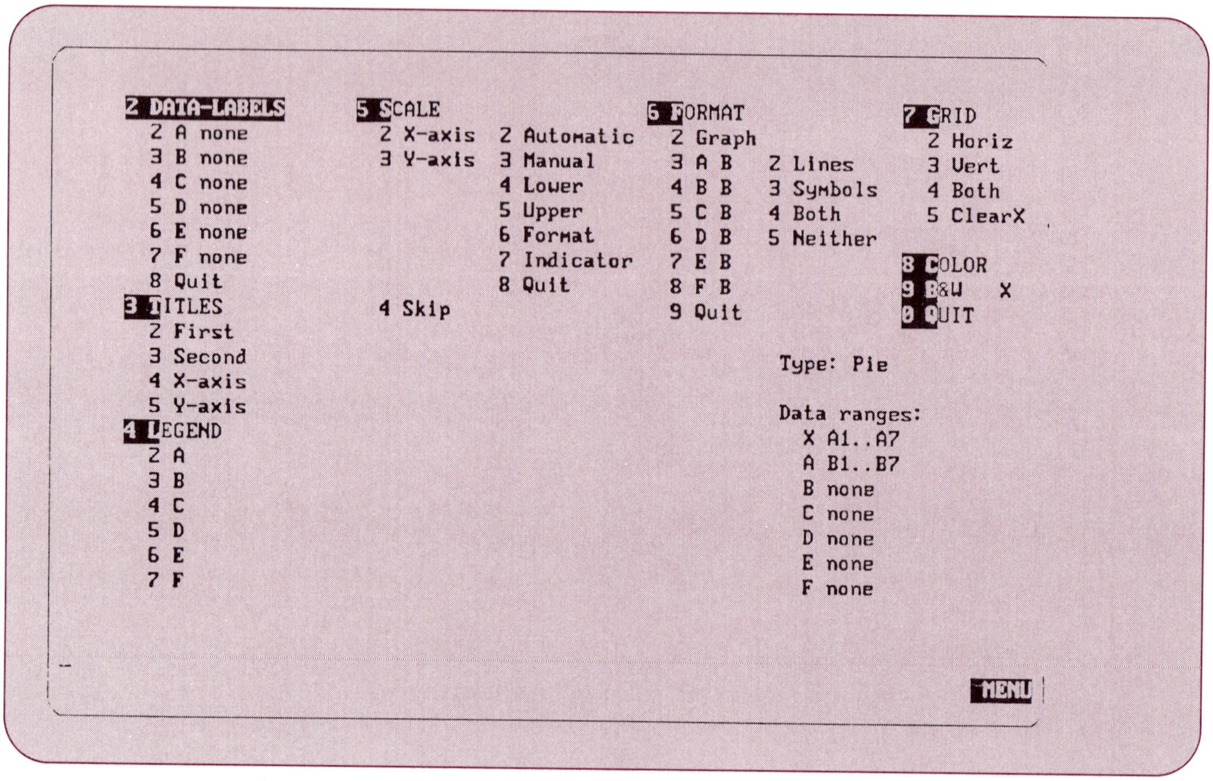

Screen Display 5-1

4 X-axis	Places text below the horizontal axis.
5 Y-axis	Places text sideways along the vertical axis.

You can enter two lines for graph title. X-axis and Y-axis options are not used for a pie chart. You will enter a one-line title, EXPENSES.

- Select **First**.

  > You are prompted to

  `Enter title:`

- Type **EXPENSES** and press ENTER.
- Select **Quit** to get back to the Graph second-level menu.
- Select **View**.

  > The graph now contains a title.

- Press any key to continue.

PRINTING A GRAPH

You can print the graph you just viewed.

- Make sure that the printer is on and is ready to use.
- Select **P**rint.

  > The graph is printed.

NAMING A GRAPH

Since you may want to work with this graph later, you should name it. Naming a graph does not save the graph itself in memory. Rather, its parameters are named and associated with the current spreadsheet. You can recreate the graph later simply by identifying the name. When you save the spreadsheet, the named parameters are saved along with it.

- Select **N**ame.

  > The following third-level options are displayed:

2 Use	Draws a graph using named parameters.
3 Create	Stores the current graph parameters.
4 Delete	Erases a stored graph name.
5 Reset	Erases all stored graph names.
6 Table	Lists all graphs that have been named for the current spreadsheet.

You are creating a new name.

- Select **C**reate.

  > You are prompted to **Enter name:**.

A name can be up to 14 characters in length. If you enter an existing name, the old one will be overwritten. Use the name PIE1.

- Type PIE1 and press **ENTER**.

  > The Graph second-level options are displayed again.

Remember, this pie chart itself was not saved. Its parameters were named PIE1 and have been associated with the current spreadsheet. These are saved when the spreadsheet is saved. You can later view the chart even if you have gone on and created several other graphs in the meanwhile.

SAVING A GRAPH

You need to save your graph if you want to use the graph itself (without retrieving the spreadsheet from the disk). For example, you may want to include the graph in a word processing document.

- Select **Save**.

  > The message appears:

  ```
  Enter file name: B:\
  ```

You are asked to give the graph a name for storage on disk. A filename can be one to eight characters in length and can include uppercase and lowercase letters, numbers, and the underscore character (—). VP-Planner Plus automatically assigns an extension .PIC.

You will save the graph as PIE1S.

- Type **PIE1S** and press **ENTER**.

  > The graph is saved on disk.

The graphs created in the rest of this lesson will not be saved; they will just be named. By loading the spreadsheet the graph is associated with, the graph can always be viewed and printed.

Now reset the graph settings to get ready for the next graph.

- Select **Reset**.

  > You have the option to reset the entire graph parameters or just the specific ones (such as X range or A range).

- Select **Graph** to reset the whole thing.
- Select **Quit** to exit the Graph command.

BAR GRAPHS

Another way to represent data graphically is with bars, or **histograms**. Bar heights indicate the magnitudes of the various items represented by the bars. Use the data you used for the pie chart once again.

- Type **/GTB** to specify you want Bar Graph.

  > The Graph second-level options are displayed.

Now you have to specify the label range (the X range, or the labels to be displayed horizontally along the bottom axis of the graph) and the values (the A range).

- Select **X**.
- Labels appear on column A, so type **A1.A7** and press **ENTER**.
- Select **A**.
- Values are on column B. Type **B1.B7** and press **ENTER**.

- Enter a one-line title, **BUDGET**, after selecting **Options, Titles**, and **First**.
- Select **Quit**.

You might have noticed that although you reset all the parameters after you created the pie chart, you really did not need to do so. The only parameter that needed changing was the graph type.

- Select **View**.

  > The graph shown in Figure 5-5 is displayed.

Note that the height of each bar is determined by the value in column B, and the label on the X-axis (horizontal line) is determined by the label entered in column A.

- Press any key to continue.

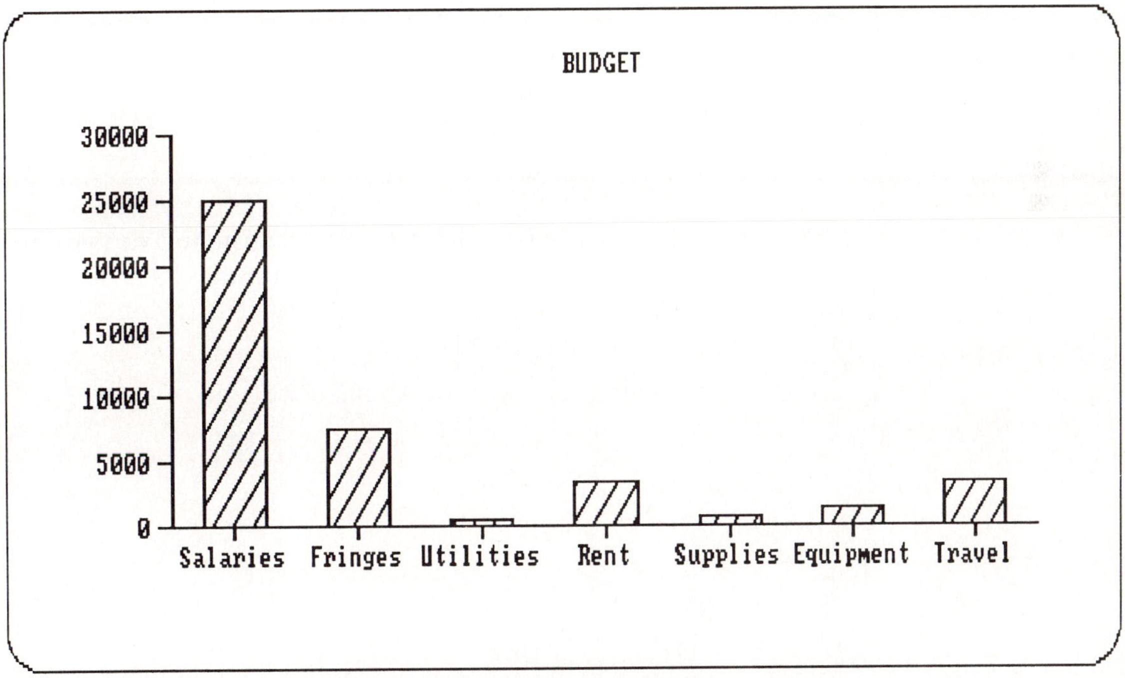

Figure 5-5 A bar graph of business expenses

PRACTICE TIME

1. Name this graph BAR1.
2. Quit the Graph command. (Do not Reset since you will use these parameters in just a while.)

Note that two graphs—PIE1 and BAR1—are now associated with the current spreadsheet. In fact, you can return to the Graph Command and use the pie chart from before.

- Type /GN for Graph Name.
- Select Use.

  > You are prompted to enter the name. A pop-up window appears that displays all the named graphs that are associated with the spreadsheet.

- Highlight PIE1 and press ENTER.

  > The pie chart is displayed.

- Press any key to continue.

PRACTICE TIME

1. Display the bar graph that was just created.
2. Press any key to continue.
3. Quit the Graph command.

The values in column B are for one month only, and you've decided to put budgets for two more months in columns C and D. Furthermore, you would like to see the values for the second and third months on the same bar graph.

- Enter the following values in the spreadsheet:

	C	D
1	25250	25200
2	7610	7600
3	425	450
4	3450	3450
5	500	825
6	1475	1500
7	3800	2875

- Type /G to enter the Graph command.

You've already specified that you want Bar Graph. Also, the X and A ranges have been specified. Now you need to specify the B range (values for the second month, column C) and C range (values for the third month, column D).

- Select B, type C1.C7, and press ENTER.
- Select C, type D1.D7, and press ENTER.
- Select View.

  > The graph shown in Figure 5-6 is displayed.

The first bar in each category represents the value for the first month (A range); the second bar, the second month (B range); and third bar, the third month (C range). It would be helpful for someone looking at the graph if the graph contained some descriptive information. This can be accomplished by adding a second line to the title, labeling both the vertical and horizontal axes, and creating a legend. A **legend** is descriptive text that identifies the patterns on a graph.

- Press any key to continue.

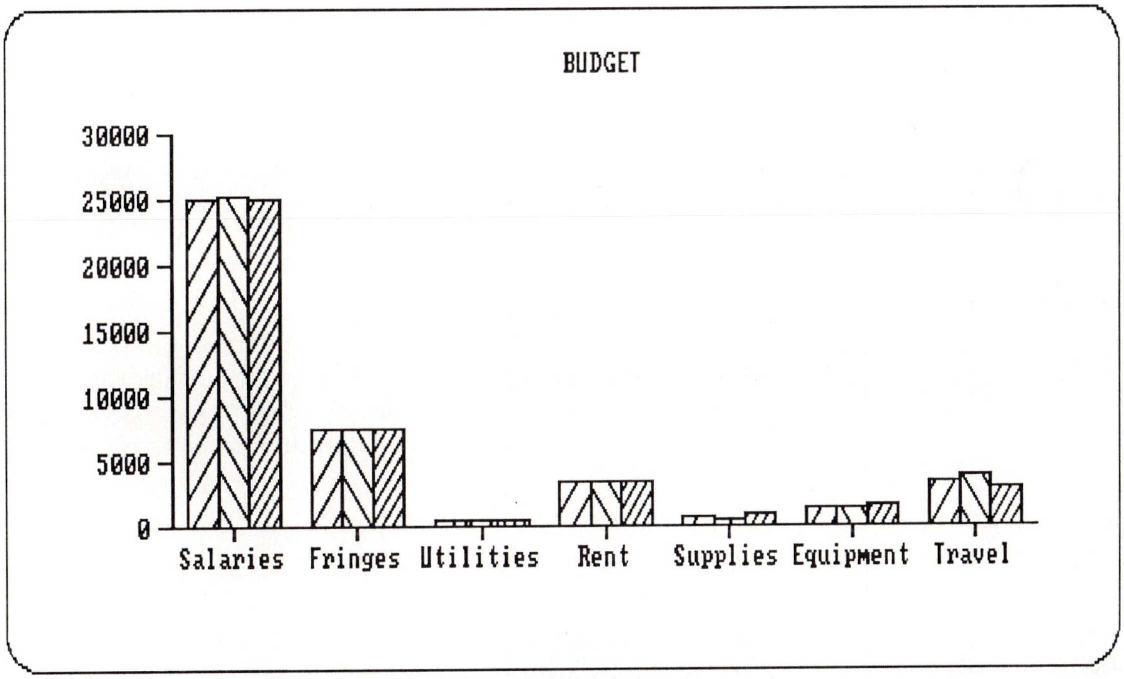

Figure 5-6 A three-month histogram

Let's assume that these figures are for the months of March, April, and May. You will first add a second line to the title.

- Select **Options, Titles**, then **Second**.

  > You are prompted to enter the text for the second line of title.

- Type **March - May** and press ENTER.

Now, to add labels to the horizontal (X) and vertical (Y) axes:

- Select **Titles**, then **X-axis**.
- Type **Expense Categories** and press ENTER.
- Select **Title**, then **Y-axis**.
- Type **Amount** and press ENTER.

You have to add legends for the A, B, and C ranges.

- Select **Legend**, then **A** range.
- Type **March** and press ENTER.
- Select **Legend**, then **B** range.
- Type **April** and press ENTER.
- Select **Legend**, then **C** range.
- Type **May** and press ENTER.
- Select **Quit** to exit to the Graph second-level menu.
- Select **View**. Your modified histogram should look like Figure 5-7.
- Press any key to continue.

PRACTICE TIME

1. Name this graph BAR2.
2. Print the graph, then exit the Graph command.
3. Save the spreadsheet as VPP7. This spreadsheet has three named graphs associated with it. When you retrieve the spreadsheet later, you can view any of these graphs by giving the name (selecting the Name, then the Use options).

STACKED-BAR GRAPHS

Rather than showing bars (for each month) side by side, the cumulative values can be seen by stacking them. You can switch to a stacked-bar graph by simply changing the graph type.

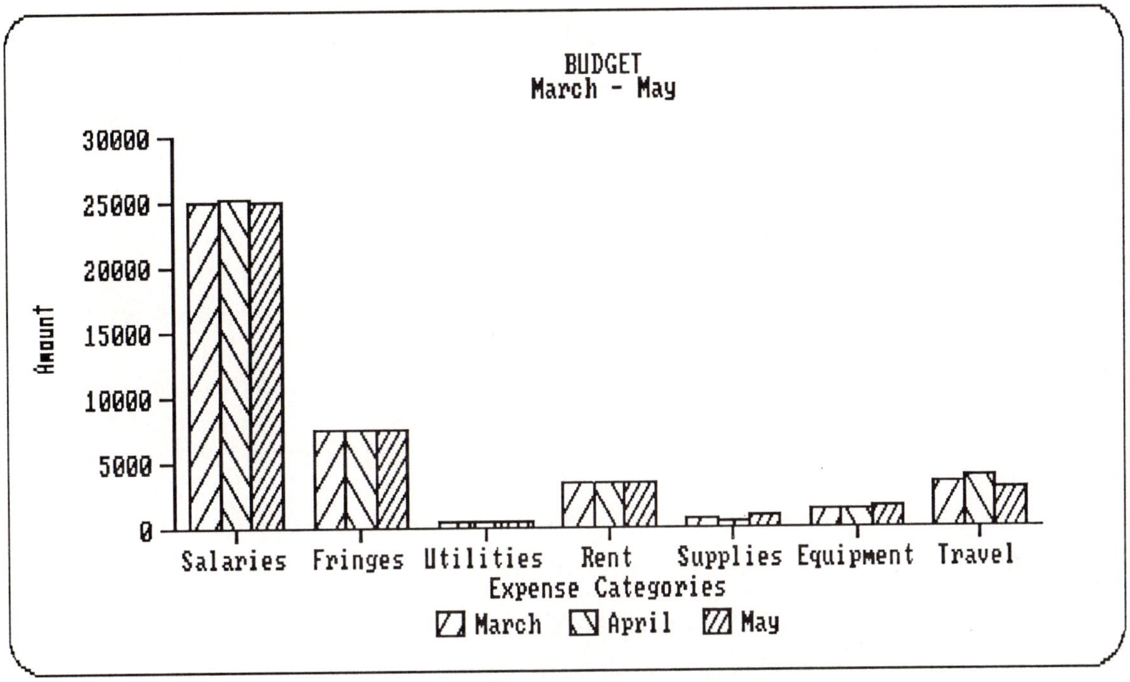

Figure 5-7 A more understandable bar graph

- Type /GT, then select Stacked-Bar.
- Now select View to look at it.

  > The graph of Figure 5-8 is displayed.

- Exit the Graph command.

LINE GRAPH

Whereas the heights of bars in a bar graph represent relative values, the lines in a line graph connect points in the X-range. To learn this concept, you will create a spreadsheet to show the projected accumulated expenses (estimated by the straight-line method), and the actual accumulated expenses associated with the Madison contract.

This contract came in on August 1, 1989, and is scheduled to be completed on March 1, 1990. The expense is not to exceed $50,000. The spreadsheet will show project status by month and year. In column A of the spreadsheet, you will enter the months label from August 1989 through March 1990. Column B will show the projected accumulated expenses, and column C will contain the actual accumulated expenses.

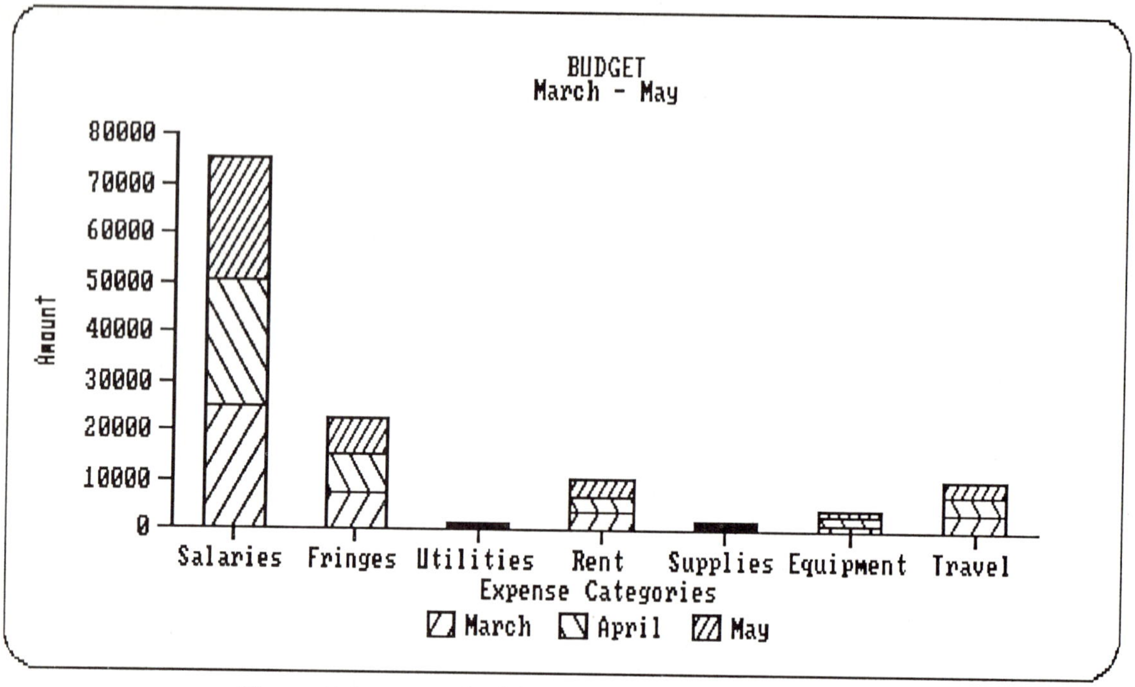

Figure 5-8 A stacked-bar graph of business expenses

Rather than typing in the actual month and year in each cell in column A, you will practice with an alternative method of entering dates.

- Clear the spreadsheet (/WEY).
- At cell A1 enter the title MONTH.
- At cell A2, enter @DATE(1989,8,1).

  > Cell A2 displays the value **32721**.

The @DATE function has three arguments: year, month, and date (1989,8,1). It returns a number in the range of –36157 (which stands for January 1, 1801) to 73050 (which stands for December 31, 2099). August 1, 1989, happens to be 32721.

NOTE ■ You can obtain today's date value by using the @NOW function. This function gives not only the date value but also the time as a fraction of a day. If you want the date value only (without the time), you enter @INT(@NOW). Both time and date are based on the computer's internal clock.

Although the first day of each month comes a variable number of days after the previous one, for your purposes you can assume 31 days. Hence, the idea is to enter date numbers in 31-day increments in cells A2 through A9, starting with 32721. This can be accomplished by using the Data Fill command.

- Type **/DF**.

  > You are prompted to enter the range of cells to fill with numbers.

- Type **A2.A9** and press **ENTER**.

  > You are prompted for a start value.

- Type **@DATE(1989,8,1)** and press **ENTER**.

  > You are prompted for an increment value.

- Type **31** and press **ENTER**.

  > You are prompted for a stop value.

Since the data fill range was specified as A2 through A9, the values will be displayed only in those cells. You are not sure of the stop value, so enter something very large.

- Type **70000** and press **ENTER**.

  > The screen shown in Screen Display 5-2 is displayed.

These date numbers do not mean much to you. You need to change the display format.

- Type **/RF**; then select **Date**.

  > The following options are displayed:

2 1=D-MMM-Y	21-Nov-89
3 2=D-MMM	21-Nov
4 3=MMM-Y	Nov-21
5 4=M/D/Y	11/21/89
6 5=D/M/Y	21/11/89
7 6=Y M D	89 11 21
8 Day	Wednesday
9 Month	November
0 Time24	24-hour (16:30)
PMtime	12-hour am/pm (4:30 pm)

Just to see what they will look like, you will select the first option.

- Select **1=D-MMM-Y**.

  > You are prompted to enter the range to format.

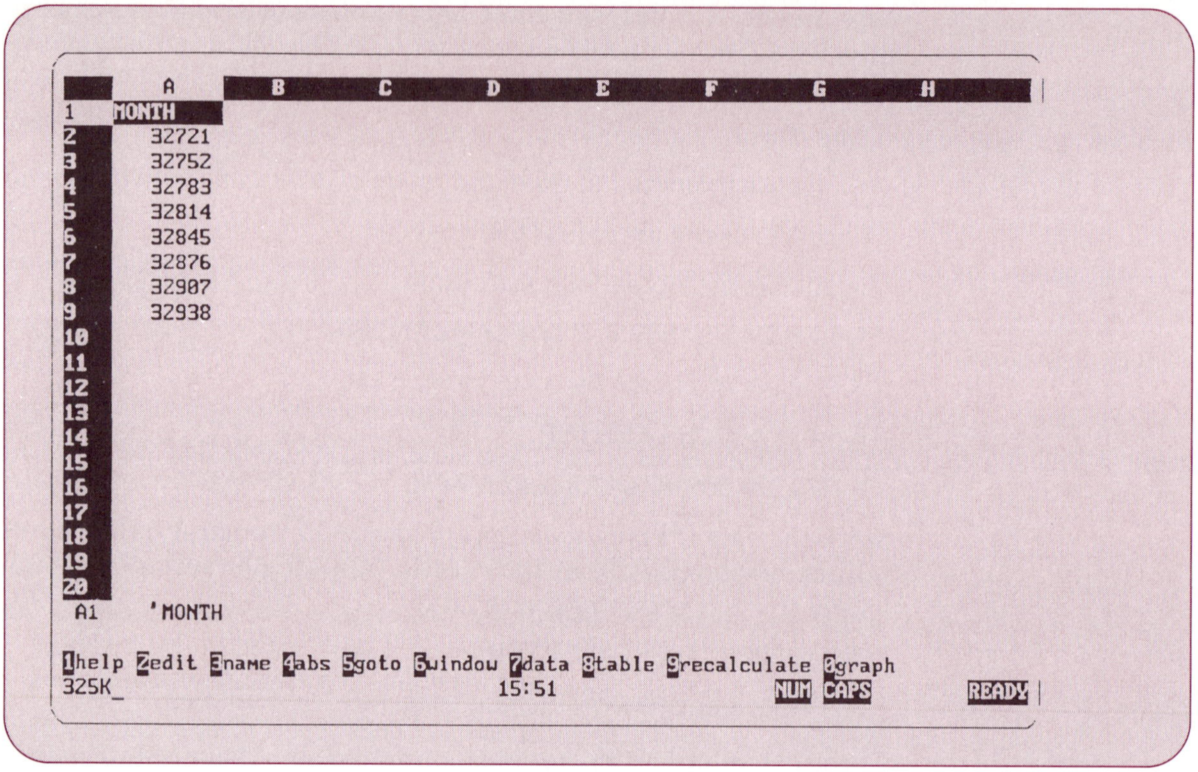

Screen Display 5-2

- Type A2.A9 and press ENTER.

  > More meaningful dates appear. Cell A2, for example, displays `01-Aug-89`.

PRACTICE TIME

For your purposes you need only the month and year, so reset the format of cells A2 to A9 to **Date, 3=MMM-Y**. The date in cell A2 should appear as **Aug-89**.

Column B will hold straight-line projections for expenses, and column C will hold the actual expenses.

- At cell B1 center the title ST. LINE.
- At cell C1 center the title ACTUAL.
- Set the display format of the range B2.C9 to **Fixed** with **0** decimal places (whole dollars).

- At cell B9 enter the contract value, **50000**.
- At cells B2 and C2 enter the value of **0** (zero), the starting value.

Straight-line method assumes that the expense is the same every month. Since the contract is 7 months long, the monthly expense is one-seventh of the total contract amount. Hence the accumulated expense each month is that of the previous month plus one-seventh of the total contract value.

- In cell B3 enter the expression **+B2+(B$9/7)**.

  > The value **7143** appears at cell B3.

Cell B9 holds the total contract value. As the formula is being copied to other cells in column B, the row number 9 in the formula must not change. The $ before 9 instructs VP-Planner Plus not to change it (in a relative manner). That is, in cell B4, for example, the formula would be +B3+(B9/7).

- Copy the formula at cell B3 to cells B4.B8.

Now enter the actual expenses in the project. You will assume that you are in mid-December, and have only the actual accumulated expenses through December 1.

- Enter the following values in column C in the appropriate rows.

Aug	0
Sep	9235
Oct	18825
Nov	26580
Dec	35320

Now you are ready to create a line graph.

- Type **/GTL** to indicate Line Graph.
- Select **X**, type **A2.A9**, then press **ENTER** to specify the X range.
- Select **A**, type **B2.B9**, then press **ENTER** to specify the A range.
- Select **B**, type **C2.C9**, then press **ENTER** to indicate the B range.
- Select **View**.

  > The graph shown in Figure 5-9 is displayed.

Because the last actual expense value is for the month of December (remember?), it is relatively easy to identify which symbol is which in this graph. Suppose, however, that you could not tell which line represents the projected expense and which represents the

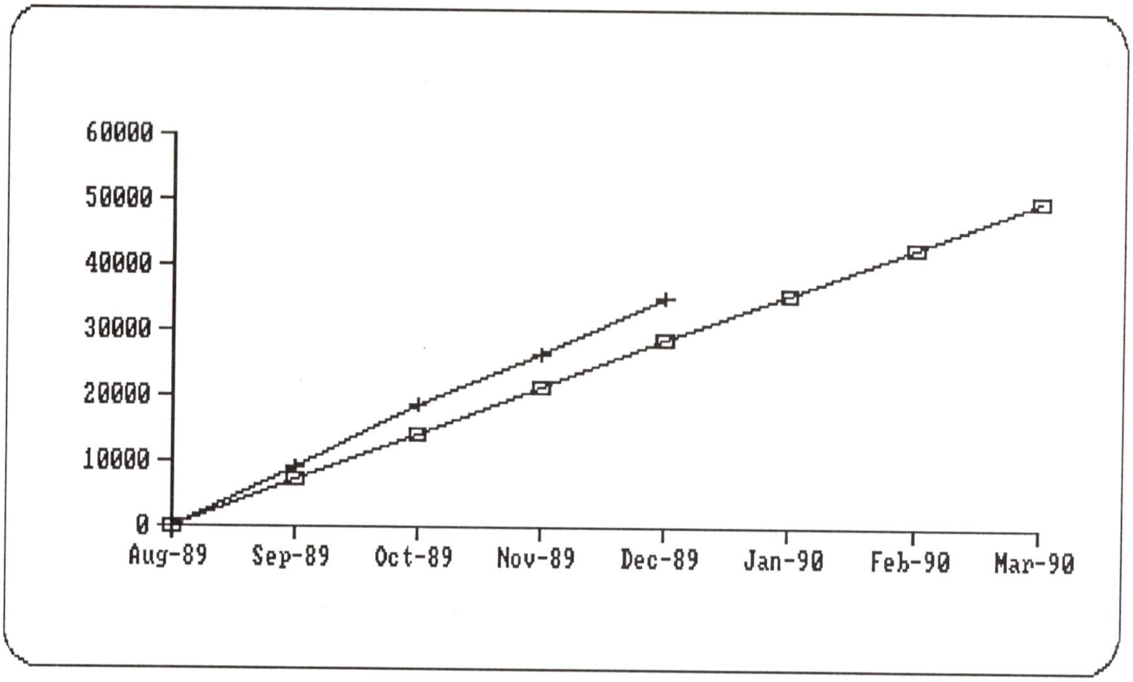

Figure 5-9 A line graph of expenses

actual expense. You need a legend to identify the symbols. You will enter two lines in the legend, one for each symbol.

- Press any key to continue.
- Select **Options**, then **Legend**.

> You are prompted to identify which ranges need legends.

A legend is needed for range A (straight-line expense) and range B (actual expenses).

- Select **A**, type **St. Line**, and press **ENTER**.
- Select **Legend** and **B**. Then type **Actual** and press **ENTER**.

PRACTICE TIME

1. Enter the title **ST. LINE VS ACTUAL** on the first line and **Madison Contract** on the second line.
2. Enter the title **Expenses** on the Y-axis.
3. View the graph. It should look like the one in Figure 5-10.

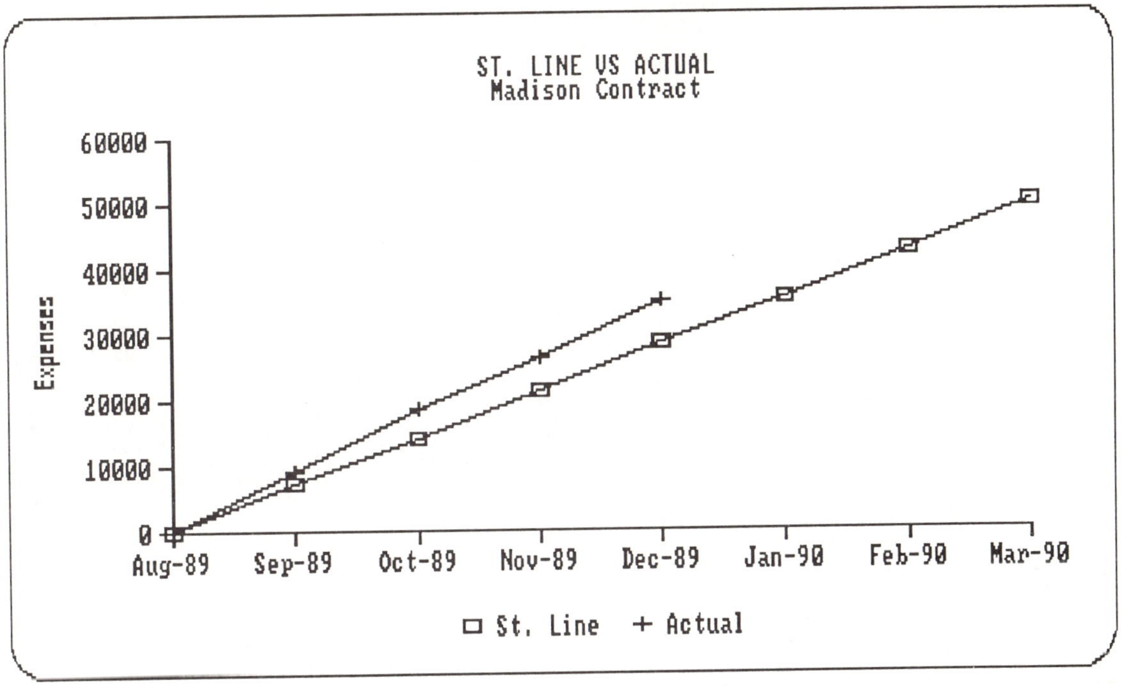

Figure 5-10 A more understandable line graph

4. Name the graph LINE1.
5. Reset all graph settings.
6. Exit the Graph command and save the spreadsheet as file VPP8.

XY GRAPHS

Up to now the X-range of all graphs has consisted of labels of one type or another. In an XY graph the X-range consists of numbers. This is useful, for example, if you are trying to see the relationships between different items of data. The following is a very simple example of how you might generate and use an XY graph.

You have conducted an advertising campaign during the past 10 months, spending widely variable amounts each month. You would like to determine the effectiveness of your campaign as reflected in your total sales.

- Clear the spreadsheet.
- Enter the following data:

	A	B	C
1		Ad Costs	Sales
2	Sep	12000	230500
3	Oct	10000	225000
4	Nov	8500	220700
5	Dec	15000	290400
6	Jan	11000	195700
7	Feb	9500	187200
8	Mar	9000	193000
9	Apr	10500	220300
10	May	13000	240500
11	Jun	11500	225100

Now let's create the XY graph.

- Type /GTX for XY Graph.

The X range is the values to be displayed along the X-axis (horizontal), and the A range is the values to be displayed along the Y-axis (vertical). You want to show the advertising cost along the X-axis and sales amounts along the Y-axis.

- Select X, type B2.B11, and press ENTER.
- Select A, type C2.C11, and press ENTER.
- Enter the title AD COSTS VS SALES on the first line and September through June on the second line.
- Enter the title Advertising Cost on the X-axis and Monthly Sales on the Y-axis.
- Select Quit to get out of the Option menu.
- Select View.

  > The graph shown in Figure 5-11 is displayed.

This graph is rather confusing, isn't it? The lines connect consecutive rows of data in the spreadsheet, and are not necessary in your analysis. The XY graph is used to see the correlation between two sets of data. In this case you want to see if money you spent on advertising had any effect on your sales. The chronological sequence has no bearing on your analysis. For this reason, you can remove the lines connecting the dots.

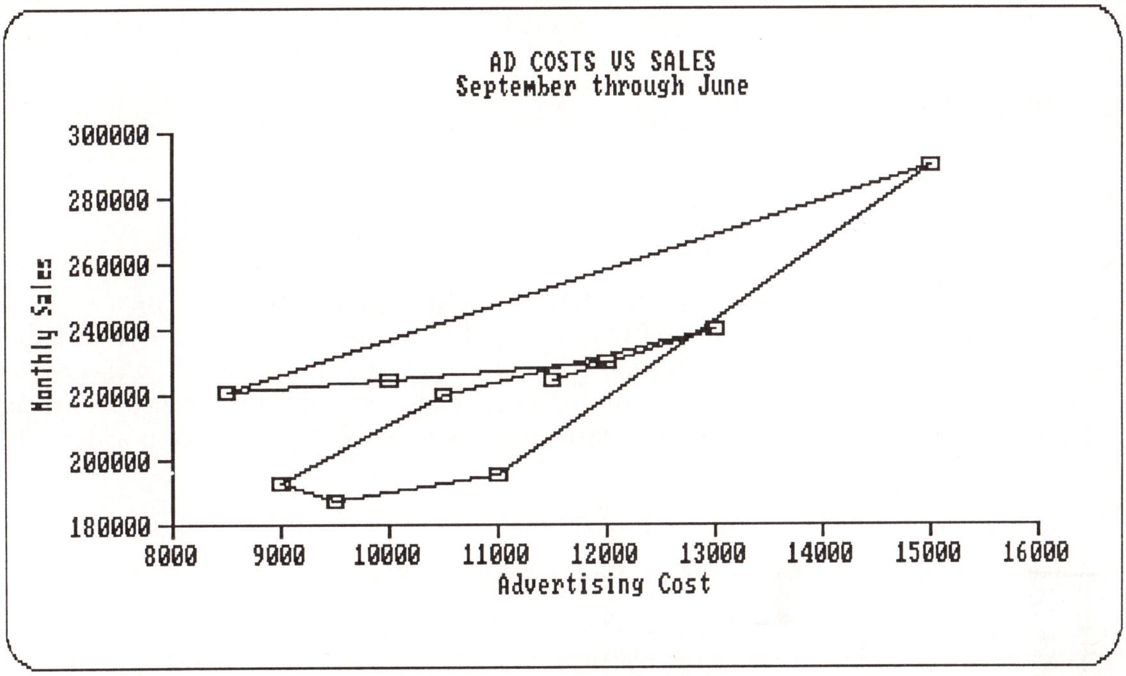

Figure 5-11 A misleading XY graph

- Press any key to go back to the Graph menu.
- Select **O**ptions.
- Select **F**ormat.
  > Format options are highlighted.

The Format option lets you control the plotting of the line on the XY graphs, either for the entire graph or for a particular data range. In your case you want to control the entire graph.

- Select **G**raph.
  > The options are highlighted:

2 Lines	Connects the points on the graph with a line.
3 Symbols	Assigns a different symbol to each range of points.
4 Both	Connects the points on the graph and uses symbols for the data points. This is the default.
5 Neither	Reset command. Turns off drawing of lines and symbols.

- Select **S**ymbols, then **Q**uit to get out of this menu.
- Select **Q**uit again to get out of the Option menu.
- Select **V**iew. Your graph should now look like Figure 5-12.

With the lines removed, there seems to be a correlation between advertising and sales. It looks like the more money spent on advertising, the better the sales! Note that the ranges of both axes are automatically calculated so that the graph fills the page.

Although this graph contains enough information to tell that it depicts the relationship between sales and advertising figures from September through June, the reader does not know which data point represents which month. You can label each data point with its month by using the information in column A.

- Press any key to continue.
- Select **O**ptions, then **D**ata-Labels.

> Options in Data-Labels are highlighted.

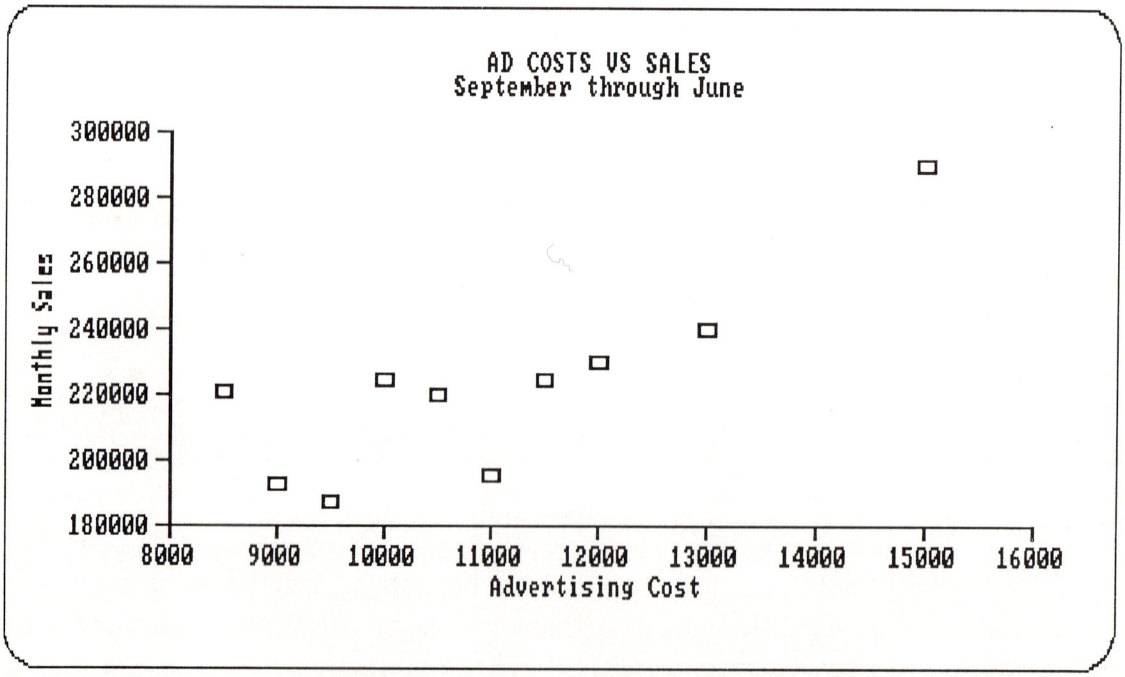

Figure 5-12 A less confusing XY graph

The range you want to label is A (there is no other range since you have specified only the X and A ranges in this XY graph).

- Select **A**.

> You are prompted to enter the data label range.

You are to specify the cells that hold the labels corresponding to the values in the A range. As you know, column A contains the labels.

- Enter the range in column A that contains the labels Sep through Jun and press ENTER.

> A pop-up window opens with a prompt to specify the position of a label relative to its corresponding data point.

- Select **Above**.
- Select **Quit** twice.
- Select **View**.

> The graph of Figure 5-13 is displayed.

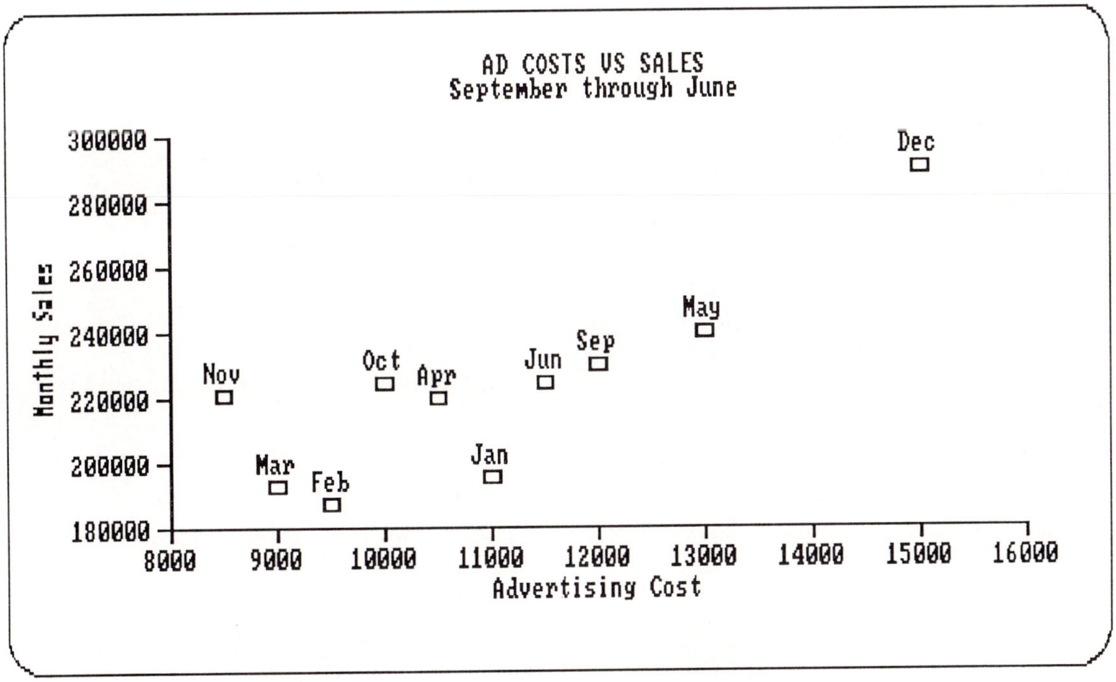

Figure 5-13 A more understandable XY graph

PRACTICE TIME

1. Name this graph XY1.
2. Print the graph.
3. Exit the graph mode, and save the spreadsheet as VPP9.

END OF LESSON 5

- Type **/QY** to exit to DOS.
- Remove the disk from the disk drive.
- Turn OFF the monitor, computer, and printer.

SUMMARY

In this lesson many of the terms and concepts that are necessary to use the spreadsheet graphics feature are discussed:

- A pie chart is a graph consisting of a circle divided into slices, much like a pie, and is used to show how resources are divided among categories.
- A bar graph uses the bar heights to indicate the magnitude of the various items represented.
- A line graph connects points in the X-range and is used to show trends of one or more quantities.
- An XY graph is a line graph that shows correlation between two sets of values.
- When a graph is named, its parameter settings are identified with a name, and the name is associated with the spreadsheet. When the spreadsheet is saved, the associated names are saved as well.
- A graph can be printed or saved on a disk.
- The @DATE function requires three arguments (year, month, and date) and returns a date value. Display format can be changed by using the Format Date option.
- The following commands are discussed:

/GN	Graph Name—names parameters for the graph.
/GOD	Graph Options Data-Labels—enters labels for each data point on a graph.
/GOL	Graph Options Legend—enters descriptive text to identify shading or symbols used in a graph.
/GOT	Graph Options Titles—specifies titles to be included in the graph.
/GP	Graph Print—prints the current graph.

/GS	Graph Save—saves the graph on a disk.
/GT	Graph Type—specifies the type of graph.
/GX, /GA - /GF	Graph Ranges—specifies various cells to use in generating a graph.
/GV	Graph View—displays a graph on the screen.
/RFD	Range Format Date—sets display format for a date.

REVIEW QUESTIONS

1. Name four (out of five) kinds of graphs that can be generated by VP-Planner Plus. ______________________________

2. What two ranges must be specified for a pie chart? ______________________________

3. What is the difference between *naming* a graph and *saving* a graph? Explain. ______________________________

4. What is a legend? ______________________________

5. What are X-axis and Y-axis? ______________________________

6. Explain the difference between a line graph and an XY graph. ______________________________

7. What are the arguments needed for @DATE function? What is the purpose of this function? ______________________________

8. How do you eliminate lines connecting symbols in an XY graph? ______________________________

9. What are data labels? When would you use them? ______________________________

10. How do you print a graph? ______________________________

EXERCISES

1. a. Retrieve the spreadsheet EX4__1 from Lesson 4.
   b. Using the distribution table on total amount, create, name, and print a bar graph, a pie chart, and a line graph.
   c. Save the spreadsheet as EX5__1.

2. a. Retrieve the spreadsheet EX4__2 from Lesson 4.
   b. Using the distribution table on average, create, name, and print a bar graph, a pie chart, and a line graph.
   c. Save the spreadsheet as EX5__2.

Lesson 6
Introducing Macros

Objectives

Upon completion of the material presented in this lesson, you should be able to do the following:

- Understand what a macro is.
- Know the difference between a label macro and an autokey macro.
- Create and invoke an autokey macro.
- Create and invoke a label macro.
- Convert an autokey macro to a label macro.
- Convert a label macro to an autokey macro.
- Create a multiple-line label macro.

STARTING OFF

Start VP-Planner Plus so that a blank worksheet is displayed on the screen. Insert a data disk into drive B and change the file directory to B.

MACROS

Think back to the previous lessons. How often did you have to insert the same series of commands? Because VP-Planner Plus is menu driven, you often have to enter several keystrokes to accomplish even a very simple task. Of course, the more keystrokes you must enter, the greater the chance of making mistakes. Wouldn't it be nice if you could use one command to invoke a whole series of frequently used keystrokes? Well, you can.

This lesson introduces the concept of macros in VP-Planner Plus. As a prefix, *macro* means large or big. In various computing languages, however, a *macro* is a block of code that can be "patched" (inserted for use) into a program at several places, each time with a single command. In VP-Planner Plus, a macro is a series of worksheet commands or data entries stored in a cell and activated with a single keystroke or a combination of keystrokes. In this sense you can think of a macro as stored keystrokes. It takes only a few keystrokes to invoke a macro once it is set up. Macros are defined for each spreadsheet and are stored and retrieved along with the spreadsheet.

TYPES OF MACROS

There are two types of macros in VP-Planner Plus: label macros and autokey macros. They are created and invoked differently. Each type has advantages and disadvantages, which you will weigh after you go through simple examples of each.

LABEL MACROS

To create and use a label macro:

1. Enter the macro (series of data and commands) as a label into a spreadsheet cell.
2. Name that cell \L, where "L" is any letter (A–Z). Lowercase letters are automatically converted to uppercase. You can also use 0 (zero), but \0 is reserved for a special kind of macro.

NOTE ■ When a macro is named \0 (zero), it is an autostart macro. An autostart macro is a macro that is invoked (executed) as soon as the spreadsheet containing it is retrieved.

3. As often as required after steps 1 and 2, invoke (execute) the macro with the Alt-L keystroke combination; that is, while holding down the Alt key, press the letter of the macro name. You may enter either an uppercase or lowercase letter. For example, to invoke macro \R, use **Alt-R** or **Alt-r**.

Suppose, for example, you want to display some numbers across 24 columns. The numbers are the integers between 0 and 99. To display all 24 columns on the screen at the same time, the width for these columns (A to X) should be set to 3. You could spend your afternoon typing **/WCS3 <ENTER> <RIGHT ARROW>** over and over again. Or, you can set up a macro that contains these keystrokes and then simply execute the macro 24 times!

- With cell cursor in A1, type (apostrophe) to indicate that this cell is a label.

- Type the following keystrokes, but do not press ENTER: /WCS3.

You probably recognized the keystrokes as *Worksheet Col-width Set 3*, the command keystrokes to set the width of the current column (the column the cell cursor is on) to 3. The next step in setting the column width is to press ENTER. However, if you were to press ENTER now, VP-Planner Plus interprets it as a signal that you've finished entering the current label. You want to enter "pressing ENTER" as a part of the label. In a label macro, the ~ (tilde) represents the pressing of ENTER.

- To represent pressing the ENTER key, type ~ (tilde).

Next you want to move the cursor one column to the right. This is accomplished by pressing the RIGHT ARROW key. In a label macro, {RIGHT} represents pressing the RIGHT ARROW key.

- To represent pressing the RIGHT ARROW key, type {RIGHT}.

The pressing of various function keys and numeric keypad keys are represented in macros by words (upper or lowercase) within braces ({}):

Key	*Macro Component*	*Key*	*Macro Component*
UP ARROW	{UP}	DOWN ARROW	{DOWN}
RIGHT ARROW	{RIGHT}	LEFT ARROW	{LEFT}
HOME	{HOME}	END	{END}
PAGE UP	{PGUP}	PAGE DOWN	{PGDN}
F2 (Edit)	{EDIT}	F3 (Name)	{NAME}
F4 (Abs)	{ABS}	F5 (GoTo)	{GOTO}
F6 (Window)	{WINDOW}	F7 (Query)	{QUERY}
F8 (Table)	{TABLE}	F9 (Calc)	{CALC}
F10 (Graph)	{GRAPH}	Alt-F5 (Relative Goto)	{GOREF}
ESCAPE	{ESC}	DELETE	{DEL}
BACKSPACE	{BKSP}	ENTER	~

- You have finished entering the macro. Press **ENTER** to complete the entry.

Once you have entered the macro, you need to name it. You name it with the Range Name command, except that a macro is named with a backslash (\) followed by one (and only one) alphabetic character.

Sometimes it's hard to come up with a meaningful name, but this macro might be named \W since it adjusts column width.

- Type /RNC for Range Name Create.
- Type \W and press ENTER to give the name.
- Press ENTER again to indicate that you are just naming the current cell.

  > Cell A1 is named, and hence the macro is named.

Now that the macro has been created and named, you will use it.

- With the cursor in column A, press Alt-W. That is, hold down the ALT key and press W.

  > The width of column A is set to 3 and the cursor moves to column B.

- Enter Alt-W 23 times more. You may have to slow down a bit and let VP-Planner Plus catch up with your blazing speed.

  > When you finish, columns A through X are each three spaces wide, and the cursor is in column Y.

- Press the Home key to move the cursor back to A1.

  > The macro is still displayed in cell A1, as seen in Screen Display 6-1.

Once you have entered and named a macro, you can edit it, or change its contents, without having to rename it. For example, suppose you decided that you need to display only 12 columns, and that columns A through L can be six spaces wide.

NOTE ■ Should you move the cell location of the macro, you will have to name it again, since a range name does not transfer.

- With cell cursor on A1 (the cell with the macro), press the F2 function key to edit the contents.
- Use the RIGHT ARROW and LEFT ARROW keys to place the cursor on the number 3.
- Press the DELETE key to erase 3, then type 6.
- Press ENTER to terminate editing the macro.
- Use the macro 12 times to change columns A through L.

These macros are part of the spreadsheet. As long as the cells containing label macros are present in the spreadsheet, the macros exist.

Let's save this worksheet so that you can retrieve the macro later.

- Save the worksheet as VPP10.
- Clear the worksheet by using /WEY.

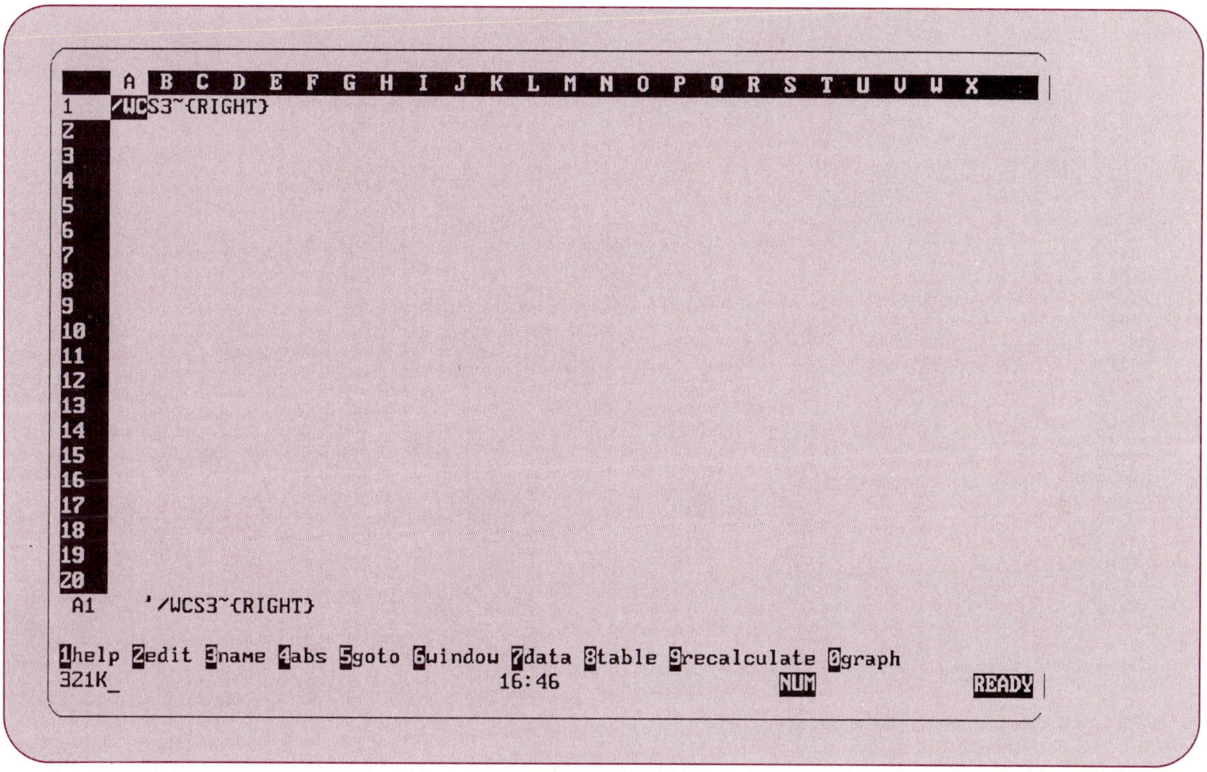

Screen Display 6-1

PRACTICE TIME

1. Retrieve the spreadsheet VPP1 from Lesson 1.
2. In cell F10 create a label macro \P to print the whole spreadsheet. The command keystrokes are **/PPGQ**. Your screen should look like the one in Screen Display 6-2.
3. Invoke macro \P.
4. Edit macro \P so that you print just the range B1.B5. Think very carefully about all the keystrokes you enter to accomplish this task. Particularly, be careful of where you need to press ENTER.
5. Save the worksheet as VPP11.

AUTOKEY MACROS

Autokey macros are created by using the 'Autokey' feature of VP-Planner Plus. This feature captures a series of command keystrokes as you enter them. This series of commands, or a macro, is assigned

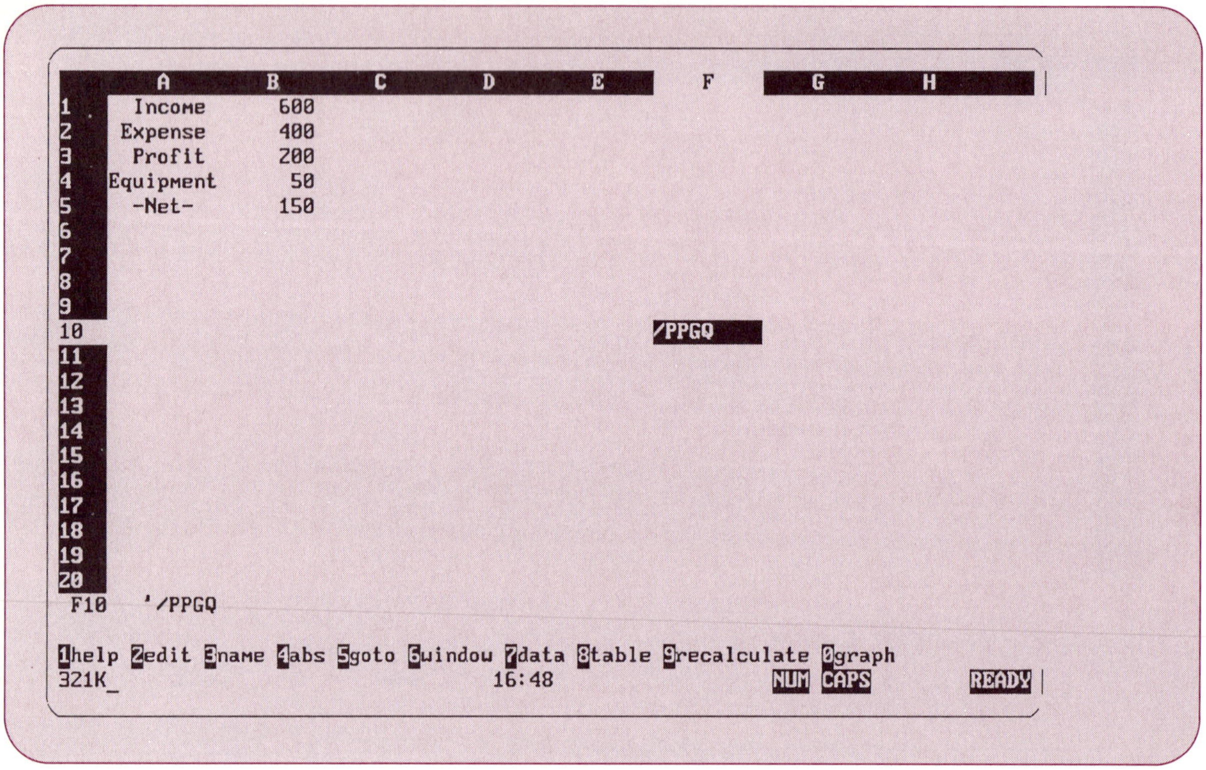

Screen Display 6-2

to a function key of your choice. You can have up to ten autokey macros (one for each function key) in a worksheet at a time. These macros are saved along with the worksheet. To create and use an autokey macro, follow these steps:

1. Enter **/WAD** for Worksheet Autokey Define.
2. Specify the function key the macro is to be assigned to. You can specify one of F1 through F10. However, function key F10 is reserved for a special purpose.

NOTE: ■ When an autokey macro is associated with the F10 function key, it is an autostart macro (like \0 in label macro). If a worksheet has both an autostart autokey macro and an autostart label macro, only the autostart autokey macro executes when the spreadsheet containing them is retrieved.

3. Give a descriptive name to the macro. This name can be up to 10 characters in length.
4. Go through all the keystrokes you want captured as the macro.

5. When you have finished capturing all keystrokes needed, specify the end to the macro definition by pressing **ALT-F10**.
6. As often as required after steps 1 through 5, invoke (execute) the macro with the CTRL-function key combination. That is, if the macro is associated with the F1 function key, for example, hold the **CTRL** key down and press the **F1** function key.

You will use the autokey feature to write a macro that sets the display format of a cell to Currency. You will enter a number into the worksheet so that you can go through and capture the actual keystroke sequence (and see the results).

- Clear the spreadsheet.
- Enter the number **100** at cell A1.
- At cell A1 type **/WA** for Worksheet Autokey.

> The following options are displayed:

2 Define	Program an autokey (F1–F10) to perform a series of keystrokes.
3 Clear	Delete an autokey macro.
4 Xecute	Execute an autokey macro.
5 Label>Macro	Convert label cells (label macro) into an autokey macro.
6 Macro>Label	Convert an autokey macro into label cells (label macro).
7 Step	Cause the autokey sequence to be executed one step (keystroke) at a time by pressing any key.
8 Run	Cancel the Step option; run the macro normally.
9 ImmedX	Execute the macro defined in the current cell (label macro).
0 Quit	Quit.
Width	Not discussed.

- Select **Define** so that you can create a macro.

> The following message appears:

```
DEFINE WHICH AUTOKEY?. Press function key.
1. 2. 3. 4. 5.
6. 7. 8. 9. 10.
```

You are asked to define an autokey, one of the function keys. You are to press a function key to indicate which one should represent this macro. You will use the F1 function key here.

- Press the **F1** function key.

  > The following message appears at the bottom.

  ```
  Enter the name for this key sequence (max 10 charac-
  ters):
  ```

This name should be descriptive so that you can tell the function of this macro later.

- Enter **CURRENCY**.

  > The following message is displayed at the bottom right corner of the screen.

  ```
  Press ALT-F10 to end. 512
  ```

From this point on, whatever you enter is saved as a part of this autokey macro that can be invoked with the F1 function key. When you no longer want to save the keystrokes, press **ALT-F10**. Your macro can have up to 512 characters. The number at the end of the message tells how many characters you can add to the macro.

You will make all the keystrokes necessary to change the display format of cell A1 to Currency.

- With the cursor on cell A1, type **/RFC2**, then press **ENTER** twice.

  > The number displayed at cell A1 changes to $100.00.

  > Your keystrokes are being saved. You will notice that the number that appears at the bottom right corner has decreased to 505.

- Since you are now through entering keystrokes for the macro, press **ALT-F10**.

You have created a macro called CURRENCY, assigned to F1. Now you will execute it.

- At cell B2 enter **12.5**.

You will change the display format of cell B2 to Currency by using the autokey macro.

- With the cursor on cell B2, enter **CTRL-F1**.

  > The cell content is displayed in the Currency format.

NOTE ■ You can also execute an autokey macro by entering **/WAX** for Worksheet Autokey Xecute, then pressing the appropriate function key.

PRACTICE TIME

1. Create for the F2 function key an autokey macro called MONTHS that inserts the months of the year (JAN, FEB, MAR, . . . , DEC) across a row, starting at the cursor position, then sends the cursor to cell A1 (HOME).
2. With the cursor on any cell invoke the macro.
3. Save the spreadsheet as VPP12.

If you make an entry error during an autokey macro creation, all the keystrokes you enter to correct the error are also stored as a part of the macro. Moreover, you cannot go back and edit the macro. The only way to change the macro is to recreate from scratch or convert it into a label macro so that it can be edited. The edited label macro can then be converted back into an autokey macro.

CONVERTING AUTOKEY MACROS TO LABEL MACROS

For practice you will convert an autokey macro you previously created to a label macro.

- Type /WA, then select **Macro>Label**.

  > You are prompted to select the autokey (the function key) you want to convert.

- Press **F1**.

  > The following prompt appears.

  ```
  Select the starting cell of the column of labels to
  be created:
  ```

As you recall, label macros are contained in cells of the worksheet.

- Clear column C by using the Range command.
- You will put this macro into column C. Enter C15.

  > The macro **/RFC2~** is now displayed in cell C15.

- Name cell C15 to make it into a label macro \C.

PRACTICE TIME

Convert the F2 autokey macro into a label macro \M starting at cell C18. Your screen might look like the one in Screen Display 6-3.

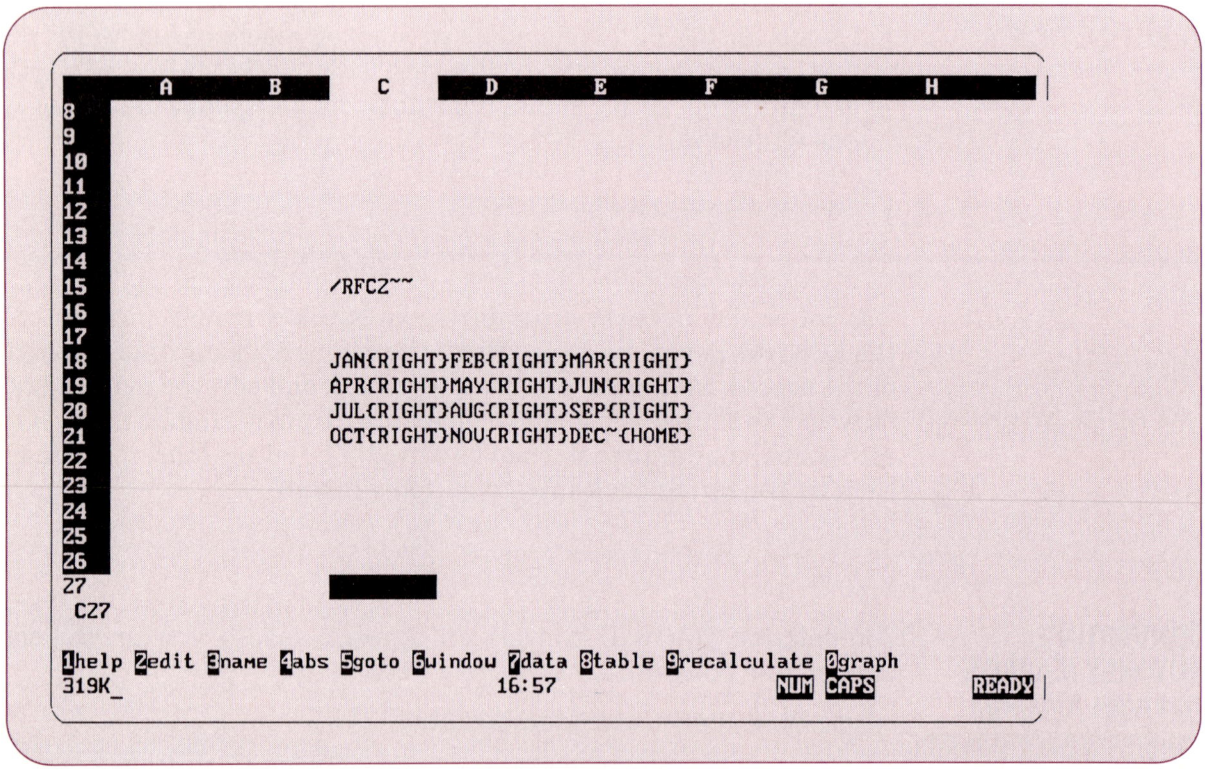

Screen Display 6-3

Notice that the macro keystrokes are entered in four cells, C18 through C21, but you name cell C18 only.

MULTIPLE-LINE LABEL MACROS

One advantage of label macros is that they can be in many lines (cells). What this means is that keystrokes need not be in one cell only. They can be broken up into little chunks and stored in consecutive cells in a column. Once the contents of the *named* cell (starting cell), for example C18, have been executed, VP-Planner Plus looks at the cell in the next row down, C19. If C19 is not blank, the macro is continued. The macro continues until it is stopped or encounters an empty cell. In the example presented in the preceding Practice Time, the macro execution will stop when the empty cell C22 is encountered.

When you create a label macro, it is a good idea to use three consecutive columns. Macro commands and keystrokes are entered in the middle column. You should limit the portion of macro in any given cell to a small chunk. You enter the name of the macro (as a label) on the cell to the left of the *named* cell (the starting cell). The cells in the third column should contain comments that describe the function of each chunk in the cells adjacent to them.

The widths of these columns should be adjusted to accommodate the longest entries. For that reason, it is a good idea to store macros in columns that will not interfere with the rest of the worksheet. You might store them in columns A, B, and C, then start the worksheet in column D. Or, you might use columns to the right of the worksheet entries. In either case, for presentation purposes, you might want to hide those columns containing macros.

You will retrieve the worksheet VPP10 prepared earlier and change the label macro \W into a multiple-line macro defined in columns A, B, and C as discussed above.

- Retrieve the spreadsheet VPP10.

The macro displayed in cell A1 is /WCS6~ {RIGHT}.

- Move the content of cell A1 to cell B1.
- Name cell B1 as \W.
- Edit the label macro at cell B1 so that cell B1 holds keystrokes to set the column width of the current cell to 6; then cell B2 contains the command to press the RIGHT ARROW key.
- Enter the label \W at cell A1. (Make sure to precede it with a label prefix character.)
- In cells C1 and C2 describe the function of keystrokes in cells B1 and B2, respectively.
- Adjust columns to appropriate widths. Your screen should look like the one in Screen Display 6-4.

This macro will stop executing when the empty cell is encountered at cell B3. You can put in a specific command {QUIT} to stop the macro execution. However, the effect of leaving cell B3 empty and having the entry {QUIT} is the same.

{QUIT} is an example of a macro command. There are many macro commands available that let you *program* macro instructions. Macro

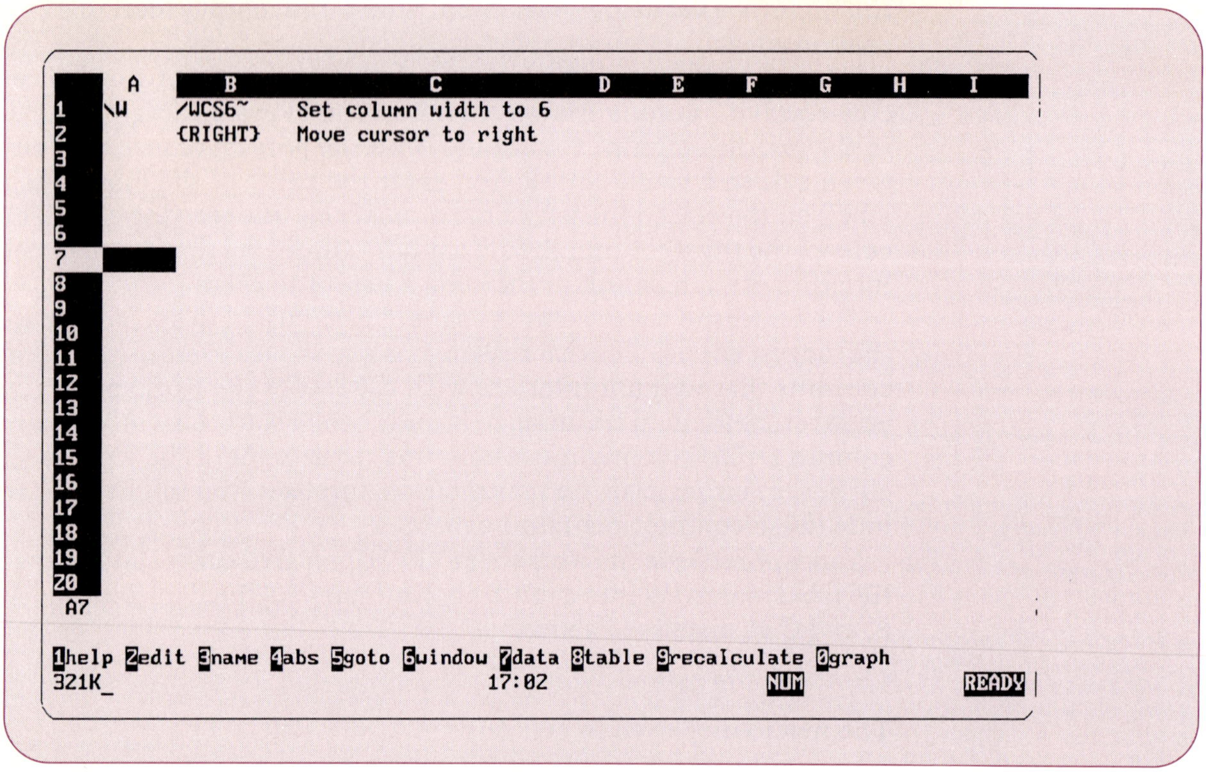

Screen Display 6-4

commands are not discussed in this manual. If you are interested in exploring macros further, you should look at Chapter 11 of the VP-Planner Plus manual.

CONVERTING LABEL MACROS TO AUTOKEY MACROS

You will now convert the label macro from the previous section to an autokey macro for practice.

- Enter /WAL for Worksheet Autokey Label>Macro.

  > The following message appears at the bottom.

```
    CHOOSE AN AUTOKEY Press function key.
1.  2.  3.  4.  5.
6.  7.  8.  9.  10.
```

You will associate this autokey macro with the F3 function key.

- Press **F3**.

  > The following message appears at the bottom of the screen:

  `Enter the name for this key sequence (Max 10 characters):`

- Enter COL-WIDTH6.

  > The following message appears at the bottom of the screen:

  ```
  Select the starting cell of the column of labels to
  be compiled:
  ```

The label macro you are converting starts in cell B1.

- Enter B1.

  > The macro has been converted.

- Save the worksheet as VPP13.

You can test the autokey macro by entering CTRL-F3.

AUTOKEY VS LABEL MACROS

Now that you have looked at both the autokey and label macros, you may have some ideas of the advantages and disadvantages of each type.

Label macros are entered directly into cells. You must be certain that the series of command keystrokes you are entering is correct. Also, you must use special symbols for ENTER, arrow keys, HOME, and other keys. The procedure is difficult, error-prone, and tedious, especially if the macro is a long one. By contrast, the procedure for entering an autokey macro is self-checking.

Names for label macros are only two characters long, with a backslash (\) for the first character. This limits the descriptiveness of the name you assign. By contrast, autokey macro names can be up to 10 characters long.

Label macros are displayed as a part of the worksheet, hence there is a possibility of someone accidentally erasing the cells containing them. You can hide them, but the possibility is still there. Autokey macros are not as visible or as vulnerable.

It might seem that autokey macros are superior to label macros. The advantages are not that one-sided, however. One advantage of label macros, for instance, is that you can define up to 27 of them (A–Z,zero). You can define only 10 autokey macros.

Autokey macros are restricted to 255 characters in length. Label macros can have several lines (cells). Documentation for label macros can be included in the spreadsheet in a separate column.

Label macros can be edited. Autokey macros cannot be edited directly, although an autokey macro can be converted into a label macro and edited, then converted back into an autokey macro.

Although not discussed in this manual, there are macro commands that can be entered into label macros that are not available to autokey macros.

Label and autokey macros provide two complementary ways for you to use VP-Planner Plus more effectively.

END OF LESSON 6

- Type /QY to exit to DOS.
- Remove the disks from the disk drives.
- Turn OFF the monitor, computer, and printer.

SUMMARY

In this lesson the concept of macro is introduced.

- A macro is a series of worksheet commands or data entries that is stored in a cell or some other memory location and is executed with a single keystroke or a combination of keystrokes.
- There are two kinds of macros in VP-Planner Plus: label macros and autokey macros.
- A label macro stores keystrokes as a label in a cell. The cell is named as \L, where "L" is one of characters A–Z or zero.
- A label macro requires that you enter ~ (tilde) to represent pressing the ENTER key; pressing other keys is represented by words within braces. For example, pressing the RIGHT ARROW key is represented by {RIGHT}.
- A label macro is invoked by using CTRL-character, where "character" is the character used in naming the macro.
- An autokey macro captures keystrokes as the actual entries are made. It is associated with a function key and is invoked by using CTRL-f, where "f" is the function key specified.
- An autokey macro can be converted into a label macro; a label macro can be converted into an autokey macro.
- A label macro can be entered into multiple rows (cells) in a column.
- The following commands are discussed:

/WAD	Worksheet Autokey Define – start the definition process of an autokey macro.
/WAM	Worksheet Autokey Macro>Label – convert an autokey macro into a label macro.
/WAL	Worksheet Autokey Label>Macro – convert a label macro into an autokey macro.
/WAX	Worksheet Autokey eXecute – execute an autokey macro.

REVIEW QUESTIONS

1. What is a macro? ______________________________

____

____

2. What are the two types of macros in VP-Planner Plus? ______________

____

3. Explain how a label macro is created. ______________

____

____

____

4. Explain how an autokey macro is created. ______________

____

____

____

5. How do you invoke a label macro? ______________

____

an autokey macro? ______________

____

6. How do you edit an autokey macro? ______________

____

7. How do you convert an autokey macro into a label macro? ______________

____

____

____

8. How do you convert a label macro into an autokey macro? ______________

____

____

____

9. How does the execution of a multiple-line label macro get stopped?

____

____

10. Give three advantages and disadvantages for each type of macro. ______

____

____

____

EXERCISES

1. a. Create an autokey macro which, given a current cell (a cell with the cursor on it) that already contains a label, edits the contents so that the label is centered.
   b. Convert the autokey macro into a label macro.
   c. Save the spreadsheet as EX6_1.
   d. Print the spreadsheet.

2. a. Create the following multiple-line label macro:
   Sets the current directory to B, retrieves the file EX1_1, then prints the entire spreadsheet.
   b. Convert the label macro into an autokey macro.
   c. Save the spreadsheet as EX6_2.
   d. Print the spreadsheet.

PROJECT 2

Use the spreadsheet you developed in Project 1 (after Lesson 3) for Wilhemina's company.

A. Generate a pie chart showing the portion of pretax profits earned by each of the four items Wilhemina manufactures. Design and print the chart as if you were making a presentation to Wilhemina's banker.

B. Wilhemina wants to increase her pretax profits to about $35,000 per year. She is not able to hire any more home workers in the area, and she is now producing and selling at the maximum capacity. Wilhemina believes it is time to increase her prices. But she wants to hold her product mix to approximately what she has now.

   She knows from experience that she cannot increase the price of the drawstring duffle. Determine two price structures that will result in yearly pretax profits of between $34,000 and $36,000 without changing the product mix or the price of the drawstring duffle.

PROJECT 3

You are starting a lawn/garden-care service, and you want to establish prices for the services you offer. You want to be sure you make a profit, even if costs change. The three standard services you offer are lawn seeding, monthly lawn care (mowing and fertilizing), and yard cleanup (pruning and raking). The yards you service are all about the same size.

- Seeding takes 4 hours of labor, 7 pounds of seeds, 6 pounds of fertilizer, and 1 round trip in the truck.
- Monthly lawn care takes 2 hours of labor, 2 pounds of fertilizer, 1 gallon of weeder, 1 cubic yard of disposal, and 5 round trips in the truck.

- Yard cleanup takes 3 hours of labor, 4 cubic yards of disposal, and 2 round trips in the truck.

When you have found the total cost of a service, you add 15 percent profit to arrive at your charge for the service. Initially, your costs are as follows:

Labor	$10.00 per hour
Seed	$ 2.25 per pound
Fertilizer	$ 0.75 per pound
Weeder	$ 9.00 per gallon
Disposal	$ 3.00 per cubic yard
Truck	$ 2.00 per round trip

You can use the spreadsheet to find the prices you will charge customers and to update the prices as your costs change.

A. Prepare a spreadsheet, using the following as a guide.

		SEEDING		*LAWN CARE*		*CLEANUP*	
Item	*Unit Cost*	*No. of Units*	*Cost*	*No. of Units*	*Cost*	*No. of Units*	*Cost*
Labor	10.00 / hr	4		2		3	
Seed	2.75 / lb	7		0		0	
Fertilizer	.75 / lb	6		2		0	
Weeder	9.00 / gal	0		1		0	
Disposal	3.00 / cu yd	0		1		4	
Truck	2.00 / trip	1		5		2	
	Total Cost						
	15% Profit						
Charge for Service							

1. Enter the labels and values as shown in the table. The column that is headed Unit Cost is actually two columns. The values are in one column under the heading of Unit, and the other information is in a second column labeled Cost.
2. Individual costs are calculated by multiplying the number of units by the unit cost.
3. For total costs, use the @SUM function to add the values in each column.
4. Profit is the total cost multiplied by the percentage that is specified at a coordinate.

C. Save the spreadsheet on a disk as file LAWNCARE.
D. Get printouts of the worksheet and the formulas.
E. After a month of service, you realize that it takes 2.5 hours of labor per month for lawn care, and the cost of disposal has been raised to $3.25 per cubic yard. Make the changes and get printouts of both the worksheet and formulas.

CONGRATULATIONS! If you have completed the exercises and projects till now, you have learned much about the use of an electronic spreadsheet program in business. Remember that the VP-Planner Plus software diskette is yours. So use the spreadsheet program whenever you have a need. It is almost certain that you will use one in business. The more comfortable you are with one (and the more innovative ways you can think of to apply one to business problems), the better prepared you will be to take your place in business.

Command Summary

This section is a quick reference for VP-Planner Plus commands covered in this manual. This is not a complete list of all VP-Planner Plus commands. However, some commands that were not covered in the lessons are listed here for your convenience. Try them on your own.

CONTROL PANEL

1. First line (status line)—displays cursor position and entry at cursor on left, and mode on right.
2. Second line (input line)—displays what is being entered in VALUE, LABEL, EDIT, or POINT mode.
3. Third line—displays the function keys and their usage.
4. Fourth line—displays availability of memory, time, mode indicator, and status indicator(s).

CURSOR MOVEMENT

1. The arrow keys located on the numeric keyboard move the cursor one position in the direction of the arrow.
2. The HOME key moves the cursor to A1.
3. The PGUP and PGDN keys move the cursor an entire screen up and down, respectively.
4. The TAB and SHIFT/TAB keys move the cursor one screen left and right, respectively.
5. Pressing the F5 function key, followed by a cell address, moves the cursor directly to the coordinate specified.

CORRECTING MISTAKES

1. /WEY clears the entire worksheet.
2. /RE <ENTER> erases the entry at the cursor position.
3. During an entry, BACKSPACE erases a character to the left of the cursor and DEL erases the character the cursor is on.
4. The Edit key (F2) can be used to change an entry in a cell.

METHODS OF SELECTING A MENU OPTION

1. Type the first character of the command you want.
2. Use the UP and DOWN ARROW keys to highlight your selection and press ENTER.
3. Press the function key with the same number.

HELP KEY

The F1 function key provides assistance in unfamiliar situations.

COMMAND STRUCTURE

2 W Worksheet commands: Commands that affect the worksheet.

- **2 G** Global commands: Commands that affect the entire worksheet.
  - **2 F** Format commands: Set the display format of numbers.
    - **2 F** Fixed: Set a fixed number of decimal points.
    - **3 S** Scientific: Exponential format.
    - **4 C** Currency: Currency format.
    - **5 ,** Commas: Commas inserted, negative values parenthesized.
    - **6 G** General: Standard format.
    - 7 +/– Plus/Minus: Horizontal bar graph.
    - **8 P** Percent: Percent format.
    - **9 D** Date: Date format.
    - **0 T** Text: Display the formula instead of the value.
    - **R** Reset: Return to default settings.
    - **H** Hide: Prevent display of cell contents.
    - **1** Custom 1 format.
    - **2** Custom 2 format.
  - **3 L** Label-Prefix commands: Position text in cell (default for entire worksheet).
    - **2 '** Left-justified.
    - **3 "** Right-justified.
    - **4 ^** Centered.
    - **5 '** Flush-right.
  - **4 C** Column-Width: Set column width for entire spreadsheet.
  - **5 R** Recalculation: Set conditions of worksheet recalculation.
  - **6 P** Protection: Turn protection on or off.
  - **7 D** Default: Define default disk and printer settings.
  - **8 Z** Zero-suppress: Turn zero suppression on and off.
- **3 I** Insert: Insert blank rows or columns.
  - **R** Row: Insert rows.
  - **C** Column: Insert columns.

- **4 D** Delete: Delete entire rows or columns.
  - **R** Row: Delete rows.
  - **C** Column: Delete columns.
- **5 C** Col-width: Set characteristics of a column.
  - **S** Set-width: Set column width.
  - **R** Reset-width: Return column width to worksheet default.
  - **H** Hide: Suppress display of specified column.
  - **D** Display: Re-enable display of specified column.
- **6 E** Erase: Erase entire worksheet.
- **7 T** Titles: Freeze titles on screen.
  - **2 B** Both: Freeze the column(s) to the left and row(s) above the cursor.
  - **3 H** Horizontal: Freeze the row(s) above the cursor.
  - **4 V** Vertical: Freeze the column(s) to the left of the cursor.
  - **5 C** Clear: Remove the previous title settings.
- **8 W** Window: Split window commands.
  - **2 H** Horizontal: Split window horizontally, just above present cursor row.
  - **3 V** Vertical: Split window vertically, just to left of present cursor column.
  - **4 S** Sync: Windows scroll synchronously.
  - **5 U** Unsync: Windows scroll independently.
  - **6 C** Clear: Return to one window.
- **9 S** Status: Display worksheet settings.
- **0 A** Autokey: Display options for recording keystrokes for macros.
- **P** Page: Insert a page-break above the cell cursor.

3 R Range: Commands that affect part of the worksheet.

- **2 F** Format: Commands that change the format of a range. (see Global Format)
- **3 L** Label: Label alignment in a range. (see Global Label-Prefix)
- **4 E** Erase: Erase a range.
- **5 N** Name: Commands dealing with range names.
  - **2 C** Create: Name or redefine a range.

- **3 D** Delete: Remove an existing range name.
- **4 L** Labels: Use the label in an adjacent cell to name a one-cell range.
- **5 R** Reset: Delete all the range names on the worksheet.
- **6 S** Show: Display a sorted list of the current range names.
- **7 T** Table: Insert a two-column table of current names and their cell reference addresses.

6 J Justify: Adjust alignment of a column of labels.
7 P Protect: Disallow changes to a range.
8 U Unprotect: Allow changes to a range.
9 I Input: Enter data into unprotected cells in a range.
0 C Col: Set the width of one or more adjacent columns.
V Value: Copy range, converting formulas to values.
T Transpose: Copy range, switching columns and rows.

4 C Copy: Copy a range to a new position in the worksheet.
From range: Range of original data.
To range: Range of copied data.

5 M Move: Move a range to a new position in the worksheet. Operates like the Copy command, except the original range is erased.

6 F File: Commands that access disk or deal with worksheet.

- **2 R** Retrieve: Retrieve a file from disk.
- **3 S** Save: Save a worksheet on disk.
- **4 C** Combine: Combine values from a specified file to the current worksheet.
- **5 X** Extract: Save a range from the current worksheet to a file on disk.
- **6 E** Erase: Erase a specified disk file.
- **7 L** List: Display filenames in current directory.
- **8 I** Import: Read text or numbers from a print file into the worksheet.
- **9 D** Directory: Display/set current directory.
- **0 U** Utility: Copy or rename disk files.

7 P Print: Commands that allow worksheet printing.
Specify one of the following destinations:

- **2 P** Printer.
- **3 F** File.

Then, the Print Menu is displayed.

- **2 R** Range: Range to be printed.
- **3 L** Line: Advance one line.
- **4 P** Page: Advance to top of page.
- **5 O** Options: Options that affect page style.
  - **2 H** Header: Specify a header line.
  - **3 F** Footer: Specify a footer line.
  - **4 S** Setup: Specify printer setup string.
  - **5 M** Margins: Specify page margins.
  - **6 B** Border: Print border columns and rows.
  - **7 P** Page-Length: Set lines per page.
  - **8 C** Copies: Specify the number of copies to be printed.
  - **9 O** Other: Additional options.
    - **2 A** As-is: Print range as displayed on screen.
    - **3 C** Cell-formulas: Print cell formulas.
    - **4 F** Formatted: Print headers, footers, and page breaks.
    - **5 U** Unformatted: Suppress printing of headers, footers, and page breaks.
    - **6 P** Page#: Print the page numbers.
    - **7 N** No-page#: Turn off page numbering.
    - **8 R** Row/Col#s: Print the row and column numbers.
    - **9 S** Stop-R/C#s: Cancel Row/Col#s.
    - **0 B** Background: Toggle background printing on or off.
    - **W** Wide-print: Toggle sideways (wide) printing on and off.
  - **0 Q** Quit: Quit Options menu.
- **6 C** Clear: Reset some or all print settings.
  - **2 A** All: Return all options and settings to default.
  - **3 R** Range: Clear the specified range.
  - **4 B** Borders: Clear the current border range.
  - **5 F** Format: Return the margins, page length, and setup string to default.
- **7 A** Align: Reset to top of page after adjusting paper.

8 G Go: Print specified range.
9 Q Quit: Quit Print menu.
0 S Status: Display the current Print command settings.
E Eject: Advance paper to the top of the next sheet.

8 G Graph: Commands that create graphs from worksheet data.
2 T Type: Set graph type.
2 L Line: Line graph.
3 B Bar: Bar graph.
4 X XY: XY graph.
5 S Stacked-Bar: Stacked-bar graph.
6 P Pie: Pie chart.
3 R Reset: Clear all or part of graph settings.
G Graph: Clear all graph settings.
X X range: Clear X-axis data.
A A range: Clear first data range.
B B range: Clear second data range.
C C range: Clear third data range.
D D range: Clear fourth data range.
E E range: Clear fifth data range.
F F range: Clear sixth data range.
Q Quit: Quit Reset menu.
4 V View: View graph.
5 P Print: Print graph.
6 S Save: Save graph on disk for later printing.
7 O Options: Commands that make a graph more presentable.
2 D Data-Labels: Set labels for data points.
3 T Titles: Set titles for graph.
2 F First: First main title.
3 S Second: Second main title.
4 X X-axis: X-axis title.
5 Y Y-axis: Y-axis title.
4 L Legends: Set legends for data ranges.
5 S Scale: Set scales for axes.
6 F Format: Control the use of symbols and lines in a line or XY graph.
2 L Line: Connect data points with a line.

- **3 S** Symbol: Assign a symbol for each data point in a range.
- **4 B** Both: Use both lines and symbols.
- **5 N** Neither: Use neither lines nor symbols, but display data labels if they are defined.

- **7 G** Grid: Set background grid.
- **8 C** Color: Display for color monitor.
- **9 B** B&W: Display for black and white monitor.
- **0 Q** Quit: Exit the Options menu.

- **8 N** Name: Graph-naming commands.
  - **2 U** Use: Make the current graph a named graph.
  - **3 C** Create: Give the current graph a name.
  - **4 D** Delete: Delete a named graph.
  - **5 R** Reset: Delete all named graphs.
  - **6 T** Table: Insert a table of graph names.
- **9 Q** Quit: Quit the Graph menu.
- **0 L** Look: Display a graph from a specified graph file.
- **X** X range: Set X-axis range of data.
- **A** A range: Set first data range.
- **B** B range: Set second data range.
- **C** C range: Set third data range.
- **D** D range: Set fourth data range.
- **E** E range: Set fifth data range.
- **F** F range: Set sixth data range.

9 D Data: Commands that deal with data manipulation.

- **2 F** Fill: Fill a range with consecutive numbers.
- **3 T** Table: Create a table of values.
- **4 S** Sort: Data-sorting commands.
  - **2 D** Data-range: Set range for sorting.
  - **3 P** Primary-key: Set primary sort key column, and specify ascending or descending.
  - **4 S** Secondary-key: Set secondary sort key column, and specify ascending or descending.
  - **5 3** 3rd-key: Set third sort key column, and specify ascending or descending.
  - **6 4** 4th-key: Set fourth sort key, and specify ascending or descending.
  - **7 R** Reset: Clear data range and keys.

8 G Go: Perform the sort.
9 Q Quit: Quit the Sort menu.
5 Q Query: Commands used for data searches.
2 I Input: Set the input data range.
3 C Criterion: Set the criterion data range.
4 O Output: Set the output data range.
5 F Find: Highlight the matches.
6 E Extract: Copy matches to output range.
7 U Unique: Copy matches to output range, eliminating duplicates.
8 D Delete: Erase matches from input range.
9 R Reset: Clear some or all search ranges.
0 Q Quit: Quit the Query menu.
6 D Distribution: Determine the distribution of the data.
7 E External: Transfer data between the current worksheet and a database file.
8 I Input: Edit, delete, and add records in a DBF FILE.
0 T Tools: Use word-processing and graphics features to enhance worksheets and printed report.
S System: Invoke the DOS command interpreter.
Q Quit: Quit the VP-Planner Plus program.
N No: Cancel the Quit command.
Y Yes: Exit to the Lotus Access System.
\ Repeating Labels: Fill a cell with a repeating character string.

FUNCTION KEYS

F1	Help
F2	Edit
F3	Name
F4	Abs
F5	GoTo
F6	Window
F7	Data
F8	Table
F9	Recalc
F10	Graph

FUNCTIONS

See the VP-Planner Plus manual for details. This is *not* a complete list of all the functions.

Mathematical Functions	@ABS(x)	absolute value of x
	@ACOS(x)	arc cosine of x
	@ASIN(x)	arc sine of x
	@ATAN(x)	arc tangent of x
	@ATAN2(x,y)	arc tangent of y/x
	@COS(x)	cosine of x
	@EXP(x)	exponential of x
	@INT(x)	integer part of x
	@LN(x)	natural logarithm of x
	@LOG(x)	logarithm base 10 of x
	@MOD(x,y)	x mod y
	@PI	pi (3.14159)
	@RAND	random number from 0 to 1
	@ROUND(x,n)	round x to n decimal places
	@SIN(x)	sine of x
	@SQRT(x)	square root of x
	@TAN(x)	tangent of x
Logical Functions	@FALSE	the value 0 (false)
	@TRUE	the value 1 (true)
	@ISNA(x)	the value 1 (true) if x has the value NA
	@ISERR(x)	the value 1 (true) if x has the value ERR
	@ISNUMBER(x)	the value 1 (true) if x is numeric
	@ISSTRING(x)	the value 1 (true) if x is string
	@IF(cond,x,y)	x if cond is true, y if cond is false
	@NA	the value NA (not applicable)
	@ERR	the value ERR (error)
Date/Time Functions	@DATE(year,month,day)	serial number of date (2 = 1 Jan 1900)
	@DATEVALUE(date)	converts date (string) into a serial number
	@DAY(date)	day number
	@MONTH(date)	month number
	@YEAR(date)	year number
	@TIME(h,m,s)	converts a time value into a serial number

	@TIMEVALUE(time)	converts time (string) to a serial number
	@NOW	current date and time as a serial number
Statistical Functions	@COUNT(list)	counts the items in list
	@SUM(list)	sums the values of items in list
	@AVG(list)	averages the values of items in list
	@MIN(list)	minimum of all items in list
	@MAX(list)	maximum of all items in list
	@STD(list)	standard deviation of all items in list
	@VAR(list)	variance of items in list
Financial Functions	@NPV(x,y)	net present value, given interest (x) and range (y)
	@IRR(x,y)	internal rate-of-return, given guess (x) and range (y)
	@PV(x,y,z)	present value of series of periodic, equal cash flows, given payment (x), interest (y), and term (z)
	@FV(x,y,z)	future value of series of equal payments, given payment (x), interest (y), and term (z)
	@PMT(x,y,z)	periodic payment amount, given principal (x), interest (y), and term (z)
	@RATE(x,y,z)	return on an investment, given future value (x), present value (y), and term (z)
	@TERM(x,y,z)	number of payment periods of an investment, given payment (x), interest (y), and future value (z)
	@CTERM(x,y,z)	number of compounding periods an investment must grow for a desired return, given interest (x), future value (y), and present value (z)
	@DDB(v,x,y,z)	double-declining-balance depreciation, given cost (v), salvage (x), life (y), and period (z)

@SLN(x,y,z)	straight-line depreciation, given cost (x), salvage (y), and life (z)
@SYD(v,x,y,z)	sum-of-the-years' digits depreciation, given cost (v), salvage (x), life (y), and period (z)

MODULE 3
dBASE III PLUS

Introduction

In business, schools, and even private homes, a great deal of information must be maintained. For example, information on correspondence must be stored, kept up to date, and retrieved as the need occurs. When paper documents are involved, this information is kept in a file cabinet and is arranged in some kind of sequence. Any method used to organize information (manual or automated) must allow for its easy retrieval.

Should the information be in alphabetical order, or should it be in numerical sequence? That all depends on how you intend to retrieve the information. Say, for example, that you are to file students' records in some order. Should the file be in alphabetical order by student name or in numerical sequence by student number? You have to consider which you will be doing more often, retrieving by student name or by student number. Let's say that you decide to file by student name since you look up students by names more often. What do you do if someone asks for information by student number? You need to have a cross reference. If you find out later that you need to look up all the students in a particular class, you will have to create another cross reference. Your filing system could become very complicated. It has been said that anybody can file; but the retrieving takes a little doing!

A *database management system (DBMS)* is a set of computer programs that provides a mean for storing, updating, and retrieving information. You can use a database management system in many ways. In its simplest use the system stores information in a *flat file*, such as a file on all students, with an individual *record* for each student. In a student file a record might consist of several *fields* of information, depending on the application. In a student record the fields might consist of student name, student number, and class number, among others. You could then retrieve the record for any student if you were given the name or student number, or you could retrieve the names of all the students in any particular class. If you would like a printed report on students, alphabetized and by classes, you could produce that, too.

A more sophisticated use of a database management system is the elimination of redundant information through the use of *relational database files*. Some information is used in different application areas within a company. For example, customer information, such as customer name, address, and telephone number, might be needed by sales, shipping, and accounts receivable departments. Rather than keeping customer information on separate databases for each of these areas, it can be kept on one customer database. (This way, should the customer move or change telephone numbers, the information needs to be updated on only one file.) In using the database for any application, given the customer number, the customer database file is accessed to obtain the name, address, and telephone number. The fact that these particular pieces of information came from another database file is *transparent* to the users, meaning that they are not aware of this, nor do they need to be.

Furthermore, the customer database file might include information needed by all application areas, but each area will see only those pieces of information needed for its application. The customer database file might include credit status. This information is needed by the accounts receivable application, but is not needed by the shipping. Hence the credit status will not, and cannot, be accessed by personnel in shipping.

dBASE III Plus is a database management system with these simple and sophisticated capabilities. It is a very powerful program capable of record retrieval, automatic updating, and report generation. With dBASE III Plus you also can write programs that enable others, less familiar with computers, to perform data entry and retrieval.

This manual covers only the simple commands of dBASE III Plus and explains just what is needed for a particular lesson. Many options and features available in dBASE III Plus can be explored on your own after you understand the basic commands. The lessons in this manual introduce the student to dBASE III Plus and to database management systems uses in general. After completing these lessons, you should find it easier to learn additional features of dBASE III Plus and to work with other database management systems and file management systems.

STARTING dBASE III Plus

To use this module, you need dBASE III Plus Sampler Demo Disks #1 and #2. You also need a formatted data disk and the BCS data disk you received with this tutorial.

Installing dBASE III Plus

Before working for the first time with the dBASE III Plus software disks that accompany this manual, you may need to *install* the software. To install means you let the software know the configuration of your computer so the software can make some adjustments. In the case of the dBASE III Plus sampler version, this involves making sure that appropriate CONFIG.SYS and CONFIG.DB files exist. There is a program called INSTALL on Sampler Disk #1 that makes all the necessary adjustments. However, before running INSTALL you should check with your instructor.

CAUTION: If you are working with a PC with 256K of RAM, the INSTALL program *replaces* CONFIG.SYS in the root directory of the DOS startup disk with CONFI256.SYS that is on the Sampler Disk #1, then *replaces* CONFIG.DB on Sampler Disk #1 with CONFI256.DB on the Sampler Disk #1.

If you are working with a PC with more than 256K of RAM, the INSTALL program *replaces* CONFIG.SYS in the root directory of the DOS startup disk with CONFIG.SYS in Sampler disk #1.

In addition, if you are using a PC with a hard disk, the INSTALL program will create a subdirectory

SAMPLER and give you instruction to copy all dBASE III Plus onto this directory.

The CONFI256.SYS specifies FILES = 20 and BUFFERS = 4; CONFIG.SYS on Sampler disk #1 specifies FILES = 20 and BUFFERS = 15. CONFI256.DB contains various parameters to adjust dBASE to the memory size (of 256K). That means if there already is a CONFIG.SYS in the root directory of the DOS start-up disk you cannot just run the INSTALL program. You need to check to find out if commands other than FILES and BUFFERS exist in the CONFIG.SYS file in the root directory. If so, rather than running the INSTALL program, you should edit the CONFIG.SYS file to make it compatible with what is stated above.

To run the INSTALL program:

1. Start the computer with DOS.
2. Insert the dBASE Sampler Demo Disk #1 in drive A (the one on the left) and close the door.
3. Type INSTALL and press ENTER.

   > The following message is displayed:

   ```
   Put Sampler disk 1 in Drive A, and your DOS disk in
   drive B (Remember to remove any write protect tab
   from disk)
   Strike a key when ready . . .
   ```

4. Just follow the instructions displayed on the screen.

   > When the installation process is completed, the following message appears on the screen.

   ```
   Now reboot your computer with your DOS disk in
   drive A (CONTROL-ALT-DEL). Then place Sampler
   Disk 1 in drive A and type DBASE.
   ```

5. You can start dBASE by following the instructions displayed.

To Start dBASE III Plus

To start dBASE III Plus on all subsequent sessions, follow the instructions given below:

1. Start the computer with DOS.
2. Insert dBASE Sampler Demo Disk #1 in drive A (the one on the left) and close the door.

3. Type DBASE and press ENTER.

   > The copyright screen appears.

4. Press ENTER to continue.
5. Remove Sampler Disk #1 from the disk drive and put it back in its envelope.
6. Insert Sampler Disk #2 in drive A and the BCS data disk in drive B. Make sure to close the door of each disk drive.
7. Press ENTER to begin use of dBASE III Plus.

USING A PRINTER

dBASE III Plus sends all its output to the LPT1 port. The manual assumes that your computer is set up accordingly.

BROWSING AN EXISTING dBASE DATABASE

In this section you will access an existing dBASE database. We developed it already and stored it on the BCS data disk you received with this tutorial. Do not expect to understand every keystroke you are about to enter. The objective is for you to experience how dBASE works. In subsequent lessons you will learn how to use dBASE to develop your own applications.

With dBASE started you will access two of the files in Figure 6-4 of *Business Computer Systems*. For your convenience, we have copied the data here in Figure I-1.

Your screen should look like Screen Display I-1 on page 208. If it does not, press ENTER.

Now follow these steps, observing the results on the screen.

NOTE ■ With dBASE you sometimes need to press two keys at one time, such as the CTRL key and the END key. We will show such a combination this way: CTRL/END.

In the first series of instructions, you will open the Customers file, scan it, then close the file. Do not be concerned if you do not understand the key sequences now.

	Type	*Results*
1.	ENTER	Disk drive submenu appears.
2.	ENTER	Drive B is selected; list of database files appears.
3.	From menu, use UP ARROW and DOWN ARROW to highlight CUSTS.DBF; press ENTER	Prompt appears asking if file is indexed.

	Type	*Results*
4.	Y	List of index files appears.
5.	Use UP ARROW and DOWN ARROW to highlight CIND.NDX; press ENTER	"Master" appears next to CIND.NDX.
6.	LEFT ARROW	Setup menu appears.
7.	Press RIGHT ARROW twice	Update submenu appears.
8.	Highlight Browse; press ENTER	Customer data from the CUSTS file appears on the screen, one record per line.
9.	Use UP ARROW and DOWN ARROW to scan the Customers file. Compare data to that in Figure 19. If you get a message at the bottom of the screen, "Add new records? [Y/N]", press either N, UP ARROW, or DOWN ARROW.	
10.	CTRL/END	Data disappears; update submenu appears.
11.	Press LEFT ARROW twice	Setup submenu appears.

Congratulations! You have successfully opened, browsed, and closed a dBASE file. The one you just looked at was the Customers file. In the next series, you will open and scan the Sales file. You will follow a procedure identical to the one you used for the Customers file.

12.	ENTER	Disk drive submenu appears.
13.	Highlight B: and press ENTER	List of database files appears.
14.	Highlight SALES.DBF and press ENTER	Prompt appears asking if the file is indexed.
15.	Y	List of index files appears.
16.	Highlight SALESIND.NDX and press ENTER	"Master" appears next to SALESIND.NDX

CUSTOMERS

Account Number	Name	Address	Phone Number	Balance
1002	Johnson, Inc.	Hartford, CT	555-1234	8,500
1009	Akim Assoc.	Wethersfield, CT	555-6901	7,000
1028	M. Dane	Springfield, MA	555-1977	5,200
2402	E. Annino	Clinton, CT	555-0652	4,900

SALES

Sale Number	Date	Amount	Customer Account Number	Salesperson Social Security Number
2347	03/14/90	2,000	1002	049-58-3112
2348	03/14/90	2,500	1028	111-22-3333
2349	03/14/90	6,000	1009	049-58-3112
2350	03/15/90	1,000	1002	286-00-0552
2351	03/15/90	2,500	2402	111-22-3333

Figure I-1 Customers and sales

	Type	*Results*
17.	LEFT ARROW	Setup menu appears.
18.	Press RIGHT ARROW twice	Update menu appears.
19.	Highlight Browse and press ENTER	Sales data is displayed on the screen.
20.	Use UP ARROW and DOWN ARROW to scan the sales data. Compare to the data in Figure 19.	
21.	CTRL/END	Data disappears; Update menu appears.
22.	Press LEFT ARROW twice	Setup menu appears.

Before continuing with the final series of keystrokes, study the data in Figure I-1. One file contains only customer data, the other

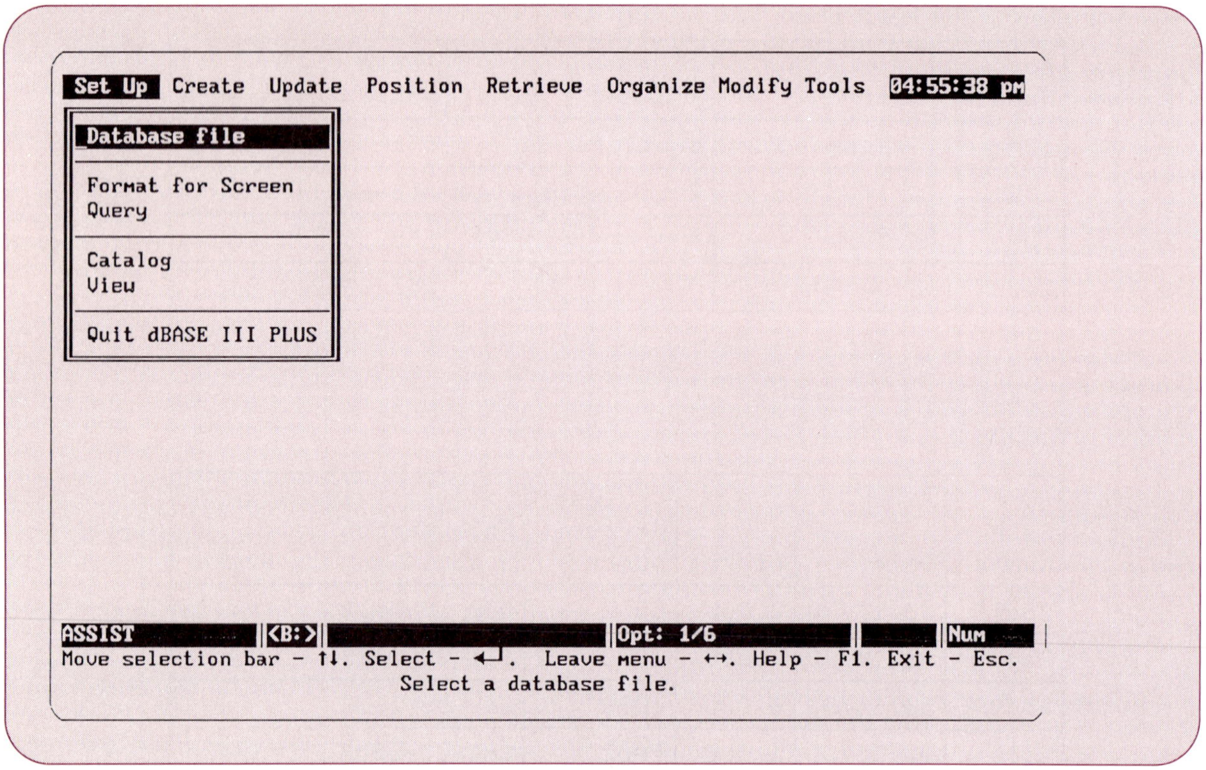

Screen Display I-1

one contains only sales data. Suppose you wanted to see a list of sales that shows the sale number, amount, customer name, and balance of the customer who made each purchase. To do this, you need to combine data from two files. In dBASE, this is accomplished by means of a *view* (you'll learn how to build views in a subsequent lesson). Figure I-2 shows how the combined data will look.

SALE_NUM	*AMOUNT*	*NAME*	*BALANCE*
2347	2000.00	Johnson, Inc.	8500.00
2348	2500.00	M. Dane	5200.00
2349	6000.00	Akim Assoc.	7000.00
2350	1000.00	Johnson, Inc.	8500.00
2351	2500.00	E. Annino	4900.00

Figure I-2 View extracted from Sales and Customers files

Type	Results
Now use dBASE to open and browse the view.	
23. Highlight View and press ENTER	Disk drive submenu appears.
24. Select B: and press ENTER	List of view files appears.
25. Highlight SALECUST.VUE and press ENTER	Setup menu appears.
26. Press RIGHT ARROW twice	Update menu appears.
27. Highlight Browse and press ENTER	Combined sale and customer data appears. The sale number and amount are from the Sales file, and the customer name and balance are from the Customers file.
28. CTRL/END	Update menu appears.
29. Press LEFT ARROW twice	Setup menu appears.

We could combine the data from the two tables in other ways, too, displaying different combinations of fields. In the next several lessons you will learn how to build your own database using dBASE.

Remove the BCS data disk from drive B.

Lesson 1
Creating Files

Objectives

Upon completion of the material presented in this lesson you should understand and do the following:

- Learn terminology used with database systems.
- Know the difference between working through ASSIST and working from the dot prompt.
- Create a database file.
- Specify fields to be included in the file.
- Enter information into a database file.
- Browse a database file.
- Sum and average numeric fields in a database.
- Count the number of records in a database.
- Switch from one database file to another.
- Print the screen display on the printer.

STARTING OFF

Start dBASE III Plus on the computer, following instructions given in the introduction to this module, so that the dBASE ASSIST screen shown in Screen Display 1-1 is displayed. Put a formatted disk in drive B.

At the top of the screen is the ASSIST *menu bar*, showing eight menu choices and the current time. The first choice, **Set Up**, is

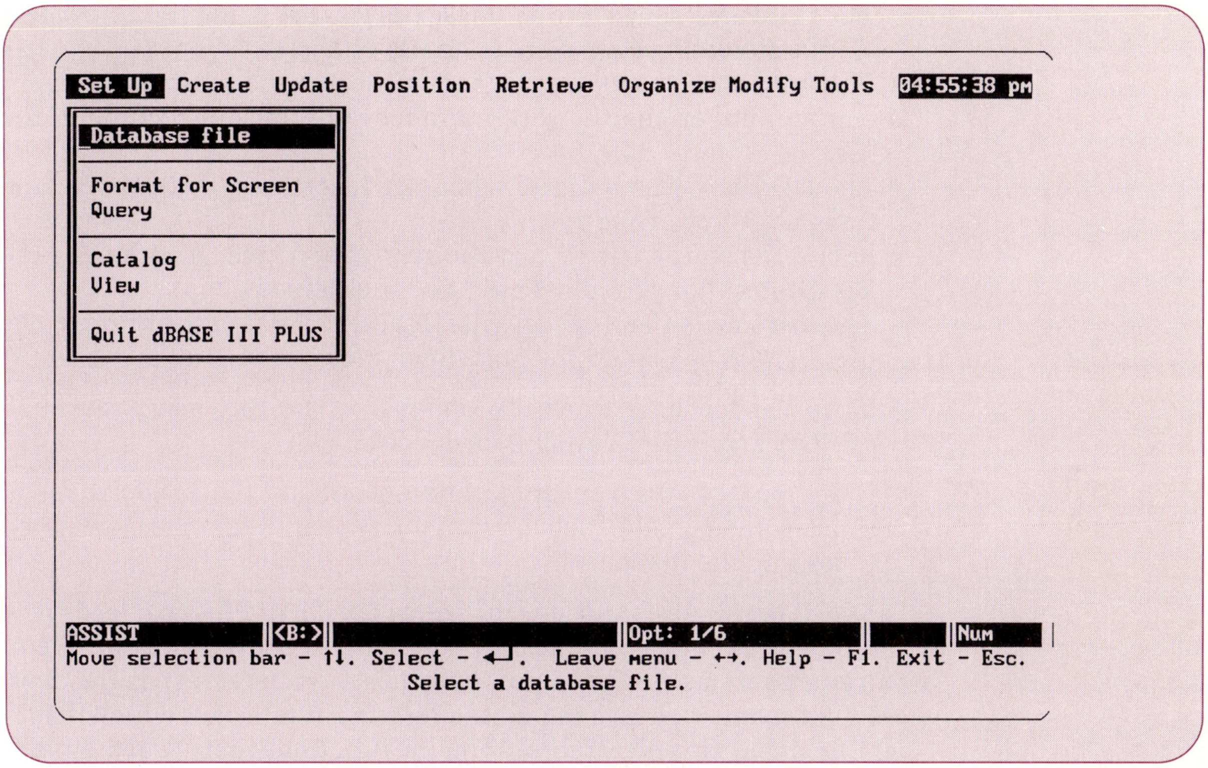

Screen Display 1-1

highlighted, and below it is a *pull-down menu* containing six options.

At the bottom of the screen are three lines of information that are always present while you are using dBASE III Plus. The first of these is the *status bar*. It is highlighted, and divided into six areas.

- The first area shows where you are: it says ASSIST, indicating that you are in the ASSIST mode.
- The second area shows <B:>, indicating that drive B is the default. That is, drive B contains the disk on which the file you create will be stored. On the dBASE Sampler, the default drive is preset to B. When you use the regular version of dBASE III Plus, the default is set initially to the drive on which the dBASE program is stored. With the commercial version you will have to change the default drive. At this point verify that B: is your default drive setting. If necessary, use the SET DEFAULT TO command to select drive B. See the dBASE III Plus manual for more specific information.

- The third area shows the database file you are using right now. It is blank, indicating that there is no file in use.
- The next area shows Opt: 1/6. It indicates the option or current record number and the total number of options or records in the file.
- The last two areas indicate when the Insert (Ins), Num Lock, and Caps Lock key are active.
- Below the status bar line is the *navigation line*. It indicates the keystrokes that you may enter, and their effects.
- The last line is the *message line*. It gives a brief description of the highlighted option on the pull-down menu.

· Move the highlight to all the options on the top, using the LEFT ARROW and RIGHT ARROW keys.

> As you move the highlight to different options, the pull-down menu blanks and another pull-down menu appears under the highlighted area on the menu bar.

ASSIST, or the *Assistant*, is a feature of dBASE III Plus that leads new users (and experienced ones) by the hand to show them the use of various commands. The menu that you see on the screen is the main ASSIST menu. Just as a menu in a restaurant tells you which dishes are available, this menu shows you the functions that are available to you at this point. The pull-down menu that is displayed when an option on the menu bar is selected shows further options you have within the highlighted category. To make a selection from the pull-down menu, you move the highlight, this time with the UP ARROW and DOWN ARROW keys, and press ENTER.

· With any selection on the menu bar, move the highlight on the pull-down menu, using the **UP ARROW** and **DOWN ARROW** keys.

Note that the message at the bottom line, the message line, changes each time you move the highlight. If, when you make a selection, there is a further selection to be made, another menu, or the sub-menu, is displayed. You move the highlight cursor with the UP ARROW and DOWN ARROW keys and select by pressing ENTER.

NOTE ▪ The RIGHT ARROW and LEFT ARROW keys are used to make selections on the menu bar. All other menu selections are made with the UP ARROW and DOWN ARROW keys. The advantage of such a menu-driven system is that there is no need for you to memorize and type in all the commands.

dBASE III Plus can be used without ASSIST. You can get out of ASSIST at any time by pressing the ESC key from the main ASSIST menu.

- From the ASSIST menu, press the **ESC** key.

  > A dot appears just above the status bar, preceded by the word (**DEMO**), and followed by a flashing underscore (_) character called the *cursor*.

The word (DEMO) appears only in the sampler or the demonstration version of dBASE III Plus. The dot, or the *dot prompt*, means that dBASE III Plus is ready for a command. The cursor shows where the characters you enter will appear on the screen. The status bar shows that the cursor is on the command line, and the message line indicates that you are to enter a dBASE III Plus command.

You can enter a command now. However, you haven't a clue of what to enter. At least with ASSIST, you can see the available commands, and the navigation and message lines give you brief directions on what you can do. All commands that can be entered from the ASSIST can be entered from the dot prompt without ASSIST. However, the reverse is not true. *Not* all commands that can be entered from the dot prompt are available through ASSIST. Hence you need to learn how to enter commands through the dot prompt in order to take advantage of all that dBASE III Plus has to offer. Also, if you are planning to learn to program in dBASE III Plus, you must use the dot prompt commands.

In these lessons you will first use ASSIST to utilize dBASE III Plus. As you enter commands in ASSIST, the *action line* on the screen (just above the status bar) shows you the equivalent dot prompt command. You will note these commands, then enter them later from the dot prompt. You will create two database files: one using ASSIST and one from the dot prompt. For the first one, you need to go back to ASSIST.

- From the dot prompt type ASSIST and press ENTER.

  > The ASSIST menu is displayed.

DATABASE FILES IN dBASE III Plus

dBASE III Plus acts on database *files*. A single file may consist of up to one billion *records* (if disk space is available). Each record can contain up to 128 *fields* of information, or 4,000 *characters*, whichever is more limiting. It is not necessary for one file to contain all your information. One file can reference information in a different file. For example, in an inventory file there may be more than one item from a particular vendor. However, a record on an item does not have to include the name and address of the vendor. Instead, it can reference the vendor by having a field containing vendor number. The vendor number, in turn, appears as a field in a separate vendor file. In this way each vendor name and address is entered only once, in the vendor file, rather than multiple times in records for inventory items. The concept of having two or more database files with related information, called a *relational model,* will be covered in Lesson 5.

Within dBASE III Plus each record is made up of a set of fields. Each field must be given a field name, which you make up to describe the contents of the field. Field names consist of one to ten characters, made up of letters (A–Z), numbers (0–9), and the underscore character (_). Each field name must begin with a letter. Letters that are entered as lowercase are converted automatically to uppercase for all field names, filenames, and dBASE III Plus commands. You may enter these as upper- or lowercase, but they are converted to uppercase for display.

There are five types of fields in dBASE III Plus. The type of information contained in the field and the types of operations that can be performed on the data depend on the field type. The field types and their uses are listed here:

- *Character* fields store character *strings* (names, telephone numbers, employee numbers, item descriptions, etc.). The strings can be compared, indexed, and sorted. However, strings (even numbers as strings) cannot be modified by or used in arithmetic expressions.
- *Numeric* fields store numbers, either as *integers* (whole numbers), or *real numbers* (includes decimals). Regardless of how a number is displayed, it maintains 12 digits of accuracy. Numeric fields can be used in calculations and can be modified by arithmetic calculations.
- *Logical* fields each hold a single character, which serves as a *flag* indicating either true or false. Logical true is represented by T, t, Y, or y (true or yes). Logical false is represented by F, f, N, or n (false or no). Logical fields can be tested in programs to determine how to process the data.
- *Date* fields store the date in the format MM/DD/YY (01/02/90). Dates can be sorted and indexed. They may be entered from the keyboard or specified as the current date. Numbers may be added to or subtracted from dates to make new dates, and one date may be subtracted from another to yield the number of days or the length of a time period. The user can determine the day of the week (i.e.,

SUNDAY), the calendar month (i.e., FEBRUARY), and the year by using built-in functions that operate on date fields.

- *Memo* fields are designed to hold large blocks of textual information, and can be up to 5,000 characters long, although each field uses only as much disk space as its content requires. Memo fields cannot be sorted or used in indexing, and cannot be manipulated, except by the screen editor. They can be entered, read, printed, and modified.

When you design a database, you need to consider not only what types of fields to use for each piece of data in a record, but also what size the field should be. The widths, or capacities, of memo, logical, and date fields are always automatically specified. For character fields you need to specify a maximum number of characters in each field. For example, one field might be for last names of people. You would specify a sufficiently large field width to hold the longest name you anticipate entering. For numeric fields you need to specify both the total width (including spaces for the minus sign and the decimal point) and the number of places to the right of the decimal point.

Now you will create a database that contains customer information. It will contain the names, addresses, telephone numbers, and credit account balance for all the customers, one customer per record. Since you may wish to use only first names (or last names) at times, you decide to store names in two fields. Summarizing the decisions you have made thus far, the fields in the record are those shown in the table.

Field No.	*Contents*
1	first name
2	last name
3	street address
4	city
5	state
6	zip code
7	telephone number
8	balance

You have to name each field and also decide what type of data each should contain. As a rule, if a field consists of numbers that are not manipulated mathematically, it is better to establish it as a character field.

The first and last names, address, city, and state should all be character fields, since these will store both alphabetic and numeric characters. Although the zip code is a number, it should be a character field because you won't use it in mathematical expressions. Similarly, the telephone number might be expressed as (916) 983-1295. If you want to include the parentheses, space, and hyphen, then you must specify it as a character field. The balance field must be specified as a numeric field since it is used in calculations.

As mentioned earlier, each field also needs to have a defined width. The width should be at least as large as the longest expected entry, and a numeric field requires definition of both width and decimal position. You could choose the following field names, types, and widths:

Field No.	*Name*	*Type*	*Width*	*Dec*
1	FIRST_NAME	CHARACTER	12	
2	LAST_NAME	CHARACTER	12	
3	ADDRESS	CHARACTER	30	
4	CITY	CHARACTER	15	
5	STATE	CHARACTER	2	
6	ZIP	CHARACTER	5	
7	TELEPHONE	CHARACTER	14	
8	BALANCE	NUMERIC	7	2

NOTE ■ The BALANCE field has the width 7 and decimal 2. This allows it to be as large as 9999.99 or as negative as −999.99.

CREATING A FILE FROM ASSIST

To create a database file, the CREATE command is used. This is how you name the file and set up its *structure*. The structure consists of the names, widths, and types for all fields within the record.

- From the ASSIST main menu select the second option on the menu bar, **Create**, by pressing the **RIGHT ARROW** key until it is highlighted.

  > The pull-down menu shows six options. **Database file** is highlighted.

- Press **ENTER** to select the highlighted option.

  > A submenu, with drive letters, appears to the right of the pull-down menu.

  > The action line (just above the status bar) displays **Command: CREATE** to inform you that the equivalent dot prompt command is CREATE.

You are to select the drive that will store the database file. You want to select drive B:, which is already highlighted.

- Make sure that your data disk is in drive B and press **ENTER**.

  > The action line shows **Command: CREATE B:**.

  > A message indicates that you are to enter a filename.

To create a new database file, you need to specify a *filename*. The name should reflect the contents of the file. A valid filename is any name from 1 to 8 characters long, consisting of letters (all lowercase letters are interpreted as uppercase letters), numbers, or any of the following symbols: !, @, #, $, %, ^, &, (,), -, __, and ~. However, within dBASE III Plus you should avoid filenames with (,), &, and - (hyphen). You should *not* specify an *extension* (a period followed by one to three additional characters) for the filename, since the extension .DBF is assigned to all database files by the dBASE III Plus program.

Since you intend to store customer information on the file, you decide to name the file ACCOUNTS.

- Type **ACCOUNTS**. If you make a mistake, use either the Del key or Backspace key to delete your error and then retype.

NOTE ■ The Backspace key deletes the character to the left of the cursor, while the Del key deletes the character the cursor is on.

- Press **ENTER**.

  > The screen shown in Screen Display 1-2 is displayed.

After you enter a filename, you are prompted to enter the structure of the database file. The structure describes the order in which fields are to appear in the record and also the specified field names, types, and widths, if necessary.

At the top the number of *bytes* (characters) remaining for the fields is displayed. Just below are several helpful cursor control commands for use in creating the structure. The status bar shows that you are still in CREATE and that the file you are working with is in drive B and is named ACCOUNTS. It also shows the number of fields that are already defined. Near the center of the screen, on the left side, are four titles: Field Name, Type, Width, and Dec. Beneath these is the number 1. This refers to the first field. The cursor is positioned on the line with the number 1, underneath the title Field Name.

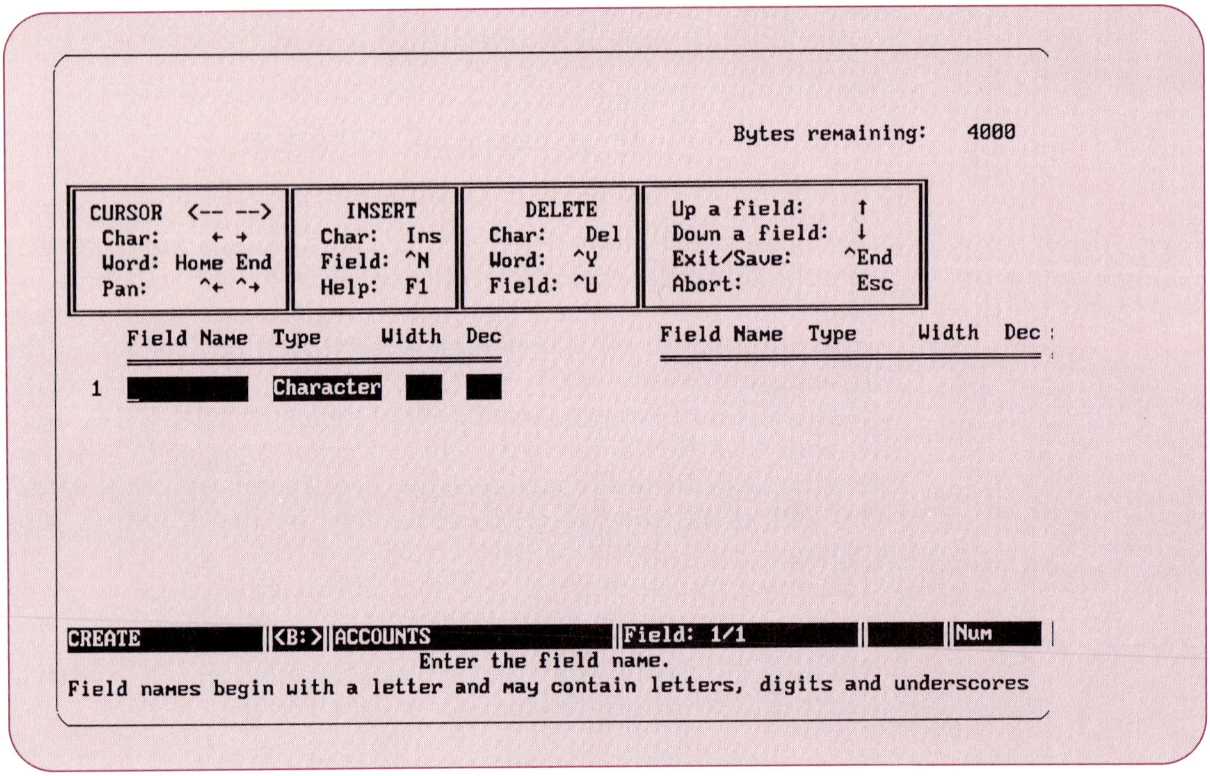

Screen Display 1-2

- Type FIRST_NAME (do not press ENTER).

  > Without pressing ENTER, you hear a beep and the cursor jumps to the next field, which contains the word Character.

When you fill an entry completely (as, for example, the entry for field name, FIRST_NAME, that contains the maximum 10 characters), dBASE III Plus automatically moves to the next entry and beeps.

You want the field to be a Character field, so you need only to press ENTER to go to the next entry.

- You accept the *default* of Character by pressing **ENTER**.

  > The cursor jumps to the Width column.

You decided earlier that the field is to be 12 characters wide.

- Type 12 and press **ENTER**.

  > Field 2 appears.

  > The status bar updates the number of defined fields, and the bytes remaining—shown at the top of the screen—changes.

Look at the screen. The cursor shows where you are. The editing and cursor navigation menu at the top of your screen shows all the commands to move the cursor and insert or delete items.

PRACTICE TIME

Enter the structure of the first seven fields, according to the information given here.

Field No.	*Name*	*Type*	*Width*
1	FIRST__NAME	CHAR	12
2	LAST__NAME	CHAR	12
3	ADDRESS	CHAR	30
4	CITY	CHAR	15
5	STATE	CHAR	2
6	ZIP	CHAR	5
7	TELEPHONE	CHAR	14

Stop when the eighth field is displayed.

You enter numeric field data very much like you enter character field data, but you also specify the decimal field.

- Type the last field name, BALANCE, and press **ENTER**.

  > The cursor jumps to the Type column.

You want to make this a numeric field.

- Press the **SPACE BAR** repeatedly. All the available field types are displayed in turn. Stop when **Numeric** is displayed again.
- Press **ENTER**.

  > The cursor jumps to the Width column.

- Type 7 and press **ENTER**.

  > The cursor jumps to the Decimal column.

- Type 2 and press **ENTER**.

When you have entered the eighth field, the program prompts you for the structure of the ninth field. Since you are finished entering the database structure, you will leave this mode.

- Enter **Ctrl/End** (hold down the **Ctrl** key while you press the **End** key—this key combination is displayed on the screen as ^END) to end creating the database structure.

> The bottom of the screen contains the message:

`Press ENTER to confirm. Any other key to resume`

- Press **ENTER** to confirm that you are finished.

> The screen displays the message:

`Input data records now? (Y/N)`

Now that you have created the structure of the file, the program is asking whether you want to enter data into the file. You have the option of either doing so or leaving the file empty. You will enter data now.

ENTERING DATA

- Type **Y** to indicate that you will enter data. *Do not press ENTER.*

> You see the form, or the *template,* of Screen Display 1-3 on the screen.

The screen is now designed to help you enter data into your file. The status bar shows that you have not yet entered any records. At

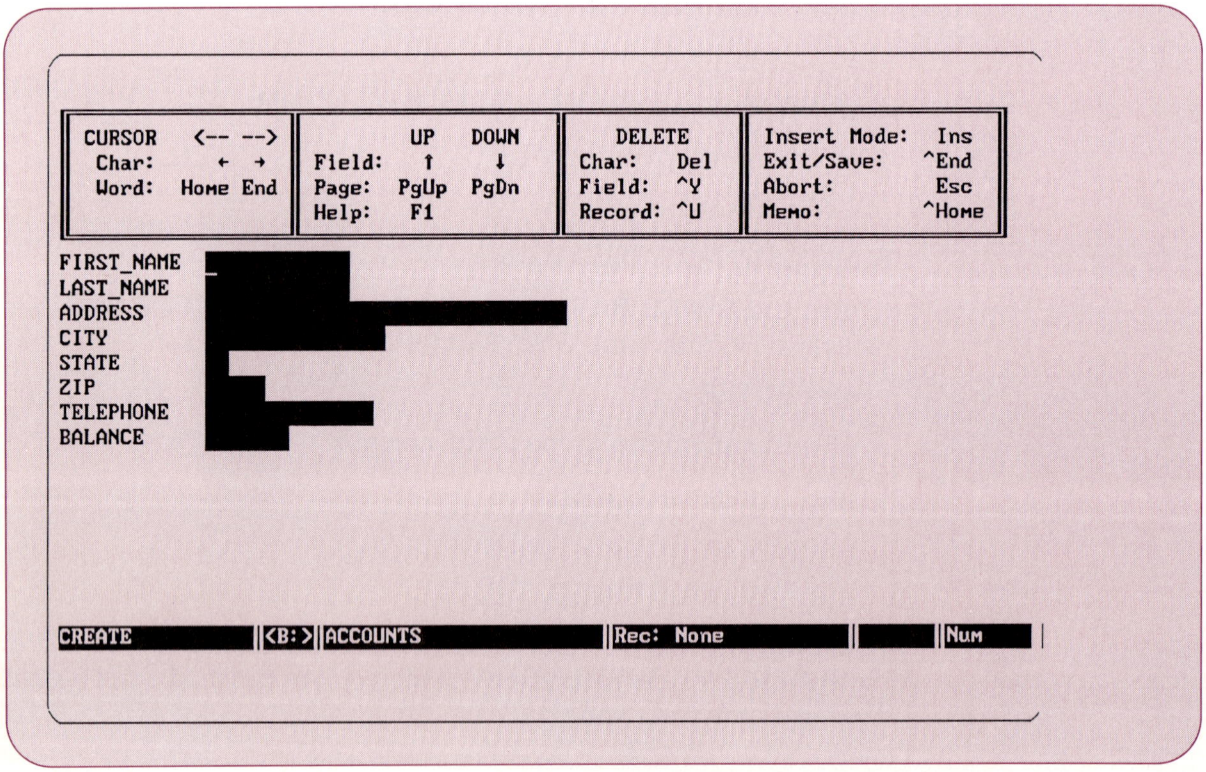

Screen Display 1-3

the top are onscreen aids to help you to move the cursor, insert, and delete. In the middle of the screen are the names of the fields in the leftmost column and some highlighted areas of various widths to the right of the field names. These highlighted areas are the widths you specified for the respective fields, and these are the positions at which you will enter the information for the various fields in the first record. If you make a mistake, you can use the cursor movement keys to go back and correct the information. For example, if you key in an incorrect letter, you can use the Del key or the Backspace key to delete it, and then key the correct character.

You will now enter the data on customers. The first customer is **Robert Castillo**, who lives at **112 South Broadway, Sparks, NV 89431**. His phone number is **(702) 358-0200**, and his balance is **247.50**. Unlike field names, the entries are not changed to uppercase. Enter them in upper- and lowercase letters, as they appear.

- With the cursor next to FIRST__NAME, type Robert in the first field and press **ENTER** to move to the next field.
- In the LAST__NAME field, type Castillo and press **ENTER** to move to the next field.

If you notice an error on a previous field, use the UP ARROW key to position the cursor where you want, and retype the entry.

- Enter the street address, 112 South Broadway, in the ADDRESS field, and Sparks in the CITY field. After each entry press **ENTER** to move to the next field.
- In the STATE field, type NV.

  > Without your pressing ENTER, there is a beep and the cursor moves to the next field. Remember, when you fill a field, dBASE III Plus automatically moves the cursor to the next field. The beep should alert you in case you have misentered data.

- Next enter 89431 in the ZIP field, and (702) 358-0200 in the TELEPHONE field.
- Finally type 247.50 in the BALANCE field. Do not press ENTER.

  > A blank template appears.

  > The status bar now shows that you have entered one record. You are ready to enter the second record.

Do you have the idea yet? If the entry for a field is as long as the field length, the computer beeps and goes to the next field automatically.

Otherwise you press ENTER to go to the next field. If you make a mistake, either use the Backspace/Delete key to erase the character and enter the correction, or use the arrow keys to position the cursor and retype the entry.

PRACTICE TIME

The remaining customer entries are given below. You are to enter them into the database. If you get out of the entry mode by mistake and end up back in the ASSIST main menu, position to UPDATE and select the APPEND option. You will be able to enter data from where you left off.

Name:	Harold Smith
Address:	885 North McCarran
City,State,Zip:	Reno, NV 89512
Telephone:	(702) 788-9120
Balance:	29.75

Judy Davenport
555 Timber Lane
Truckee, CA 95734
(916) 966-0722
178.90

Irene Orwell
12575 Sun Valley Blvd.
Sun Valley, NV 89433
(702) 673-9800
860.00

Jonathan Handel
1001 East Fourth Street
Reno, NV 89501
(702) 786-0905
76.24

Chico Juarez
72 Mill Road
Floriston, CA 96111
(916) 479-3205
312.12

Sandy O'Dell
2219 Carson Highway
Carson City, NV 89701
(702) 234-0776
4.49

Julio Chavez
225 Forest Hill Road
Truckee, CA 95734
(916) 968-2335
782.38

Larry Fisher
315 California Avenue
Reno, NV 89509
(702) 329-4405
278.98

Jennifer Bacon
975 Lake Drive
Chilcoot, CA 95926
(916) 477-6705
142.45

Cindy Beard
P.O. Box 10733
Reno, NV 89510
(702) 323-6220
923.40

Abdel Ahmad
417 Miner Street
Virginia City, NV 89440
(702) 847-3562
9.80

Mandy Vario
P.O. Box 37
Dayton, NV 89403
(702) 246-0171
442.45

When you have finished entering data, press **ENTER** again at the next blank form to exit the Data Entry mode. You return to the ASSIST menu.

BROWSE COMMAND

You have just finished entering the names, addresses, telephone numbers, and account balances for customers. Perhaps you would like to check the entries to verify that they were captured correctly. You can do so by using the BROWSE command. The BROWSE command allows you to look at all the data in all the records, and to modify the information if you choose. The data is displayed in a *multirecord format*—that means one record per line on the screen.

- Highlight the **Update** option on the menu bar.
- Highlight the **Browse** option on the pull-down menu and press **ENTER**.

 > The action line displays **Command: BROWSE** for a split second.

 > The screen shown in Screen Display 1-4 is displayed:

Notice that only the last record entered in the file is displayed.

- Press the **UP ARROW** key repeatedly.

 > Soon records 1 through 11 (to 13 on some screens) are displayed on the screen, as seen in Screen Display 1-5.

When the onscreen help menu shows at the top, dBASE III Plus displays only 11 (to 13 on some screens) records. To display 17 (to 20

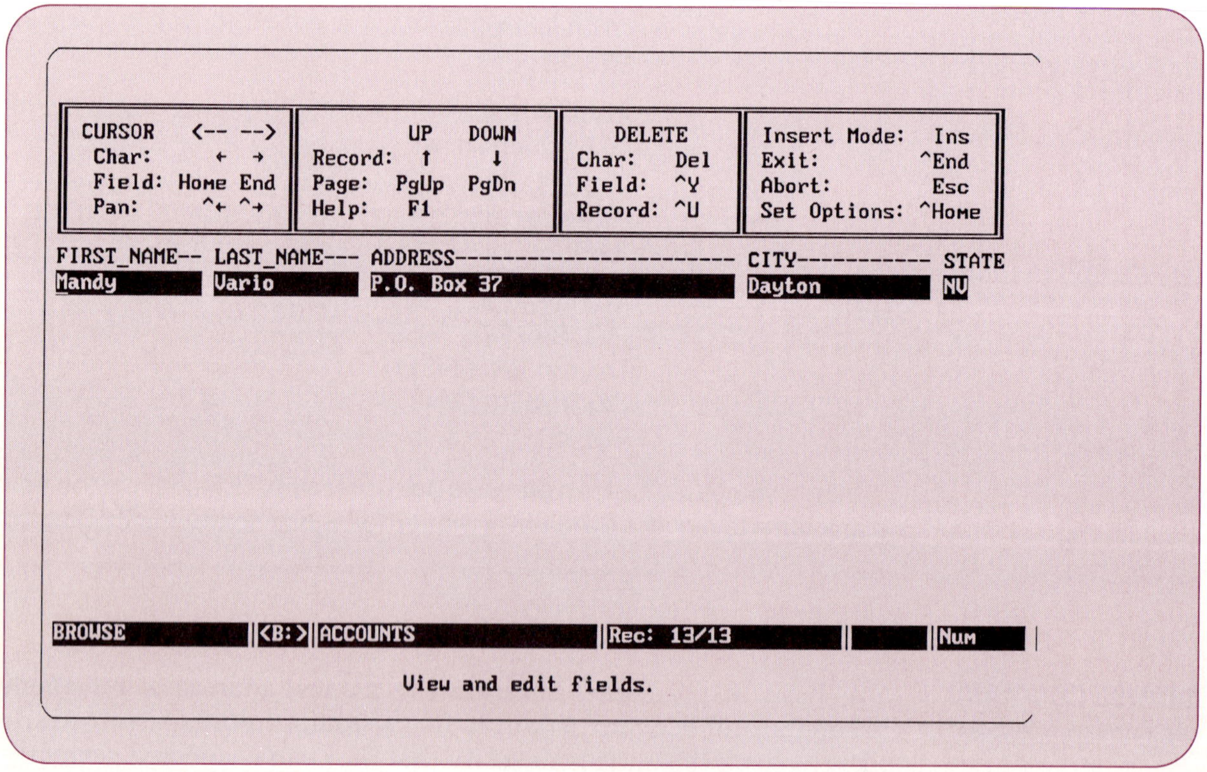

Screen Display 1-4

```
 CURSOR    <-- -->  |        UP    DOWN  |    DELETE       | Insert Mode:    Ins
  Char:      ←   →  | Record:  ↑     ↓   | Char:    Del    | Exit:          ^End
  Field:  Home End  | Page:   PgUp  PgDn | Field:   ^Y     | Abort:          Esc
  Pan:      ^←  ^→  | Help:    F1        | Record:  ^U     | Set Options:  ^Home

FIRST_NAME-- LAST_NAME--- ADDRESS--------------------- CITY---------- STATE
Robert       Castillo     112 South Broadway           Sparks         NV
Harold       Smith        885 North McCarran           Reno           NV
Judy         Davenport    555 Timber Lane              Truckee        CA
Irene        Orwell       12575 Sun Valley Blvd.       Sun Valley     NV
Jonathan     Handel       1001 East Fourth Street      Reno           NV
Chico        Juarez       72 Mill Road                 Floriston      CA
Sandy        O'Dell       2219 Carson Highway          Carson City    NV
Julio        Chavez       225 Forest Hill Road         Truckee        CA
Larry        Fisher       315 California Avenue        Reno           NV
Jennifer     Bacon        975 Lake Drive               Chilcoot       CA
Cindy        Beard        P.O. Box 10733               Reno           NV
Abdel        Ahmad        417 Miner Street             Virginia City  NV
Mandy        Vario        P.O. Box 37                  Dayton         NV

BROWSE       |<B:>|ACCOUNTS        |Rec: 1/13      |      |Num

                         View and edit fields.
```

Screen Display 1-5

on some screens) records, or in this case the entire file, press the **F1** function key. The menu at the top disappears, and you can see all the records. Press the F1 key a second time to get the menu back.

Only the first five fields are displayed. To see the other fields to the right, or *pan* to these fields, hold down the **CTRL** key while you press the RIGHT ARROW key (denoted CTRL/RIGHT ARROW). To move back to previous fields, you use CTRL/LEFT ARROW.

If you notice any mistakes, now is a good time to correct them. Use the cursor movement keys to position the cursor at the proper field and then enter the correct data. You will notice that what you type replaces the existing entries in the same position.

PRACTICE TIME

Practice moving around the file by using the cursor move and pan commands until you become familiar with the commands given on the onscreen help menu and you can place the cursor in any field you choose.

SCREEN PRINTOUTS

There are several ways to get hard copies of the information when you are in dBASE III Plus. The simplest way is explained here. Other ways are described in subsequent lessons.

- Check that the printer is on and ready to print.
- Turn off the help menu by pressing the **F1** function key since you do not want the menu to show up in the printout.
- Position the data on the screen so the leftmost field is displayed, and all the records are displayed.
- When you want a printout of the information on the screen, you press the **PrtSc** (Print Screen) key while holding down the **SHIFT** key, denoted **SHIFT/PrtSc**.

Since the record is wider than the screen width, you will need to pan to the right and get a second printout of the file for side-by-side display.

SUM, AVERAGE

Let's do some fancy but easy information retrieval from the database file.

- Exit BROWSE by entering **CTRL/END**.

  > The ASSIST menu is displayed.
- Highlight **Retrieve** on the menu bar.
- Highlight **Sum** on the pull-down menu and press **ENTER**.

  > The action line displays **Command: SUM**.

  > A submenu appears to the right. The **Execute the command** option is already highlighted.

You will see this same submenu a number of times during the next lesson. It will not be discussed here.

- Accept the highlighted option by pressing **ENTER**.

  > The following appears at the bottom of the screen.

```
  13 records summed
BALANCE
4288.46
```

The SUM command (without any options) sums up all the numeric fields on all records and prints the result on the screen. In this case there was only one numeric field, BALANCE, and 13 records.

Now try the AVERAGE option.

- Press any key to get back to the ASSIST menu.

  > **Retrieve** is already selected.

- Highlight **Average** and press **ENTER**.

  > The action line displays **Command: AVERAGE**.

- Press **ENTER** to select the highlighted option.

  > The following is displayed at the bottom of the screen.

```
     13 records averaged
BALANCE
 329.88
```

The AVERAGE command (without any option) calculates the average amount for all the numeric fields for all the records. In this case the average for the BALANCE field for the 13 records was calculated.

- Press any key to get back to the ASSIST menu.

COUNT

The Count option in Retrieve gives the number of records contained in the file. Try it on your own. As you do so, note the dot prompt command displayed on the action line.

WORKING FROM THE DOT PROMPT

You will now go through a similar process of creating a database file, but from the dot prompt. You will see that once you know the commands, entering them from the dot prompt command is not difficult at all. In fact, it is much easier in some cases.

If you recall, the first thing you had to do when creating a file was to tell the computer where (which drive) to store the database file, that is, to specify the default drive. The default drive is set to B.

- From ASSIST, press the **ESC** key to get to the dot prompt.

You will now create a database file called INVENTRY, which is an inventory file. If you recall from the action line (during ASSIST), the command is CREATE. You just have to specify what file you are creating.

- Type CREATE and press **ENTER**.

  > The message **Enter the name of the new file:** appears on the next line.

- Type INVENTRY and press **ENTER**.

  > The screen for specifying database structure is displayed. It is the same screen as the one you saw in ASSIST.

NOTE ■ You could have typed CREATE INVENTRY on one line.

PRACTICE TIME

1. Enter the following structure for the INVENTRY file.

Field No.	*Name*	*Type*	*Width*	*Dec*
1	ITEM_CODE	C	5	
2	DESCRIPTN	C	40	
3	PRICE	N	6	2
4	QUANTITY	N	5	0
5	LAST_SOLD	D	8	

2. Enter the following data. When entering the date, you do not type /'s. Notice that /'s already appear on the screen. To enter 12/21/89, for example, you type 122189.

Item Code:	DX104
Description:	IMwriter ribbon
Price:	5.50
Quantity:	3522
Date Last Sold:	12/21/89
	DX500
	IMwriter, 4 color
	19.00
	496
	11/24/89
	VR502
	K.Itoh 8510 ribbon
	9.25
	400
	12/04/89
	ML799
	Micro 193 ribbon
	8.49
	250
	11/16/89

DX524
Maxon EX800 ribbon
12.75
1250
12/05/89

DX045
Maxon FX80 ribbon
4.40
155
12/01/89

DX250
Disento II ribbon, multistrike
5.09
450
11/28/89

DX460
Galaxy NL10 ribbon
7.75
702
12/01/89

DX205
Mann Tally 1000 ribbon
4.50
654
11/29/89

DX750
Spirit 7 ribbon, multistrike
7.95
325
11/22/89

DX300
NIC P-565 ribbon
10.25
244
11/11/89

DX119
SAM 1300 ribbon, multistrike
4.15
200
11/14/89

When you have finished entering, press **ENTER** again to exit the data entry mode. You return to the dot prompt.

To browse the newly created database file, you use the BROWSE command.

- Type BROWSE and press **ENTER**.

  > You see the browse screen again.

- Check to make sure that it looks as it did when you entered from ASSIST.

PRACTICE TIME Obtain a hard copy of the contents of the database INVENTRY by using **SHIFT/PrtSc**.

- Exit BROWSE by entering **CTRL/END**.

To obtain the sum and average of numeric fields, you use the SUM and AVERAGE commands, as you noted earlier. If you recall, SUM and AVERAGE functions (without any options) work on all numeric fields in the file.

- Type SUM and press **ENTER**.

  > The following is displayed.

```
  12 records summed
PRICE QUANTITY
99.08    8648
```

- Now type AVERAGE and press **ENTER**.

```
  12 records averaged
PRICE QUANTITY
8.26     721
```

Once you know the commands, it is much faster to issue commands through the dot prompt.

USING ANOTHER DATABASE FILE ON THE DISK

From the Dot Prompt

You can use the file ACCOUNTS that was created by using the ASSIST. Note that the third area in the status bar displays INVENTRY.

- Type USE ACCOUNTS and press **ENTER**.
  > The third area on the status bar now displays **ACCOUNTS**. That is, the file ACCOUNTS is now the one in use.

PRACTICE TIME

Issue the SUM and AVERAGE commands from the dot prompt.

Using ASSIST

Now, you will switch back to the INVENTRY file, but this time through ASSIST.

- Type ASSIST and press **ENTER**.
  > The ASSIST screen is displayed.
  > The **Set Up** option is highlighted.
- Highlight **Database file** and press **ENTER**.
  > A submenu, with drive letters, appears to the right.
- Press **ENTER** to accept B.
  > Another submenu appears. This time database files ACCOUNTS.DBF and INVENTRY.DBF are listed, with **ACCOUNTS.DBF** highlighted.
- Highlight **INVENTRY.DBF** and press **ENTER**.
  > A message is displayed, asking **Is this file indexed? [Y/N]**.
- This will be explained in the next lesson. For now press **N** (do not press ENTER).
  > Notice the third area on status bar has changed to **INVENTRY**.

Now you can use the INVENTRY database file. Notice how many more commands it took in ASSIST to switch from one database file to another. The advantage of ASSIST is that you do not have to know the commands (since all the options are listed). Once you are familiar with the commands, however, it is much faster to work through the dot prompt.

END OF LESSON 1

You are now at the end of the first lesson. You must exit the dBASE III Plus program properly to close all the active files. If you exit in any other manner (such as shutting the computer off), you might damage files and lose data. You can exit either through ASSIST or from the dot prompt.

From ASSIST

- Select the **Set Up** option on the menu bar.
- Highlight the last option, **Quit dBASE III PLUS**, and press **ENTER**.
- Remove the disks from both drives.
- Turn OFF both the monitor and the computer.

From the Dot Prompt

- Type QUIT and press **ENTER**.
- Remove the disks from both drives.
- Turn OFF both the monitor and the computer.

SUMMARY

In this lesson many of the terms and concepts that are necessary to use a database management system are introduced.

- A database file is composed of records, which in turn are composed of fields.
- Each field must be given a field name, type, and width.
- A valid field name can be up to 10 characters long. The first character must be a letter, and the name can contain letters, numbers, and underscore (_).
- The commands in dBASE III Plus can be given through ASSIST or from the dot prompt.
- A field can be in one of five types: Character, Numeric, Logical, Date, and Memo.
- ASSIST, or the Assistant, is a feature of dBASE III Plus that leads users through the program from a series of menus.
- Once a user is familiar with commands in dBASE III Plus, commands can be entered at the dot prompt.
- A valid filename is any name from 1 to 8 characters long, consisting of letters, numbers, or any of the following symbols: !, @, #, $, %, and ^. dBASE III Plus automatically adds the extension .DBF to database files.
- SHIFT/PrtSc is used to get a hardcopy of screen display at any time.
- The following commands are discussed:

CREATE	Creates a database file, defines its structure, and allows entry of records

BROWSE	Displays the database in a multiple-record format, one row per record
SUM	Sums all or specified numeric fields for all or specified records in a database
AVERAGE	Averages all or specified numeric fields for all or specified records in a database
COUNT	Counts the number of records in a database that meet specified conditions
SET DEFAULT TO	Instructs dBASE III Plus which drive to use as default for all data files
USE	Specifies which database from disk to use, or to make active
QUIT	Exit to DOS

REVIEW QUESTIONS

1. Explain how fields, records, and files relate to each other. __________

2. What are the five types of fields in dBASE III Plus? __________

3. How do you decide on the width of a character field? a numeric field?

4. What is the advantage of using dBASE III Plus through ASSIST? disadvantages? __________

5. What command lets you exit from the creating structure mode (during CREATE)? __________

6. What does it mean to "pan"? Why do you need to pan? How do you pan?

7. What does it mean during data entry when, before pressing the ENTER key, the computer beeps and the cursor jumps to the next field? ______

8. What can you do during BROWSE? ______

9. Explain the process involved in switching from one database file to another, using ASSIST: ______

From the dot prompt: ______

10. What command can you use to get a printout of what is displayed on the screen? ______

EXERCISES

Exercise 1

1. Create a database file, DB1EX1, of items in inventory. The file is to contain the following fields:

Field No.	*Name*	*Type*	*Width*	*Dec*
1	CODE	C	4	
2	DESCRPTION	C	15	
3	PRICE	N	5	2
4	VENDOR	C	10	
5	QTY	N	4	0

2. Enter the following records:

Code	*Description*	*Price*	*Vendor*	*Qty*
M013	3.5 DISK SSDD	3.22	MemoryRex	720
M073	3.5 DISK DSDD	4.55	MemoryRex	420
F220	5.25 DISK DSDD	2.14	MemoryRex	600

M025	3.5 DISK SSDD	3.40	Maxwell	90
M045	3.5 DISK DSDD	4.22	Maxwell	260
F240	5.25 DISK DSDD	3.10	Maxwell	580
F320	5.25 DISK DSDD	2.85	Dylan	500
M006	3.5 DISK SSDD	3.25	ThreeDee	210
M067	3.5 DISK DSDD	4.38	ThreeDee	740
F144	5.25 DISK DSDD	2.12	ThreeDee	110
M001	3.5 DISK SSDD	2.98	Generic	260
M059	3.5 DISK DSDD	4.04	Generic	520
F153	5.25 DISK DSDD	1.57	Generic	690

3. Browse the records and print the screen display, using SHIFT/PrtSc.
4. Exit dBASE III Plus properly.

Exercise 2

1. Create a database file, DB1EX2, of business people with whom you work. The file is to contain the following fields:

Field No.	*Name*	*Type*	*Width*	*Dec*
1	FIRST__NAME	C	12	
2	LAST__NAME	C	12	
3	COMPANY	C	30	
4	ADDRESS	C	30	
5	CITY	C	15	
6	STATE	C	2	
7	ZIP	C	5	

2. Enter the following records:

Name:	Barry Davenport	Michael Wyndham
Company:	Market Research Inc.	Man of the Future
Address:	226 S. Foothill Dr.	Ten North Madison
City:	Davis	Lake Oswego
State:	CA	OR
Zip:	95616	97034
	Jennifer Barkley	Terry Buchanan
	CPI Consulting	Pomona HiTech
	1000 W. Seventh, Ste. 202	5965 Birch Ave.
	Fullerton	Pomona
	CA	CA
	92634	91767

Mitch Norman	Dallas Hough
Management Consultants	Development Insight
5000 Greenbelt Road	2350 34th Ave.
College Park	Los Angeles
MD	CA
20740	90025
Sandra Donohue	Amber Green
Systematics	Green Improvements
220 Georgia	7501 N. Marquette
Silver Spring	Washington
MD	DC
20901	20022

3. Browse the records and print the screen display using SHIFT/PrtSc.
4. Exit dBASE III Plus properly.

Exercise 3

1. Create a data base file, DB1EX3, of inventory items. The file is to contain the following fields:

Field No.	*Name*	*Type*	*Width*	*Dec*
1	NUMBER	C	5	
2	TYPE	C	3	
3	DESCRPTION	C	25	
4	COST	N	8	2
5	PRICE	N	8	2
6	QUANTITY	N	5	0
7	LOCATION	C	3	

2. Enter the following records:

Number	*Type*	*Description*	*Cost*	*Price*	*Qty*	*Loc*
L1003	UPS	200 watt capacity	195.00	389.00	325	A-8
L1011	UPS	325 watt capacity	240.00	479.00	72	C-1
L1029	UPS	450 watt capacity	315.00	625.00	46	B-1
L1037	UPS	1000 watt capacity	625.00	1249.00	12	A-2
L0005	SSS	modem surge protector	30.00	59.90	880	A-6
L1045	UPS	200 watt capacity	185.00	369.00	470	C-8
L1052	UPS	325 watt capacity	230.00	459.00	112	B-3

L1060	UPS	450 watt capacity	300.00	599.00	35	A-3
L1078	UPS	675 watt capacity	450.00	899.00	60	B-6
L0013	UPS	1800 watt capacity	150.00	299.00	0	A-5
L0047	SSS	2-outlet box	25.00	49.95	1480	C-4
L0054	SSS	4-outlet strip	29.00	57.95	2257	A-7
L0062	SSS	6-outlet strip	33.00	65.95	1326	B-7
L0104	SSS	2-outlet box	33.00	64.95	775	C-7
L0112	SSS	6-outlet strip	38.00	75.95	1843	A-4
L4502	SSS	power controller	50.00	99.85	422	C-5
L4510	SSS	power controller	85.00	169.95	633	B-9

3. Browse the records and print the screen display, using SHIFT/PrtSc.
4. Exit dBASE III Plus properly.

Lesson 2
Manipulating the Data

Objectives

Upon completion of the material presented in this lesson you should be able to do the following:

- Display/list selected records/files in a database.
- Understand the concept of a record pointer and move it around.
- Display/list the database structure.
- Sort records in a database.
- Index records in a database.
- Seek records in an indexed database.
- Delete/recover/pack records in an existing database.
- Add records to an existing database.

STARTING OFF

Start dBASE III Plus on the computer, following instructions given in the introduction to this module, so that the dBASE ASSIST screen is displayed. Insert the data disk from the previous lesson into drive B.

In completing the first lesson, you created and entered information into two database files. You used the BROWSE command to view the contents of each file, and you found out how to use COUNT, SUM, and AVERAGE. Finally, you learned how to print out the screen image.

In this lesson you will see how to retrieve the records you are looking for and how to sort records in alphabetic or numeric order, based on one or more fields. You will also learn how to print selected records and fields in a file. These commands get lots of use in dBASE III Plus, and by using them you should begin to feel more comfortable using the program. Again, commands are entered by using both the ASSIST and the dot prompt.

DIRECTORY

The first thing you normally want to do is to let the program know which database file you plan to use. Do you remember the name of the file you created in the first lesson? dBASE III Plus has a command that allows you to print the names of files on your disk.

From ASSIST

- Highlight the option **Tools**.
- Highlight **Directory** and press **ENTER**.
  > The action line displays **Command: DIR**.
  > A submenu appears to the left, listing disk drives.
- Highlight the drive **B** and press **ENTER**.
  > The action line displays **Command: DIR B:**.
  > The disk drive submenu is replaced with the one giving 10 options for file type.

dBASE III Plus is asking you if you want to display the names of only a specific type of file or all filenames. dBASE III Plus generates nine different file types, identified by the extensions in their filenames. Database files have the extension .DBF. As other file types are introduced, they will be described. Right now you want to display the names of only the database files.

- Select **.dbf Database Files**, which is already highlighted, by pressing **ENTER**.
  > The screen shows the names of the database files that are on drive B.
  > **ACCOUNTS.DBF** and **INVENTRY.DBF** are listed.
- Press any key to continue.
  > The ASSIST menu is displayed.

From the Dot Prompt

The command to display the directory is similar to the one used in DOS. You may even use the wildcard character *.

- Press the **ESC** key to exit to dot prompt.

- Type DIR *.DBF and press **ENTER**.

  > The files with .DBF extensions are listed.

Database files on a disk are like a collection of files (in file folders) in a file cabinet. When you want to use a file that is in a file cabinet, you get the file from the cabinet, place it on your desk, and open the folder to begin using the file. When you are finished using the file, you place all the papers back into the folder, close the folder, and place it back into the file cabinet. Similarly, to use a database file that is on disk, you need to place it into the computer's memory so that it is open for you to work with. This process is called *opening a file*. A file is opened when you select it for use. When a file is no longer needed, then it should be recorded back onto the disk, so that its changes are stored properly. This is called *closing the file*. A file is automatically closed either when you open another file for usage or when you exit dBASE.

OPENING A FILE

You want to open the file ACCOUNTS. You will recognize that you've done this once before in Lesson 1, when switching to another database file on the data disk. You can open the file either through ASSIST or from the dot prompt.

From ASSIST

- Make sure that you are in ASSIST.

  > The option **Set Up** is highlighted.

- Highlight **Database file** and press **ENTER**.
- Highlight **B:** for drive B and press **ENTER**.
- Highlight **ACCOUNTS.DBF** and press **ENTER**.
- Type N (do not press ENTER) to the question about index.

  > The status bar shows the file named **ACCOUNTS** has been opened.

From the Dot Prompt

- Make sure that you are in the dot prompt mode.
- Type USE ACCOUNTS and press **ENTER**.

THE DISPLAY/LIST COMMANDS

If you do not remember the data entered into the file in the first lesson, you can use the DISPLAY or LIST command to review file content. The DISPLAY and LIST commands allow you to look at the data in the file. Unlike BROWSE, you cannot change data or enter new records through the use of the DISPLAY or LIST command.

The DISPLAY and LIST commands are almost identical. The difference is that DISPLAY is geared more for displaying on the screen, and LIST is used for listing on the printer. In fact, when you are in ASSIST, you *cannot* send the result of DISPLAY to the printer; you can send the result to the printer only from LIST. Also, when you use the DISPLAY command, the program pauses when the screen is full, and a message appears at the bottom of the screen asking you to press any key to continue. This message appears even when you send the output to the printer (and you probably do not want the message printed). The LIST command lists all the records without pausing. If you list a large database file to the screen, the information will scroll right through!

From ASSIST

- From the ASSIST menu highlight **Retrieve**.
- Highlight **Display** and press **ENTER**.

  > The action line shows **Command: DISPLAY**.

  > A submenu appears to the right.

The submenu shows five options you have at this point. The first option carries out the command DISPLAY. Let's see what happens when you carry out the command right now.

- With **Execute the command** highlighted, press **ENTER**.

  > Only the first record is displayed.

The other options in the submenu let you specify what you want displayed. The program keeps track of all the records and their record numbers. Furthermore, there is a record pointer that is moved as the program carries out the command. When you issue the DISPLAY command without setting the other options, the program displays only the record the pointer is set to, or the *current record*. The present position of the pointer is displayed on the fourth area of the status bar: 1/13 – the first of thirteen records.

Let's specify other options.

- Press any key to continue.
- Highlight **Display** (in Retrieve) and press **ENTER**.

  > Note the action line.

- Highlight **Specify scope** and press **ENTER**.

  > A submenu appears below the previous menu.

This is where you specify the scope of records to display. If the scope is omitted, the display refers only to the current record. Right now you want to see all the records.

- Highlight **ALL** and press **ENTER**.

  > The action line shows **Command: DISPLAY ALL**.

  > The words **Specify scope** change coloring on the menu, indicating that you have set the scope. This selection is no longer available for the current DISPLAY command option.

- Highlight **Execute the command** and press **ENTER**.

  > The screen shown in Screen Display 2-1 appears.

The contents of the first 7 records in the file are displayed on the screen, two lines per record. At the bottom is the message:

```
Press any key to continue. . .
```

```
 Set Up  Create  Update  Position  Retrieve  Organize Modify Tools  05:38:25 pm



Record#  FIRST_NAME   LAST_NAME    ADDRESS                         CITY
  STATE ZIP   TELEPHONE      BALANCE
      1  Robert       Castillo     112 South Broadway              Sparks
  NV    89431 (702) 358-0200  247.50
      2  Harold       Smith        885 North McCarran              Reno
  NV    89512 (702) 788-9120   29.75
      3  Judy         Davenport    555 Timber Lane                 Truckee
  CA    95734 (916) 966-0722  178.90
      4  Irene        Orwell       12575 Sun Valley Blvd.          Sun Valley
  NV    89433 (702) 673-9800  860.00
      5  Jonathan     Handel       1001 East Fourth Street         Reno
  NV    89501 (702) 786-0905   76.24
      6  Chico        Juarez       72 Mill Road                    Floriston
  CA    96111 (916) 479-3205  312.12
      7  Sandy        O'Dell       2219 Carson Highway             Carson City
  NV    89701 (702) 234-0776    4.49
Press any key to continue..._
ASSIST          ||<B:>||ACCOUNTS             ||Rec: 1/13          ||      ||Num
```

Screen Display 2-1

- Press any key.

  > The screen scrolls up, and the last five records of the file are displayed.

NOTE ■ Another difference between the LIST command and the DISPLAY command is that the default display for the DISPLAY command is the current record, while the default display for the LIST command is ALL.

The screen is merely an output device, not a record of everything that exists in memory. If the screen is full and the program has more information to display on the screen, the screen scrolls up. That means that the information on the screen moves up one line, so that the bottom line is available for the new information to be displayed. The information that was previously on the top line of the screen has scrolled off.

- Press any key to go back to the ASSIST menu.

PRACTICE TIME

Do the same with the LIST command. Notice that the program does not pause when the screen is full.

From the Dot Prompt

Do you recall the equivalent dot prompt command that was displayed on the action line?

- Press the **ESC** key to get to the dot prompt.
- Type DISPLAY ALL and press ENTER.

  > The first eight records are displayed.

- Press any key.

  > The rest of the records are displayed.

  > A dot prompt is displayed.

- Now type LIST ALL and press ENTER.

THE HELP COMMAND (F1)

You may wonder just how to enter a command for certain results, or, as now, how to enter the command you used in ASSIST from the dot prompt. The dBASE manual is one way to find out. There is also a useful HELP command (F1) that can show you the information you might usually need.

Try this with the DISPLAY command.

- From the ASSIST menu, highlight **Retrieve**.
- Highlight **Display**, but do not press ENTER.
- Press the **F1** function key.

  > The screen shown in Screen Display 2-2 appears.

The F1 function key gives the help for the command you have highlighted on the ASSIST menu. The screen is designed to be self-explanatory, but it may take a certain amount of experience before you can understand all the options. The parts enclosed in brackets, [], are optional. The words given in uppercase are keywords. A keyword is a reserved word that dBASE III Plus recognizes as a part of the command. Keywords are used to indicate certain options of the command. They include ALL, TO PRINT, OFF, FIELDS, FOR, and WHILE.

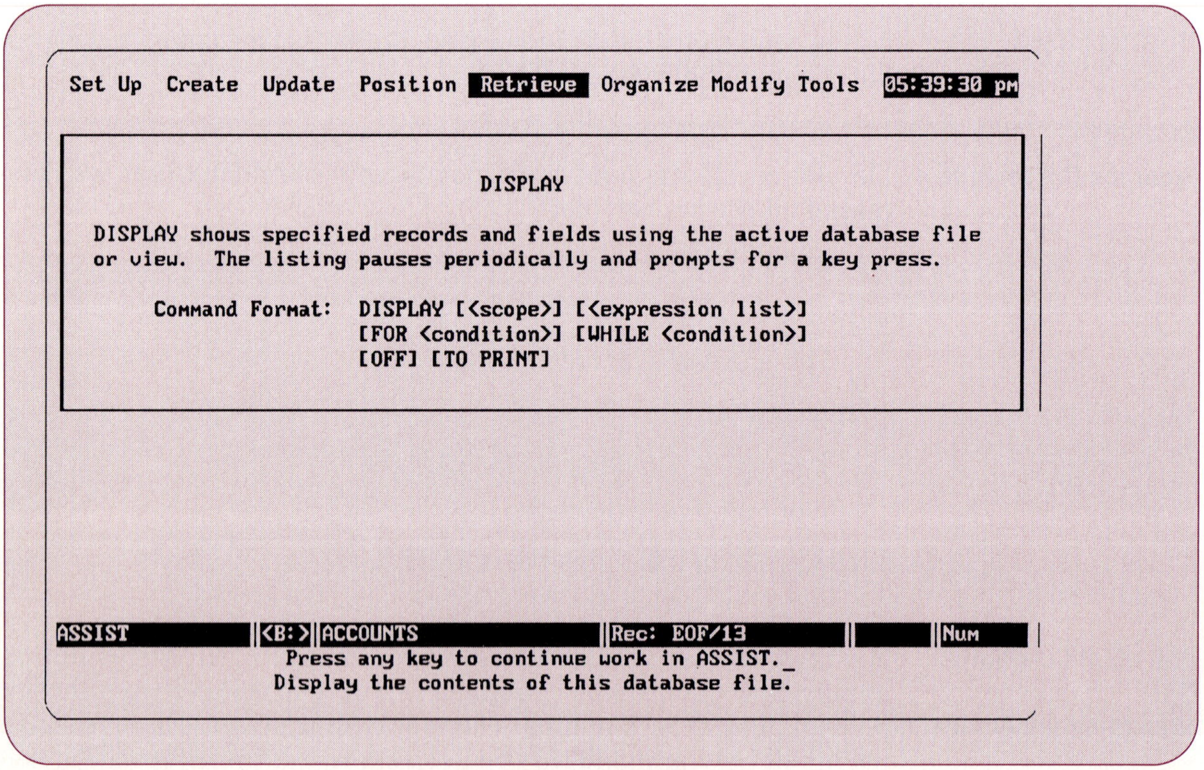

Screen Display 2-2

In the DISPLAY command, everything except the command itself is enclosed in brackets [is optional]. You specify the level of detail you need. The following is a summary of the various options available for the DISPLAY command:

- [<scope>] allows the user to choose a scope for display. If the scope is omitted, the display refers only to the current record. Possible entries for scope are ALL, NEXT *n*, and RECORD *n*, where *n* is a number. NEXT 5 means to display the next 5 records, beginning with the current record, and RECORD 8 means to display only record number 8.
- [<expression list>] allows you to name the fields or functions you want displayed. The field list is a series of field names, separated by commas, to be displayed.
- [FOR <condition>] means that all records that meet the specified condition are displayed.
- [WHILE <condition>] means that all records are displayed until the first record is reached where the specified condition is not met, and all subsequent records are not displayed, regardless of whether or not they meet the condition.
- [OFF] means do not precede the records with the record numbers.
- [TO PRINT] means to direct the output to the printer (rather than to the screen). This is not available when issuing the DISPLAY command through ASSIST.

- Press any key to go back to ASSIST.

RECORD POINTER

As noted previously, dBASE III Plus keeps track of the records in the database file. That is, you could ask it to display record 3 if you choose. dBASE III Plus also has a record pointer, which points to the current record. The current record number is displayed on the fourth area in the status bar.

PRACTICE TIME

Display the current record, either from ASSIST or from the dot prompt. That is, issue the DISPLAY command without any options. You should get just the headings for the fields without any data.

When the DISPLAY ALL command is carried out, as a record is displayed, the record pointer moves down the records in the file. When done, the record pointer points below the last record in the file.

In fact, the fourth area on the status bar shows EOF/13, meaning that the record pointer is on EOF (End of File) of 13 records.

You need to reposition the record pointer, probably to the beginning of the file. The pointer can be moved by using the GOTO, SEEK, and DISPLAY commands, which are options of the Position command of the ASSIST menu.

THE GOTO COMMAND

From ASSIST

- Highlight **Position** on the menu bar.
- Highlight the last option, **Go to Record**, and press **ENTER**.
  > The action line displays **Command: GOTO**.

  > A submenu appears to the right with three options: **TOP**, **BOTTOM**, and **RECORD**.

TOP sends the record pointer to the first record in the file, BOTTOM sends the record pointer to the last record in the file, and RECORD sends the pointer to whichever record you want (you get to specify which record).

You want to send the pointer to the TOP. Notice the status bar saying EOF/13.

- Highlight **TOP** and press **ENTER**.
  > The action line displays **Command: GOTO TOP** for a split second.

  > The ASSIST menu is displayed again as though nothing happened, but the fourth area on the status bar shows 1/13, meaning that the record pointer is on the first record of the 13-record file.

From the Dot Prompt

- From the dot prompt type GOTO BOTTOM and press **ENTER**.
  > The status bar shows 13/13.
- Now type GOTO RECORD 7 and press **ENTER**.
  > The status bar shows 7/13.
- Display the current record.
  > The record on Sandy O'Dell is displayed.
- Type GOTO TOP to send the cursor to the beginning of the file.

PRACTICE TIME

You may use either ASSIST or the dot prompt command.

1. Display the current record. The first record, that of Robert Castillo, should be displayed.
2. Change the position of the record pointer and display the current record again. Do this several times until you feel comfortable with the procedure.

DISPLAYING SELECTED FIELDS

So far you have not indicated which fields in the record you want displayed. Hence all the fields in the record at the record pointer were shown. There is an option to specify which fields.

NOTE ▪ All options specified for DISPLAY apply also to the LIST command. DISPLAY is used here since most of the output is to the screen.

From ASSIST

- Highlight **Retrieve** on the menu bar.
- Highlight **Display** on the pull-down menu and press ENTER.

  > The Action line displays **Command: DISPLAY**.

The third option on the submenu is for specifying the fields.

- Highlight **Construct a field list** and press ENTER.

  > Another submenu appears to the left, listing all the fields on the record.

  > A box in the middle gives information about the field that is highlighted.

You are to specify which fields you want displayed. Let's say that you want to display only the first name, last name, and telephone number for all the customers. Fields will be displayed in the order they were selected.

- Highlight FIRST__NAME and press ENTER.

  > The coloring of FIRST__NAME on the submenu changes, indicating that this field has been selected for display.

  > The Action line displays **Command: DISPLAY FIRST__NAME**.

  > The cursor moves to the next field.

- Similarly, highlight and press **ENTER** for fields **LAST__NAME** and **TELEPHONE**.

  > The Action line displays **Command: DISPLAY FIRST__NAME, LAST__NAME, TELEPHONE**.

- Press either the **LEFT ARROW** or the **RIGHT ARROW** key to leave this menu.

  > The selection **Construct a field list** has changed coloring on the submenu.

PRACTICE TIME

1. Specify the scope to ALL. Make sure to note what appears on the Action line.
2. Execute the command. Your screen should look like the one in Screen Display 2-3.

```
 Set Up  Create  Update  Position  Retrieve  Organize Modify Tools  05:40:32 pm






Record#  FIRST_NAME   LAST_NAME    TELEPHONE
      1  Robert       Castillo     (702) 358-0200
      2  Harold       Smith        (702) 788-9120
      3  Judy         Davenport    (916) 966-0722
      4  Irene        Orwell       (702) 673-9800
      5  Jonathan     Handel       (702) 786-0905
      6  Chico        Juarez       (916) 479-3205
      7  Sandy        O'Dell       (702) 234-0776
      8  Julio        Chavez       (916) 968-2335
      9  Larry        Fisher       (702) 329-4405
     10  Jennifer     Bacon        (916) 477-6705
     11  Cindy        Beard        (702) 323-6220
     12  Abdul        Ahmad        (702) 847-3562
     13  Mandy        Vario        (702) 246-0171
ASSIST          ||<B:>||ACCOUNTS            ||Rec: EOF/13      ||      ||Num
                  Press any key to continue work in ASSIST._
```

Screen Display 2-3

From the Dot Prompt

Let's try the same command from the dot prompt.

- From ASSIST press the **ESC** key.
- Type DISPLAY FIRST_NAME, LAST_NAME, TELEPHONE ALL and press **ENTER**.

  > You get the same result.

Now you will use the LIST command to display the same records and the same fields, but you will send the result to the printer.

- Make sure that the printer is turned on and is ready to use.
- Type LIST FIRST_NAME, LAST_NAME, TELEPHONE ALL TO PRINT and press **ENTER**.

  > The selected records are printed on the printer.

NOTE ■ You might notice that the last record that was displayed on the screen was not printed on the printer. This is a little problem with the dBASE III Plus program. To get the last record printed, type **EJECT** and press **ENTER**.

DISPLAYING SELECTED RECORDS

You also have the option of specifying only some of the records rather than all of them. If you want to select some records, you must first position the record pointer at the top of the file, since the search for a selection begins at the current record.

PRACTICE TIME

Position the record pointer at the beginning of the file.

Suppose you are to display fields LAST_NAME, FIRST_NAME, and TELEPHONE for only those customers who reside in California. You can use the **Build a search condition** option on the submenu.

From ASSIST

This time you will use the LIST command and send the result to the printer.

- Highlight **Retrieve** on the menu bar.
- Highlight **List** on the pull-down menu and press **ENTER**.
- Highlight **Construct a field list** and press **ENTER**.
- Select **FIRST_NAME, LAST_NAME**, and **TELEPHONE** fields to be displayed and press either **LEFT ARROW** or **RIGHT ARROW** key.

- Highlight **Build a search condition** and press ENTER.
  > A submenu appears, listing all the fields in the record, and a box in the middle describes the field that is highlighted.

You want to select all the records for which the STATE field is CA.

- Select **STATE** and press **ENTER**.
  > The Action line displays **Command: LIST FIRST__NAME, LAST __NAME, TELEPHONE FOR STATE**.

  > A submenu appears, listing all the logical operators.

You are looking for the equals condition.

- Select **= Equal To** and press **ENTER**.
  > The Action line displays **Command: LIST FIRST__NAME, LAST __NAME, TELEPHONE FOR STATE='**.

  > The following message appears:

  ```
  Enter a character string (without quotes):
  ```

You want the records where the state is equal to CA. When you enter the comparison value, it must match exactly, both with regard to the character string, and with regard to upper- and lowercase letters.

- Type CA (no ENTER).
  > The computer beeps and a submenu appears to the right of the screen asking if there is more than one condition to be met by the records selected.

  > The Action line displays **Command: LIST FIRST__NAME, LAST __NAME, TELEPHONE FOR STATE='CA'**.

There are no other conditions.

- Select **No more conditions** and press **ENTER**.
- Highlight **Execute the command** and press **ENTER**.
  > A box appears with the question **Direct the output to the printer? [Y/N]**.

If you answer N, the result is sent to the screen. You want them to be printed.

- Make sure that the printer is turned on and is ready to use.
- Type Y (do not press ENTER).
  > Selected records are printed.

NOTE ■ Again, you might notice that the last record that meets the condition is not printed. (There should be four records.) Exit to the dot prompt and enter **EJECT**.

From the Dot Prompt

You will use the DISPLAY command this time.

- Type DISPLAY FIRST_NAME, LAST_NAME, TELEPHONE FOR STATE='CA' and press **ENTER**.

THE DISPLAY/LIST STRUCTURE COMMAND

When you are interested in displaying some fields in your database file, there may be a problem if you have forgotten the field names. There are several ways you could find out the field names. One way is to display the structure of the file. This gives the field names, types, and widths.

From ASSIST

- Highlight **Tools** on the menu bar.
- Highlight **List structure** on the pull-down menu and press **ENTER**.

> The Action line displays **Command: DISPLAY STRUCTURE**.

> The following message is displayed:

```
Direct the output to the printer? [Y/N]
```

dBASE wants to know if you want this information printed. You want it on the screen.

- Type N (no ENTER).

> The screen shown in Screen Display 2-4 is displayed.

- Press any key to return to ASSIST.

From the Dot Prompt

- Type DISPLAY STRUCTURE and press **ENTER**. (If you want it to print to the printer, you type **DISPLAY STRUCTURE TO PRINT**.)

PRACTICE TIME

Use the DISPLAY command to accomplish the following tasks. You may use either ASSIST or the dot prompt commands. Remember, you may have to reposition the record pointer at the top of the file between DISPLAY commands.

1. Display all the customer names.
2. Display all records, but only the last name, first name, and balance for each customer.

3. Display only the fields last name, first name, and balance for only those records with balance less than or equal to 500.00.
4. Display all fields for record number 6.

THE SORT COMMAND

Sometimes it is necessary to arrange the records of a file in a particular sequence. A file consisting of golfers' scores at a tournament might be arranged in ascending order (from lowest to highest) to find out who finished in which place. As an alternative, it might be necessary to print out the names in alphabetical order. Such arranging of records in a particular order is called *sorting*. There are two ways that dBASE III Plus arranges files in order. You will be introduced to both methods.

The first way is the SORT command, which sorts a file on one or more fields, in ascending or descending order, as you choose. The accompanying diagram shows how SORT works. The filenames shown in these boxes serve to indicate that two files are involved.

```
 Set Up  Create  Update  Position  Retrieve  Organize Modify Tools  05:41:50 pm






Structure for database: B:ACCOUNTS.dbf
Number of data records:       13
Date of last update   : 05/21/89
Field  Field Name  Type       Width    Dec
    1  FIRST_NAME  Character     12
    2  LAST_NAME   Character     12
    3  ADDRESS     Character     30
    4  CITY        Character     15
    5  STATE       Character      2
    6  ZIP         Character      5
    7  TELEPHONE   Character     14
    8  BALANCE     Numeric        7      2
** Total **                      98

ASSIST          ||<B:>||ACCOUNTS           ||Rec: EOF/13       ||      ||Num
                    Press any key to continue work in ASSIST._
```

Screen Display 2-4

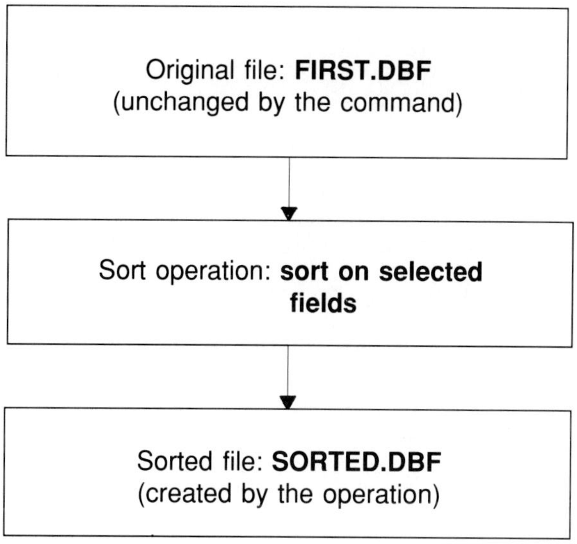

When the SORT command is performed on a file in use, a new database file is created, which consists of all the data in the original database file. However, the records in the new file are arranged in the sorted sequence. If you change the contents of a record or add records to the original file, the sorted file is not updated unless you issue the SORT command again.

The sorted file is created on disk. That is, it is not open. If you want to use the sorted file, you have to specify it for use. If the new file has the same name as an existing database file, it overwrites the previous contents.

You will now SORT the ACCOUNTS file so that the entries are alphabetical by last name. You will call the sorted file CUSTNAME.

From ASSIST

- From the ASSIST menu highlight **Organize** on the menu bar.
- Highlight **Sort** on the pull-down menu and press **ENTER**.

  > The Action line displays **Command: SORT ON**.

  > A submenu listing all the field names is displayed along with a box describing the field name that is highlighted.

dBASE III Plus wants to know which field to sort on. You want the file alphabetized by last name.

- Select **LAST_NAME** and press **ENTER**.

  > The Action line displays **Command: SORT ON LAST_NAME**.

> The coloring of **LAST__NAME** changes on the submenu, indicating that the field has been selected.

- Press either the **RIGHT ARROW** or **LEFT ARROW** key to leave the menu.

> A submenu appears to the right, showing disk drives.

You want the sorted file created on the data disk in drive B.

- Select **B:** and press **ENTER**.

> The Action line displays **Command: SORT ON LAST__NAME TO B:**.

> A box appears in the middle, requesting that you enter the name for the sorted file to be created on the disk in drive B.

- Type CUSTNAME and press **ENTER**.

> The Action line displays **Command: SORT ON LAST__NAME TO B:CUSTNAME** for a split second.

> After a little while the following message appears just above the status bar.

```
100% Sorted        13 Records sorted
```

The file ACCOUNTS is still open. CUSTNAME is stored on disk. To see what happened, you need to open file CUSTNAME.

- Press any key to continue work in ASSIST.
- Highlight **Set Up** on the menu bar.
- Highlight **Database file** on the pull-down menu and press **ENTER**.
- Highlight **B:** and press **ENTER**.
- Highlight **CUSTNAME.DBF** and press **ENTER**.
- Type N (no ENTER) in response to the question **Is the file indexed?**

> The status bar indicates that **CUSTNAME** is the file in use.

- Display just the last name for all records.

> The file is in alphabetical order by last name, as shown in Screen Display 2-5.

From the Dot Prompt

Rather than sorting on the same field (LAST__NAME), you will now sort in ascending order by balance. Before doing so, you must specify the usage of ACCOUNTS file again.

```
 Set Up  Create  Update  Position  Retrieve  Organize Modify Tools  05:43:10 pm




Record#  LAST_NAME
      1  Ahmad
      2  Bacon
      3  Beard
      4  Castillo
      5  Chavez
      6  Davenport
      7  Fisher
      8  Handel
      9  Juarez
     10  O'Dell
     11  Orwell
     12  Smith
     13  Vario
ASSIST          ||<B:>||CUSTNAME           ||Rec: 1/13        ||      ||Num  |
                    Press any key to continue work in ASSIST._
```

Screen Display 2-5

- Type USE ACCOUNTS and press ENTER.

You can place the sorted file on the file CUSTNAME once more, but if you do, you overwrite the existing information. You will place the sorted records on the file CUSTBAL.

- Type SORT ON BALANCE TO CUSTBAL.
- Type USE CUSTBAL.
- Display LAST__NAME and BALANCE fields for all customers.

  > The file is in order by balance amount, as seen in Screen Display 2-6.

You can also sort on multiple fields. That is, you can specify more than one field as sort key. If there are several records with identical values for the first field, the second field is used to break the tie. For example, suppose you would like a list by city and state (all cities in one state, with states in alphabetical order, followed by all cities in the next state, and so on); then you want the file sorted by state and city, in that order.

```
(DEMO) . use accounts
(DEMO) . sort on balance to custbal
  100% Sorted             13 Records sorted
(DEMO) . use custbal
(DEMO) . display last_name, balance all
Record#  last_name     balance
      1  O'Dell           4.49
      2  Ahmad            9.80
      3  Smith           29.75
      4  Handel          76.24
      5  Bacon          142.45
      6  Davenport      178.90
      7  Castillo       247.50
      8  Fisher         278.98
      9  Juarez         312.12
     10  Vario          442.45
     11  Chavez         782.38
     12  Orwell         860.00
     13  Beard          923.40
(DEMO) . _
Command Line  ||<B:>||CUSTBAL               ||Rec: EOF/13    ||     ||Num    |

                         Enter a dBASE III PLUS command.
```

Screen Display 2-6

In ASSIST, as you specify the sort fields, make sure to select fields in the order you want the sort performed. In the example just stated, make sure to select STATE first, then CITY. From the dot prompt it is just a matter of stating the sort fields in order, separated by commas (e.g., SORT ON STATE, CITY TO . . .).

PRACTICE TIME

You may do the following in either the ASSIST mode or the dot prompt command.

1. Sort the file ACCOUNTS by zip code and place the sorted file on CUSTZIP.
2. Sort the file ACCOUNTS by state and city, and place the sorted file on CUSTCITY.

Make sure to display the sorted file to check the result.

THE INDEX COMMAND

In addition to the SORT command, dBASE III Plus contains an Index command that performs sequencing in a different way. While Sort actually rearranges records in the file and creates a new database file, Index creates an index file (extension .NDX) that allows records in the database file to be displayed in the specified sequence. When an index file is active, if you change an entry or enter a new record, the index file is updated automatically, and the records are still displayed in the specified sequence.

To index a file requires two steps. First, you Index the file, establishing an .NDX file. If you wish, you can Index the file several times, establishing different .NDX files for different fields. Second, you have to specify which index file is being used (made active). You can have more than one index file active at a time, but only the first index file is the master index. (The records in the database are displayed, based on this index.) The other index files are set active to keep them current (updated) if any changes are made to the database file. This may seem confusing at first, but you should be able to get the hang of it fairly soon. You will now index the file ACCOUNTS on last names.

From ASSIST

- Make sure that ACCOUNTS is in use.
- From the ASSIST menu, highlight **Organize** on the menu bar.
- Highlight **Index** on the pull-down menu and press **ENTER**.

  > The Action line shows **Command: INDEX ON**.

  > A box appears in the middle of the screen, asking you for the name of the field to index on.

NOTE ■ If you forget the field names, press the F10 function key. The field names and the description of the highlighted field appear on the screen. You can select the fields in the usual manner.

You want to index on the last names, LAST_NAME field.

- Type LAST_NAME and press **ENTER**.

  > The Action line displays **Command: INDEX ON LAST_NAME TO**.

  > A submenu appears to the right, listing disk drives.

You want the .NDX file to be created on the disk in drive B.

- Select **B:** and press **ENTER**.

> The Action line displays **Command: INDEX ON LAST_NAME TO B:**.

> A box appears, asking you to enter a name for the .NDX file.

You will call this file LAST.

- Type LAST and press **ENTER**.

> The Action line displays **Command: INDEX ON LAST_NAME TO B:LAST** for a split second.

> The following message appears on the screen.

```
100% indexed        13 Records indexed
```

- Press any key to continue work in ASSIST.

So far you have set up an index file, LAST.NDX, which you can use to place your database file in alphabetical order by last name. You will now see how to make the index file active so it can continually keep ACCOUNTS alphabetized.

dBASE III Plus automatically sets the index file just created active. If any other index files were active when you created a new index, they are no longer active.

- From the ASSIST menu, highlight **Set Up** on the menu bar.
- Highlight **Database file** on the pull-down menu and press **ENTER**.
- Select drive **B:** and press **ENTER**.
- Select **ACCOUNTS.DBF** and press **ENTER**.
- To the question **Is the file indexed?**, answer by typing **Y** (no ENTER).

> A submenu listing all the .NDX files appears on the screen.

- Select **LAST.NDX** and press **ENTER**.

> The action line displays **Command: USE B:ACCOUNTS INDEX LAST**.

> The word **Master** appears next to **LAST.NDX**, indicating the ACCOUNTS file is sequenced by using this index.

Other .NDX files you might make active at this time will be used only to keep them updated.

Now let's see whether you have alphabetized the file.

- Use **RIGHT ARROW** or **LEFT ARROW** key to exit the submenu.

- Display fields LAST__NAME and FIRST__NAME on all records in the file ACCOUNTS. Your screen should look like the one in Screen Display 2-7.

Notice that the record numbers on the first column are not in numerical sequence although the records are displayed in alphabetic order by last name. This is because the records were not physically rearranged.

To be sure that the index file is always working, let's see what happens if you change an entry that affects the sequencing of the file. You will see this in BROWSE. Do you remember how to get into BROWSE?

- Press any key to continue.
- From the ASSIST menu highlight **Update** on the menu bar.
- Highlight **Browse** on the pull-down menu and press **ENTER**.

  > Only the very last record is displayed.

```
 Set Up  Create  Update  Position  Retrieve  Organize  Modify  Tools  05:48:32 pm




Record#  LAST_NAME    FIRST_NAME
     12  Ahmad        Abdul
     10  Bacon        Jennifer
     11  Beard        Cindy
      1  Castillo     Robert
      8  Chavez       Julio
      3  Davenport    Judy
      9  Fisher       Larry
      5  Handel       Jonathan
      6  Juarez       Chico
      7  O'Dell       Sandy
      4  Orwell       Irene
      2  Smith        Harold
     13  Vario        Mandy
ASSIST        ||<B:>||ACCOUNTS           ||Rec: 12/13        ||      ||Num    |
             Press any key to continue work in ASSIST._
```

Screen Display 2-7

- Press the **F1** function key.
- Press the **UP ARROW** key repeatedly until all 13 records are displayed.
- Place the cursor on the record for Castillo, using the **DOWN ARROW** key.
- Place the cursor on the "C" of "Castillo" by using the **RIGHT ARROW** or **LEFT ARROW** key, then type Woodrum.
- Press the **UP ARROW** key once.

  > Robert Woodrum's record (no longer Robert Castillo's) moved to the bottom of the screen, thus keeping the display of records in alphabetical sequence by last name.

- When you understand how the file behaves, change Woodrum's last name back to **Castillo** and again press the **UP ARROW** key once.
- Press **CTRL/END** to get back to ASSIST.

From the Dot Prompt

You will index the file ACCOUNTS on city.

- Type INDEX ON CITY TO CITY.
- Display fields LAST_NAME, CITY, and STATE for all records. Your screen should look like the one in Screen Display 2-8.

Suppose you want the names within a city in alphabetic order. This is similar to sorting CITY in LAST_NAME sequence. With the Sort command, you specified the fields in sort order, separated by a comma. This time you specify the fields with a plus sign (+) placed in between.

You will re-index to the CITY.NDX file.

- Type INDEX ON CITY+LAST_NAME TO CITY and press **ENTER**.

  > The message **CITY.ndx already exists, overwrite it? (Y/N)** appears.

- Type Y (do not press ENTER).
- Display fields LAST_NAME, CITY, and STATE for all records.

PRACTICE TIME

Make CITY.NDX and LAST.NDX active, with CITY.NDX as the master. You can use the dot prompt or the ASSIST. If you use the dot prompt, the CITY.NDX must be specified first. If you use the ASSIST, the CITY.NDX must be selected first. An index file that is not made active will not be updated when the database changes. Hence if it is made the master index at some later time, the result is unpredictable.

THE SEEK COMMAND

Earlier, you learned how to move the record pointer to a specific record, using the GOTO command. That command only lets you point to a record number, the beginning of the file, or the end of the file. It does not let you point to a record by specifying its contents. For example, given a database file on inventory, you may want to point to a record that contains a specific part number. When a file is indexed, you can use the SEEK command to locate a record containing a specific expression for the field that is indexed.

You will now move the record pointer to the record that contains Dayton as the city. Make sure that you have specified the ACCOUNTS file for usage and CITY.NDX as the master index file. SEEK works only on the content of the master index field.

```
(DEMO) . index on city to city
  100% indexed          13 Records indexed
(DEMO) . display last_name, city, state all
Record#  last_name    city            state
      7  O'Dell       Carson City     NV
     10  Bacon        Chilcoot        CA
     13  Vario        Dayton          NV
      6  Juarez       Floriston       CA
      2  Smith        Reno            NV
      5  Handel       Reno            NV
      9  Fisher       Reno            NV
     11  Beard        Reno            NV
      1  Castillo     Sparks          NV
      4  Orwell       Sun Valley      NV
      3  Davenport    Truckee         CA
      8  Chavez       Truckee         CA
     12  Ahmad        Virginia City   NV
(DEMO) . _
Command Line  ||<B:>||ACCOUNTS          ||Rec: EOF/13       ||     ||Num

                 Enter a dBASE III PLUS command.
```

Screen Display 2-8

```
(DEMO) . index on city+last_name to city
city.ndx already exists, overwrite it? (Y/N) Yes
  100% indexed           13 Records indexed
(DEMO) . display last_name, city, state all
Record#  last_name    city           state
      7  O'Dell       Carson City    NV
     10  Bacon        Chilcoot       CA
     13  Vario        Dayton         NV
      6  Juarez       Floriston      CA
     11  Beard        Reno           NV
      9  Fisher       Reno           NV
      5  Handel       Reno           NV
      2  Smith        Reno           NV
      1  Castillo     Sparks         NV
      4  Orwell       Sun Valley     NV
      8  Chavez       Truckee        CA
      3  Davenport    Truckee        CA
     12  Ahmed        Virginia City  NV
(DEMO) .
Command Line    ||<B:>||ACCOUNTS          ||Rec: EOF/13       ||       ||Num

                     Enter a dBASE III PLUS command.
```

Screen Display 2-9

From ASSIST

- From the ASSIST menu highlight **Position** on the menu bar.
- Highlight **Seek** on the pull-down menu and press **ENTER**.
  > The action line displays **Command: SEEK**.
  > The following message appears:

  `Enter an expression:`

It wants to know what expression for the field CITY you are looking for. You are looking for the city of Dayton. Since Dayton is not numeric, it must be enclosed in either apostrophes or quotes (' or "). Also, upper and lowercase do matter here.

- Note the fourth area in the status bar that shows the current location.
- Type 'Dayton' and press **ENTER**.
  > Nothing happens.
- Press any key to get back to the ASSIST menu.
  > The status bar now shows 13/13.

Now that the record pointer is positioned, let's see if it's on the record with CITY = 'Dayton.' Do you remember how to display the current record?

- Highlight **Retrieve** on the menu bar.
- Highlight **Display** on the pull-down menu and press **ENTER**.
- Select **Execute the command**, which is already highlighted, and press **ENTER**.
  > Mandy Vario's record is displayed. She lives in Dayton and is the 13th record.

From the Dot Prompt

You will seek a record based on the last name field. The person you are looking for is Jennifer Bacon.

- Make the index file LAST the master index.
- Type SEEK 'Bacon' and press **ENTER**.

PRACTICE TIME

1. Display fields LAST__NAME, FIRST__NAME, and TELEPHONE for Jennifer Bacon's record.
2. Get a hard copy of her record by using either the TO PRINT option or SHIFT/PrtSc.

The SEEK command is a fast way to search through large database files. It is, however, restricted to search for data in the indexed field only.

KEEPING A DATABASE CURRENT

A database is a dynamic thing. One of the features of dBASE III Plus is the ability to update data in the database, to keep it current. You have seen some of the features of dBASE III Plus. Now you will find out how dBASE III Plus handles the deletion and insertion of individual records in a database.

THE DELETE COMMAND

You have just found out that Larry Fisher does not want to do business with you anymore. He paid up the balance, and there is no purpose in continuing to carry his record in the database. You will delete it.

From ASSIST

- From the ASSIST menu highlight **Update** on the menu bar.
- Highlight **Delete** on the pull-down menu and press **ENTER**.

> The action line displays **Command: DELETE**.

> The same submenu you saw in the DISPLAY and LIST commands appears, except that **Construct a field list** option has different coloring, indicating that this option is not available. You cannot delete specific fields through this option.

You want to delete the record for which LAST__NAME = Fisher.

- Highlight **Build a search condition** and press **ENTER**.
- Highlight **LAST__NAME** and press **ENTER**.
- Highlight **= Equal To** and press **ENTER**.
- Type Fisher and press **ENTER**.
- Highlight **No more conditions** and press **ENTER**.

> The action line displays **Command: DELETE FOR LAST__NAME='Fisher'**.

- Highlight **Execute the command** and press **ENTER**.

> The message **1 record deleted** appears at the bottom of the screen.

- Press any key to return to the ASSIST menu.

From the Dot Prompt

You will also delete the record for Judy Davenport.

- Type DELETE FOR LAST__NAME='Davenport' and press **ENTER**.

> You get a dot prompt.

- DISPLAY ALL (You should know how to do this by now.)

Records for Larry Fisher and Judy Davenport are still there, but preceded by * (asterisk). The asterisks indicate that these records have been marked for deletion.

THE RECALL COMMAND

The DELETE command marks the record for deletion. It does not actually remove the record. With a record in this marked state, you can change your mind and restore the record. This is done by using the RECALL command. The RECALL command is reached through Update and Recall.

PRACTICE TIME

Try figuring out the RECALL command on your own, either through ASSIST or from the dot prompt. Recall only Judy Davenport's record.

THE PACK COMMAND

Finally, records are deleted from the file permanently by using the PACK command. The PACK command takes a while to do its job, especially on large files, so it is advisable to mark all records that are to be deleted, and then to perform PACK once. Make sure that the record for Larry Fisher is still marked for deletion.

- From the ASSIST menu select **Update**, then **Pack**. Press **ENTER**.

  > Since your file is not very big, you get the following messages back almost immediately:

```
    12 records copied
Rebuilding index - B:LAST.ndx
  100% indexed             12 Records indexed
]Rebuilding index - B:CITY.ndx
  100% indexed             12 Records indexed
```

The file now contains 12 records instead of 13. Also, the two active index files were updated as well. To issue this command from the dot prompt, you just type PACK and press ENTER.

THE APPEND COMMAND

Now that you have only twelve customers, you frantically advertise for more customers. In the process you recruit two new customers. Now you need to add them to the database. To do so, you use the APPEND command. Since your database is indexed (and the index files are active), it doesn't matter where you add the new records. APPEND adds records physically at the bottom of the file, but the index file lets you display the records in the order you want. You will enter one customer from ASSIST and the other from the dot prompt.

From ASSIST

- From the ASSIST menu highlight **Update**, then **Append**. Press **ENTER**.

  > The empty template that appeared when you first entered data reappears.

You are to enter the data into these fields. When you are finished with the entry and see a blank template, press **ENTER** to exit, saving the data.

- Enter the following data into the database:

```
John Losser
885 Greenstone Drive
Reno, NV 89512
(702) 323-5005
378.45
```

From the Dot Prompt

- Type APPEND and press **ENTER**.

  > The same template appears.

- Enter the following data into the database:

```
Jim Winston
784 Rhinestone Road
Reno, NV 89503
(702) 747-8997
0.00
```

- Display all to see that the records are indexed by last name.

END OF LESSON 2

This is the end of the second lesson. You will close the database file that has been in use and then shut down the computer.

From ASSIST

- From the ASSIST menu highlight **Set Up**.
- Highlight **Quit dBASE III PLUS** from the pull-down menu and press **ENTER**.
- Remove disks from the drives.
- Turn OFF the computer, monitor, and printer.

From the Dot Prompt

- Type QUIT and press **ENTER**.
- Remove disks from the drives.
- Turn OFF the computer, monitor, and printer.

SUMMARY

In this lesson many of the terms and concepts that are necessary to use a database effectively are introduced.

- A database file must be opened before it can be used, and closed when finished.
- dBASE III Plus keeps track of the records in the database file by using a record pointer.
- To specify which fields to take action on (list, display, delete, etc.), use the **Construct a field** option through ASSIST or list the names of the fields, separated by commas, in the dot prompt command.
- To specify which records to take action on (list, display, delete, etc.), use the **Build a search condition** option through ASSIST or the **FOR** statement in the dot prompt command.
- Sorting actually rearranges the records, putting them in order in a new database file.

- Indexing creates an index file that allows the database to be manipulated or displayed in specified order.
- The following commands are discussed:

APPEND	Add records to the database file
DELETE	Mark specified records for deletion from the database file
DIR	List the files on the default drive
DISPLAY	List specified records and fields to the monitor or printer, pausing when the screen is full
GOTO	Position the record pointer at the beginning or end of the open database file, or at any specified record
HELP	Give onscreen help
INDEX	Create an index file (.ndx) that keeps the database file organized on an expression (usually a single field), even when changes are made to the database file
LIST	Display specified fields and records to the monitor or printer, without any pauses
LIST STRUCTURE	Display to the monitor or printer the structure of the active database file
PACK	Copy all records not marked for deletion, creating a new version of the same database file, but without any marked records
RECALL	Unmark specified records (selected for deletion)
SEEK	Quickly locate an expression in the field for which the database is indexed in the master index file
SORT	Create a copy of the database file that is sorted on one or more fields, in ascending or descending order

REVIEW QUESTIONS

1. What are the differences between the DISPLAY and LIST commands?

2. How do you select fields to be displayed?

3. How do you select records to be displayed?

4. How do you send your output from the LIST command to the printer?

5. How do you move the record pointer around in a database file?

6. What command do you use to look at the database structure?

7. What is the difference between arranging records by using the SORT and INDEX commands?

8. After you append records to a database file, how do you keep records in arranged order when the file is sorted?

   When the file is indexed?

9. Can you SEEK a sorted file? Explain. ______________________

____

____

____

10. Are the records deleted once they are marked for deletion? Explain. __

____

____

____

EXERCISES

Exercise 1

1. Open the database file DB1EX1 you prepared in Lesson 1.
2. Index the file on the CODE field.
3. Make the following changes.
   - Delete the record for Dylan diskettes.
   - Append the following:

Code	*Description*	*Price*	*Vendor*	*Qty*
M033	3.5 DISK SSDD	1.94	Nashville	500
M094	3.5 DISK DSDD	2.40	Nashville	500
F433	5.25 DISK DSDD	1.03	Nashville	500

4. Get a hard copy of the file by using SHIFT/PrtSc.
5. List to the printer the fields CODE, DESCRPTION, and PRICE of all records.

Exercise 2

1. Open the database file DB1EX2 you prepared in Lesson 1.
2. Sort DB1EX2 on the field LAST__NAME to a new file DB2EX2.
3. Open DB2EX2.
4. List to the printer the fields LAST__NAME and COMPANY for all records.
5. Append the following record:

Name:	Jerry Weinstein
Company:	Productivity Booster
Address:	15 East Buffalo Bill
City:	Boulder
State:	CO
Zip:	80307

6. Delete the record for Dallas Hough.
7. List to the printer the fields LAST__NAME, FIRST__NAME, and COMPANY of just those people living in California (CA).
8. Pack the file.

Exercise 3

1. Open the database file DB1EX3 you prepared in Lesson 1.
3. Index the file on product number (NUMBER).
4. Seek the item with the product number L0047 and get a hard copy.
5. Index the file on LOCATION.
6. Make the product number the master index, but make sure to keep the location index active.
7. Make the following changes to the database file:
   - Delete the records for all products with cost greater than $400.
   - Move item L1078 from B-6 to B-2.
8. Make the location index the master index.
9. List to the printer the fields NUMBER and LOCATION for all records.

Lesson 3
Importing Spreadsheet Data

Objectives

Upon completion of the material presented in this lesson you should be able to do the following:

- Recall how to use VP-Planner Plus.
- Import VP-Planner Plus spreadsheet data into a dBASE III Plus database file.
- Articulate some of the problems encountered when sharing data between nonintegrated software products.

When you studied VP-Planner Plus, you learned how to use a spreadsheet to store and manipulate data. Although spreadsheets can be used for limited data storage, database management software is more suited for that purpose. In this lesson, you will learn how to import VP-Planner Plus spreadsheet data into a dBASE III Plus database file, and then use dBASE III Plus to manipulate the data. As we begin this lesson, you will probably benefit from a brief review of VP-Planner Plus.

STARTING OFF

For this lesson you will need the VP-Planner Plus disk and the data disk on which you stored your VP-Planner Plus files. You also will need your dBASE III Plus diskettes. We will start by locating the VP-Planner Plus spreadsheet you'll need for this lesson.

1. Load DOS.
2. Load VP-Planner Plus: insert the VP-Planner Plus disk into drive A, type VPP, and press ENTER.
3. Insert the data diskette into drive B.

4. Retrieve the file called VP5 (you created it during VP-Planner Plus Lesson 5, titled "Using a Spreadsheet for Data Management"). Type /FR. When the list of files appears, highlight VP5 and press ENTER.

   This spreadsheet contains inventory data. You should have 17 rows in the spreadsheet (not counting the column headings). If you do not, please turn back to VP-Planner Plus Lesson 5 and correct your errors.
5. On a sheet of paper, write the name, data type, and width of each column. For numeric fields, note the number of decimal positions.
6. Exit from VP-Planner Plus, by typing /QY.
7. Remove the VP-Planner Plus disk from drive A.

That spreadsheet, VP5, is the one you are going to import into dBASE. To accomplish that, you need to create the dBASE file structure for this soon-to-be imported data.

1. Load dBASE III Plus from the dBASE III Plus Sampler Demo Disks.
2. Using ASSIST, select Create Database file. Name this file DBINVENT.
3. Choose appropriate field names, such as *number, type, descrip,* and so forth. Use the field widths and data types you wrote down when you reviewed the spreadsheet.
4. When you have defined all 8 fields, take a moment to check your work, ensuring that it matches the spreadsheet column widths and data types. Then press CTRL/END. You do not want to add records now. Get back to ASSIST.

At this point you have the structure of a dBASE file defined, but it contains no records. Those records are stored on the diskette in drive B in VP-Planner Plus format. Now you need to load those spreadsheet rows into the dBASE file. This is done from the dot prompt using the APPEND command.

1. Press ESC to get to the dot prompt.
2. Carefully type the following command:

   APPEND FROM B:VP5.WKS TYPE WKS

   Press ENTER.

   The APPEND command tells dBASE III Plus where it will get the data and what format the data is stored in. The file is called VP5.WKS, and it is on drive B; thus, the file designation is B:VP5.WKS. dBASE III Plus can import data in many different formats (from various spreadsheet programs, word processors, and other data management programs). Therefore it needs to know which format the incoming data is in so it can convert it properly; hence the option TYPE WKS.

At this point, dBASE issues a message such as "18 records copied."

Now you have a dBASE III Plus file called DBINVENT that contains the data from the VP-Planner Plus spreadsheet. Get to the ASSIST menu. Select Update, then Browse. Press the UP ARROW until the top record appears. Press F1 for a full screen display.

Note that the column headings in the VP-Planner Plus spreadsheet row 1 were imported along with the other "legitimate" data. Like any software product, dBASE III Plus cannot surmise which spreadsheet fields contain desirable data, so it copies all of the entries. Also notice that imported column headings that appear here in numeric fields (such as the imported column heading for weight) contain bogus numeric data. The entire record is useless and superfluous. You must delete it.

1. Highlight the first record.
2. Type CTRL/U and press ENTER.

   Notice that the status bar says "Del" in the next-to-last field, indicating that this record has been marked for deletion.
3. Type CTRL/END to go back to ASSIST.
4. Select Pack, and press ENTER.

   The message says that 17 records were copied. Press any key.
5. Select Browse again.

   Note that this time only actual data records appear.

At this point you can manipulate the inventory data however you choose.

PRACTICE TIME

1. Build an index for the DBINVENT database file on the Number field; call the index INVNUM.
2. Build an index for the DBINVENT database file on the Location field; call the index LOCATION.
3. Build an index for the DBINVENT database file on the Description field; call the index DESCR.
4. In turn, make each index the master index and then seek, retrieve, and display a specific record based on a value of that index. For example, with INVNUM.NDX as the master index, seek and display the record for inventory item number L0047.

END OF LESSON 3

Quit dBASE III Plus, remove all diskettes, and store them properly. Turn OFF the computer, printer, and monitor.

SUMMARY

In this lesson you learned how to import VP-Planner Plus spreadsheet data into a dBASE III Plus file. Once there, imported data can be stored and manipulated with the database program just as if you had entered it through the database program.

- Imported data is often stored in a format different from the one used by the database software. For instance, VP-Planner Plus spreadsheets are stored in .WKS format.
- To import data you must first establish the database structure that will hold the imported records.
- Import data by means of the APPEND command, which you execute from the dot prompt.
- Mark for deletion any superfluous imported "data," such as column headers, from the spreadsheet. Then pack the file.

REVIEW QUESTIONS

1. In preparing to import VP-Planner Plus data into dBASE, why did you first retrieve the spreadsheet file and write the name, data type, and width of each column? ____________________

2. What is the difference between creating a database file structure and loading database data? ____________________

3. In this command, what is the file designation?

   APPEND FROM B:VP5.WKS TYPE WKS __________

4. What dBASE command would you issue to load data from a VP-Planner Plus spreadsheet on drive B called PAYROLL? ____________________

5. The inventory worksheet in this lesson contained 17 data records, yet dBASE III Plus imported 18 data records. Explain the discrepancy. ____________________

6. How do you resolve the discrepancy noted in question 5? ____________________

7. Which index would you use for the imported inventory file if you wanted to seek and display the item in warehouse bin C-4? ____________________

8. Which index would you use for the imported inventory file if you wanted to see all the records for six-outlet strips? ______________

____

9. Why is a spreadsheet program not as well suited for data management as a database program is? ______________________

____

10. Describe two problems with importing VP-Planner Plus spreadsheet data into dBASE III Plus. ______________________

____

EXERCISES

Exercise 1

Using VP-Planner Plus, retrieve the VP5 inventory spreadsheet you used in this lesson. Review how to perform a data query in VP-Planner Plus. From this spreadsheet, select all items that cost $100.00 or more.

Using dBASE III Plus, retrieve the imported inventory file, DBINVENT. From this file, extract all items that cost $100.00 or more.

Exercise 2

In exercise 1, which software (if either) was better suited for the task of doing a random query of stored data? Explain. Suppose there were 5,000 inventory items in the file. Which software (if either) would be better suited then? Explain your answer.

Lesson 4
Creating Labels and Reports

Objectives

Upon completion of the material presented in this lesson you should be able to do the following:

- Understand the concept of report format.
- Create a label file.
- Print, using a label file.
- Modify a label file.
- Create a report file.
- Print, using a report file.
- Modify a report file.
- Print subtotals on a report.
- Modify the structure of a database file.

STARTING OFF

Start dBASE III Plus on the computer by following instructions given in the introduction to this module so that the dBASE ASSIST screen is displayed. Insert the data disk from the previous lesson into drive B.

So far you have seen several features that are common to most database management systems. That is, most systems have ways to enter data, sort records on one or more fields, display data, and obtain printouts. Another common feature is generation of printouts formatted according to your specifications. In this lesson you learn to prepare labels and reports from information in the database.

Two types of printouts can be *formatted*, or laid out on paper according to a specific design. A *label* output lets you indicate which fields are to be placed on each line, and how many columns of labels are to be printed on each page. A good example of the use of a label output is to produce mailing labels from the information in a database.

The second type of output, the *report,* produces table-style output, with titles at the top of each page and column and the contents of each column reflecting information from the fields in the database.

CREATING LABELS

A label is a formatted output of one or more fields printed in specified blocks on the page. A variety of gummed label sheets can be used with most printers. Some sheets contain a series of 1- by 3-inch labels, either one, two, or three labels across. Other sheets contain various label sizes. Labels also come on continuous forms. The labels do not need to be mailing labels. They could be inventory labels, labels for internal distribution within an office or company, or any other type of information from a selected set of records that meets a particular need.

dBASE III Plus has a flexible label-printing capability that can handle many different label-making needs. Two steps are required to produce labels. The first step involves designing a label file, which is saved and can be used repeatedly. The label file describes how the output is formatted on the page, and which fields are to be printed in each label. Label files on disk have the extension .LBL. A label file does not contain the actual labels, but rather the lists of the fields to be used to produce the different lines in the label. The second step is the actual printing of the labels.

You may have various label files, either serving different database files or formatting different types of labels for a particular database file. Each of these files must have a unique filename. You will now create the label filename, ACCOUNTS.

The two files, ACCOUNTS.DBF and ACCOUNTS.LBL, have different extensions, which indicate their different purposes. If you have only one label file for a particular database file, it may be helpful to give it a name that avoids confusion with other database files on the data disk.

The task of creating labels, whether from the dot prompt or from ASSIST, is identical after the initial command is entered. You can use either method, depending on what you feel comfortable with.

- Specify the database file ACCOUNTS for usage with active index files LAST.NDX (Master) and CITY.NDX.

From ASSIST

- Highlight **Create** on the menu bar.
- Highlight **Label** on the pull-down menu and press **ENTER**.
- Highlight **B:** as the drive to create the label file on and press **ENTER**.

  > The following message appears on the screen:

  ```
  Enter the name of the file:
  ```

- Type ACCOUNTS and press **ENTER**.

From the Dot Prompt

- Type CREATE LABEL ACCOUNTS and press **ENTER**.

> The screen shown in Screen Display 4-1 displays the label file structure.

The box at the top contains some parameters to establish the size and spacing of the labels. The limits and defaults (already defined for labels measuring $3\frac{1}{2} \times \frac{15}{16}$ inch) for these parameters are given in the table.

Parameter	*Limits*	*Default size*
Width of label:	1 - 120	35 characters
Height of label:	1 - 16	5 lines
Left margin:	0 - 250	0
Lines between labels:	0 - 16	1
Spaces between labels:	0 - 120	0
Number of labels across:	1 - 5	1

If you are using $1 \times 3\frac{1}{2}$-inch labels in a strip, then the default is appropriate for you. For now, however, you will be printing onto the usual printer paper so you will see how to program the printing of multiple labels per line. For example, suppose you had a sheet of 1×4-inch labels, two across on a line. This means an $8\frac{1}{2} \times 11$-inch sheet contains 22 labels. Also, suppose your printer prints 10 characters per inch. You want to change the default shown on your screen so that there are two labels across and 5 spaces between labels.

- Highlight **Spaces between labels** and press **ENTER**.

  > An arrow appears next to the value 0.

- Type **5** and press **ENTER**.

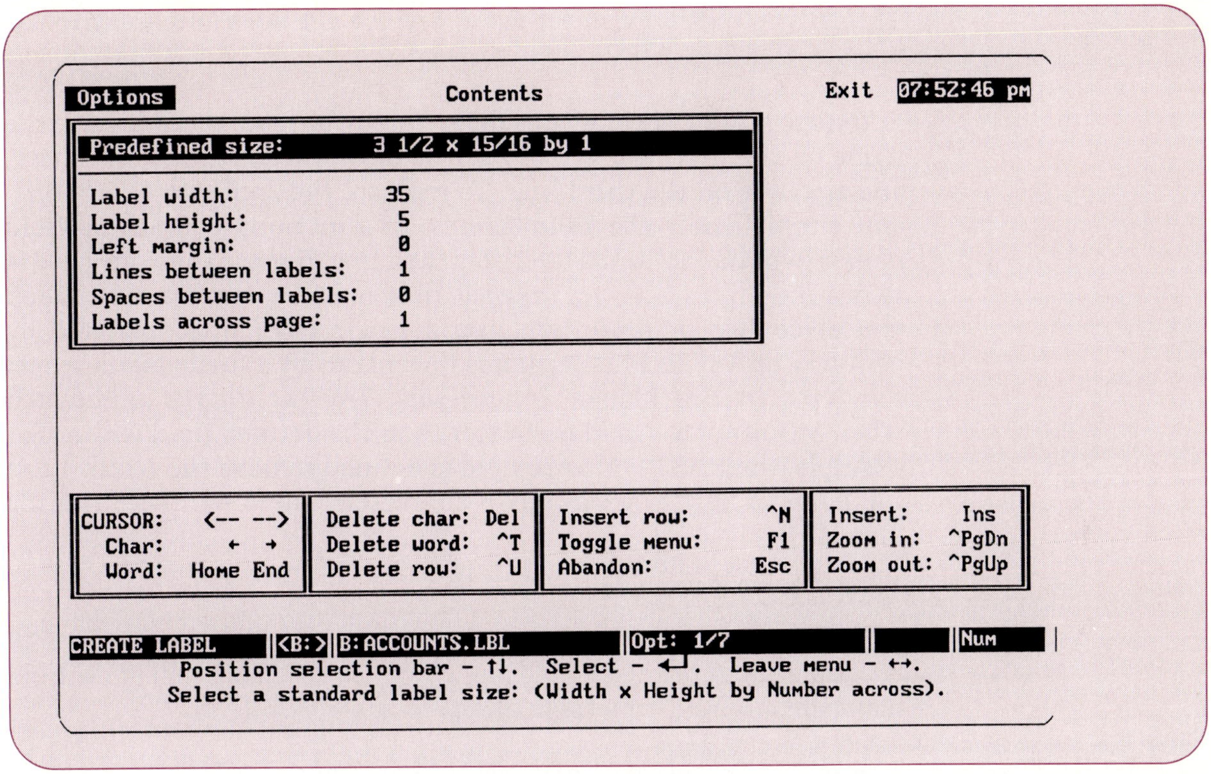

Screen Display 4-1

- Press the **DOWN ARROW** key once more to select **Labels across page** and press **ENTER**.
- Type **2** and press **ENTER**.
- Press the **RIGHT ARROW** key to continue.

> A box appears to the right for you to specify the label contents.

You accepted the default value of five lines in the label. Thus the screen shows five lines.

NOTE ■ dBASE III Plus requires all information in the labels to be character fields. If you have other types of fields, you need to enter the appropriate conversion functions, as indicated below.

Type of Field	*Conversion Function*
numeric	STR() keeps only the integer part
date	DTOC() if you want date printed
date	CDOW() if you want day of week
date	CMONTH() if you want month printed

Thus if you have a numeric field, BALANCE, it is entered into the label as STR(BALANCE), but the fraction (cents) part is lost.

You are producing mailing labels. You would like them to have the name on the first line, street address on the second, and city, state, and zip code on the third line. To indicate the contents of any line, you simply enter the field names, or functions containing field names (will be explained later), for each line. If more than one field is to be printed in a line, separate the field names with commas. When you place two or more fields on a single label line separated by commas, dBASE III Plus separates the entries by a single blank space, removing trailing blanks as necessary. *Trailing blanks* are created when an entry in a field is shorter than the defined field width. For example, the LAST__NAME field is defined to have the width 12. If the name is Smith, with only 5 characters, there will be 7 trailing blanks.

- Press **ENTER** to select the first line.

NOTE ■ If you do not remember the field names, press the **F10** function key. A box with field names appears. You can select the field names by highlighting them and pressing **ENTER**.

- Type FIRST__NAME, LAST__NAME and press **ENTER**.
- Highlight the second line, then press **ENTER**.
- Type ADDRESS and press **ENTER**.
- Highlight the third line, then press **ENTER**.
- Type CITY, STATE, ZIP and press **ENTER**.

You have now finished specifying the label format.

- Press the **RIGHT ARROW** key.

  > A submenu appears to the right, asking if you want to save this label file.

- Highlight **Save** and press **ENTER**.

You have completed the first part of printing labels: you have prepared the label form ACCOUNTS. Now you get to print them.

From ASSIST

- Highlight **Retrieve**.
- Highlight **Label** from the pull-down menu.

- Specify that the label file reside in drive B by selecting **B:** and pressing **ENTER**.
  > The names of all the label files on the disk in drive B are displayed.
- Highlight **ACCOUNTS.LBL** and press **ENTER**.
  > The familiar submenu appears on the screen.
- With **Execute the command** highlighted, press **ENTER**.
  > A message appears in the middle of the screen, asking if you want your output sent to the printer.
- Make sure that the printer is turned on and ready to use.
- Type **Y** (no ENTER).
  > The labels are printed.
- Press any key to get back to the ASSIST menu.

From the Dot Prompt

- Make sure that the printer is turned on and ready to use.
- Type LABEL FORM ACCOUNTS TO PRINT and press **ENTER**.

The labels look as follows:

Abdel Ahmad 417 Miner Street Virginia City NV 89440	Jennifer Bacon 975 Lake Drive Chilcoot CA 95926
Cindy Beard P.O. Box 10733 Reno NV 89510	Robert Castillo 112 South Broadway Sparks NV 89431
Julio Chavez 225 Forest Hill Road Truckee CA 95734	Judy Davenport 555 Timber Lane Truckee CA 95734
Jonathan Handel 1001 East Fourth Street Reno NV 89501	Chico Juarez 72 Mill Road Floriston CA 96111
John Losser 885 Greenstone Drive Reno NV 89512	Sandy O'Dell 2219 Carson Highway Carson City NV 89701

Irene Orwell 12575 Sun Valley Blvd. Sun Valley NV 89433	Harold Smith 885 North McCarran Reno NV 89512
Mandy Vario P.O. Box 37 Dayton NV 89403	Jim Winston 784 Rhinestone Road Reno NV 89503

Are you beginning to get the hang of this? Once you become familiar with the questions that dBASE III Plus is asking, you can set up a label file and have it print either all the records in a file or only certain selected records.

PRACTICE TIME

Create mailing labels for those customers residing in California.

(*Hint:* You do not need to create a new .LBL file.)

MODIFYING LABELS

It is possible to change the format of labels defined in ACCOUNTS.LBL. Perhaps you have a different roll of labels, with different size than your original design specification, or you may have paper with two or three labels across the page. You may have decided to change the label by spacing the fields differently, or by adding and/or subtracting fields from the original specification.

To modify a label, be sure that the database using the label is in USE.

- Make sure that ACCOUNTS is the database file in use.

From ASSIST

- Highlight **Modify** on the menu bar.
- Highlight **Label** and press **ENTER**.

  > The submenu for drive specification shows.
- Highlight **B:** and press **ENTER**.

  > All the valid .LBL files on the disk are displayed.
- Highlight **ACCOUNTS** and press **ENTER**.

From the Dot Prompt

- Type **MODIFY LABEL ACCOUNTS** and press **ENTER**.

> The menu shows the Options screen. It is as you set it.

You can change any options as though you were creating a new label format.

PRACTICE TIME

Change the labels to three across. Change the label width to 23.

NOTE ■ Since the address field is set to 30 width, any addresses longer than 23 characters would be truncated (cut off).

- Highlight **Contents** on the menu bar.

> The Contents screen appears, as it had been previously created.

Suppose you want to insert a comma between the city and state.

- Highlight the third row, and press **ENTER**.
- Use the **LEFT ARROW** key to move the cursor so that it is on top of the comma after CITY. Make sure that **INS** shows at the right side of the status bar. If not, press the **Ins** key to turn it on.
- Type +"," so that the line reads: **CITY+",",STATE,ZIP**. Press **ENTER**.

By placing any character or text within apostrophes or quotes, that text is printed on the label. So here you told it to add, or *concatenate* (+), the character comma (,) right after CITY. If you had changed it to read CITY,",", a blank space would have been inserted between CITY and the comma.

- Highlight **Exit**, then **Save**. Press **ENTER**.

PRACTICE TIME

Print the labels again. Note how the positioning of labels on the page is changed, and note the comma between the city and state. But also note the blank spaces between the city and the comma, as well as the truncated zip codes.

Abdel Ahmad	Jennifer Bacon	Cindy Beard
417 Miner Street	975 Lake Drive	P.O. Box 10733
Virginia City , NV 894	Chilcoot , CA 959	Reno , NV 895
Robert Castillo	Julio Chavez	Judy Davenport
112 South Broadway	225 Forest Hill Road	555 Timber Lane
Sparks , NV 894	Truckee , CA 957	Truckee , CA 957
.	.	.
.	.	.
.	.	.

When you concatenate, or add on, to a field by using a plus sign, the trailing blanks are not removed. To remove the trailing blanks here, you need to use a function called TRIM. A *function* is a process built into dBASE III Plus to manipulate data.

PRACTICE TIME

1. Modify the label ACCOUNTS as follows. Change the content of the last line to read TRIM(CITY) + ",",STATE,ZIP.
2. Exit, then save the label file.
3. Print the label.

Abdel Ahmad	Jennifer Bacon	Cindy Beard
417 Miner Street	975 Lake Drive	P.O. Box 10733
Virginia City, NV 89440	Chilcoot, CA 95926	Reno, NV 89510
Robert Castillo	Julio Chavez	Judy Davenport
112 South Broadway	225 Forest Hill Road	555 Timber Lane
Sparks, NV 89431	Truckee, CA 95734	Truckee, CA 95734
.	.	.
.	.	.
.	.	.

CREATING REPORTS

The other type of printout is the *Report*. Creating reports also takes two steps. The first step is to design a report file, and the second step is the actual printing. Report files on disk have the extension .FRM.

You will now prepare a report containing customer names and balances. You will include their telephone numbers, so that you can call them, if you wish. It is important that you have an idea of what kind of report you want to produce. Some planning with pencil and paper is necessary before doing the task on the computer.

At the top the report heading can range from a simple "Customer Account Balances" to a more elaborate heading of up to four lines.

The columns of the report should contain the first name, last name, telephone number, and balance. You would like the balance field totaled at the bottom. The report might look something like the following:

Customer Account Balances

Customer Name		Telephone	Balance
John	Losser	(702) 323-5005	378.45
.			
.			
.			

You want to index the report by the balance amount; that is, you want customer names listed in ascending order by balance amount. The report fields can have simple headers, or titles, such as shown above.

The first step is to get the records in the right sequence.

PRACTICE TIME

Index your database file ACCOUNTS by BALANCE. You can call the .NDX file whatever you wish. Make sure this index is the master index of the file.

From ASSIST

- Highlight **Create**.
- Highlight **Report** on the pull-down menu and press **ENTER**.
- Highlight **B:** and press **ENTER** to indicate that drive B contains the disk to store the report file.

  > The screen instructs you to enter a filename, which can consist of one to eight letters or digits.

- Type BALANCES and press **ENTER**.

From the Dot Prompt

- Type CREATE REPORT BALANCES and press **ENTER**.

> The screen of Screen Display 4-2 is displayed.

```
 Options        Groups        Columns          Locate          Exit  08:04:18 pm
 ┌──────────────────────────────────────┐
 │ Page title                           │
 │ Page width (positions)        80     │
 │ Left margin                    8     │
 │ Right margin                   0     │
 │ Lines per page                58     │
 │ Double space report           No     │
 │ Page eject before printing    Yes    │
 │ Page eject after printing     No     │
 │ Plain page                    No     │
 └──────────────────────────────────────┘

 CURSOR   <-- -->  │ Delete char:    Del │ Insert column: ^N │ Insert:    Ins
  Char:    ←   →   │ Delete word:     ^T │ Report format: F1 │ Zoom in:  ^PgDn
  Word:  Home End  │ Delete column:   ^U │ Abandon:      Esc │ Zoom out: ^PgUp

CREATE REPORT  ║<B:>║B:BALANCES.FRM       ║Opt: 1/9         ║Ins  ║NumCaps
         Position selection bar - ↑↓.  Select - ↵.  Leave menu - ←→.
 Enter up to four lines of text to be displayed at the top of each report page.
```

Screen Display 4-2

In the bottom box are the edit and cursor move commands. At the top is a box containing various parameters for the report. The top line in the box, which is highlighted, lets you enter the title for the report.

- Press **ENTER**.

  > A box appears with several blank lines.

You may enter up to four lines of 80 characters each for a heading to be placed at the top of each page. At the end of each line press the ENTER key to move to the next line. When you have completed your entry, press CTRL/END.

- Type Customer Account Balances and press **ENTER**.
- Press **CTRL/END**.

The parameters presented in the menu are self-explanatory. A report on 8½-inch-wide paper will usually have a line width of 80 characters. The left and right margins are used to keep the report from going all the way to the edges of the paper. Similarly, the choice of 58 lines per page allows eight lines (four each) for the top and bottom margins. You also have the option of double spacing the report if you choose. You will go ahead and use the preset values of these parameters.

- Highlight Columns on the menu bar.

  > The screen shown in Screen Display 4-3 appears.

The final task of designing the report is to lay out the headers and contents of the various fields in the report. Initially, the report has a width of 80 character spaces, of which 8 are taken by the left margin (unless you changed the margins in Options). For each column of the report, or the report field, you enter field names. If you need to see the edit–cursor-move menu, press the F1 key. You press the F1 key the second time to get back to this screen.

The first line within the box at the bottom shows the number of columns taken up by the left margin and thc number remaining. The > characters on the left show character spaces reserved for the

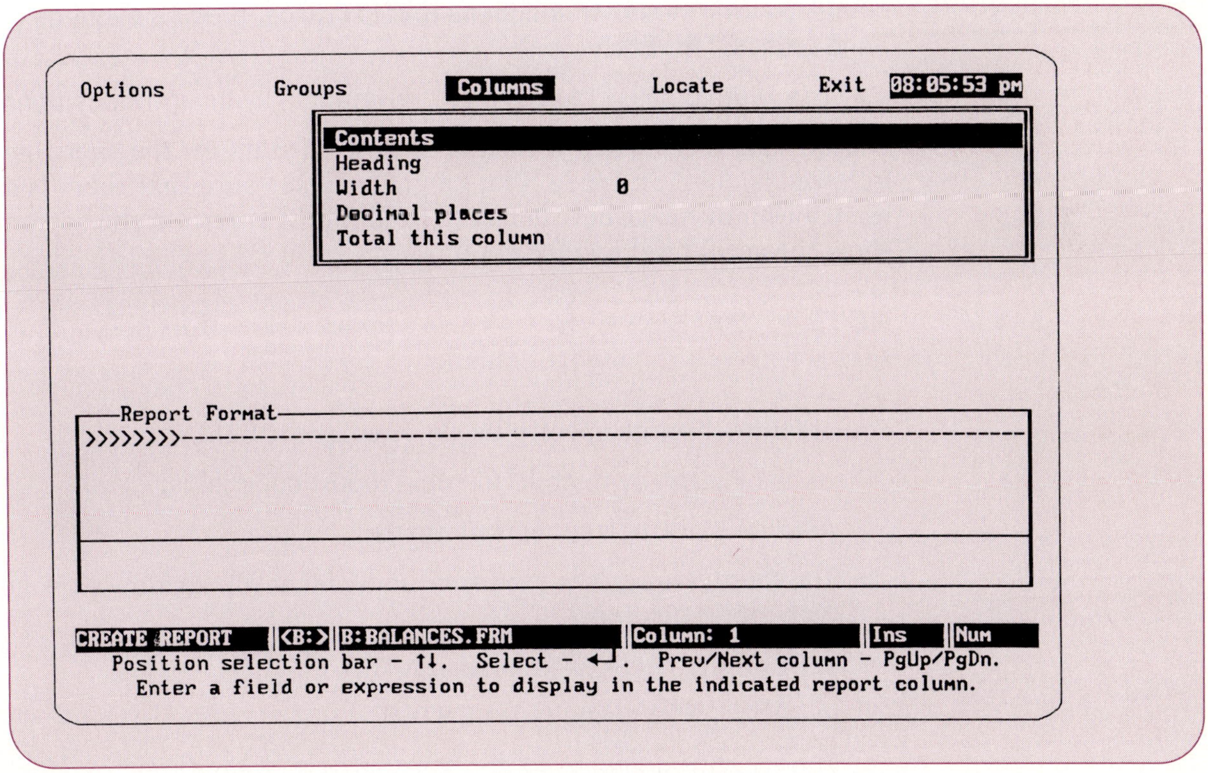

Screen Display 4-3

margin, and the hyphens show columns left for the fields you can specify.

The top box contains parameters to specify the contents of a report field. Try the first column.

- With **Contents** highlighted, press **ENTER**.

  > An arrow appears within the highlight, followed by the cursor.

You are to enter a field name. You want the first name to appear on the first column.

- Type FIRST_NAME and press **ENTER**.

  > The field width specified changes to **12**.

  > **X**'s appear in the bottom box.

The column heading is to be Customer Name.

- Highlight **Heading** and press **ENTER**.

  > A box opens up for you to enter the heading.

- Type Customer Name and press **ENTER** twice, type 13 hyphens (-), and press **CTRL/END**.

  > The width changed to 13 since this heading takes up 13 positions.

Notice that the header you entered now appears on the first line, followed by a blank space. The program makes sure that there is at least one blank space between each field. The X entries at the bottom show the actual field width.

NOTE ▪ You can set the width to a larger value, thus giving more spaces between the report fields.

You are now through specifying the first report field.

- Press the **PgDn** key to go to the next report column.

  > Another blank box appears at the top.

  > The fourth area on the status bar shows that you are now working with report column 2.

- With **Contents** highlighted, press **ENTER**.
- Type LAST_NAME and press **ENTER**.

  > The width changes to **12** and **X**'s appear in the bottom box.

- Highlight **Heading** and press **ENTER**.
- Press **ENTER** twice, type 15 hyphens (-), and press **CTRL/END**.

PRACTICE TIME

Enter the other two report fields, **TELEPHONE** and **BALANCE**.

TELEPHONE will have the heading **Telephone** with 25 hyphens (-) on the second line.

BALANCE will have the heading **Balance** with 9 hyphens (-) on the second line.

Notice that, since BALANCE is a numeric field, this box contains **Decimal places** and **Total this column** as added options. You will use the preset, or default, values: **2** for decimal places and **Yes** for the total (report will display the column total for this field).

You have now specified all the report fields. Let's save this report file.

- Highlight **Exit** on the menu bar.

  > The pull-down menu asks you if you want to save the file.
- Highlight **Save** and press **ENTER**.

Now do the second step: print the report.

From ASSIST

- Highlight **Retrieve**.
- Highlight **Report** and press **ENTER**.
- Select **B:** and press **ENTER** to indicate that the report file is found in drive B.

  > A submenu appears, listing all the .FRM files on the disk in drive B.
- Highlight **BALANCES.FRM** and press **ENTER**.
- With **Execute the command** highlighted, press **ENTER**.

  > A message appears, asking you if you want output sent to the printer.
- Make sure that the printer is turned on and is ready to use.
- Type Y (no RETURN).

NOTE ■ If you do not select Y, then the output will be sent to your screen only.

From the Dot Prompt

- Make sure that the printer is turned on and is ready to use.
- Type REPORT FORM BALANCES TO PRINT and press **ENTER**.

> The report is printed.

Page No. 1
12/07/89

Customer Account Balances

Customer Name		Telephone	Balance
Jim	Winston	(702) 747-8997	0.00
Sandy	O'Dell	(702) 234-0776	4.49
Abdel	Ahmad	(702) 847-3562	9.80
Harold	Smith	(702) 788-9120	29.75
Jonathan	Handel	(702) 786-0905	76.24
Jennifer	Bacon	(916) 477-6705	142.45
Judy	Davenport	(916) 966-0722	178.90
Robert	Castillo	(702) 358-0200	247.50
Chico	Juarez	(916) 479-3205	312.12
John	Losser	(702) 323-5005	378.45
Mandy	Vario	(702) 246-0171	442.45
Julio	Chavez	(916) 968-2335	782.38
Irene	Orwell	(702) 673-9800	860.00
Cindy	Beard	(702) 323-6220	923.40
*** Total ***			
			4387.93

In these examples you did not specify a scope, build a search condition, or build a scope condition in producing reports. You could have. Just as you did in the labels output, you could have used the submenu to make reports for only those customers from California, or only those customers who owe you more than $500.00. Remember, any options with dim coloring are not available to you at that point.

PRACTICE TIME

Design, create, and print a report that lists all customers from Nevada who owe you more than $300.00. The report is to contain the customer name, address, and balance.

MODIFYING REPORTS

You can change the format specified in a report file. In the previous report, names were placed in two columns. You would like them placed both in the same column, last name first, separated by a comma.

- Make sure that ACCOUNTS is in use.

From ASSIST

- Highlight **Modify**.
- Highlight **Report** and press **ENTER**.
- Highlight **B:** and press **ENTER**.
- Highlight **BALANCES** and press **ENTER**.

From the Dot Prompt

- Type MODIFY REPORT BALANCES and press **ENTER**.

> The Options screen appears.

You don't want to change Options or Groups.

- Highlight **Columns**.

> The screen shows the information you entered previously.

Right now you want to delete column 1 and modify column 2 (which will become column 1).

- With Column 1 displayed (first names), press **CTRL/U**. That is, hold down the **CTRL** key and press the **U** key.

The first column no longer appears. Column 1 now contains the last names. You want to change the content of this column so that it displays both the last name and the first name. In a report format you cannot place more than one field in a column by specifying the field names separated by commas, as you did in labels. You have to concatenate fields, using plus (+) signs. When you concatenate, trailing blanks are not removed and field contents are not separated by blank spaces. So you must use the TRIM function on the LAST_NAME field and insert a blank space between the comma and the first name.

- With **Contents** highlighted, press **ENTER**.

> The contents are **LAST_NAME**.

- Change the line as follows:

  `TRIM(LAST_NAME)+", "+FIRST_NAME`

  and press **ENTER**.

You also need to modify the heading.

- Highlight **Heading** and press **ENTER**.
- Type **Customer Name** and press **ENTER** twice.
- Type 26 hyphens (-) and press **CTRL/END**.

PRACTICE TIME

Save the report file, then print the report.

Page No. 1
12/07/89

Customer Account Balances

Customer Name	Telephone	Balance
Winston, Jim	(702) 747-8997	0.00
O'Dell, Sandy	(702) 234-0776	4.49
Ahmad, Abdel	(702) 847-3562	9.80
Smith, Harold	(702) 788-9120	29.75
Handel, Jonathan	(702) 786-0905	76.24
Bacon, Jennifer	(916) 477-6705	142.45
Davenport, Judy	(916) 966-0722	178.90
Castillo, Robert	(702) 358-0200	247.50
Juarez, Chico	(916) 479-3205	312.12
Losser, John	(702) 323-5005	378.45
Vario, Mandy	(702) 246-0171	442.45
Chavez, Julio	(916) 968-2335	782.38
Orwell, Irene	(702) 673-9800	860.00
Beard, Cindy	(702) 323-6220	923.40
*** Total ***		
		4387.93

PRINTING SUBTOTALS

Sometimes you need to have subtotals within a report. For example, in the report you prepared, you may need to have subtotals for each state as well as the final total. Printing subtotals in dBASE III Plus is very simple.

To print subtotals, however, the file arrangement must be based on the field on which subtotals are to be printed. In this case that field is

STATE. The idea is that every time the content of the STATE field changes, a subtotal is written for the previous group.

PRACTICE TIME

1. Make sure that the ACCOUNTS file is in use.
2. Index on STATE. You can name the .NDX file whatever you choose.
3. Make sure that STATE is the master index.
4. Create a report file STATE, which has the same entries in the Content section as the BALANCES.FRM file.
5. Enter the report title **"Customer Account Balances"** on the first line, and **"by State"** on the second line.

Now you will specify the printing of subtotals. You want it subtotaled on STATE.

- Highlight **Groups**.

  > A box appears for subtotal specifications.

NOTE ■ There are two levels of subtotals available (group/subgroup). Only one level is discussed here.

- Highlight **Group on expression** and press **ENTER**.
- Type STATE and press **ENTER**.
- Exit and save.

PRACTICE TIME

Now print the report.

Page No. 1
12/08/89

Customer Account Balances
by State

Customer Name	Telephone	Balance
** CA		
Davenport, Judy	(916) 966-0722	178.90
Juarez, Chico	(916) 479-3205	312.12
Chavez, Julio	(916) 968-2335	782.38
Bacon, Jennifer	(916) 477-6705	142.45
** Subtotal **		
		1415.85

** NV		
Castillo, Robert	(702) 358-0200	247.50
Smith, Harold	(702) 788-9120	29.75
Orwell, Irene	(702) 673-9800	860.00
Handel, Jonathan	(702) 786-0905	76.24
O'Dell, Sandy	(702) 234-0776	4.49
Beard, Cindy	(702) 323-6220	923.40
Ahmad, Abdel	(702) 847-3562	9.80
Vario, Mandy	(702) 246-0171	442.45
Losser, John	(702) 323-5005	378.45
Winston, Jim	(702) 747-8997	0.00
** Subtotal **		
		2972.08
** Total **		
		4387.93

MODIFYING THE STRUCTURE OF A DATABASE FILE

No matter how well you planned your database file structure, there are times when you need to modify it. A name field may be too short, a new field may be necessary, or perhaps an existing field is found not to be necessary anymore. You can modify the structure of a dBASE file to accommodate these changes without losing any data you already have. (There is an exception that will be mentioned later.)

- Make sure that the database file ACCOUNTS is specified for usage with LAST.NDX as the master index.
- Display the database structure to the screen, as shown in Screen Display 4-4.

The file consists of name, address, telephone, and balance information. You have decided that (since your business is expanding so quickly) you need to add an account number field. Since you will not be doing any calculation on the account number field, it will be a character field, and you decide on the width of 3 characters.

The task of modifying a database structure, whether from the dot prompt or from ASSIST, is identical after the initial command is entered. You can use either method.

From ASSIST

- Highlight **Modify** on the menu bar.
- Highlight **Database file** on the pull-down menu and press **ENTER**.

```
Set Up  Create  Update  Position  Retrieve  Organize Modify Tools  08:42:55 pm

Structure for database: B:ACCOUNTS.dbf
Number of data records:       14
Date of last update   : 05/22/89
Field  Field Name  Type       Width    Dec
    1  FIRST_NAME  Character     12
    2  LAST_NAME   Character     12
    3  ADDRESS     Character     30
    4  CITY        Character     15
    5  STATE       Character      2
    6  ZIP         Character      5
    7  TELEPHONE   Character     14
    8  BALANCE     Numeric        7      2
** Total **                      98

ASSIST          ||<B:>||ACCOUNTS              ||Rec: 11/14      ||Ins    ||Num    |
                       Press any key to continue work in ASSIST._
```

Screen Display 4-4

From the Dot Prompt

- Type MODIFY STRUCTURE and press ENTER.

> The screen you used to create the database appears, with the present database structure displayed.

You can add the account number field anywhere in the structure, but here you will insert it as the first field, shifting down the remaining fields. All you have to do to insert a field is to place the cursor where you would like the new field inserted (if it is to be the third field, place it on the third field) and enter CTRL/N.

- With the cursor on the first field, press **CTRL/N** to insert a new field.

> Space for a new field opens up, with all the existing fields moving down one row on the display.

- Enter the following structure for the new field:

```
ACC__NUMBER     Character     3
```

- Exit the Modify Structure with **CTRL/END**.
- Press **ENTER** to confirm.

  > dBASE informs you that the file has been copied, with the data preserved for all fields with the same name. The LAST index file is also rebuilt.

PRACTICE TIME

1. From the BROWSE screen enter the following account numbers for the records in the file.

205	Robert Castillo
025	Harold Smith
203	Judy Davenport
053	Irene Orwell
201	Jonathan Handel
072	Chico Juarez
128	Sandy O'Dell
066	Julio Chavez
105	Jennifer Bacon
051	Cindy Beard
170	Abdel Ahmad
150	Mandy Vario
088	John Losser
100	Jim Winston

2. Index on ACC__NUMBER to the file ACC__NO.

NOTE ■ You could have changed the field length and field names as well just by typing the new values over the existing values. When you execute this command (to modify the structure), dBASE III Plus creates a backup database, and after the structure is modified, the data in the backup database file is loaded to the new database automatically. However, if a field name *and* the field length are changed, the data will not be loaded to the new database. If both must be changed, you must use the MODIFY STRUCTURE twice. Change the field name on the first pass and change the field length on the second pass.

PRACTICE TIME

1. Specify for use the database file INVENTRY created in Lesson 1.
2. Index on ITEM__CODE to CODE.NDX.

3. Modify the structure, adding a field RETAIL after the PRICE field. The RETAIL field is to be numeric, width 7, decimal 2. (Values will be entered into this field in Lesson 5.)

END OF LESSON 4

From ASSIST

- From the ASSIST menu highlight **Set Up**.
- Highlight **Quit dBASE III PLUS** on the pull-down menu and press **ENTER**.
- Remove the disks from both drives.
- Turn OFF the monitor, computer, and printer.

From the Dot Prompt

- Type Quit and press **ENTER**.
- Remove disks from the drives.
- Turn OFF the monitor, computer, and printer.

SUMMARY

In this lesson many of the terms and concepts that are necessary to print reports from the information on a database are discussed.

- Output can be formatted as a label or a report.
- Two steps are involved in creating an output:
  1. Create a label or report file.
  2. Print, using the label or report file.
- A report filename has extension .FRM, and a label filename has extension .LBL.
- After a label or report file is created, it can be modified.
- When creating a label file, you can specify more than one field on a line by listing the field names, separated by commas. This removes all trailing blanks and inserts a blank space between the fields.
- Fields and characters are concatenated by using the plus (+) sign. Concatenation does not remove the trailing blanks.
- The TRIM function removes the trailing blanks from the field entry.
- A report can include subtotals and totals.
- A database structure can be modified without losing data.
- The following commands are discussed:

CREATE LABEL file	Create a label file, file, for the database in use.

CREATE REPORT file	Create a report file, file, for the database in use.
LABEL FORM file	Produce label style output for the database in use, using the label file file.
MODIFY LABEL file	Modify the label file file.
MODIFY REPORT file	Modify the report file file.
MODIFY STRUCTURE	Modify the structure of the database file in use.
REPORT FORM file	Produce report style output for the database in use, using the report file file.

REVIEW QUESTIONS

1. What is a report format? ______________________________

2. Define label and report formats, and give an example of each. ______________________________

3. What is a trailing blank? ______________________________

4. When specifying fields to be printed, what happens when the field names are separated by commas? ______________________________

5. What does "concatenate" mean? When and how do you do it? ______________________________

6. What does the TRIM function do? ______________________________

7. Does the database file have to be in any particular order when printing subtotals? Explain. ______________________________

8. Summarize steps required to print subtotals in a report. ______

9. Can you modify a structure of a database that contains data? Explain.

10. When modifying a structure, how do you insert a new field? ______

EXERCISES

Exercise 1

1. Retrieve DB1EX1. Make sure it is indexed on CODE.
2. Create a report similar to the following:

MEMORY MAGIC, INC.
Disk Inventory Report

ITEM CODE	DESCRIPTION	PRICE	VENDOR	QUANTITY IN STOCK
F144	5.25 DISK DSDD	2.12	ThreeDee	110
F153	5.25 DISK DSDD	1.57	Generic	690
F220	5.25 DISK DSDD	2.14	MemoryRex	600
.				
.				
.				
M094	3.5 DISK DSDD	2.40	Nashville	500
Total				
				6700

3. Print a report for all records
4. Print a report for 3.5-inch disks only. (*HINT:* You can use the search condition: DESCRIPTION = "3.5".)
5. Create labels for a 3½ × 15/16 by 2 label sheet, with each entry similar to following:

3.5 DISK SSDD
Item Code: M013
Vendor: MemoryRex
Price: $3.22

Note the text that needs to be entered within quotes in Contents.

6. Print labels for all records.
7. Modify labels so that Vendor is on the line above Item Code.
8. Print labels for all 3.5-inch disks.

Exercise 2

1. Retrieve DB2EX2.
2. Index on state and city in one index file.
3. Create address labels for 3½ × 15/16 by 2.
4. Print labels for all records.
5. Print labels for zip code >= 90000.
6. Modify DB2EX2 database structure: add fields

    EMPLOYEES N 4 0
    INS_POLICY L

    Add the following data to records:

Company	Employees	Ins_Policy
CPI Consulting	24	T
Pomona HiTech	320	T
Market Research Inc.	10	F
Systematics	95	T
Green Improvements	205	T
Development Insight	5	F
Management Consultants	40	T
Man of the Future	8	T
Productivity Booster	15	F

7. Print labels for all companies without policies (INS_POLICY is false).
    Hint: This cannot be done from ASSIST (ASSIST can do only for INS_POLICY true). The search condition is FOR .NOT. INS_POLICY (note the periods around NOT).

Exercise 3

1. Retrieve DB1EX3 indexed on part number, location. These index files may already exist.
2. Create a report similar to the following:

THE POWER LINE

Current Inventory Report

Item Number	Type	Description	Cost	Price	Quantity	Loc.
L0005	SSS	modem surge protector	30.00	59.90	880	A-6
L0013	UPS	1800 watt capacity	150.00	299.00	0	A-5
L0047	SSS	2-outlet box	25.00	49.95	1480	C-4
.						
.						
.						
L4510	SSS	power controller	85.00	169.95	633	B-9
*** Total ***						
					10748	

---

3. Print the report for only type SSS.
4. Create a label that prints 3-across like this:

UPS 200 watt capacity
L1003
A-8

---

5. Print for all A locations.

(*Hint:* Specify the search condition LOCATION = 'A'.)

Lesson 5
Advanced Features of dBASE III PLUS

Objectives

Upon completion of the material presented in this lesson you should be able to do the following:

- Use multiple database files at the same time.
- Set up relations between database files.
- Generate and use custom screen formats for data entry.
- Create a command (program) file.

STARTING OFF

Start dBASE III Plus on the computer by following instructions given in the introduction to this module so that the dBASE ASSIST screen is displayed. Insert the data disk from the previous lesson into drive B.

USING TWO DATABASE FILES SIMULTANEOUSLY

So far you've used only one database file at a time. When you wanted to use INVENTRY after using ACCOUNTS, you had to specify the usage of INVENTRY, closing the ACCOUNTS file. Actually, you can have up to ten database files opened at the same time in dBASE III Plus. This feature, however, can be accessed only through the dot prompt, as are many of the other advanced features of dBASE III Plus.

Picture yourself in a large office, with ten desks at your disposal. You can spread a different piece of work or file on each desk and move from one desk to the other, sometimes passing information on one desk to another. dBASE III Plus has ten work areas you can use, and you can open one database file in each. You select the work area to use, then you can use the file in that work area.

The work areas in dBASE III Plus are identified as A through J *or* 1 to 10. Here you will use letters A through J. The work area you are initially placed in is A, and you stay in A until you issue a SELECT command to specify another work area. That means you are now in area A.

- With drive B as the default, specify INVENTRY for usage with CODE.NDX as the master index.

  > You see **INVENTRY** listed on the status bar.

Suppose you move to area B and open the ACCOUNTS file there.

- Make sure you are at the dot prompt.
- Type SELECT B and press **ENTER**.

  > On the status bar INVENTRY is no longer indicated.

- Specify **ACCOUNTS** for usage with **ACC_NO.NDX** as the master index.

To find out what files you have opened in what area and what index you are using with each file, you can use the DISPLAY STATUS command.

- Type DISPLAY STATUS and press **ENTER**.

  > The screen shown in Screen Display 5-1 is displayed.

The status of each work area is displayed on the screen. This command is your window as to where open files are kept in the system.

- Press **ENTER** to continue.

  > More information is displayed. This is not discussed here.

- Return to the first work area by typing SELECT A and pressing **ENTER**.

  > The status bar indicates that **INVENTRY** is in use.

NOTE ■ The commands could have been entered as SELECT 1 and SELECT 2 instead of SELECT A and SELECT B. The two forms are equivalent.

In an office environment with ten desks that you can use, as discussed earlier, it is not too likely that you will work on ten completely independent pieces of work at the same time. It's more likely that you have more than one related piece of information

```
(DEMO) . select b
(DEMO) . use accounts index acc_no, last
(DEMO) . display status

Select area:  1, Database in Use: B:INVENTRY.dbf   Alias: INVENTRY
    Master index file:  B:CODE.ndx  Key: item_code

Currently Selected Database:
Select area:  2, Database in Use: B:accounts.dbf   Alias: ACCOUNTS
    Master index file:  B:acc_no.ndx  Key: acc_number
           Index file:  B:last.ndx  Key: LAST_NAME

File search path:
Default disk drive: B:
Print destination:  PRN:
Margin =     0
Current work area =    2

Press any key to continue..._
Command Line     ||<B:>||ACCOUNTS                ||Rec: 2/14          ||      ||Num

                        Enter a dBASE III PLUS command.
```

Screen Display 5-1

spread out on different desks so that you can pass or share information from one to another. It is the same with the ten work areas in dBASE III Plus. The purpose of having ten work areas is to have two or more databases for a single system in use at the same time.

You will now set up a third file, SALES, which relates to both the ACCOUNTS and INVENTRY database files. Rather than using a third area, you will place this file in area A, thus closing the INVENTRY file.

PRACTICE TIME

1. Make sure that you are in work area A. (**SELECT A**)
2. Create the database file SALES with the following structure.

Field No.	*Field Name*	*Type*	*Width*	*Dec*
1	TRANS_DATE	Date		
2	ACC_NUMBER	Character	3	
3	ITEM_CODE	Character	5	
4	QUANTITY	Numeric	4	0

3. Enter the following data:

TRANS__DATE	ACC__NUMBER	ITEM__CODE	QUANTITY
07/11/89	051	DX460	24
07/12/89	066	DX524	120
07/13/89	025	DX750	48
07/10/89	066	DX460	64

4. Index on TRANS__DATE to SALES.NDX.

To close all database files (in all areas), you use the command CLOSE DATABASE.

- Type CLOSE DATABASE and press **ENTER**.

SETTING A VIEW

When we create a file for customer account data we normally store items such as the customer's name, address, telephone number, and current balance. When we create a file for sales data, we normally store items such as the date, what was sold, how many, and to whom. To indicate to whom each sale was made, we could place a customer's name and address in each sale record. But that data is already stored in the accounts file. Normally, we avoid duplicating stored data whenever possible.

If we don't duplicate that data in each sale record, then how do we know the name and address of the customer to whom the company made a sale? A number of techniques can be used, but a common one is to assign each customer a unique account number, then place the appropriate account number in each sale record. You saw an illustration of this in Chapter 6 of *Business Computer Systems*. Thus, the connection between a particular sale record and a particular customer record is made by means of the value of the customer account number.

In dBASE, we establish such a connection—which in dBASE is called a *relation*—by means of a special construct called a *view*.

Let's look at the current example; each record in the SALES file contains information on a sale that was made. The SALES file contains the fields TRANS__DATE, ACC__NUMBER, ITEM__CODE, and QUANTITY. The field ITEM__CODE can be used to relate the SALES file to the INVENTRY file. A *view* can be set up so that all information about an item code is displayed on the screen along with the information on the SALES file. The fact that the information is coming from two database files is transparent to the user. Since it has an ACC_NUMBER field, the SALES file can be related to the ACCOUNTS database file as well. Thus a view can be constructed to see the customer name and balance, as though those fields were included in SALES. Because the clerk is processing the sales information (and in the process, needs information from the ACCOUNTS file), the SALES file is said to be the *parent* file and the ACCOUNTS file is called the *child*, and the field that controls the access is ACC_NUMBER. For the relation to work, the child file must be indexed on the control field. In this case, the ACCOUNTS file must have the ACC_NO.NDX (index on ACC_NUMBER) as the master index.

NOTE ■ Although the field QUANTITY appears in both SALES and INVENTRY files, they are not related. The one in INVENTRY is the quantity that is left on inventory; the one in SALES is the quantity sold.

All of these views are created and saved as files with the extension .VUE. Because dBASE III Plus does not allow more than one child file per parent file, both of these views cannot be set up in a single view. You will set them up as two separate views. The dBASE III Plus command that sets up the view is the VIEW command. It is a *high-level command*, meaning that, once it is set up, it does a lot of things automatically. For example, when a user activates a view, the user does not need to specify which database files and index files to use, nor does the user need to specify which fields should be displayed. These are all defined in the view. Hence a certain amount of planning should be done before setting up a view, so that the informational requirements of the user are satisfied.

Let's set up a view that relates the SALES file with the ACCOUNT file. You want to display all fields in the SALES file and names and balance fields from the ACCOUNTS file.

From ASSIST

- Highlight **Create** on the menu bar.
- Select **View** on the pull-down menu.
- Select drive **B** and enter a filename for the view. Enter **CUSTOMER**.

From the Dot Prompt

- Type **CREATE VIEW CUSTOMER** and press **ENTER**.

> The Create View screen is displayed, as seen in Screen Display 5-2.

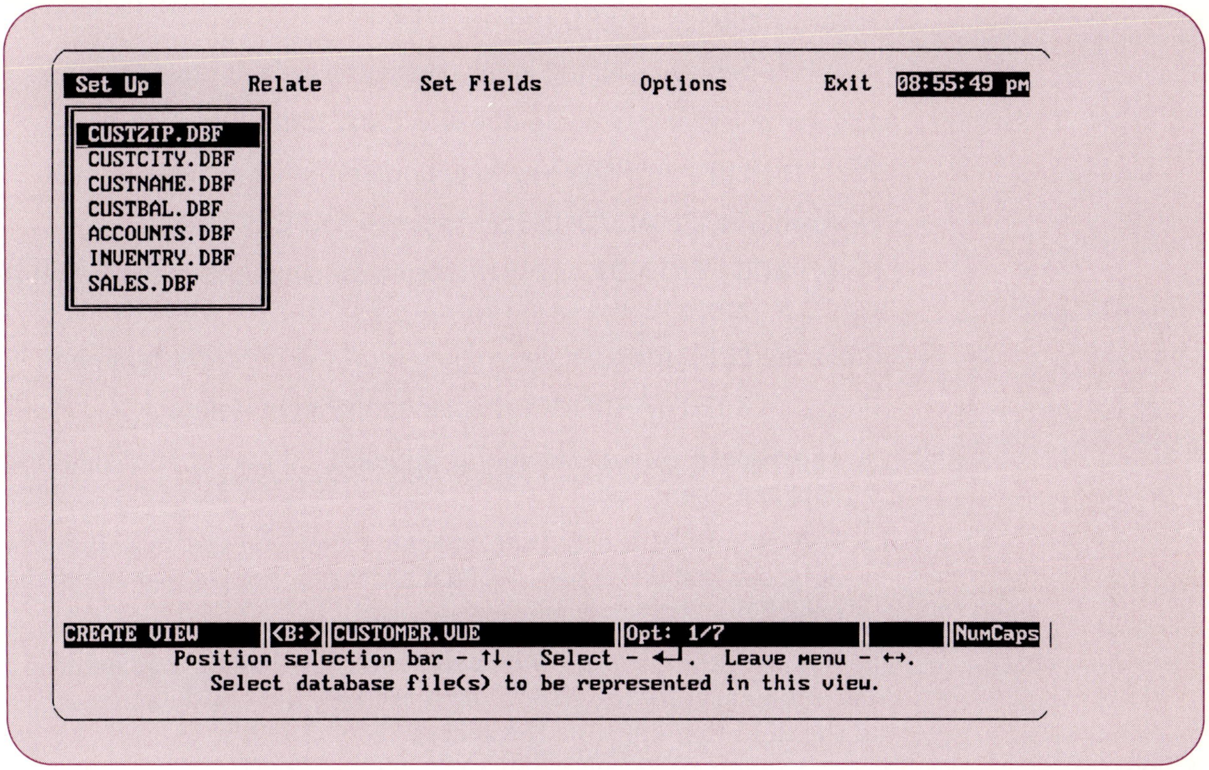

Screen Display 5-2

Like ASSIST and some other commands you have used, it is a menu-driven process. Along the top are the main menu selections. *Set Up* is used to select the database files and appropriate index files for use in the view. *Relate* is used to specify the parent file and to indicate which field in that file controls the record in the child file. The *Set Fields* option is used to specify which fields in the related files are to be displayed. (*Options* is not discussed here.)

- Highlight **Set Up**.

  > A pull-down menu displaying all the database files in the default drive appears.

If any database file is in use, there is a triangle to the left, marking it as selected. Otherwise there is no triangle. Triangles are toggled on and off by moving the highlight to the file and then pressing the ENTER key. When you select a file, a submenu appears that allows you to select the index files you want to be active in the view. Select the Master index for the file first. When finished, press the LEFT ARROW or RIGHT ARROW key to continue selecting database files.

- Highlight the file **SALES** and press **ENTER**.

  > A box displaying all the index files in the default drive appears.

SALES is not indexed, so do not select any index file with it.

- Press the **LEFT ARROW** key to get out of the index file submenu.
- Highlight the file **ACCOUNTS** and press **ENTER**.
- Select **ACC_NO.NDX** as the master index since this is the field that controls access to ACCOUNTS (from SALES).
- Press the **LEFT ARROW** key to get out of the index file submenu.
- Press the **RIGHT ARROW** key again to highlight **Relate**.

  > The Relate pull-down menu appears, showing the selected database filenames.

  > The prompt at the bottom indicates that you are to select the database that will initiate the relation, that is, the file that will be the parent.

The Relate option is used to *link* the two files that were selected. To do this, you specify the parent database file, the child database file, and the field that controls the access.

- Highlight **SALES** and press **ENTER**.

  > Immediately, another submenu opens for selecting the database that will accept the relation, that is, the child database.

Since this view contains only two database files, dBASE III Plus indicates that ACCOUNTS is the child database.

- Press **ENTER**.

  > A triangle appears to the right of the filename. The prompt line informs you that the master key expression (for ACCOUNTS) is **ACC_NUMBER**. You are to enter the field name in the parent file (SALES) that is the equivalent. That field is ACC_NUMBER.

- Press the **F10** function key for a list of the field names in SALES.

  > A submenu of field names appears.

- Highlight **ACC_NUMBER** on the submenu and press **ENTER**.
- Press **ENTER** again to terminate the linking expression.

The child file is now linked by the contents of ACC_NUMBER to the parent file. Note the action line, which shows the relation chain.

- Press the **RIGHT ARROW** or **LEFT ARROW** key to leave the Relate submenu.

Having related the files, you need to select which fields from each of the files are to be included in the view (to be displayed on the screen). Here you want to show all the fields in SALES, but just fields FIRST__NAME, LAST__NAME, and BALANCE from the ACCOUNTS file.

NOTE ■ In another view you might want to select other fields.

- Highlight **Set Fields**.

  > The pull-down menu shows the selected filenames in the view.

By selecting each in turn, another submenu appears with the field names for you to select or de-select as you have done previously.

- Highlight **SALES** and press **ENTER**.

  > All the fields in SALES are displayed. Note that all fields are initially selected. (There are triangles next to all fields.)

If you want *not* to display some of the fields, highlight those and press ENTER. In this case, however, you want to show all of them.

- Press the **RIGHT ARROW** key to leave the submenu.
- Highlight **ACCOUNTS** and press **ENTER**.
- De-select (so that the triangles do not appear) fields ACC__NUMBER and ADDRESS through TELEPHONE.
- Return to the main menu and select **Exit**, followed by **Save**.

You have completed specification of files, relations, and fields. The view has been created and is active now.

- Now BROWSE the file.

  > The screen of Screen Display 5-3 appears.

You recognize the four fields in SALES, but then you see the name fields and the balance from ACCOUNTS. Note that Julio Chavez is listed twice, since he placed two orders.

Let's try a little experiment.

- Position the cursor on the **ACC__NUMBER** field on the first record.
- Change the account number to 000, which is not in the ACCOUNTS database.

```
CURSOR   <-- -->  |       UP    DOWN  |  DELETE       |  Insert Mode:   Ins
 Char:     ←   →  | Record:  ↑    ↓   | Char:   Del   |  Exit:         ^End
 Field: Home End  | Page:  PgUp  PgDn | Field:  ^Y    |  Abort:         Esc
 Pan:     ^←  ^→  | Help:   F1        | Record: ^U    |  Set Options: ^Home

TRANS_DATE ACC_NUMBER ITEM_CODE QUANTITY FIRST_NAME-- LAST_NAME--- BALANCE
07/11/89   201        DX460           24 Jonathan     Handel         76.24
07/12/89   066        DX524          120 Julio        Chavez        782.38
07/13/89   025        DX750           48 Harold       Smith          29.75
07/10/89   066        DX460           64 Julio        Chavez        782.38

BROWSE          ||<B:>||SALES          ||Rec: 1/4        ||     ||NumCaps

                         View and edit fields.
```

Screen Display 5-3

> Nothing happens.

- Move the cursor down a record, then back to the first record.

  > The name and balance fields are now blank. There was no record in ACCOUNTS that matched the account number given.

- Now change the account number to **051**. Then move the cursor down a record, then back to the first record.

  > Now you see **Cindy Beard** in the name field.

The information displayed under VIEW is kept current at all times.

- Enter **CTRL/END** to exit BROWSE.
- From ASSIST highlight **Retrieve**, then **Display**, and press **ENTER**.
- Highlight **Construct a field list** and press **ENTER**.

  > All seven field names are displayed.

- Display all records to the screen.

It is as though you are working with one database file.

PRACTICE TIME

Create a Sales Transaction Report that looks similar to the following:

Page No. 1
07/11/89

SALES TRANSACTION REPORT

TRANSACTION DATE	ACCOUNT NUMBER	CUSTOMER NAME	ITEM CODE	QUANTITY SOLD
07/11/89	051	Beard, Cindy	DX460	24
07/12/89	066	Chavez, Julio	DX524	120
07/13/89	025	Smith, Harold	DX750	48
07/10/89	066	Chavez, Julio	DX460	64
*** Total ***				
				256

NOTE ■ In creating the column information, note that the Contents of a report column when a View is active consist of both the filename and the field name, linked by the characters "–>". This is to avoid confusion if the same field name appears in multiple database files.

- Close all database files.

If later you decide that you want to use the view again, you can set the view through ASSIST by selecting Set Up/View and specifying the view file CUSTOMER, or from the dot prompt by typing SET VIEW TO CUSTOMER. Also, the view can be changed through ASSIST by selecting Modify/View and specifying the view file CUSTOMER, *or* from the dot prompt by typing MODIFY VIEW CUSTOMER.

PRACTICE TIME

You will now relate the SALES file with the INVENTRY file.

Before you start, index SALES on TRANS__DATE to the index file SALES.NDX, and modify the structure of INVENTRY.DBF so that the width of DESCRPTION is 30.

The view file is to be named WAREHAUS. The SALES file is the parent file, indexed on SALES.NDX, and INVENTRY is the child file. Make sure that CODE.NDX is the master index for the INVENTRY file since ITEM__CODE is the field that controls the access.

You are to display the fields TRANS__DATE, ACC__NUMBER, ITEM __CODE, and QUANTITY in SALES, and the DESCRIPTN and PRICE fields in INVENTRY.

When finished, do BROWSE to see the file. It should look like the one in Screen Display 5-4.

```
 CURSOR    <-- -->  |         UP    DOWN  |    DELETE      | Insert Mode:   Ins
  Char:       ←  →  | Record:  ↑      ↓   | Char:    Del   | Exit:         ^End
  Field:  Home End  | Page:   PgUp  PgDn  | Field:   ^Y    | Abort:         Esc
  Pan:        ^← ^→ | Help:    F1         | Record:  ^U    | Set Options: ^Home

TRANS_DATE ACC_NUMBER ITEM_CODE QUANTITY DESCRIPTN-------------------- PRICE-
07/10/89   066        DX460           64 Galaxy NL10 ribbon              7.75
07/11/89   051        DX460           24 Galaxy NL10 ribbon              7.75
07/12/89   066        DX524          120 Maxon EX800 ribbon             12.75
07/13/89   025        DX750           48 Spirit 7 ribbon, multistrike    7.95

BROWSE          |<B:>|SALES               |Rec: 4/4        |      |NumCaps|

                          View and edit fields.
```

Screen Display 5-4

You have created views of two database files. Views of up to ten files can be created, provided that they are appropriately linked. In the above example you might have a PURCHASE file, where you record purchased parts that go into inventory. This file will contain vendor code and item__code, which will relate it to the VENDOR file (where information about each vendor is kept) and to the INVENTRY file. Each record of INVENTRY, too, might contain a VENDOR field so you know where these were purchased. As you can see, as you create more complex relations, there is a need for planning.

- Close all database files.

GENERATING CUSTOM SCREEN FORMATS FOR DATA ENTRY

Up to now you have used the default screen to enter data into database files. You can create a custom screen by creating a format file for the screen. The screen format file is associated with a database file, and has the extension .SCR when it is being created.

When the format is saved, however, the file will have the extension .FMT.

- Specify database file SALES for use with no index.

From ASSIST

- Highlight **Create**.
- Highlight **Format** and press **ENTER**.
- Select drive **B:**, then type the filename SALES

From the Dot Prompt

- Type CREATE SCREEN SALES and press **ENTER**.

> The Create Screen subprogram is displayed, as shown in Screen Display 5-5.

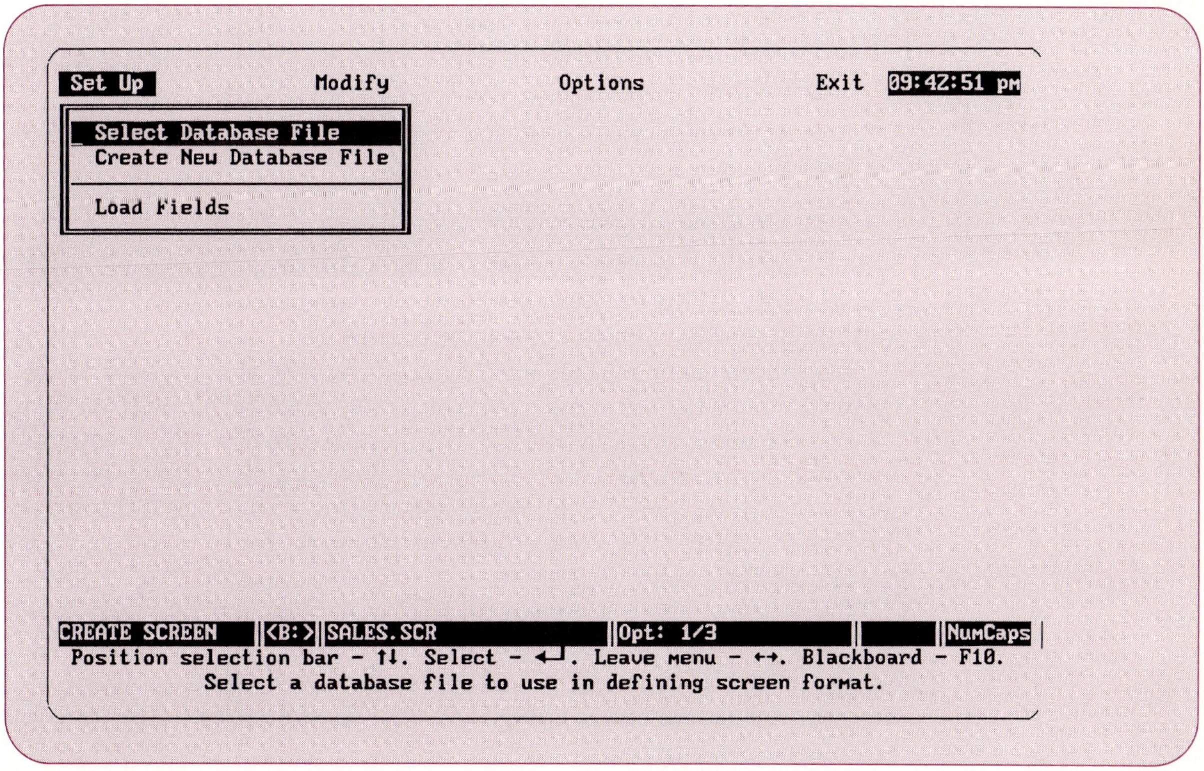

Screen Display 5-5

Create Screen is partially menu-driven, and partially a blackboard for you to lay out the screen display. Think of this subprogram as having two sides: blackboard and menu. Now you are on the menu side.

- Press the **F10** function key.

  > You are now on the blackboard side.

You toggle the two sides by using the F10 function key.

- Press the **F10** function key again to return to the menu side.

The menu side has four main menu options: Set Up, Modify, Options, and Exit. Set Up is used to select fields for the blackboard. Modify lets you specify the input *template* and whether the field is read-only or changeable. These terms will be explained.

- Highlight Set Up.
- Highlight the Load fields option on the pull-down menu and press ENTER.

  > All fields in the SALES file are displayed.

- Select all four fields (Highlight the field and press ENTER so that triangles appear.)
- When done, exit the sub-menu with the LEFT ARROW or RIGHT ARROW key.

  > You are now in the blackboard, as shown in Screen Display 5-6.

When you first load the fields, you automatically move to the blackboard. All other times you will toggle between the menu board and the blackboard with the F10 function key.

The fourth area of the status bar indicates the page, row, and column where the cursor is. Rows on a page are numbered from 00 to 24, and columns across a line are numbered from 00 to 79. If you have a database with many entries, you can design a multiple-page entry form. The main part of the blackboard shows the four field names and their width. The first thing you want to do is to move them around so they look nice.

The field names that appear on the screen are just labels. It is the highlighted areas to the right of the field names that are the actual entry fields. In creating a custom screen, you need to move the highlighted area around. Labels can be whatever you choose and can be entered anywhere.

You want to design the input screen form so that it looks something like the following:

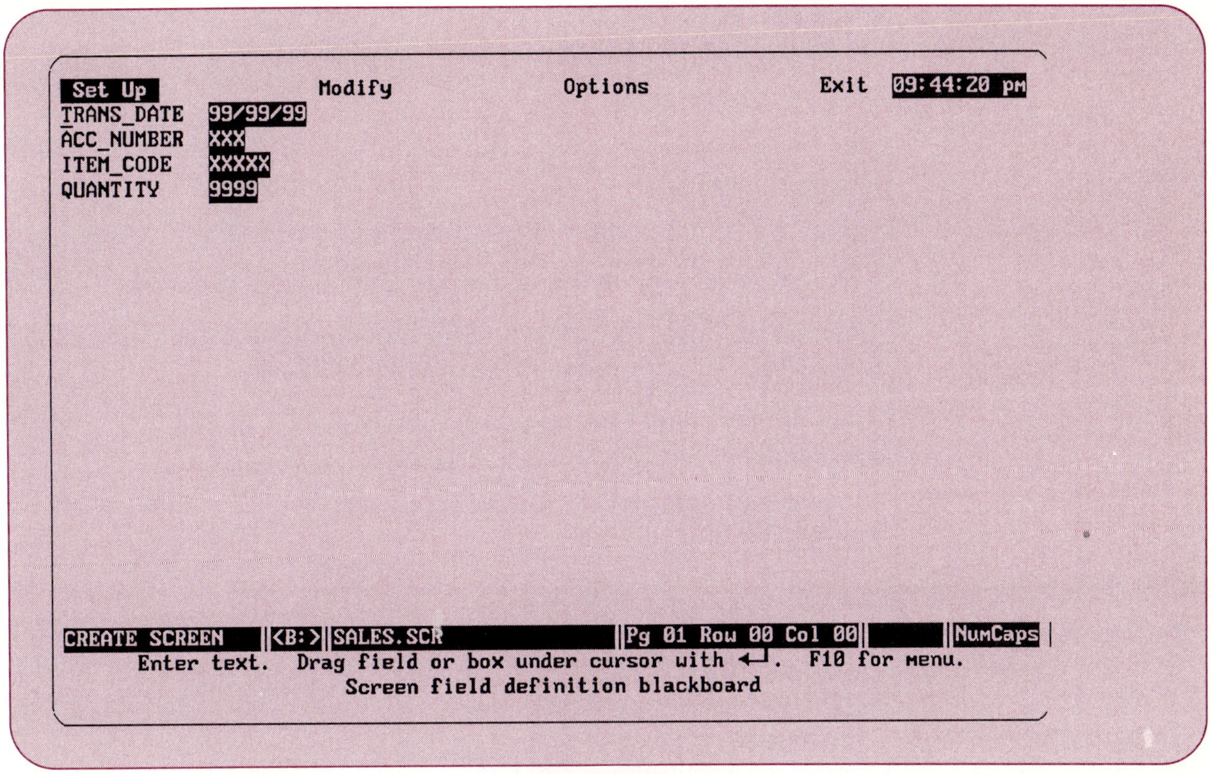

Screen Display 5-6

ACME DISTRIBUTIONS SALES

DATE: mm/dd/yy

CUSTOMER ACCOUNT NUMBER: 999

PART NUMBER ORDERED: !!999

QUANTITY ORDERED: 9999

- Before starting, make sure that the INS key is off.
- Use the cursor-move keys to move the cursor to the highlighted region to the right of QUANTITY.

  > At the bottom of the screen the Navigation and Prompt lines indicate that you can drag the field to another place on the screen.

- Press the **ENTER** key to *hook* the field onto the cursor, so the field can be *dragged* to another place on the blackboard.

  > Nothing happens.

- Use the arrow keys to move the cursor to row 14, column 45 (check the fourth area on the status bar to see where you are).
- When the cursor is there, press ENTER again to drop the field.

  > The field moves so that its first position is at the cursor.

- Now go to row 14, column 25, and type the label QUANTITY ORDERED:. Do not press ENTER when finished.

You no longer need the field name QUANTITY at the upper left of the screen.

- Move the cursor to where QUANTITY is displayed, and delete the field name using the DEL key.

PRACTICE TIME

1. Move the ITEM__CODE input field to row 12, column 46, and enter the title **PART NUMBER ORDERED:** beginning at row 12, column 24. Then delete the field name ITEM__CODE from the left edge of the screen.
2. Move the account number field to row 9, column 48; enter the label **CUSTOMER ACCOUNT NUMBER:** starting on column 22.
3. Move the date field to row 7, column 36; enter the label **DATE**: starting on column 29.
4. Make sure to delete the old field names at the left.
5. Enter the screen title on row 4, starting on column 24.

NOTE ■ You can move what is displayed on the screen. Turn the INS key on. If you were to place the cursor in the space before the field name or the highlight and press ENTER, the field name or the highlight would move to the right. If you were to press the DEL key, the field name or the highlight would move to the left.

At this point you could quit and have a serviceable input screen, but you want to make it even better. There are several things you can do to improve the input screen. For example, you can draw boxes around some information on the screen or specify which types of characters or numbers can be entered into fields (input template).

Template

One of the most common causes of errors in a database is the incorrect data that was input. Often referred to as "garbage-in, garbage-out (GIGO)," if any incorrect data was entered, the information you get out is also in error. In custom designing a screen format for data entry, you can build in some kind of error checking. The template is one such way to do this. Using a template, you get to restrict the type of data that might be entered into a field. In this case you will restrict data that can be entered into the part number field (ITEM_CODE) to two uppercase letters followed by three numbers.

- Place the cursor on the input field for part number (highlighted area), and press the **F10** function key to toggle to the other screen.

  > Modify screen is displayed for **ITEM_CODE** field.

- Highlight **Picture Template** and press **ENTER**. Your screen should look like the one in Screen Display 5-7.

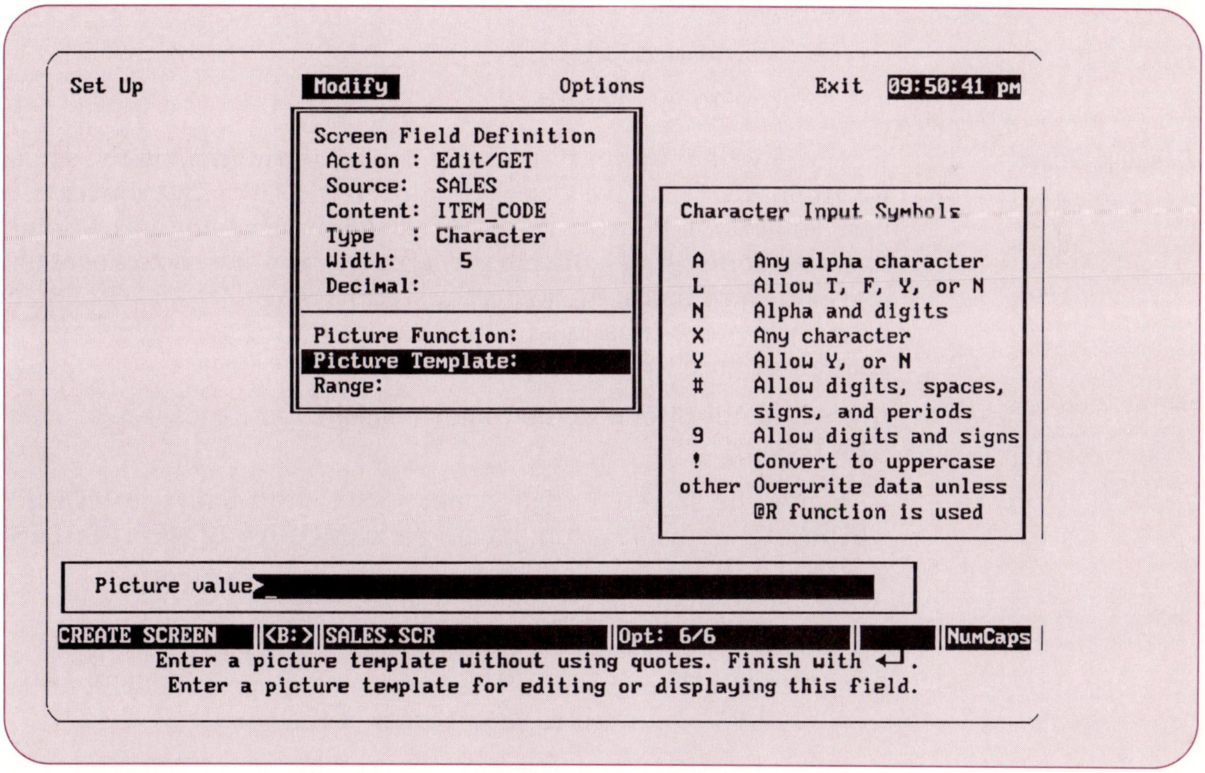

Screen Display 5-7

The Picture Template option allows you to indicate, on a position-by-position basis, which types of input are allowed. The help menu at the right indicates the allowable template symbols. You want the display to be two uppercase letters and three digits: The ! symbol forces alphabetic entries to uppercase letters (and precludes entry of lowercase letters); the 9 symbol forces entry of digits. The Picture value box, just above the status bar, is where your entry is made.

- Type !!999 to specify two positions of uppercase, followed by three digit positions. When finished, press **ENTER** and then **F10** to return to the blackboard.

  > Notice that **!!999** appears within the highlight.

- Move the cursor to the account number field (ACC_NUMBER), which is to be three digits.
- Press the **F10** function key.

  > The Modify screen for the ACC_NUMBER field is displayed.

- Highlight **Picture Template** and press **ENTER**.
- Type 999 and press **ENTER**.
- Press the **F10** function key.

Drawing Boxes

Now you will draw boxes around certain information on the screen for emphasis. First take a word of caution and save what you have, in case something doesn't work out correctly. Drawing boxes is not hard, but sometimes students get confused, and draw boxes over text and data entry fields. By saving the screen format before drawing the boxes, you prevent having to do the work to this point over again if something goes wrong.

- Move to the Menu screen and highlight **Exit**, then **Save**. Press **ENTER**.
- Reenter the screen through either ASSIST (this time use **MODIFY, FORMAT**) or the dot prompt command (**MODIFY SCREEN SALES**).
- Highlight the **Options**, then **Double Bar**. Press **ENTER**.

  > You return to the blackboard.

(*CAUTION:* The cursor is "live" now, so don't press ENTER unless you want to set a corner of the box.)

In drawing a box, you need to specify the top left and bottom right corners of the box. You just have to be careful not to place the box on top of the text. Here the top left will be row 3, column 10; and the bottom right will be row 16, column 62.

- Position the cursor at row 3, column 10, using the arrow keys, and press **ENTER**.

  > At the prompt line you are instructed to locate the opposite corner of the box and press ENTER.

- Move the cursor to row 16, column 62 and press **ENTER** again.

  > The double box is drawn around your input form, as seen in Screen Display 5-8.

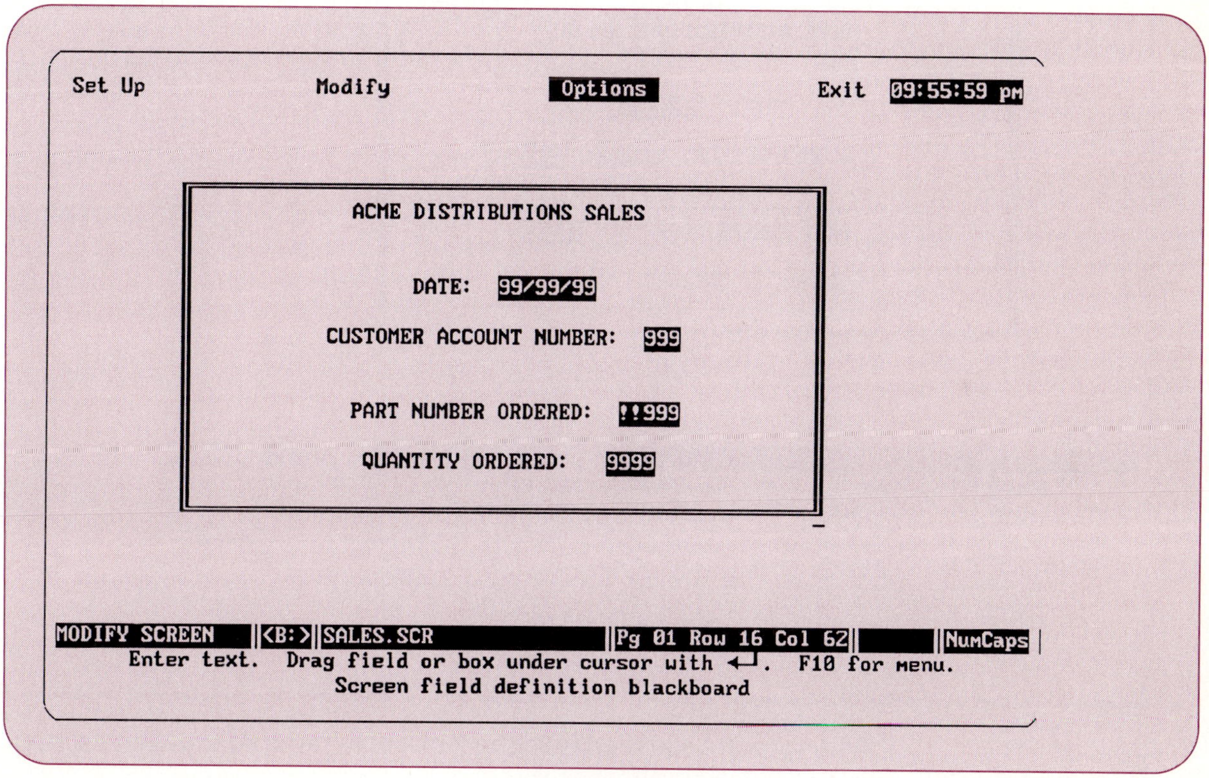

Screen Display 5-8

PRACTICE TIME

Draw a single box around the text and fields for part number and quantity. Remember, the horizontal lines have to be on different rows from the text. You might use row 11, column 18 as the top left corner and row 15, column 55 as the bottom right corner. Your screen should look like the one in Screen Display 5-9.

NOTE ■ If you decide you placed a box in the wrong place, with the cursor on the corner you just placed, press ENTER again. The box can be changed like a rubber band, by moving the cursor with the arrow keys. It is again set by pressing ENTER. This is true even after you have done other editing on the blackboard.

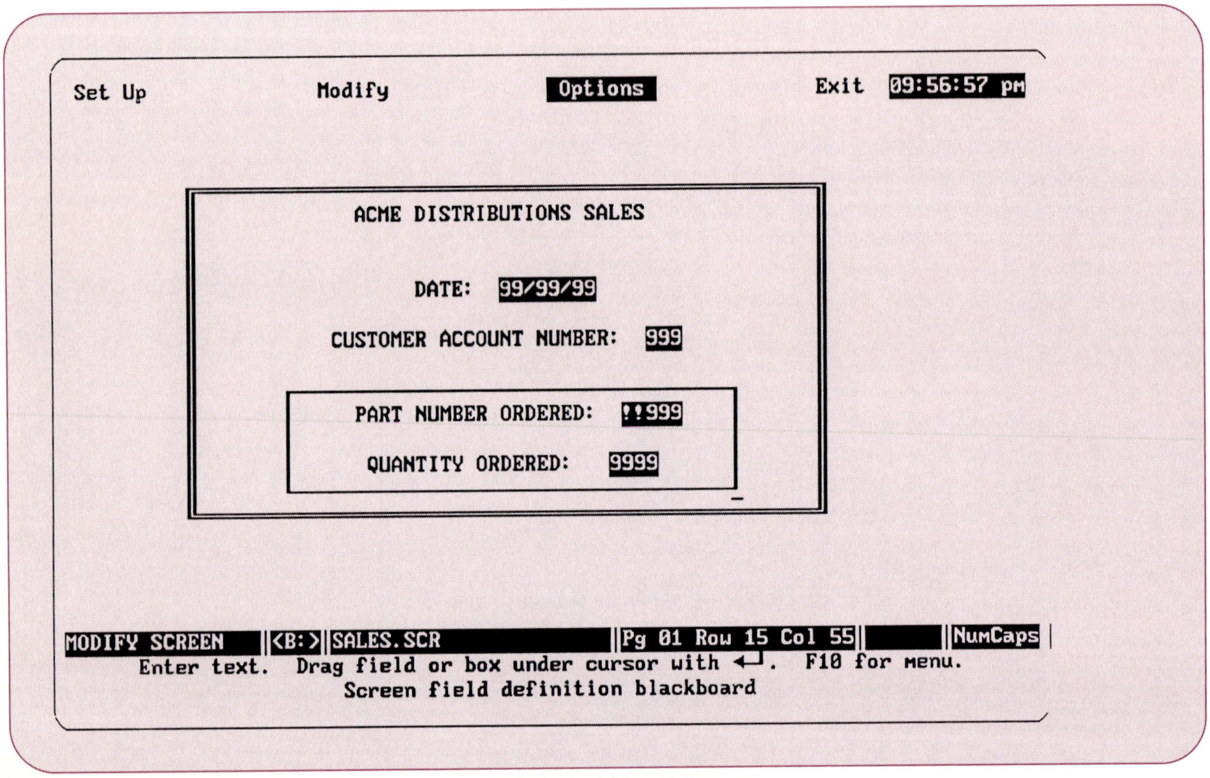

Screen Display 5-9

- When you are satisfied with the looks of it, move to the Menu screen, and exit, saving the changes.

USING CUSTOM SCREEN FORMATS FOR DATA ENTRY

The screen format is active right now. If you are to APPEND to the file, the custom screen is displayed. When you quit dBASE or otherwise close the file, then when you return to using the file, you need to specify the Format again.

- Close database files.
- Specify the database file **SALES** with **SALES.NDX** as the master index.

As mentioned earlier, when you are creating a custom screen, the file being used has the extension .SCR. Once it is created, however, to activate the screen you use the file with the extension .FMT.

From ASSIST

- Highlight **Set Up**.
- Highlight **Format for Screen** and press **ENTER**.
- Highlight **B:** and press **ENTER**.
- Highlight **SALES.FMT**.

From the Dot Prompt

- Type **SET FORMAT TO SALES** and press **ENTER**.

Now you get to enter data.

PRACTICE TIME

1. APPEND the following data to the file. (From ASSIST highlight **Update/Append**; from the dot prompt, type **APPEND**.) As you enter the data, try entering some letters for account number, or entering lowercase letters for the item code. As you should see, you have designed an input screen that can help prevent mistakes in data entry.

DATE	*ACC_NUMBER*	*ITEM_CODE*	*QUANTITY*
07/25/89	128	ML799	120
07/25/89	150	DX119	48
07/25/89	150	DX460	24
07/25/89	100	DX300	90

2. Activate a view, either CUSTOMER or WAREHAUS, then BROWSE.
3. Close all files.

4. Create a report that requires the WAREHAUS view, as shown below:

Page No. 1
12/12/88

SALES REPORT

DATE OF SALE	PART NUMBER	DESCRIPTION	QUANT.	PRICE	AMOUNT OF SALE
07/10/89	DX460	Galaxy NL10 ribbon	64	7.75	496.00
07/11/89	DX460	Galaxy NL10 ribbon	24	7.75	186.00
07/12/89	DX524	Maxon EX800 ribbon	120	12.75	1530.00
07/13/89	DX750	Spirit 7 ribbon, multistrike	48	7.95	381.60
07/25/89	ML799	Micro 193 ribbon	120	8.49	1018.80
07/25/89	DX119	SAM 1300 ribbon, multistrike	48	4.15	199.20
07/25/89	DX460	Galaxy NL10 ribbon	24	7.75	186.00
07/25/89	DX300	NIC P-565 ribbon	90	10.25	922.50
*** Total ***					
					4920.10

Note the last report column, where the amount of sale is printed. This column is generated by specifying QUANTITY * PRICE in the Contents for that field. Use the F10 function key to select the fields, so that the appropriate filenames are also included in the field specifications.

COMMANDS ON THE DOT PROMPT

Suppose that you are about to begin a procedure of data entry into the file SALES. What commands do you need to enter through the duration of the session?

(1) Set the default drive.
(2) Specify the SALES file for use with the appropriate index.
(3) Set the screen format to SALES.
(4) Give the APPEND command to enter data.
(5) Turn off the screen format.
(6) Review the data with the view for customer accounts active, to verify that the customer numbers that were entered are valid. That means, set the view, then browse.
(7) Repeat the data review with the view for inventory (WAREHAUS).
(8) List the SALES file to the printer.
(9) Close the database file.

That is a long list of things. You know how to do all those things, and more. But it may take time looking up the particular file names in various steps, and misspelled commands can be confusing at times.

It is possible for you to put all the commands that you need to carry out a procedure such as the one mentioned above into a single file, called a *command file,* or *program file.* All commands entered must be dot prompt commands. You can cause the commands in the command file to be executed, or performed, by issuing a single command. This is a tremendous advantage when you have a procedure that you want executed the same way, over and over. Command files have the extension .PRG.

Before creating a command file, you must identify which commands need to be in it. So you should step through all the commands required to carry out the procedure you need to do, and write them in a list so that you can enter them into a command file later. The procedure is the one that is mentioned above. Remember, all the commands are issued from the dot prompt.

- Have a pencil and paper ready.
- For step (1), type SET DEFAULT TO B and press **ENTER**. Make sure to write it down on the paper as well.
- For step (2), type USE SALES INDEX SALES and press **ENTER**. Write it down.
- For step (3), type SET FORMAT TO SALES and press **ENTER**. Add it to your list.
- For step (4), type APPEND and press **ENTER**. Write it down.

If this were a real data entry session, you could enter data at this point. Right now, however, you don't really have anything to append to the SALES database file.

- Press **ESC** to abort APPEND. There is no need to write this down.
- For step (5), type SET FORMAT TO and press **ENTER**. Include this in your list.

NOTE ■ By leaving the filename blank in the SET FORMAT TO command, you turn off the screen format that was set previously.

The next two steps are for verifying the data entry. The best way to make sure that the account numbers were entered correctly is to compare the entry against the ones in the CUSTOMER database. If it exists, it is a valid account. If it does not exist (name fields will be blank), there is an error. The same thing is true of the item code. By checking it against the entries in the INVENTRY database file, you can verify the validity. In each case you will set the view and then browse.

- Type SET VIEW TO CUSTOMER and press **ENTER**.
- Type BROWSE and press **ENTER**. Write these down as step (6).

  > You should see seven fields as you did in the previous lesson. If any of the names and balance fields appear blank, the account number is in error. You can correct it now.

- Enter **CTRL/END** to exit BROWSE. There is no need to write this down.
- Type SET VIEW TO WAREHAUS and press **ENTER**.
- Type BROWSE and press **ENTER**. Put these in your list for step (7).
- Enter **CTRL/END** to exit BROWSE. There is no need to write this down.

The way to turn off the view is to close all files. You will then open the SALES file before going on to step (8).

- Type CLOSE DATABASE and press **ENTER**.
- Type USE SALES INDEX SALES and press **ENTER**. Although these are not some of the numbered steps, you will probably find it helpful to write them on your list.
- For step (8), make sure that the printer is on and is ready to use. Then type LIST ALL TO PRINT and press **ENTER**. Put this on your paper.
- For the last step, type CLOSE DATABASE and press **ENTER**.

Did you write everything down on the paper?

INVOKING THE COMMAND EDITOR

dBASE III Plus has a built-in text editor, which is useful for entering and editing command files. The command MODIFY COMMAND filename is used for initial entry of the commands, as well as for later editing of the commands. As mentioned earlier, the command file has a .PRG extension.

- Type MODIFY COMMAND DATAENTR and press **ENTER**.

  > The screen of Screen Display 5-10 appears.

The Help menu at the top can be toggled on and off with the F1 function key. Keep it on for now, while you get used to the editor.

- Make sure that the word **Ins** appears on the top line. If it does not, press the **INS** key.

```
Edit: DATAENTR.prg                                   NumCaps

 CURSOR:  <-- -->  |           UP  DOWN | DELETE          | Insert Mode:      Ins
  Char:      ← →   | Line:     ↑    ↓   | Char:     Del   | Insert line:      ^N
  Word:  Home End  | Page: PgUp  PgDn   | Word:      ^T   | Save: ^W  Abort:Esc
  Line:     ^← ^→  | Find:    ^KF       | Line:      ^Y   | Read file:        ^KR
  Reformat: ^KB    | Refind:  ^KL       |                 | Write file:       ^KW

_
```

Screen Display 5-10

NOTE ■ There are two modes of typing: insert and replace. Here the lesson assumes that Insert is active. When you are familiar with the editor, you may select whichever is more comfortable.

Commands may be entered in upper- or lowercase. Here commands are presented in uppercase for clarity. As you enter commands, press ENTER at the end of each line. If you need to make corrections, use the cursor key to move to the location you want to change, and press the appropriate key to accomplish the task. CTRL/Y deletes a line, pressing the DEL key erases the character at the cursor, and pressing the BACKSPACE key erases the character to the left of the cursor.

- Enter the commands you wrote down:

```
SET DEFAULT TO B
USE SALES INDEX SALES
SET FORMAT TO SALES
APPEND
```

```
SET FORMAT TO
SET VIEW TO CUSTOMER
BROWSE
SET VIEW TO WAREHAUS
BROWSE
CLOSE DATABASE
USE SALES INDEX SALES
LIST ALL TO PRINT
CLOSE DATABASE
```

When you have completed entering the commands, you exit the editor by pressing CTRL/END. If you don't want to keep the changes you made, you can abort the session with the ESC key.

- Enter **CTRL/END** to save the entries you made, and exit.

EXECUTING A COMMAND FILE

Now it is important that you step through the commands to make sure they work. The command to invoke the command file is DO filename, where filename is the command filename (without the extension). You should know what to expect when you execute the command file.

If there is an error in the commands, a message will appear indicating what to fix. In addition, a message **Cancel, Ignore, or Suspend? (C, I, or S)** appears at the bottom of the screen. You will most likely type C to cancel the execution of the command file. At that point you may have to redo a database file, an index file, or a view file, or you may have to correct the command file.

To correct the command file, enter **MODIFY COMMAND DATAENTR**, find the incorrect command, and use the editing keystrokes to correct it. Save changes by **CTRL/END** and try invoking the command file again.

When this command file is working, you are first presented with the screen format you previously generated. Later you will enter data. For now just press the ESC key to go on. When you see the BROWSE screen, make sure to exit by using the CTRL/END.

After the printout has completed, the status bar becomes blank, indicating that the databases have been closed. That is when you know that command file has finished execution.

- Make sure that the printer is on and is ready to use.
- Type DO DATAENTR and press **ENTER**.

MODIFYING FIELD CONTENTS FROM THE DOT PROMPT

The database files presented in these lessons can be used to update, for example, the quantity for each part in the inventory and the customer balance in accounts. However, more advanced programming is required to do these things automatically. For now the concept of changing values in a database by using a dot prompt command is briefly presented.

- Use **INVENTRY** with **CODE** indexed.

In Lesson 3 the RETAIL field was added to the structure, but no data was entered into that field. If you browse, the field shows 0.00 for all records. The company policy at ACME is to retail items for 1.75 times the wholesale cost, which is in PRICE. You would like to enter these new values into RETAIL. The dBASE command that modifies the contents of a database field is the REPLACE command. You may enter the command HELP REPLACE at the dot prompt to see its structure, if you like. For now you specify the scope as ALL.

- Enter the command REPLACE ALL RETAIL WITH 1.75 * PRICE
- BROWSE, to see the effects of the REPLACE command you just performed.

PRACTICE TIME

1. Modify the view WAREHAUS to include RETAIL in INVENTRY.
2. Modify the report you created earlier in this lesson where amounts of sale are computed, to compute the sales amount as QUANTITY * RETAIL.
3. Create a command file, DATAREPT, which uses the two views and prints the two reports you created while using those views.
4. Check the command file, making sure it works.

END OF LESSON 5

From ASSIST

- From the ASSIST menu highlight **Set up**.
- Highlight **Quit dBASE III PLUS** on the pull-down menu and press **ENTER**.
- Remove the disks from both drives.
- Turn OFF the monitor, computer, and printer.

From the Dot Prompt

- Type QUIT and press ENTER.
- Remove disks from the drives.
- Turn OFF the monitor, computer, and printer.

SUMMARY

In this lesson many advanced terms and concepts are discussed.

- dBASE III Plus lets you have up to ten work spaces, with ten database files opened. These work areas are identified as A through J *or* 1 through 10.
- A view sets up the usage of multiple database files transparent to users.
- You can set up a custom data entry screen to be used with a database file. Furthermore, this screen can have a field that is displayed or restricted to read-only, or it can check for the type of data input into a field. You can even draw double- or single-line boxes on the screen to emphasize some texts.
- Series of commands can be stored in a command file. They can then be executed by using a single command.
- The following commands are discussed:

CREATE SCREEN file	Creates a custom screen file file.
CREATE VIEW file	Creates a view file file that sets up the relationship between multiple database files.
DISPLAY STATUS	Shows, among other things, which files are opened in which area and what database indexes are used.
DO file	Executes the command file named file.
MODIFY COMMAND file	Lets you create or change the command file file.
MODIFY SCREEN file	Lets you change the format of a custom screen.
MODIFY VIEW file	Lets you change a view file file.
REPLACE [<scope>] field WITH <expression>	Lets you modify the contents of a field in a database file.
SELECT	Lets you select a work area to use.

REVIEW QUESTIONS

1. What is a work area? How many work areas can you have in dBASE III Plus? ______

2. When setting up a relation between two database files, do you need to index either file? Explain. ______

3. How do you select/de-select database files and field names? ______

4. How do you activate a view? ______

5. When creating a custom screen, how do you move the highlighted entry area? ______

6. What is the purpose of a template? ______

7. How do you specify where to draw a box when creating a custom screen? ______

8. Explain the meaning of file extensions .FMT, .SCR, and .VUE. ______

9. What is the purpose of a command file? ______________________

____

____

____

10. How do you invoke a command file? ______________________

____

____

EXERCISES

Exercise 1

1. Create file EX1VENDR. The file structure is given below:

Vendor	C	10
Address	C	20
City	C	12
State	C	2
Zip	C	5
Contact	C	20

Enter the following data:

Vendor	Address	City	State	Zip	Contact
MemoryRex	1000 S. Sam Houston	Dallas	TX	75214	Tricia Reubenstein
Nashville	7095 Presley Way	Memphis	TN	38102	Wanda Clark
Generic	200 Firestone, Ste.1	Los Angeles	CA	90038	Betty West
ThreeDee	3 Dee Street	St. Paul	MN	55125	Paul Meyers
Maxwell	P.O. Box 50144	Tallahassee	FL	32301	Bobby Ressol

2. Index on Vendor
3. Create a View with DB1EX1 as Parent and EX1VENDR as child, with all fields except EX1VENDR–>Vendor.
4. Create a report similar to the following:

MEMORY MAGIC, INC.
Inventory Vendor List

Description	Code	Quantity	Vendor	City	ST	Contact
5.25 DISK DSDD	F144	110	ThreeDee	St. Paul	MN	Paul Meyers
5.25 DISK DSDD	F153	690	Generic	Los Angeles	CA	Betty West
5.25 DISK DSDD	F220	600	MemoryRex	Dallas	TX	Tricia Reubenstein

.
.

3.5 DISK DSDD	M073	420	MemoryRex	Dallas	TX	Tricia Reubenstein
3.5 DISK DSDD	M094	500	Nashville	Memphis	TN	Wanda Clark

5. Print the report for Qty < 300.
6. Modify the structure of EX1VENDR: add phone field.

   Enter the following data:

MemoryRex	(214) 322-0900
Nashville	(901) 747-9500
Generic	(213) 699-1524
ThreeDee	(612) 833-25019
Maxwell	(904) 955-1500

7. Modify View to include phone.
8. Modify Report: remove the columns for city and state; add phone after Contact.
9. Print the report for all records in the view.

Exercise 2

1. Create the database file POLICY. The structure of the file is as shown:

Policy	Character	5	
Amount	Numeric	8	0
Company	Character	30	
Premium	Numeric	6	2
Exp_date	Date		

Enter the following data:

Policy	Amount	Company	Premium	Exp_date
DR459	500000	Market Research Inc.	750.00	09/30/89
GY801	1000000	CPI Consulting	950.00	09/15/89
VR004	300000	Development Insight	250.00	11/15/89
DR055	400000	Pomona HiTech	350.00	12/15/89
TV883	750000	Man of the Future	875.00	09/20/89
GY900	250000	Man of the Future	300.00	04/01/90
DR195	100000	CPI Consulting	125.00	11/01/89
VR125	625000	Man of the Future	575.00	12/01/89

2. Use the database DB2EX2.
3. Index it on Company.
4. Create a View.
5. Create a report similar to the following:

DOUBLE INDEMNITY, LTD.
Listing of Active Policies

Policy Number	Amount	Client	Contact	Expires on
DR459	500000	Market Research Inc.	Barry Davenport	09/30/89
GY801	1000000	CPI Consulting	Jennifer Barkley	09/15/89
VR004	300000	Development Insight	Dallas Hough	11/15/89
DR055	400000	Pomona HiTech	Terry Buchanan	12/15/89
TV883	750000	Man of the Future	Michael Wyndham	09/20/89
GY900	250000	Man of the Future	Michael Wyndham	04/01/90
DR195	100000	CPI Consulting	Jennifer Barkley	11/01/89
VR125	625000	Man of the Future	Michael Wyndham	12/01/89

6. Print the report for expiration dates before 11/10/89. (This can be done from ASSIST if you choose.)
7. Print the report for expiration dates before 90 days after 09/15/89. [This needs to be done from the dot prompt. The search condition is as follows: FOR exp__date <= CTOD('09/15/89') + 90].

Exercise 3

1. Use DB1EX3 with indexes on NUMBER and LOCATION active.
2. Costs have risen 5 percent. Update all COST fields. From the dot prompt the command is REPLACE ALL COST WITH COST * 1.05.
3. Print out the report created in Exercise 3 for Lesson 3.
4. A new company policy is being implemented. Beginning immediately, the new price (retail) is 1.8 times the cost. Update all PRICE fields in the database. (*HINT:* Use one command to do this.)
5. Create a database file named TRANSACT with the following structure:

DATE	Date		
CUSTOMER	Character	10	
ITEM__NO	Character	5	
AMT__ORDER	Numeric	4	0

Enter the following data:

Date	Customer	Item	Amt
03/05/89	Mt Vernon	L1011	24
03/10/89	Washoe Med	L4502	144
03/15/89	Fancy Free	L0047	120
03/20/89	Fancy Free	L0112	24
03/25/89	Washoe Med	L0005	30

6. Create a view to link the files DB1EX3 and TRANSACT. TRANSACT is the parent.
7. Create a report similar to the following:

THE POWER LINE
Recent Transaction Data

Date of Sale	Customer	Item	Description	Quantity	Unit Price	Amount of Sale
03/05/89	Mt Vernon	L1011	325 watt capacity	24	453.60	10886.40
03/10/89	Washoe Med	L4502	power controller	144	94.50	13608.00
.	Washoe Med	L0005	modem surge protector	30	56.70	1701.00
.						
.						
03/25/89						
*** Total ***						
						33589.08

8. Print the report for all records in TRANSACT.

Projects

PROJECT 1

1. Design and create a database file that can be used to inventory valuables in a home. Include the following information in fields: item description, brand, serial number, date purchased, purchase price, and location.
2. Enter at least 15 records into the database (for example, furniture, jewelry, camera, stereo equipment, appliances, and sporting goods).
3. Create a report that prints the item description, brand, and purchase price.
4. Print the report, sorted (or indexed) by purchase price.
5. Modify the structure to include another field in the database, called CATEGORY. This will indicate the general category of the item. Typical categories are furniture, jewelry, camera, stereo, appliance, and sporting.
6. Update the database to enter data into each category.
7. Modify the report to group the report on category.
8. Print the report with the category grouping (after properly sequencing the database file).
9. Create and print inventory labels, which include all fields, one per line. The labels may be two across if you choose. You decide the label dimensions.

PROJECT 2

In Chapter 6 of *Business Computer Systems* you studied an application in which one person (Jeff) scheduled umpires for a baseball league. In this project, you will design and implement part of that application.

1. Design and create a database file in which you will store data about games, including the date, home team, visiting team, and umpire name.
2. Enter this data in the game file:

DATE	*HOME*	*VISITOR*	*UMPIRE*
9/15	RHAM	Lyme	Juarez
9/15	Guilford	Madison	Wellman

9/15	Westbrook	Saybrook	Hall
9/15	Middlefield	Newington	Burke
9/18	Saybrook	Lyme	Burke
9/18	RHAM	Newington	Juarez
9/18	Madison	Guilford	Hall
9/22	Lyme	Saybrook	Burke
9/22	Newington	Westbrook	Wellman
9/24	Middlefield	RHAM	Burke

3. Design and create a database file in which you will store data about umpires, including their name, their phone number, and whether or not the umpire is certified.
4. Enter this data in the umpire file:

NAME	*PHONE NUMBER*	*CERTIFIED*
Burke	555-0000	Y
Hall	555-1111	N
Juarez	555-2222	Y
Wellman	555-3333	Y

5. Establish whatever report formats, indexes, and views are needed to produce the following reports:
   a. A master schedule in date order showing all the details for every game, including the umpire's phone number and certification status.
   b. A schedule for each team (printed on separate pages) showing only those games in which the team is playing. Include the date, home team, visiting team, umpire, and umpire's phone number.
   c. A schedule for each umpire (printed on separate pages) in date order, showing the date, home team, and visiting team.

PROJECT 3

1. Design and create a database for your school's public service club. The database should contain each member's name, address, telephone number, office held (if any), and a membership number.
2. Enter at least 20 records into the file, including at least five officers.
3. Design and create a label form for mailing labels. Use the standard label size, two across ($^{15}/_{16}$ x 3½ inches by 2).

4. Print two sets of labels on regular paper. The first set includes all club members. The second set includes only the club officers.
5. Create a second database, for use with the first, of committee assignments. The database has two fields: membership number and committee.
6. Enter 15 records into the committee assignment database, with valid membership numbers (records in the first file) in three committees: Social, Finance, and Projects. Some members may be on two committees.
7. Create a view of the two files, containing all the fields.
8. Design and create a report of committee member names and addresses, grouped by committee. Print the report.

Command Summary

This section is a quick reference for dBASE III Plus commands covered in this manual. This is not a complete list of all dBASE III Plus commands or of options for each command. However, some commands that were not covered in the lessons are listed here for your convenience.

DOT PROMPT COMMANDS

The following conventions are used in this summary to show the correct form for each command:

[ ]	Optional parameter
<condition>	Specifies a limited range for the command (e.g., FOR LNAME = "Smith")
<scope>	Expression to specify how much of the database to use in the command (e.g., NEXT 10, ALL, RECORD 3)
<keyexpression>	A field name or combination of fields (e.g., LAST_NAME, LAST_NAME + FIRST_NAME)
uppercase letters	Indicate a command keyword
/	Indicates when either of several commands may be used
<prompt>	Displayed character string
<fieldlist>	A list of one or more data fields
<filename>	The name of a file, including the drive designator
<filetype>	Type of file (e.g., Database)
<drive>	Drive designator (e.g., A, B, C)
<workarea>	One of ten work areas (e.g., 1, 2, A, B)

APPEND Adds a record to the end of a database file

ASSIST Switches dBASE III Plus to the menu-driven mode

AVERAGE Computes the arithmetic mean of all numeric fields

BROWSE Menu-driven full-screen database edit

CLEAR Erases the screen

CLOSE ALL <filetype> Closes the specified file type, such as DATABASE

COUNT Tallies the number of records

CREATE <filename> Defines a new dBASE III Plus database file

CREATE LABEL <filename> Creates a file to define a form for printing mailing labels

CREATE REPORT <filename> Creates a file used to define a report

CREATE SCREEN <filename> Creates a screen format file (.FMT) and custom screen format (.SCR)

CREATE VIEW <filename> Creates a relation between files as a working environment and saves it to a file

DELETE [<scope>] [WHILE <condition>] [FOR <condition>] Marks for deletion records in a database that meet the specified conditions

DISPLAY [OFF] [<scope>] [<fieldlist>][WHILE <condition>][FOR <condition>] [TO PRINT] Displays the records and fields in the current database; pauses between screen displays; OFF suppresses the record numbers from the display

DISPLAY STATUS [TO PRINT] Displays current status information about active databases, indexes, alternative files, and system parameters

DISPLAY STRUCTURE [TO PRINT] Displays the structure of the current active database

DO <filename> Executes a program or procedure

EJECT Executes a form feed on the printer

FIND <string> <number> Positions the record pointer in an indexed database to the first record that meets the specified condition

INDEX ON <keyexpression> TO <filename> Creates an index for a database on a specified key

LABEL FORM <filename> [<scope>][SAMPLE][TO PRINT] [WHILE <condition>][FOR <condition>][TO FILE <filename>] Prints labels, using the specified label form file; the SAMPLE clause prints a sample of the label format so you can check paper alignment

LIST [OFF][<scope>][<fieldlist>][WHILE <condition>][FOR <condition>][TO PRINT] Lists records from the database meeting the specified conditions

LIST STRUCTURE [TO PRINT] Lists structure of current active database

LOCATE [<scope>][FOR <condition>][WHILE <condition>] Positions record pointer to first record in a database meeting the specified condition

MODIFY COMMAND <filename> Creates or modifies a program by using dBASE III Plus's internal editor

MODIFY LABEL <filename> Modifies a file that defines a label

MODIFY REPORT <filename> Modifies a report form file

MODIFY SCREEN <filename> Modifies the specified screen file

MODIFY STRUCTURE [<filename>] Modifies the structure of a database without losing the data within the database, if possible

MODIFY VIEW <filename> Modifies the specified View file

PACK Removes all records in the database that are marked for deletion

QUIT Closes all files and exits dBASE III PLUS

RECALL Unmarks specified records that were previously marked for deletion

REPORT FORM <filename> [<scope>][FOR <condition>][WHILE <condition>][TO PRINT] Creates a report, using a previously created report form from the current database

SEEK <expression> Position the record pointer to the first record in an indexed file with a key value matching the specified expression

SELECT <workarea> Switches dBASE III Plus between active work areas; up to 10 work areas can be defined for database files

SET DEFAULT TO <drive> Defines the default drive for all programs and databases and all file accesses

SET FORMAT TO Closes a format file

SET FORMAT TO [<filename>] Opens a format (.FMT screen) file used for formatted input and editing

SET INDEX TO Closes all index files

SET INDEX TO [<filelist>] Opens the specified index files

SET VIEW TO <filename> Opens a View file

SORT TO <filename> ON <field> Creates a database with records sorted in the specified sort order

SUM Computes the sums of numeric fields

USE [<filename>][INDEX <filename list>] Opens the specified database in the current work area

COMMANDS IN ASSIST

Set Up	**Database file**	Open a database file that exists on disk and optionally set one or more index files active
	Format for screen	Use a custom screen for data entry and edit
	Query	Use a query file
	Catalog	Activates catalog file
	View	Open a view file
	Quit dBASE III PLUS	End the session of dBASE III Plus
Create	**Database file**	Create a database file, define its structure, and allow entry of records
	Format	Create a custom screen for data entry and edit
	View	Create a relation between files as a working environment and save it to a file
	Query	Create a filter condition and store it in a query file
	Report	Create a report form that contains the information on report layout
	Label	Create a label form that contains information on the label layout and fields
Update	**Append**	Add records to the database file
	Edit	Edit (modify) database records, viewed one record at a time
	Display	List specified records and fields to the monitor or printer, pausing when the screen is filled
	Browse	Display the database in a multiple-record format, one row per record
	Replace	Change contents of the specified database fields
	Delete	Mark specified records for deletion from the database file
	Recall	Unmark specified records
	Pack	Copy all unmarked records, creating a new version of the same database file, but without any marked records

Position	**Seek**	Quickly locate an expression in the field for which the database is indexed in the master index file
	Locate	Position the pointer to the first record in a database meeting a specified condition
	Continue	Continue to search for the next record, using the condition specified by a LOCATE command
	Skip	Move the pointer backward or forward by the amount specified
	Goto Record	Position the record pointer at the beginning or end of the open database file or at any specified record
Retrieve	**List**	Display specified fields and records to the monitor or printer, without any pauses
	Display	Display specified fields and records to the monitor, with pauses when the screen is filled
	Report	Use a report form to prepare a report of selected records
	Label	Use a label form to prepare labels of selected records
	Sum	Sum numeric fields for specified records in a database
	Average	Average numeric fields for specified records in a database
	Count	Count the number of records in a database that meet specified conditions
Organize	**Index**	Create an index file (.NDX) that keeps the database file organized on an expression (usually a single field), even when changes are made to the database file
	Sort	Create a copy of the database file that is sorted on one or more fields in ascending or descending order
	Copy	Duplicate any type of file
Modify	**Database file**	Change the structure of an existing database

	Format	Change an existing custom screen format
	View	Change an existing view file
	Query	Change an existing query file
	Report	Change an existing report form (.FRM)
	Label	Change an existing label form (.LBL)
Tools	**Set drive**	Set the default drive for the data disk
	Copy file	Copy files, such as for backup purposes
	Directory	Display the names of files that are on the data disk
	Rename	Rename a disk file
	Erase	Delete a disk file
	List structure	Display to monitor or printer the structure of the active database file
	Import	Create dBASE files from PFS files
	Export	Create PFS files from dBASE III Plus files

MODULE 4

WordPerfect

Introduction

In the next three lessons you will get a taste of what you can do by using a word processing program. A word processing program is a computer program that helps you create, change, and print text.

You enter (type) text just as you would on a typewriter, except you don't have to worry about pressing the carriage return at the end of each line. When you reach the right margin, you can just keep on typing, and the computer will automatically place the text on the next line down for you.

The text you entered is stored on the computer. Then special word processor commands make it a simple task to insert, delete, or change characters, words, and lines. You can print the text when you are ready. The text can also be stored on a disk for later use.

When printing the text, the format can be adjusted to your needs. You can have automatic page numbering or specified headers and footers printed. Form letters or other repetitive documents can be printed with names, addresses, and other personalizing information automatically inserted as printing occurs.

What a word processor does is to take the drudgery out of making changes. Without a word processor, making changes means having to erase and write in new words, or rewrite or retype a document. You can concentrate on the creativity of writing the document and not let the mechanical process of preparing a presentable output get in the way.

The word processing systems that seem to be growing at the fastest rate right now are word processing for microcomputers. There are more than 100 packages available, such as WordPerfect, Microsoft Word, Displaywrite 4, WordStar, and MultiMate. Most word processing packages offer similar features. They include the following:

- Insert and delete words, lines, and paragraphs
- Copy and/or move sentences and paragraphs
- Search/replace text
- Superscript/subscript
- Underline, boldface, and italics
- Change to capital letters or lowercase letters
- Center
- Header/footer
- Pagination
- Hyphenation
- Reformatting
- Decimal alignment
- Justify text
- Merge letters
- Widow/orphan

More comprehensive software packages may offer such additional features as these:

Footnotes	Forms
Indentation	Macros
Column operations	Split screen
Index creation	Windowing
Table of contents creation	Sort
Outlining feature	Proportional spacing
Math	Type-to-printer
Undelete or undo	Thesaurus
Word count	Spell checker
Various fonts	Desktop publishing

Many of these features may not have much meaning to you right now. Some of them are explained in the lessons that follow.

The word processing package used in this manual is **WordPerfect 4.2.** It is judged by many as one of the best word processing packages on the market today. Although this is not the latest release of WordPerfect (the latest is 5.0), it offers most of the features listed above. Only a very limited amount is covered in this manual. You will learn enough to get started. It is up to you to explore the rest.

STARTING WORD PERFECT 4.2

To use this module, you need a copy of the WordPerfect 4.2 Training Version that accompanied this manual and a formatted data disk. To start WordPerfect:

1. Start up the computer with a DOS disk.
2. Insert the WordPerfect program disk into drive A and the formatted data disk into drive B.
3. Following the DOS A> prompt, type **B:** and press ENTER to change the default drive to B.

   In this way when WordPerfect needs the data disk to store or retrieve documents, it looks automatically at the disk in drive B.
4. Type **A:WP** and press ENTER to start WordPerfect. The A, W, and P can be entered either in upper- or lowercase letters.

   > The WordPerfect 4.2 Training Version copyright message and the explanation on how the training version differs from the regular version appear on the screen.

The training version is limited in the following ways:

- Saved documents are limited in size to about 50,000 characters.
- Printed output is unlimited, but occasionally contains the notation ***WPC.**
- Advanced printing features are not available.
- You cannot select a printer. LPT1 (PRN) is the only port that can be used for printing.

5. Press any key to continue.

   > A blank WordPerfect document screen is displayed.

Lesson 1
Creating Documents

Objectives

Upon completion of the material presented in this lesson you should be able to understand the following aspects of WordPerfect:

- Word processing terminology
- Entering text
- Giving WordPerfect commands
- Moving the cursor without affecting the text
- Marking a block of text
- Deleting a block of text
- Moving/Copying a block of text
- Inserting/Replacing text in an existing document
- Using the Speller
- Using the Thesaurus
- Saving a file on a disk
- Displaying the directory
- Retrieving a file from the disk
- Printing the text

STARTING OFF

Start WordPerfect on the computer by following instructions given in the introduction to this module so that the screen in Screen Display 1-1 is displayed.

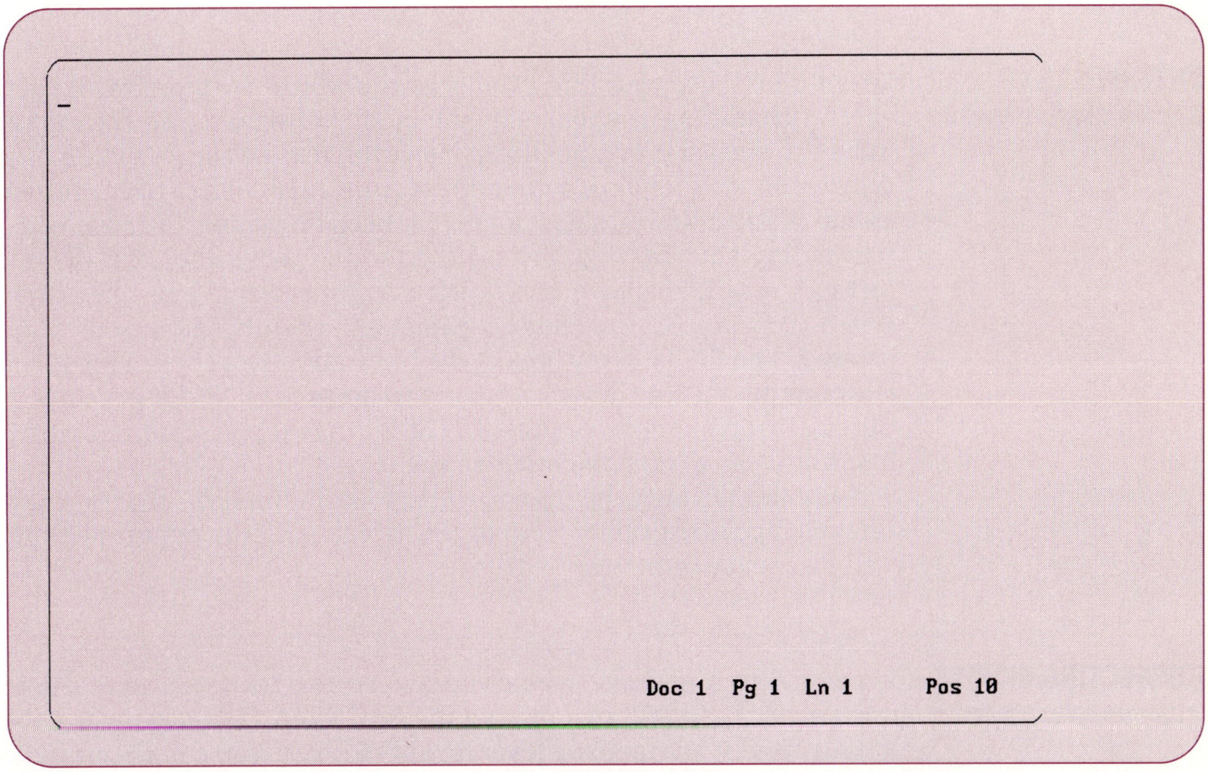

Screen Display 1-1

This is the screen on which you can enter new text, review what you have already entered, or change what is there. Of course, since you have not entered anything yet, it is blank.

The blinking underline character is the *cursor*. The cursor shows the position on the screen at which your entries are made.

The bottom line of the screen is the *status line*. The status line displays the position of the cursor. It is currently on page 1 of the first document. You can work on two documents at the same time in WordPerfect. This feature is discussed in the next lesson. The cursor is on line 1, but the position (or column) is 10! Why is it not on position 0 or 1? This is because of the default setting for the left and right margins. The *defaults,* or the preset values, for these margins are 10 and 74, respectively. WordPerfect presets certain screen and page formats so that you can just start typing. These settings can be changed at any time, but do not worry about this right now because this topic, too, is discussed in the next lesson.

ENTERING TEXT

To enter text, use your IBM PC just as you would a typewriter. As you enter a character, it appears at the cursor position, and the cursor moves to the right one position. However, unlike the keyboard on a typewriter, this keyboard does not require entry of a carriage return as you fill up a line on the screen. Just keep on typing, because when the cursor gets beyond the right margin (remember the default setting), it will reappear at the left margin setting, one line down. When you come to the end of a paragraph, the ENTER key must be pressed. The ENTER key breaks the line and moves the cursor to the left margin, one line down. You have to press the ENTER key once at the end of a paragraph, or press ENTER twice if you want to insert a blank line between paragraphs in the text.

If your text fills up the screen, the text will *scroll up*—that is, a new line will appear at the bottom of the screen, and the uppermost line will disappear from view.

CORRECTING ERRORS

If you make a mistake when you are typing text, you may delete unwanted characters by pressing the BACKSPACE key, which is the left arrow key found just above the ENTER key. You can then retype the text.

UPPERCASE LETTERS

To enter uppercase letters, simply hold the SHIFT (large up arrow) key down while you press the character—as you would on a typewriter. If you want to type several characters in uppercase, as when you enter a title, press the CAPS LOCK key, just as you would do with the shift lock key on a typewriter. To get back into lowercase, simply press the CAPS LOCK key again. When you enter certain special characters, you have to hold the SHIFT key down regardless of whether the CAPS LOCK key has been pressed.

You can tell whether you are in the uppercase mode or lowercase mode by looking at the word **Pos** on the status line. When you are in the uppercase mode, the word appears in all uppercase, that is, **POS**. When you are in the lowercase mode, it appears as **Pos**.

PRACTICE TIME

Enter the following text:

> Records of transactions, contracts, and inventories form the basis that allows business to be conducted in an orderly manner. Scribes have been used through the ages to produce copies of business contracts. Inventions which have lowered the cost or increased the speed for an individual to write a document have resulted in increased business productivity. These inventions include paper, ball point pens, and typewriters. The personal computer did not become a success until it became useful for business. Today, word processing is the most common business use of personal computers.

As you typed in this paragraph, you might have noticed the phenomenon called *wordwrap*. This means that as the text gets to the right margin, a word that is too long to fit on the line is moved down to the next line. Words are not split between two lines. This feature is included to make reading and text creation easier.

WORDPERFECT COMMANDS

Before you go any further, you will look at the way commands are entered in WordPerfect. Commands are the way you get the attention of the WordPerfect program. Many of the commands are given through use of the functions keys by themselves or in conjunction with the CTRL, SHIFT, and ALT keys. When you see CTRL/F3, for example, you are to hold down the key marked CTRL and press the F3 function key; and when you see ALT/F4, you hold down the key marked ALT and press the F4 function key.

This is where a function key template helps you. It is hard to remember what combination generates which key. If you place the template over the function keyboard, there is no need to memorize all the combinations.

NOTE ■ Should you lose the template, you can use the F3 function key to see the template on the screen. When you are through, press the SPACE BAR to return to the document.

There are other keys, such as arrow keys, that also are used to issue commands, again either by themselves or in conjunction with the three keys previously mentioned.

```
  WordPerfect 4.2 Template (IBM Layout)                    WP 4.2 *      05/01/87_

    ┌──────────────────┬──────────────────┐
    │      Shell       │      Spell       │
  F1│ SUPER/SUBSCRIPT  │    <-SEARCH      │F2
    │    Thesaurus     │     Replace      │
    │_____Cancel_______│_____Search->_____│
    │     Screen       │      Move        │            Legend:
  F3│     SWITCH       │   ->INDENT<-     │F4
    │  Reveal Codes    │      Block       │             Ctrl + Function Key
    │______Help________│_____->Indent_____│            SHIFT + FUNCTION KEY
    │   Text In/Out    │    Tab Align     │              Alt + Function Key
  F5│      DATE        │     CENTER       │F6            Function Key alone
    │   Mark Text      │   Flush Right    │
    │___List Files_____│______Bold________│
    │    Footnote      │      Print       │
  F7│     PRINT        │   LINE FORMAT    │F8
    │  Math/Columns    │   Page Format    │
    │______Exit________│____Underline_____│
    │   Merge/Sort     │   Macro Def.     │
  F9│    MERGE E       │  RETRIEVE TEXT   │F10
    │  Merge Codes     │      Macro       │
    │    Merge R       │    Save Text     │
    └──────────────────┴──────────────────┘
```

Screen Display 1-1A

Some commands are *toggles*. That means the command turns a feature ON and OFF each time you enter it. Others display a menu. A *menu*, like a menu in a restaurant, offers a choice of commands for the user. Still other commands begin a feature that is ended when the ENTER key is pressed. Some commands require additional information from you, such as what name to call a document.

Not all commands are covered in this manual. Furthermore, the manual explains just what is needed for a particular lesson. Many options and features available in WordPerfect can be explored on your own after you understand the basic commands.

CURSOR MOVEMENT

Suppose, as you read what you typed earlier, you find a mistake or, better yet, you decide to change the text to include an improvement. If the change you want to make is at the beginning of the text, and if you use the BACKSPACE key to erase all unwanted characters starting at the cursor position, you will have to retype almost the whole text. This is no improvement over using a typewriter. A word processor has a better way. To make corrections like this, you need to learn how to move the cursor without affecting the text.

- Press the **UP ARROW** key.

  > The cursor moves up one line.

- Press the **RIGHT ARROW** key.

  > The cursor moves to the right one position.

To move the cursor, use the four arrow keys located to the right of the main keyboard. The cursor will move in the direction of the arrow, one position at a time.

NOTE ■ If a number appears when an arrow key on the numeric keyboard is pressed, you have to press the NUM LOCK key. The NUM LOCK is a toggle key. After pressing NUM LOCK once, you can generate the characters that appear on the upper half of keys in the numeric keypad. Press it again to generate the characters on the bottom half of the numeric keys (the arrows).

When the numeric keypad is active, the **Pos** indicator at the lower right corner of the screen blinks. If the arrow keys are active, the **Pos** is not blinking.

If you have a long text, you cannot see all of it on the screen at any one time. With the UP ARROW and DOWN ARROW keys you can read new information or retrieve information that has scrolled off the screen. If you keep pressing the UP ARROW key, the text will scroll down (that is, new lines will appear at the top); and if you keep pressing the DOWN ARROW key, the text will scroll up (new lines will appear at the bottom).

NOTE ■ You will quickly learn that the movement of text on the screen is in the direction opposite to the label on the key. The UP ARROW key lets you view text that was *above* the screen, and the DOWN ARROW key brings into view text that was *below* the screen.

It is also possible to move the cursor a little faster. All you have to do is hold the key down, and the key will keep repeating. If you hold down the DOWN ARROW key, the cursor will zoom down the page. You can return to the top of the page by using the UP ARROW key. You will notice, however, that you cannot move the cursor past the beginning or the end of the text.

You can move the cursor to the left or right, one word at time, by holding down the CTRL key and pressing the LEFT ARROW or RIGHT ARROW key, respectively.

PRACTICE TIME

Try using the up, down, right, and left cursor movement commands.

You can move the cursor to the beginning of the document by pressing the HOME key twice and then pressing the UP ARROW key, and to the end of the document by pressing the HOME key twice and then pressing the DOWN ARROW key.

PRACTICE TIME

1. Move the cursor to the end and then to the beginning of the document.
2. Place the cursor somewhere in the middle of the document.
3. Press the **HOME** key, then press either the **LEFT ARROW** or the **RIGHT ARROW** key. Do this several times, alternating **LEFT ARROW** and **RIGHT ARROW** keys. What happens?

You also can scroll the text up or down one page at a time by using the PgUp and PgDn keys. The text you see on the screen right now is not long enough for you to try these keys. Just remember them for the future.

DELETING TEXT

As you recall, if you make a mistake in typing text, you can correct it immediately in this way:

- Press the BACKSPACE key to remove unwanted characters.
- Type the correct text.

You may delete unwanted characters *anywhere* in the text by adding one step:

- Move the cursor to the immediate right of the character you wish to delete.
- Press the BACKSPACE key to erase unwanted characters.
- Type the correct text.

The BACKSPACE key removes the characters to the left of the cursor. You can delete text in other ways, too:

- Remove the character the cursor is on by pressing the DELETE (DEL) key.
- Remove the word the cursor is on by entering CTRL/BACKSPACE; that is, hold down the CTRL key and press the BACKSPACE key.

- Remove the text from the cursor to the end of line by entering CTRL/END; that is, hold down the CTRL key and press the END key.
- Remove the text from the cursor to the end of page by entering CTRL/PgDn. You will be asked to confirm.

You can also delete a section, or *block*, of text. To do so, you first have to mark the block. You will delete a block in the current text.

- Place the cursor on the first character of the second sentence. That is, the character "S" of "Scribes have. . . ."
- Enter the Block command, which is **ALT/F4** (hold down the **ALT** key and press the **F4** function key).

  > The words **Block on** flash on the status line, as seen in Screen Display 1-2.

```
Records of transactions, contracts and inventories form the basis
that allow business to be conducted in an orderly manner.
Scribes have been used through the ages to produce copies of
business contracts.  Inventions which have lowered the cost or
increased the speed for an individual to write a document have
resulted in increased business productivity.  These inventions
include paper, ball point pens, and typewriter.  The personal
computer did not become a success until it became useful for
business.  Today, word processing is the most common business use
of personal computers.

Block on                                    Doc 1  Pg 1  Ln 3      Pos 10
```

Screen Display 1-2

- Press the **RIGHT ARROW** key a few times.

  > As you press the RIGHT ARROW key, the characters the cursor passes over are *highlighted.*

- Either press the **RIGHT ARROW** key or press the **RIGHT ARROW** key while holding down the **CTRL** key, until the text "Scribes have been used through the ages to produce copies of business contracts.   " is highlighted, as seen in Screen Display 1-3.

NOTE ■ If you went past the end of the text, use the LEFT ARROW key to move back. You will notice that this removes the highlight from the character. You can also start over by canceling the whole block operation by pressing the CANCEL key—the F1 function key.

- Press the **BACKSPACE** key.

```
Records of transactions, contracts and inventories form the basis
that allows business to be conducted in an orderly manner.
Scribes have been used through the ages to produce copies of
business contracts. Inventions which have lowered the cost or
increased the speed for an individual to write a document have
resulted in increased business productivity.  These inventions
include paper, ball point pens, and typewriter.  The personal
computer did not become a success until it became useful for
business.  Today, word processing is the most common business use
of personal computers.











Block on                                  Doc 1  Pg 1  Ln 4      Pos 30
```

Screen Display 1-3

> The message

```
Delete Block? (Y/N) N
```

appears at the bottom left.

- Type Y (no ENTER).

> The highlighted text disappears, as shown in Screen Display 1-4.

- Do not move the cursor.

RESTORING DELETED TEXT

If you change your mind about deleting the text after you've marked the block (but before pressing the BACKSPACE key), you simply cancel the command by pressing the F1 function key, and the text remains unchanged.

The F1 function key is also an *undo* key. If you realize you didn't mean to remove the text after you've deleted it, you can restore it by using the F1 function key. WordPerfect saves up to three deletions.

```
Records of transactions, contracts and inventories form the basis
that allow business to be conducted in an orderly manner.
Inventions which have lowered the cost or
increased the speed for an individual to write a document have
resulted in increased business productivity.  These inventions
include paper, ball point pens, and typewriter.  The personal
computer did not become a success until it becanc uscful for
business.  Today, word processing is the most common business use
of personal computers.




                                        Doc 1  Pg 1  Ln 3      Pos 10
```

Screen Display 1-4

When you restore the text, however, it is inserted at the cursor position, not where you deleted the text.

- Press the **F1** function key.
  - > The text you have just deleted appears at the cursor position, highlighted.
  - > The following menu appears at the bottom of the screen:

    `Undelete: 1 Restore; 2 Show Previous Deletion: 0`

Your options are these:

0	Cancel the command. Just press ENTER.
1	Restore the highlighted text at the cursor position.
2	Show what was deleted previous to the last delete.

If you were to select 2, the text deleted previous to the last delete would appear at the cursor position. Right now you want just to restore the most recently deleted text.

- Type 1 (do not press ENTER).
  - > The text is restored.

PRACTICE TIME Delete the second sentence again as a block operation.

REWRITE THE SCREEN

You probably noticed that, when you deleted the sentence, the next sentence moved over, but the text one line down was not moved up. However, as soon as you move the cursor, the screen is rewritten so that the changes fit into the format of specified margins.

- Press any arrow key.

MOVING TEXT

Block is used for much more than deleting text. Once you mark a block, you can make the whole block appear in uppercase or lowercase, make the block come out in bold characters or underlined, move or copy the block, and much, much more. Right now you will move the last sentence as a block.

- Move the cursor to the first character of the last sentence; that is, to the character "T" of the word "Today."

- Enter the **Block** command, which is **ALT/F4**.

  > The words **Block on** flash on the status line.

NOTE ■ When marking a block, if you were to press a character key, the text is blocked to the first occurrence of that character. For example, if you were to press the period (.) key now, the entire sentence is marked (since the first occurrence of the period is at the end of the sentence).

- Mark the block. That is, highlight the sentence "Today, word processing is the most common business use of personal computers." Your screen should look like the one in Screen Display 1-5.
- Enter the **Move** command, which is **CTRL/F4**.

  > The following message is displayed on the status line:

  `1 Cut Block; 2 Copy Block; 3 Append; 4 Cut/Copy Column; 5 Cut/Copy Rectangle: 0`

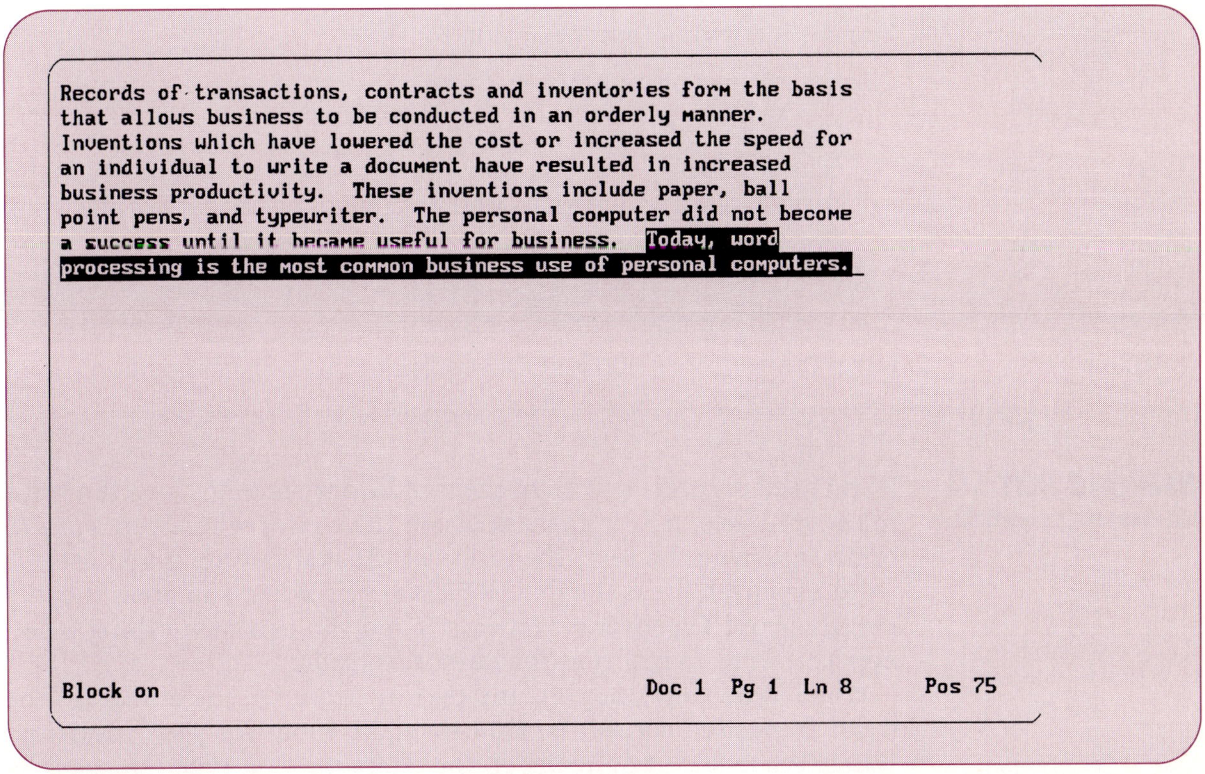

Screen Display 1-5

WordPerfect is asking if you want to "cut" the block or "copy" the block, among other options that are not discussed here. When you *cut* a block, it is physically moved out of the present location; whereas when you *copy*, the original text stays where it is and a copy of it can be inserted elsewhere. You want to cut it.

- Type **1** (do not press ENTER).

  > The block disappears.

Now, you have to move the cursor to where you want to insert this sentence.

- Move the cursor to the space just before the fourth sentence—that is, after the word "typewriter."
- Enter the **Move** command, **CTRL/F4**, again.

  > The following message appears:

```
Move 1 Sentence; 2 Paragraph; 3 Page; Retrieve 4
Column; 5 Text; 6 Rectangle: 0
```

You are retrieving text, or option 5.

- Type **5** (do not press ENTER).

  > The marked block is moved to the cursor position, as shown in Screen Display 1-6. You may have to insert or delete spaces to make the document look good, but do not be concerned about the text format right now.

PRACTICE TIME Move the sentence you just moved back to its original position.

INSERTING TEXT

If you need to insert a word in the middle of a sentence, or a sentence in the middle of a paragraph, position the cursor where you want to begin inserting the text, then look at the status line. If you see the word **Typeover**, press the INSERT (INS) key. When you press the INS key, the word **Typeover** disappears. Then you can start typing whatever you want to insert at the cursor position.

When **Typeover** is not on, any text in "front" of the cursor (to the right) is pushed across the line to make room for your insertion. When Typeover is on, however, the character you type replaces the character the cursor is on. INSERT is a toggle command. The feature is turned on and off each time you press the INS key.

```
Records of transactions, contracts and inventories form the basis
that allow business to be conducted in an orderly manner.
Inventions which have lowered the cost or increased the speed for
an individual to write a document have resulted in increased
business productivity.  These inventions include paper, ball
point pens, and typewriter.  Today, word processing is the most
common business use of personal computers.  The personal computer
did not become a success until it became useful for business.




                                   Doc 1  Pg 1  Ln 6      Pos 39
```

Screen Display 1-6

- Place the cursor just before the word "Inventions" in the second sentence.
- Insert the following text just as it appears (with spelling errors):

  `The earliest writing, cuneiform inscriptoins on clay tablets, often kept business recrds.`

- Press any arrow key to rewrite the screen.

SPELLING CHECKER (SPELLER)

The Speller helps you proof the document on the screen by comparing each word in the document with a list of correctly spelled words, known as a *dictionary*. On a regular version of WordPerfect, the dictionary contains more than 100,000 words. However, on this training version, the dictionary contains just those words necessary for you to get through the lessons, exercises, and projects. When you issue the Spell command, the program scans the document, flags those words that are not in the dictionary, and for each of these words, displays words from the dictionary that you might have meant.

You entered some words with spelling errors in the current document. You will now enter the Spell command to correct them.

- Enter the **Spell** command, which is **CTRL/F2**.

  > The following is displayed on the status line:

  ```
  Check: 1 Word; 2 Page; 3 Document; 4 Change
  Dictionary; 5 Look Up; 6 Count
  ```

You would enter 1 to check the spelling of the word the cursor is on; 2 to check spelling of the words on the page the cursor is on; and 3 to check the entire document. If you want to cancel the spelling check operation, simply press ENTER.

You want to check the entire document.

- Type 3 (do not press ENTER).

  > The message

  ```
  * Please Wait *
  ```

  appears at the bottom of the screen until the spelling checker finds a word that is not in the dictionary. After a while the screen display should look like that shown in Screen Display 1-7.

The word "inscriptoins" is highlighted and the message at the bottom tells you that it was not found in the dictionary. Just below the double line is a list of possible alternate spellings. This list includes those words in the dictionary that are different by a single letter or two letters typed out of sequence. (Sometimes, as the Speller program searches the list, a word on the list qualifies to be shown on the screen by meeting two different criteria.)

If a word on the alternative list is the correctly spelled word, type the letter preceding it. Option 1, Skip Once, leaves this word alone, and goes on to find the next word not found in the dictionary. Option 2, Skip, causes the Speller program to ignore all other occurrences of the word. Option 3, Add Word, is used if the word currently highlighted is spelled correctly and you want to add it to the dictionary. Option 4, Edit, lets you correct the spelling of the word manually. Use the arrow keys, DEL, and BACKSPACE keys to correct the error. When done, press the ENTER key. Option 5 is not discussed here.

- Since the correct spelling appears on the screen as option A, type A (do not press ENTER).

```
Records of transactions, contracts and inventories form the basis
that allows business to be conducted in an orderly manner.  The
earliest writing, cuneiform inscriptoins on clay tablets, often
kept business recrds.  Inventions which have lowered the cost or
increased the speed for an individual to write a document have
resulted in increased business productivity.  These inventions
include paper, ball point pens, and typewriter.  The personal
computer did not become a success until it became useful for
business.  Today, word processing is the most common business use
of personal computers.

================================================================================

  A. inscriptions







Not Found!  Select Word or Menu Option (0=Continue): 0
1 Skip Once; 2 Skip; 3 Add Word; 4 Edit; 5 Look Up; 6 Phonetic
```

Screen Display 1-7

> The misspelled word is replaced by the selected word from the alternative list.

> Now "recrds" is highlighted.

PRACTICE TIME

Correct the spelling of "recrds."

NOTE ■ When finished, the Spell displays the number of words checked and asks you to press any key to continue.

NOTE ■ After you finish entering text, always run it through the spelling checker. It does not catch all your mistakes (for example, if you used "their" for "there," since the word is spelled right, the mistake is not caught), but it is still a good aid in creating an accurate document.

THESAURUS

One more feature that is available in many word processors should be mentioned: the Thesaurus. Many times, when you are writing a document, you need help finding a word so you can express yourself more clearly. The Thesaurus displays synonyms and other words that point to the same idea.

NOTE ■ The WordPerfect Thesaurus also displays the antonyms, or the words with the opposite meaning.

The Thesaurus that is available on the training version is extremely limited. It is used here only to give you an idea of what it can do.

- Place the cursor at the end of the text.
- Press **ENTER** twice to insert blank lines.
- Type the following:

```
Form letters no longer need to be typed in a rush.
```

You read the sentence over and decide that the word "rush" is not quite the word you had in mind.

- Place the cursor on the word **rush**.
- Enter the **Thesaurus** command, **ALT/F1**.

> The screen of Screen Display 1-8 appears.

The screen displays those words you might want to use instead of "rush." The category **rush (v)** indicates "rush" used as a verb, **(n)** indicates "rush" used as a noun, and the **(ant)** category shows those words that are antonyms. Within each category the words are divided into subgroups, or groups of words with the same connotation.

If you find the word you are looking for in this list, type **1** (replace word) and the letter found in front of the word. For example, if the word you want to use is "dash," you type **A** (do not press ENTER). The word "rush" in the text is replaced by "dash."

If you did not find the word you are looking for in this list, you can continue the search one step further. Those words that have a dot in front of them, such as "hurry" and "race," are *headwords.* That means they can be looked up in the Thesaurus.

- Type **C** to look up "hurry."

> The second column displays those words that are found in the Thesaurus under "hurry."

If you want to clear those columns that were added to the screen (by looking up "hurry"), type **4**.

```
of personal computers.

Form letters no longer need to be typed in a rush.


rush=(v)
 1 A  dash                    rush-(ant)
   B  hasten                   5   •crawl
   C •hurry                        slow
   D •race
                               6   trickle
 2 E  accelerate
   F  expedite
   G  advance

 3 H  blitz
   I  charge
   J  sally

rush-(n)
 4 K  gush
   L  surge
   M  torrent

1 Replace Word; 2 View Doc; 3 Look Up Word; 4 Clear Column: 0
```

Screen Display 1-8

- Press **ENTER** (select option 0) to exit Thesaurus.

PRACTICE TIME

1. Use Thesaurus and replace the word "rush" with "hurry."
2. Delete the sentence "Form letters no longer need to be typed in a hurry."

SAVING YOUR WORK

The text that you have just entered is stored only in the main memory of the computer. If you quit for the day and turn off the computer, you will lose that text. To keep the text for future use, you must save your file on a disk. There are a couple of ways to save your work. One method is shown now; another is covered in the next lesson.

- Press the **EXIT** key, which is the **F7** function key. The following message appears on the status line:

```
Save Document? (Y/N) Y
```

The cursor will be on the second Y. You want to save the document. You can simply press ENTER.

- Press **ENTER**.

  > The following appears on the status line:

  ```
  Document to be Saved:
  ```

You are to enter a name under which the document is to be saved.

A valid name for the document, known as the *filename*, is one to eight characters in length, followed by an optional extension. The extension is a period (.) and one to three additional characters. Do not use an asterisk (*), colon (:), or question mark (?), or a blank space in your filename and do not begin a filename with a period.

Use the name MYFILE. It will be saved on the disk in drive B since you made drive B the default in the start-up procedure.

- Make sure that the data disk is in drive B.
- Type MYFILE and press **ENTER**.

  > The message

  ```
  Saving B:\MYFILE
  ```

  appears on the status line as the red light in front of disk drive B goes on.

  > When the light in front of the drive goes off, the following message appears on the status line:

  ```
  Exit WP? (Y/N) N    (Cancel to return to document)
  ```

WordPerfect is asking if you want to exit the program. If you answer Y, you are back in DOS. If you answer N, you remain in WordPerfect, but the document you are working on is erased from the main memory. That is, you are ready to start on another document. If you want to stay in WordPerfect and continue working on the same document, press the Cancel key, the F1 function key.

- Select N so that you remain in WordPerfect but with a clean screen.

  > A blank WordPerfect screen appears.

Many people who are saving a file for the first time worry about whether the file has really been saved on the disk. You can check the disk directory first to see if your file's name is on it. Then you can check the contents of the file.

- Enter the **List Files** command, which is the **F5** function key.

  > The status line displays the following message:

  `Dir B:\*.*`

WordPerfect is asking if you want to display all files on the disk in drive B. You do.

- Press **ENTER**.

  > A list showing the files stored on the disk in drive B is displayed as shown in Screen Display 1-9.

MYFILE, as you can see, is one of the files stored on the disk.

So there is a file with your filename on the disk. Does that mean it is the right file? You can retrieve the contents of the file.

- Use the arrow key to highlight the listing for **MYFILE**.
- Type 1 (do not press ENTER).

  > The text is retrieved.

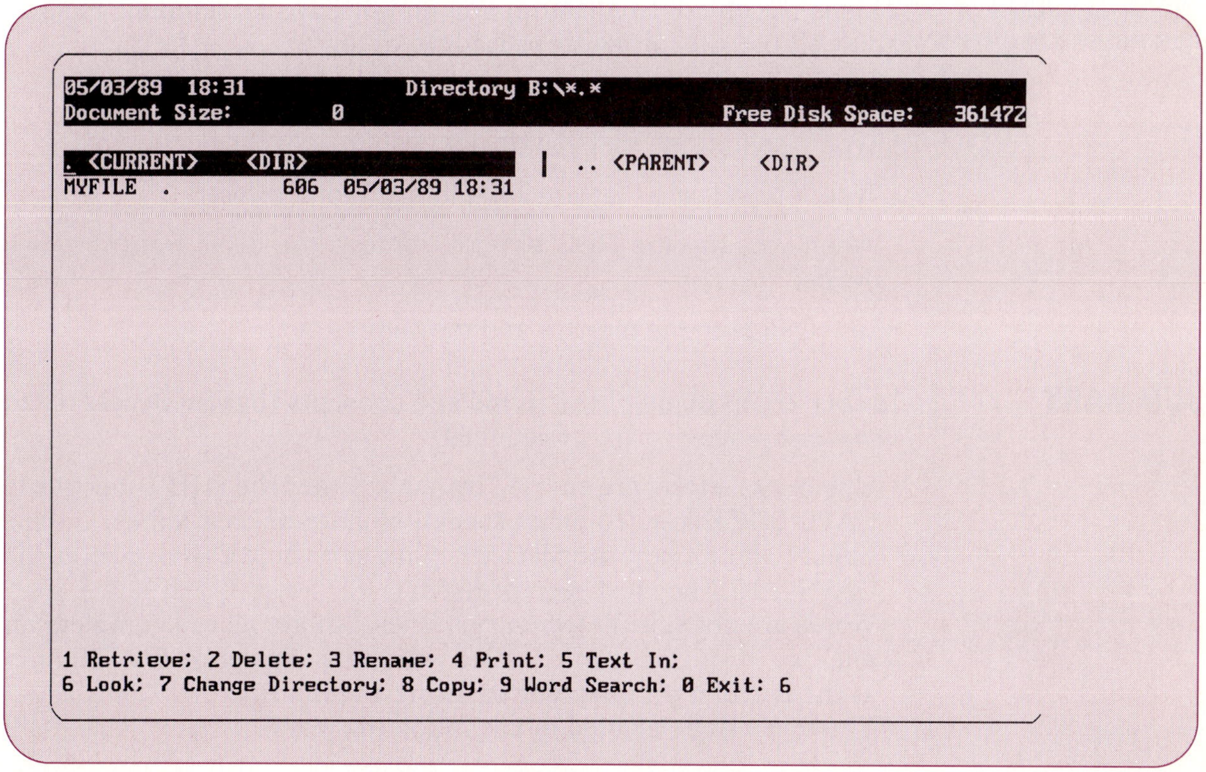

Screen Display 1-9

This text file is stored on the disk. It will not be erased even when you turn the computer off. You can always load it back into the computer (started with the IBM DOS and running WordPerfect). You will do this in the next lesson.

PRINTING TEXT

You will now print the text.

- Make sure that your printer is turned ON and is ready to use.
- Enter the **Print** command, which is **SHIFT/F7**.

  > The following is displayed on the status line:

  ```
  1 Full text; 2 Page; 3 Options; 4 Printer Control;
  5 Type-thru; 6 Preview: 0
  ```

You want to print the full document.

- Type 1 (do not press ENTER).

  > The text for MYFILE starts to print.

END OF LESSON 1

This is the end of this lesson. You do not have a document to save. You will use the following procedure to quit.

- Enter the **Exit** command, **F7**.
- Type N to indicate that you do not wish to save the document.
- Type Y to indicate that you want to exit WordPerfect.
- When you see the DOS prompt, remove the disks from the disk drives.
- Turn OFF both the monitor and the computer.

SUMMARY

In this lesson many of the terms and concepts that are necessary to use word processor are introduced.

- Uppercase letters are entered by using either the SHIFT key or the CAPS LOCK key. To enter special characters that appear on the upper half of a key, the SHIFT key must be held down, even if the CAPS LOCK key has been pressed.
- Words are not split between two lines, but are placed complete on one line through a feature called wordwrap. You press ENTER only at the end of a paragraph or to insert a blank line.
- The text can be deleted in the following ways:

DELETE	The character the cursor is on
BACKSPACE	The character to the left of the cursor
CTRL/BACKSPACE	The word the cursor is on
CTRL/END	Text from the cursor position to the end of the line
CTRL/PgDn	Text from the cursor position to the end of the page

- The cursor can be moved in the following ways:

UP ARROW	Up one line
DOWN ARROW	Down one line
LEFT ARROW	Left one position
RIGHT ARROW	Right one position
CTRL/LEFT	Left one word
CTRL/RIGHT	Right one word
HOME,HOME,UP ARROW	Beginning of the document
HOME,HOME,DOWN ARROW	End of the document
HOME,LEFT ARROW	Left edge of the document
HOME,RIGHT ARROW	Right edge of the document
PgUp	The first line of the text on the previous page
PgDn	The first line of the text on the following page

- If the text is too long to fit on the screen, you can still see it all as it scrolls up or down when the UP ARROW or DOWN ARROW key is pressed.
- Pressing the INS key toggles between "typeover" and "insert" mode. In typeover mode, the character you type replaces the one the cursor is on, whereas in insert mode, the character the cursor is on and those to the right move over.
- Spelling can be checked by using the Spell program.
- Thesaurus can be used to find an alternative word.
- A valid filename is one to eight characters in length, followed by an optional extension. Do not use an asterisk (*), colon (:), or question mark (?) in a filename.
- Commands in WordPerfect are given through the use of function and other special keys, by themselves, or in conjunction with the CTRL, SHIFT, and ALT keys.

- The following commands are presented:

ALT/F4	Mark a block
F1	Cancel a command previously given or undo an unwanted command
CTRL/F4	Move a marked block
F7	Exit (WordPerfect or a command screen)
CTRL/F2	Enter Spell
ALT/F1	Enter Thesaurus
F5	Display directory (List files)
F5,1	Retrieve a file from disk
SHIFT/F7,1	Print the document currently on the screen

REVIEW QUESTIONS

1. Why should you not press the ENTER key while entering text? When should it be pressed? ______

2. What keys move the cursor without affecting the text? ______

3. How can you correct typing errors? ______

4. How do you mark a block of text to be deleted? ______

5. What does it mean to say that the text "scrolls"? ______

6. What is the maximum number of characters that can be used in a filename? ______

7. Define "wordwrap." ______

8. What does "typeover" mean? ______

9. Why do you have to save files? ______________________________

____

____

10. Can the Speller find all your errors? Explain ______________________

____

____

EXERCISES

Exercise 1

1. Enter the text below. (Your document need not look exactly as it appears here.)
2. Check the spelling.
3. Save the file as WP1EX1.
4. Print the document.

MEMORANDUM

DATE: September 14, 1989

FROM: Lonnie Waters, Social Chairperson

SUBJECT: Fall Picnic

Don't forget to attend this year's fall picnic, to be held at the Forest Glade Regional Park on Saturday, September 23, 1989, from 11:00 am to 6:00 pm.

There will be lots of events for the entire family. We'll hold a fishing derby, and there will be races and games for all ages.

You can't beat the price: the food is free to employees and their families. Sign up by the cafeteria.

And don't forget to bring your umbrellas and rain coats, in case it rains as it did at last year's picnic.

Exercise 2

1. Enter the text below. (Your document need not look exactly as it appears here.)
2. Check the spelling.
3. Save the file as WP1EX2.
4. Print the document.

September 29, 1989

Mrs. Mildred Adams, Librarian
American Historical Society
1776 Freedom Road
Philadelphia, PA

Dear Mrs. Adams:

I am writing a term paper on quotations of American presidents, focusing on their views of how government should be run. It is easy to find famous quotations for some presidents. Washington, Lincoln, both Roosevelts, and Kennedy are well represented in my research notes.

Could you help me find other noteworthy, if obscure, quotes of the presidents? I've tried Bartlett's "Quotations" and several history textbooks in the school library.

Thank you for your time and patience.

Sincerely,

Donna Lee Light

Exercise 3

1. Enter the text below. (Your document need not look exactly as it appears here.)
2. Check the spelling.
3. Save the file as WP1EX3.
4. Print the document.

Product Initiative Report:
Water Saddle

Al Jenkins, Product Development

Our department is pleased to announce its latest product invention, for advanced testing and market analysis. For years, Cowpokes, Inc. has led the industry in developing innovative products for cattle ranches and rodeos. Recently, our department took a look at dude ranches, and found that the demand is growing despite a very low return rate. One of the most frequently mentioned complaints of guests was saddle sores.

Therefore, we initiated design and preliminary testing of a revolutionary new water saddle. Like a water bed, its shape conforms to that of the rider, eliminating those bruising pressure points and reducing the tendency to slide about, causing chafing.

The water bag is double sealed in flexible but durable vinyl which simulates the look of cowhide. Preliminary testing indicates more comfort to the rider, but a need to reduce wave oscillations. We have some ideas, but this is a subject for advanced testing.

Lesson 2
Formatting Documents

Objectives

Upon completion of the material presented in this lesson you should be able to do the following:

- Recognize the default format for printing.
- Specify various printing options:

tab set	fonts
margins	line indentation
line spacing	paragraph indentation
justification	centering text
paper size/type	underline
page numbering	bold

- Understand revealed codes
- Quickly save text
- Switch to the second document on WordPerfect
- Print in "hanging" paragraph format

STARTING OFF

Start WordPerfect on the computer by following the instructions given in the introduction to this module. The data disk from the first lesson should be in drive B.

Let's retrieve a document file onto the computer. The file to retrieve is MYFILE, which you saved at the end of the previous lesson. You retrieved it once before, using the List Files command, F5, and the Retrieve option. You will use a different method this time since you know the name of the file to be retrieved.

- Enter the **Retrieve** command, which is **SHIFT/F10**.

> The message **Document to be Retrieved:** appears on the status line.

- Type MYFILE and press **ENTER**.

> The text from the previous lesson is displayed on the screen.

DEFAULT FORMAT FOR PRINTING

You might have noticed that when you printed the text at the end of the first lesson, it was printed just about the way it was displayed on the screen. The only difference was that the text was printed *right justified,* or aligned at the right margin by having the proper number of spaces embedded between words. Since the screen display and print formats you used were preset by WordPerfect (you were using the default settings), the document may not have been printed in the format you had in mind.

You can change any of the default settings by entering *codes* into the document. Different codes govern margins, spacing, tab set, and so forth. These codes tell WordPerfect how the document should look on the screen or on the printout. Codes are embedded in the text and affect the text that follows, until another code is embedded to change the format again. It is possible to view both the text and the embedded codes at the same time, and you will be doing this a little later. You can delete embedded codes just as you would delete any character.

There are three different formats to consider: Line, Page, and Print. **Line format** includes the tab settings, margins, and line spacing. **Page format** includes the size of the printed page, top margin, and page numbering. **Print format** includes lines per inch and justification (alignment of text on the right margin). The latter two formats do not affect the way the text is displayed on the screen, just the way it is printed.

LINE FORMAT

You will work with the line format first.

- Enter the **Line Format** command, which is **SHIFT/F8**.

> The following is displayed on the status line:

```
1 2 Tabs; 3 Margins; 4 Spacing; 5 Hyphenation;
6 Align Char: 0
```

You want to look at three items: tabs, margins, and spacing.

Setting Tabs

- Select option **1** (do not press ENTER) to look at tabs.

  > The screen of Screen Display 2-1 appears. Notice the bottom half.

A ruler line is shown displaying all column numbers. On the dotted line "L" entries indicate where the tabs are set initially. They are preset for every five spaces.

- To set a tab, all you have to do is either type the column number where you want to set the tab *or* move the cursor to the column where you want to set the tab and type **L.**
- To clear a tab, you move the cursor to the L you wish to delete and press the DEL key.
- To clear all tabs, enter the Delete EOL command, which is CTRL/END.

You will delete all tabs, then set tabs at columns 15 and 20. You will then delete the tab at column 20.

```
Records of transactions, contracts and inventories form the basis
that allows business to be conducted in an orderly manner. The
earliest writing, cuneiform inscriptions on clay tablets, often
kept business records.  Inventions which have lowered the cost or
increased the speed for an individual to write a document have
resulted in increased business productivity.  These inventions
include paper, ball point pens, and typewriter.  The personal
computer did not become a success until it became useful for
business.  Today, word processing is the most common business use
of personal computers.










L....L....L....L....L....L....L....L....L....L....L....L....L....L....L....L...
0123456789012345678901234567890123456789012345678901234567890123456789012345678
         20        30        40        50        60        70        80
Delete EOL (clear tabs); Enter number (set tab); Del (clear tab);
Left; Center; Right; Decimal; .= Dot leader; Press EXIT when done.
```

Screen Display 2-1

- Enter **CTRL/END**. That is, hold down the key marked **CTRL** and press the **END** key.

  > All the L's disappear from the ruler line.

- Press the **RIGHT ARROW** key five times, then type L.

  > An L appears on column 15 of the ruler line.

- Now type 20 and press **ENTER**.

  > An L appears on column 20 of the ruler line.

- Now place the cursor on column 20 and press the **DEL** key.

  > The L on column 20 disappears.

- Press the **Exit** key, **F7**, to exit the tab screen.

NOTE ■ Tabs can also be set by pressing R, C, or D, instead of L. The effect of setting tabs by using characters R and D is discussed in the next lesson. The effect of using C is not discussed.

Display Ruler Line

If you want to see the tab settings while you are working on a document, you can display the *tab ruler line* at the bottom of the screen.

- Enter the **Screen** command, which is **CTRL/F3**.

  > The following options appear on the status line:

  ```
  0 Rewrite; 1 Window; 2 Line Draw; 3 Ctrl/Alt
  keys; 4 Colors; 5 Auto Rewrite: 0
  ```

The message and options displayed are not explained here since they do not pertain to the current topic.

- Type 1 (no ENTER) for Window.

  > The message

  ```
  # Lines in this Window: 24
  ```

  appears on the status line.

- Press the **UP ARROW** key.

  > The tab ruler line is displayed at the bottom of the screen, as seen in Screen Display 2-2.

A triangle indicates a tab setting; a bracket ([or]) indicates a margin setting. When a tab and margin setting are in the same position, a brace ({ or }) is displayed.

```
Records of transactions, contracts and inventories form the basis
that allows business to be conducted in an orderly manner. The
earliest writing, cuneiform inscriptions on clay tablets, often
kept business records.  Inventions which have lowered the cost or
increased the speed for an individual to write a document have
resulted in increased business productivity.  These inventions
include paper, ball point pens, and typewriter.  The personal
computer did not become a success until it became useful for
business.  Today, word processing is the most common business use
of personal computers.




# Lines in this Window: 23
```

Screen Display 2-2

- Press ENTER.

Margin Settings

Let's leave the tab ruler line on the screen as you look at the margin settings.

- Place the cursor at the beginning of the document by using **HOME, HOME**, and **UP ARROW**.
- Enter the **Line Format** command, **SHIFT/F8**.
- Type **3** to look at the margin settings.

  > The following is displayed on the status line:

  `[Margin Set] 10 74 to Left =`

The default setting for the left margin is 10, and the right margin is 74. Since there are 85 columns on an 8½-inch paper (10 columns to an inch), the default setting for both margins is 1 inch. Let's change these to column numbers 20 and 60.

- Type 20 and press **ENTER**.

  > Now it asks for the right margin.

- Type 60 and press **ENTER**.

  > The tab ruler line reflects the new margin settings.

  > The first column of the screen is now the column 20 of the printed document. The width of the text on the screen shrinks.

The margin settings will remain at 20 and 60 until you embed another code to change them. If you want to know what the margin settings are at a specific position in the text, leave the tab ruler line in view at the bottom of the screen and move the cursor to that position. The tab ruler line always indicates the tab and margin settings at the cursor position.

PRACTICE TIME Get a printout of the document on the computer.

Line Spacing

Let's look at one more item in the Line format: spacing.

- Position the cursor at the very beginning of the text.
- Enter **SHIFT/F8**, then type **4**.

  > The message

  ```
  [Spacing Set] 1
  ```

  appears on the status line.

That means it is now on single spacing, or 1. If you want to change the spacing to double spacing, type **2** and press ENTER. If you want triple spacing, type **3** and press ENTER. You can try changing it on your own. Just make sure to set it back to 1 before going on.

PAGE FORMAT

- Enter the **Page Format** command by entering **ALT/F8**.

  > The page format menu shown in Screen Display 2-3 is displayed.

You will look at the page length and top margin to examine the default values. You will also learn how to print page numbers.

```
Page Format

     1 - Page Number Position

     2 - New Page Number

     3 - Center Page Top to Bottom

     4 - Page Length

     5 - Top Margin

     6 - Headers or Footers

     7 - Page Number Column Positions

     8 - Suppress for Current page only

     9 - Conditional End of Page

     A - Widow/Orphan

Selection: 0
```

Screen Display 2-3

Page Length

- Type 4.

  > The screen of Screen Display 2-4 is displayed.

Currently the settings are 66 for page length and 54 lines of text per page. If you want to change a setting, you can type **1** (letter paper, which is the current setting), **2** (for legal size paper), or **3** (if you'd like to set it to something else). Since you do not wish to change any setting, just press ENTER.

- Press **ENTER**.

  > The Page Format menu appears again.

Top and Bottom Margins

- Type 5.

  > The message **Set half-lines (12/inch) from 12 to** appears on the bottom line.

The top margin and bottom margins are counted in half-lines. There are 12 half-lines per inch, (6 lines per inch). The top margin is

```
Page Length

     1 - Letter Size Paper: Form Length = 66 lines (11 inches)
         Single Spaced Text lines = 54 (This includes lines
         used for Headers, Footers and/or page numbers.)

     2 - Legal Size Paper: Form Length = 84 lines (14 inches)
         Single Spaced Text Lines = 72 (This includes lines
         used for Headers, Footers and/or page numbers.)

     3 - Other (Maximum page length = 108 lines.)

Current Settings

     Form Length in Lines (6 per inch):  66

     Number of Single Spaced Text Lines: 54




Selection: 0
```

Screen Display 2-4

currently set to 1 inch (12 half-lines). Again, you do not wish to change this default.

- Return to the text by pressing **ENTER** twice.

Paging

When you have a long, multiple-page document, WordPerfect shows you where the printer will advance to a new page. These are known as *soft page breaks* and are shown as a line of hyphens on the text on the screen. As you look over the document, you may find that a soft page break will occur at some inappropriate place. For example, you do not want a page break to occur after printing just one line of a paragraph or in the middle of a table. In such a case you need manually to enter a page break, known as a *hard page break*. A hard page break is inserted by entering CTRL/ENTER at the appropriate place.

- Place the cursor at the beginning of the second to the last sentence. That is on "T" of "The personal computer did not become a success until it became. . . ."
- Enter **CTRL/ENTER**.

> The paragraph is split into two paragraphs, and a double line appears between the two paragraphs as seen in Screen Display 2-5.

- Print MYFILE.

> The two paragraphs are printed on separate pages.

Page Numbering

When you are creating a multiple page document, you may want to print the page number on each page.

- Send the cursor to the beginning of the text.
- Enter the **Page Format** screen by entering **ALT/F8** followed by **1** (do not press ENTER).

> The screen shown in Screen Display 2-6 appears.

The page numbers can be requested to be printed in one of eight positions. You will have it printed on bottom center, which is option 6.

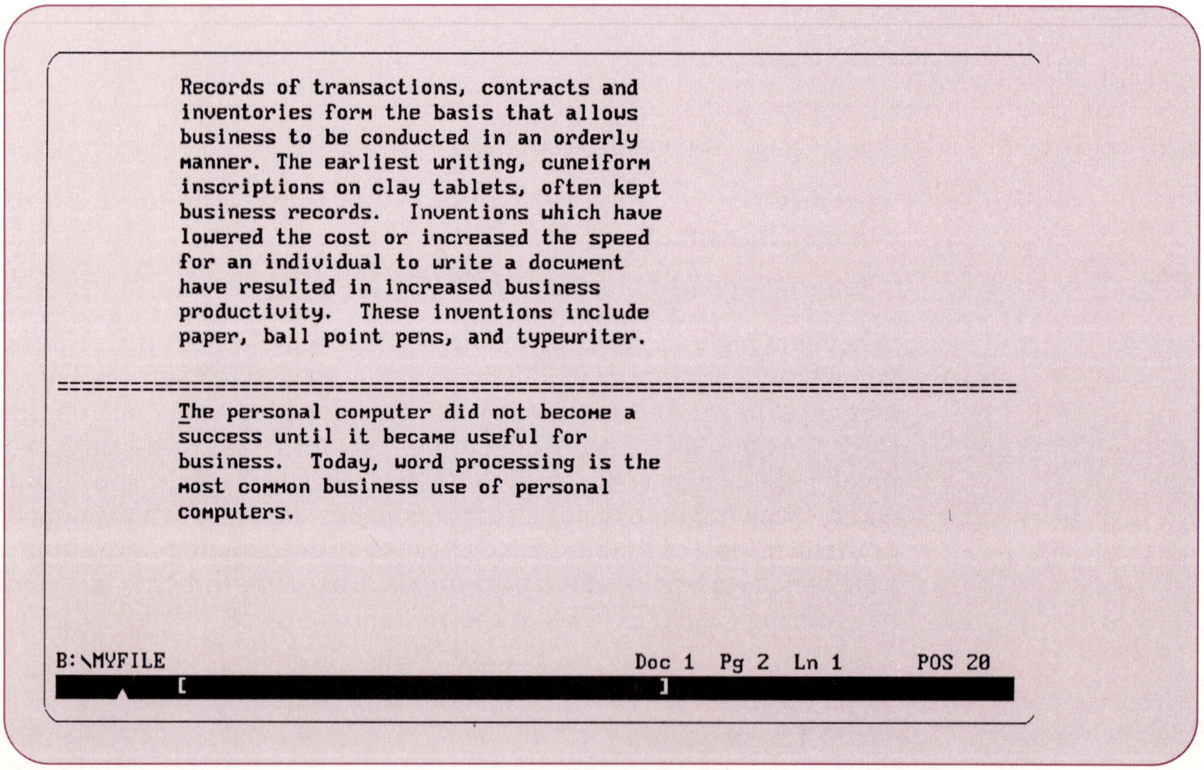

Screen Display 2-5

```
Position of Page Number on Page

     0 - No page numbers

     1 - Top left of every page

     2 - Top center of every page

     3 - Top right of every page

     4 - Top alternating left & right

     5 - Bottom left of every page

     6 - Bottom center of every page

     7 - Bottom right of every page

     8 - Bottom alternating left & right


Selection: 0
```

Screen Display 2-6

- Type 6 (do not press ENTER).

  > The Page Format screen is displayed.

- Press **ENTER** to return to the document.

PRACTICE TIME Print the text to look at the page numbering.

PRINT FORMAT

- Enter the **Print Format** command, **CTRL/F8**.

  > The Print Format menu of Screen Display 2-7 appears on the screen.

Characters/Lines per Inch

The number of characters per inch is the *pitch*. As you can see, the pitch is 10. That is, currently, the printer prints 10 characters per inch. Similarly, the number of lines per inch is set to 6.

```
Print Format

     1 - Pitch                          10
         Font                           1

     2 - Lines per Inch                 6

   Right Justification                  On
     3 - Turn off
     4 - Turn on

   Underline Style                      5
     5 - Non-continuous Single
     6 - Non-continuous Double
     7 - Continuous Single
     8 - Continuous Double

     9 - Sheet Feeder Bin Number        1

     A - Insert Printer Command

     B - Line Numbering                 Off

Selection: 0
```

Screen Display 2-7

Justification

You will notice that the Right Justification is ON. Although the screen display does not reflect it, when the text is printed, the right margin is aligned. That is, enough blank spaces are inserted in each line so that the right margin is flush.

You want to change the justification setting.

- Type 3 (do not press ENTER) to select "no justification."

  > The word ON that appeared to the right of Right Justification changes to OFF.

- Press **ENTER** to return to the text.

PRACTICE TIME

1. Get a printout of the document on the computer and compare it to the previous printout.
2. Change the Justification back to **Yes** (by typing **4** on the Print Format menu).
3. Return to the text.

REVEALING CODES

Before going any further, let's look at the codes that have been embedded in your document.

- Enter the **Reveal Codes** command, which is **ALT/F3**.

  > The tab ruler line moves to the middle of the screen, and beneath it is the same text that appears above the tab ruler line, except with embedded codes revealed, as seen in Screen Display 2-8.

You can see the codes embedded in the rest of the document by scrolling, using the arrow keys.

What a mess! Every time you changed a setting you inserted some code. The tab settings and margins that were changed at the beginning of the document embedded the codes **[Tab Set: L0,L5,L15]** and **[Margin Set:20,60]**. Since you turned the justification OFF and then ON, you see **[Rt Just Off]** followed immediately by **[Rt Just On]**. If you changed spacing, there are codes indicating that, too. The code **[HRt]** (Hard Return) shows where you pressed the ENTER key. The code **[SRt]** (Soft Return) shows where word wraparound took place. The

```
_         Records of transactions, contracts and
          inventories form the basis that allows
          business to be conducted in an orderly
          manner. The earliest writing, cuneiform
          inscriptions on clay tablets, often kept
          business records.  Inventions which have
          lowered the cost or increased the speed
B:\MYFILE                                    Doc 1  Pg 1  Ln 1      POS 10
[Pos Pg#:6][Rt Just Off][Rt Just On]_[Tab Set:L0,L5,L15][Margin Set:20,60]Record
s of transactions, contracts and[SRt]
inventories form the basis that allows[SRt]
business to be conducted in an orderly[SRt]
manner. The earliest writing, cuneiform[SRt]
```

Screen Display 2-8

hard page break you entered inserted **[HPg]**. (Soft page breaks embed **[SPg]**.) For page numbering, the code is **[Pos Pg#:6]**.

It was mentioned earlier that it is possible to remove an embedded code as though it were a character. You will start by changing the margin settings back to default values.

NOTE ■ Obviously, you will leave in those codes needed to format the document the way you want.

- Place the cursor to the right of the margin code, **[Margin Set:20,60]**, using the arrow keys.
- Press the **BACKSPACE** key.

  > The margin code disappears.

  > The text appearing above the tab ruler line widens.

When you deleted the code for the new margin setting, the text went back to the default margin setting, which is 10,74.

PRACTICE TIME

Delete other embedded codes as well, such as [Tab Set. . .], [Rt Just Off], [Rt Just On], etc. Leave [HRt] and [SRt] only.

- Press the **SPACE BAR** to return to normal screen.

SWITCH SCREEN

To illustrate the rest of the topics, you will start a second document without erasing the first from the main memory.

- Enter the **Switch** command, which is **SHIFT/F3**.

  > A blank WordPerfect screen appears. Notice the status line. You are now in **Doc 2**.

You can switch from one document to the other by using the Switch command.

- Switch back to **Doc 1** by entering **SHIFT/F3**.

  > The first document is displayed again. You can work on it if you choose to do so.

- Switch to **Doc 2**. You will enter a new document.

LINE INDENTATION

Suppose that you want to indent the first line of a paragraph five spaces. You accomplish this by setting the tab stop five spaces in from the left margin. Then, before you type the text, you press the TAB key, just as you would on a typewriter.

The default setting for the tab is every 5 positions, as you can see on the tab ruler line.

- Enter the following text. Make sure to indent the first line of the paragraph five spaces, using the TAB key.

When a computer is instructed to do a job, it handles the task in a very special way. It accepts the information. It stores the information until it is ready to use it. It processes the information. Then it gives out the processed information.

Now look at the embedded codes to see what was inserted.

- Enter the **Reveal Codes** command, **ALT/F3**. Press the **UP ARROW** key until the entire document can be seen below the tab ruler line.

  > The screen shown in Screen Display 2-9 is displayed.

Notice the code [TAB] that was embedded at the beginning of the paragraph. Should you decide not to indent the first line of this paragraph any more, you could change it by deleting the tab code (place the cursor to the right of [TAB] and press the BACKSPACE key).

- Return to the normal screen by pressing the **SPACE BAR**.

SAVING A FILE

Suppose that you decide to save this file (second document) on a disk very quickly before working with it some more. You can do this with the Save command.

- Enter the **Save** command, the **F10** function key.

  > The message

  `Document to be Saved:`

  appears on the status line, followed by the cursor.

- Type a filename, say FILE2, that you make up yourself and press **ENTER**.

```
_    When a computer is instructed to do a job, it handles the
task in a very special way.  It accepts the information.  It
stores the information until it is ready to use it.  It processes
the information.  Then it gives out the processed information.



                                        Doc 2  Pg 1  Ln 1      Pos 10
{                                                        ]
_[TAB]When a computer is instructed to do a job, it handles the[SRt]
task in a very special way.  It accepts the information.  It[SRt]
stores the information until it is ready to use it.  It processes[SRt]
the information.  Then it gives out the processed information.[HRt]
```

Screen Display 2-9

> The second document is saved on the data disk in drive B with filename FILE2, and the document is still displayed on the screen.

NOTE ■ When you save a document by using the F7 key, you first save and then exit the document. That is, the screen is cleared. When you save a document by using the F10 key, you save it and can continue to work on the same document.

When you are working on a document, it is a good idea to save it to a disk periodically. Remember, the document you are working with is in the main memory of the computer, which is not a permanent storage. You could lose the document or at least all work done on it since it was last saved.

PARAGRAPH INDENTATION

Sometimes you need to indent a whole paragraph for emphasis, such as when you are quoting from a book. What you want to do is change the value of the left margin for a little while. You could reset the left and right margins, but there is an easier way.

- Place the cursor at the end of the text, FILE2, by pressing **HOME, HOME,** and the **DOWN ARROW** key, if it isn't already there.
- Press the **ENTER** key as many times as needed to insert a blank line.
- Press the **Indent** key, which is the **F4** function key.

  > The cursor moves to the right five spaces.

Every time you press the F4 function key, the left margin is indented to the next tab stop setting. The left margin setting remains indented until ENTER is pressed.

- Type the following:

The concept behind word processing is a fascinating one. The typewriter has become archaic, stricken by a single technological blow. The concepts of training and productivity have changed, too. The more productive worker is the one who can insert text changes, make corrections, move blocks of text, and otherwise process text rewrites efficiently.

- Press **ENTER**.

  > The cursor jumps back to the original left margin, thus indicating that the paragraph indentation is no longer in effect.

Let's see what codes were embedded this time.

- Enter the **Reveal Codes** command, **ALT/F3**.

  > Screen Display 2-10 shows what is displayed below the tab ruler line.

The indentation code embedded at the beginning of the paragraph is **[->Indent]**. Let's delete it and see what happens.

- Place the cursor to the right of the indentation code.
- Press the **BACKSPACE** key.

  > The text, as it appears above the tab ruler line, is no longer indented.

- Press the **SPACE BAR** to return to normal screen.

And now let's indent it again.

```
the information.  Then it gives out the processed information.


_     The concept behind word processing is a fascinating one.
      The typewriter has become archaic, stricken by a single
      technological blow.  The concepts of training and
      productivity have changed, too.  The more productive worker
B:\FILE2                                        Doc 2  Pg 1  Ln 7       Pos 10
the information.  Then it gives out the processed information.[HRt]
[HRt]
[HRt]
_[->Indent]The concept behind word processing is a fascinating one. [SRt]
The typewriter has become archaic, stricken by a single[SRt]
technological blow.  The concepts of training and[SRt]
productivity have changed, too.  The more productive worker[SRt]
```

Screen Display 2-10

- Place the cursor at the beginning of the paragraph.
- Enter the **Indent** command, **F4**, and press the **DOWN ARROW** key.

  > The paragraph is indented again.

NOTE ■ If you have a function key template, you will notice that there are two Indent commands: F4 and SHIFT/F4. F4 generates the code [->Indent] and indents the left margin to the next tab setting. SHIFT/F4 generates the code [->Indent <-] and indents both the left margin (to the next tab setting) and the right margin (the same number of spaces as the left margin indentation).

CENTERING TEXT

There are times when you need to center a text, such as when entering a title. Let's try it.

- Send the cursor to the beginning of the text by using **HOME, HOME,** and **UP ARROW**.
- Press **ENTER** a couple of times to insert blank lines, and then place the cursor on the first line.

- Enter the **Center** command, which is **SHIFT/F6**.

  > The cursor jumps to the middle of the line.

- Type LESSON 2 EXAMPLE and press **ENTER**.

  > The title is centered, as seen in Screen Display 2-11.

PRACTICE TIME

1. Reveal the codes with **ALT/F3**. Can you tell what codes were embedded for centered text? There is **[C]** where the text to be centered starts, and **[c]** where the text to be centered ends. [C] and [c] work together. If you delete one, the other is deleted as well.
2. Return to normal screen.
3. Save the text as **FILE3** using the F10 function key so that you can continue to work on the same document.

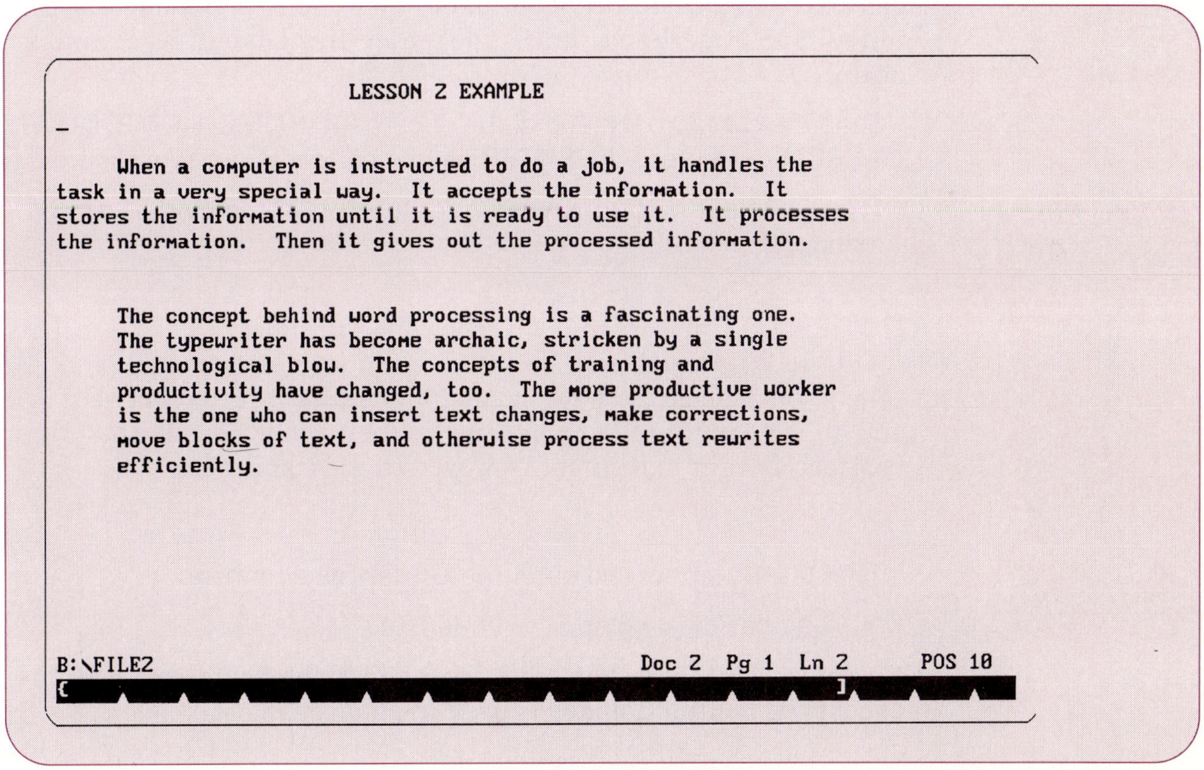

Screen Display 2-11

UNDERLINE

Let's say that you want to underline the title. Since it has already been typed in, you have to mark the title as a block and then give the Underline command.

Do you remember how you mark a block?

- Move the cursor to the first character you want underlined—in this case, "L" of "LESSON."
- Enter the **Block** command, **ALT/F4**.
- Move the cursor to the space beyond the last character to be underlined.

  > The title is highlighted.

- Enter the **Underline** command, the **F8** function key.

  > The block, or the title in this case, is now underlined.

The embedded codes for underline are **[U]**, at the beginning of the underlined text, and **[u]**, at the end of the underlined text. You can reveal the codes and verify this if you wish.

If you decide to underline characters as you are typing them in, you can enter the Underline command, F8. Then the characters that follow are underlined, until you enter the Underline command again.

- Send the cursor to the end of the document (**HOME, HOME, DOWN ARROW**) and press the **ENTER** key twice to insert a blank line.
- Type **This text is to be underlined**, then enter the **Underline** command, **F8**.

NOTE ■ If you were to reveal the codes at this point, you see **This text is to be underlined [U][u]** with the cursor between [U] and [u]. When you type a character at this point, it is inserted between [U] and [u], causing it to be underlined. When you enter the Underline command again, the cursor is moved to the right of [u].

- Type **starting now** and enter the **Underline** command.

  > The text "starting now" is underlined.

Printing with bold characters works just the same as underline, except the F6 function key is used in place of F8.

PRACTICE TIME

Change the text of FILE3 in the following manner:

1. Insert proper codes to make the title "LESSON 2 EXAMPLE" appear in bold characters.
2. Send the cursor to the beginning of the document.
3. Change the left margin setting to 20.
4. Change the right margin setting to 60.
5. Delete the second and third paragraphs. You can mark them as a block and then press BACKSPACE. Make sure to reply correctly to questions on the status line.
6. Insert ENTERs, numberings, and tabs so that the text looks like the following:

```
     When a computer is instructed to do
a job, it handles the task in a very
special way.

1.   It accepts the information.
2.   It stores the information until it
is ready to use it.
3.   It processes the information.
4.   Then it gives out the processed
information.
```

7. Save the file (using F10) on disk in drive B as file **FILE4**.

"HANGING" PARAGRAPH FORMAT

When you number a sentence, and it runs on to more than one line, the subsequent lines look better indented. For example, item 2 in the preceding list should look like this:

```
2.  It stores the information until it
    is ready to use it.
```

When a sentence or item is in this format, it is said to be in *hanging paragraph format*. A hanging paragraph indents all but the first line of the paragraph.

Since the indentation is dependent on the tab setting, you will start by putting tab stops at positions 20 and 24 prior to the first line that needs to be reformatted.

- Place the cursor on the blank line above the line starting with the number "1" (1. It accepts the information.).

- Clear all tabs, then set tabs at positions 20 and 24.

Now you are ready to change the format of those numbered paragraphs with turnover lines, that is, multiple lines.

- Place the cursor on the "2" of "2. It stores the information. . . ."
- Press the **Indent** key, **F4**.

  > The first line of the paragraph moves to the first tab setting.

- Now release the margin (for the first line) by pressing **SHIFT/TAB**.

  > The first line jumps back to the left margin.

- Press the **DOWN ARROW** key.

  > The format changes to hanging paragraph.

- Do the same for "4." Your screen should look like the one in Screen Display 2-12.

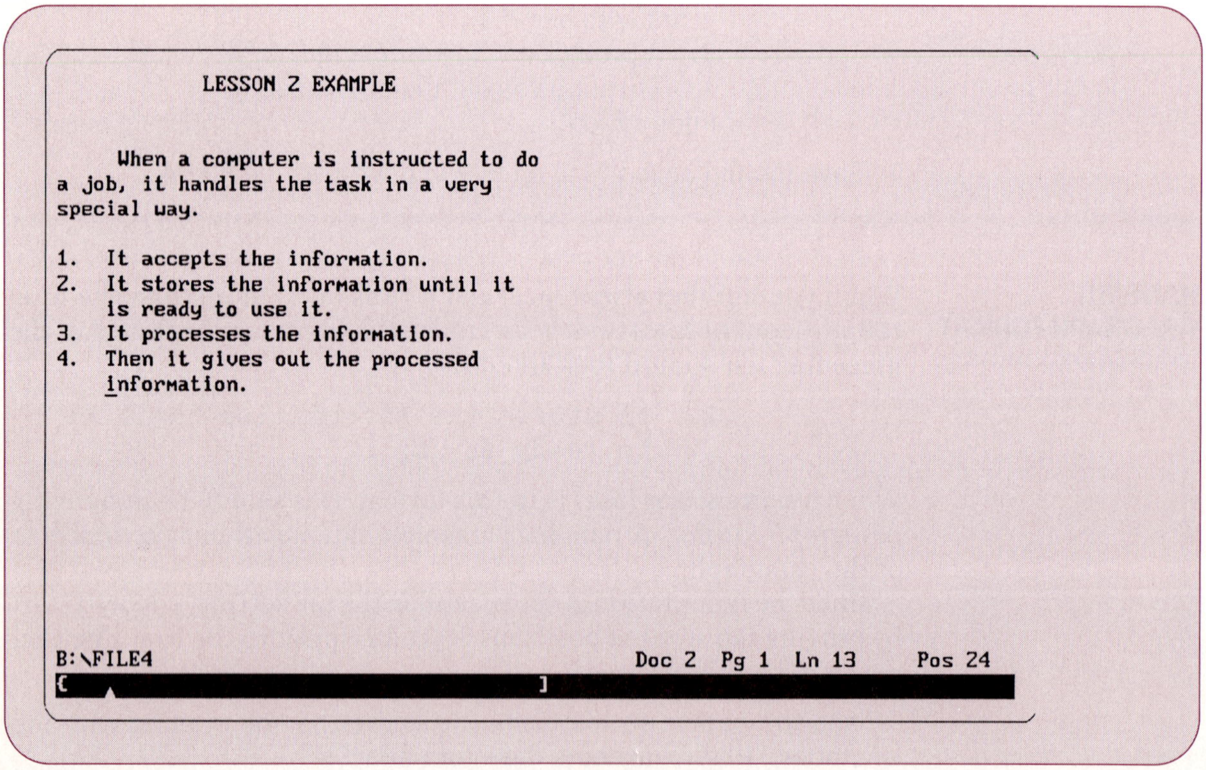

```
             LESSON 2 EXAMPLE


      When a computer is instructed to do
a job, it handles the task in a very
special way.

1.   It accepts the information.
2.   It stores the information until it
     is ready to use it.
3.   It processes the information.
4.   Then it gives out the processed
     information.







B:\FILE4                                 Doc 2  Pg 1  Ln 13    Pos 24
[                                      ]
```

Screen Display 2-12

Reveal the embedded codes. Each time you pressed F4, the code **[->Indent]** was inserted, and each time you pressed SHIFT/TAB, the code **[<-Mar Rel:4]** was inserted.

END OF LESSON 2

- Enter the **Exit** command, **F7**.

  > WordPerfect asks you if you want to save the current text.

- Type Y (do not press ENTER).

  > The message

  `Document to be saved: B:\FILE4`

  appears on the screen.

- Press **ENTER** to accept the filename FILE4.

  > The message

  `Replace B:\FILE4? (Y/N)`

  appears on the screen.

Since you last saved this document as FILE4, WordPerfect asks you if you want to replace the document already on the disk (with the same name): If you choose not to replace the existing document with the current one, that is, if you want to keep both the document already on the disk *and* this modified document, then you have to answer N and enter another filename. You will, however, simply replace it.

- Type Y (do not press ENTER).

  > The message

  `Exit Doc 2? (Y/N)`

  appears on the screen.

- Type Y and press **ENTER**.

  > You return to Doc 1.

- Exit from Doc 1 (using F7) without saving the file.
- When you see the DOS prompt, remove the disks from the disk drives.
- Turn OFF both the monitor and the computer.

SUMMARY

In this lesson many of the terms and concepts that are related to how text appears on the printout are introduced.

- The default values set by the WordPerfect program dictate how a document appears on the screen and on printouts. These values can be changed through the various Format commands (SHIFT/F8, ALT/F8, CTRL/F8).
- The following commands are presented:

SHIFT/F10	Retrieve a file from the disk when you know the filename
F10	Save a document on the disk and still continue to work with it
SHIFT/F8	Line format
Option 1 - Tabs	
Option 3 - Left and right margins	
Option 4 - Spacing	
ALT/F8	Page format
Option 1 - Page numbering	
Option 4 - Page length	
Option 5 - Top margin	
CTRL/F8	Print format
Option 1 - Pitch	
Option 2 - Lines per inch	
Option 3 - Justification off	
Option 4 - Justification on	
CTRL/F3,1,UP ARROW	Display tab ruler line at the bottom of the screen
CTRL/ENTER	Insert a hard page break
ALT/F3	Reveal (display on the screen) codes that are embedded in the document
SHIFT/F3	Switch from Doc 1 to Doc 2 and back
TAB	Indent a line to the first tab setting
F4	Indent an entire paragraph to the first tab setting
SHIFT/F4	Release the indentation (TAB or F4) for just the first line of a paragraph, thus forming a hanging paragraph.
SHIFT/F6	Center text
F8	Underline text
F6	Print text in bold characters

REVIEW QUESTIONS

1. What is the difference between soft return and hard return? Soft page break and hard page break? ______

2. Why would you want to show the tab ruler line? ______

3. If you do not specify left or right margin, what values are used?]1 ______

4. What does "justification" mean? ______

5. What does "hanging" paragraph mean? What commands do you give to create a hanging paragraph? ______

6. How do you indent an entire paragraph? ______

7. How do you underline characters? Center them? Make them bold? ______

8. How do you save a text and still continue to work with it? ______

9. How do you switch from working with one document to another? ______

10. Give the keystrokes needed to make page numbers appear at the top right corner of each page. ______

EXERCISES

Exercise 1

1. Retrieve the letter saved in the previous lesson as WP1EX2.
2. Make the following changes:
   - Center the date on the first line.
   - Make the text unjustified.
   - Change the left margin to 45 just before "Sincerely."
   - Remove the quotation marks from the book title, "Quotations." Underline it instead.
3. Save it on disk as WP2EX1.
4. Get a printout.

Exercise 2

1. Enter the following text. (Your text need not look exactly as it appears here. However, you should set new tabs before entering the recipe.)
2. Check the spelling.
3. Save it on the disk as WP2EX2.
4. Get a printout.

Dear Jill:

I've just come across the most wonderful spaghetti sauce recipe.

1 pound	Italian hot sausage
1 can (4 ounces)	sliced mushrooms, drained
¾ cup	shredded carrot
1	medium onion, grated
½ cup	chopped parsley
1 pound	ground beef
1 can (28 ounces)	Italian style tomatoes
2 cans (6 ounces)	tomato paste
1 cup	dry red wine
1	bay leaf
2 teaspoons	salt
1 teaspoon	basil leaves
¼ teaspoon	pepper
1 pound	spaghetti

In a large pan, cook sausage in ¼ cup water for 10 minutes, tightly covered, stirring occasionally. Remove sausage. In that pan, saute mushrooms, carrot, onion, celery, and parsley in sausage drippings until crisp and tender. Remove. Add beef. Cook, stirring frequently, until lightly browned. Remove any excess fat. Return sausage and vegetables to pan. Add tomatoes, tomato paste, wine, bay leaf, salt, basil and pepper. Cover and simmer 30 minutes. Uncover and simmer 2 hours, stirring occasionally. Remove bay leaf. In the meanwhile, cook spaghetti according to directions on package. Serve with grated Parmesan cheese.

Sounds great, doesn't it? It tastes delicious.

Your friend,

Jackie

Exercise 3

1. Enter the following text. (Your text need not look exactly as it appears here.)
2. Check the spelling.
3. Save it on the disk as WP2EX3.
4. Get a printout.

IDEA PROCESSING

The phrases "word processing" and "data processing" are becoming more and more prevalent in common language. In the mid-1970's, who owned a word processor? What these phrases actually refer to is idea processing. With the recent growth in computer technology available to consumers, idea processing has rapidly evolved.

In many ways, idea processing has opened previously inaccessible avenues for businesses and individuals:

* Point-of-entry data terminals in a store can immediately register sales and provide data for efficient inventory and management decisions.

* Financial models can show a board of directors the cold figures which, in past times, were available only after the decision-making had taken place.

* Form letters no longer need to be individually typed, using so much secretarial time.

* Since businesses and individuals can obtain immediate access to a variety of data sets over phone lines, the possibilities for idea processing seem limited by the mind only.

And the mind is indeed the crucial element in idea processing. For, without an accurate financial model, the best available data are worthless; without proper thought, inventory and management decisions can be detrimental to the company's well-being; without a specific and detailed method for how data are to be processed, access to timely data is worthless.

Lesson 3
Editing Documents

Objectives

Upon completion of the material presented in this lesson you should understand the following "shortcuts" in WordPerfect:

- Splitting the window
- Copying a block of text from one word processing file to another
- Entering text flush right, decimal aligned, and character aligned
- Including current date
- Finding a particular word or combination of words in a text
- Replacing a particular word or combination of words in a text with a specified word or combination of words
- Using mail merge

STARTING OFF

Your IBM PC should be booted up and WordPerfect started. Make sure that you have the data disk from Lesson 2 in disk drive B. You will start by retrieving MYFILE and FILE3 from Lesson 2.

PRACTICE TIME

1. Retrieve MYFILE as Doc 1.
2. Switch to Doc 2 by using **SHIFT/F3**.
3. Retrieve FILE3 as Doc 2.
4. Switch to Doc 1.

MOVING A BLOCK OF TEXT BETWEEN DOCUMENTS

Sometimes you need to take a passage of text out of one document and insert it into another. In WordPerfect moving a block between two documents is no different from moving a block within a document. In doing so, perhaps it will help to be able to view both documents on the screen at the same time. This can be accomplished by splitting the screen into two parts.

NOTE ■ The screen is also referred to as a *window*.

Splitting the Window

- Enter the **Screen** command, **CTRL/F3**.

  > The choices are

  ```
  0 Rewrite; 1 Window; 2 Line Draw; 3 Ctrl/Alt
  keys; 4 Colors; 5 Auto Rewrite: 0
  ```

You want to change the window.

- Type 1 (do not press ENTER).

  > The message at the bottom of the screen reads

  ```
  # Lines in this Window: 24.
  ```

It is saying that this window (the one the cursor is on) shows 24 lines of display. You want to reduce the number of lines in this window so that another window can be displayed at the bottom. You reduce by pressing the UP ARROW key.

- Press the **UP ARROW** key once.

  > The number of lines changes to 23 and the tab ruler line appears. (Remember? You did this in the previous lesson.)

- Keep on pressing the **UP ARROW** key until the number of lines reduces to 9.

  > As the number of lines in this window reduces, the second window appears below the tab ruler line. You can see Doc 2—FILE3—displayed.

- Press **ENTER** to set the number of lines.

You can switch from one document to the other by using the Switch command, SHIFT/F3.

- Switch to Doc 2, FILE3.

Notice the triangles on the tab ruler line (that show tab settings). When you switch to Doc 2, they point down.

Copying a Block Between Two Documents

You will mark the second paragraph of FILE3 as a block so that it can be included in MYFILE.

- Place the cursor on the first character of the second paragraph.
- Enter **ALT/F4** to turn the Block command on.
- Use the arrow keys to block the whole second paragraph, but do not press ENTER.
- Enter the **Move** command, **CTRL/F4**.

The block can be cut (option 1) or copied (option 2). When you cut a block, the text is no longer in the original location. When the block is copied, however, the original stays intact. Since you do not want to remove this paragraph from FILE3, you will use the copy option.

- Type **2** (do not press ENTER).

Now move the cursor to where you want to copy the block.

- Switch to Doc 1, MYFILE.
- Use the arrow keys to place the cursor at the end of the document.
- Enter **CTRL/F4**.
- Type **5** (do not press ENTER).

> The passage from FILE3 is now included in MYFILE, as shown in Screen Display 3-1.

NOTE ■ The format of the inserted document (the passage from FILE3) is changed to style contained in Doc 1 (MYFILE).

PRACTICE TIME

1. Copy the first paragraph from MYFILE to FILE3, inserting it just after the first paragraph.
2. Change back to one window. You can either be in the top window and press the **DOWN ARROW** key, or be in the bottom window and press the **UP ARROW** key. The number of lines must be incremented to 24.
3. Erase FILE3 from Doc 2 (**F7,N,Y**).

ENTERING TEXT FLUSH RIGHT

Most of the time, you enter text by starting with the left margin. That is, other than line indentation, you want your lines at the left margin. If you also want the text aligned at the right margin, you turn the

```
include paper, ball point pens, and typewriter.  The personal
computer did not become a success until it became useful for
business.  Today, word processing is the most common business use
of personal computers.

The concept behind word processing is a fascinating one.  The
typewriter has become archaic, stricken by a single
technological blow.  The concepts of training and productivity
have changed, too.  The more productive worker is the one who can
B:\MYFILE                                 Doc 1  Pg 1  Ln 15     Pos 10
[                                                   ]
task in a very special way.  It accepts the information.  It
stores the information until it is ready to use it.  It processes
the information.  Then it gives out the processed information.


     The concept behind word processing is a fascinating one.
     The typewriter has become archaic, stricken by a single
     technological blow.  The concepts of training and
     productivity have changed, too.  The more productive worker
     is the one who can insert text changes, make corrections,
     move blocks of text, and otherwise process text rewrites
     efficiently.

B:\FILE3                                  Doc 2  Pg 1  Ln 16     POS 27
```

Screen Display 3-1

justification on. There are times, however, when you want the text to be entered **flush right** (aligned with the right margin) without any regard to the left margin. An example might be when you are entering the date at the beginning of a letter.

- Switch to Doc 2.
- Enter the **Flush Right** command, **ALT/F6**.
- Type **December 14, 1989** and press ENTER.

  > The text is entered flush right—even with the right margin.

INCLUDING THE CURRENT DATE

Your PC keeps track of time when it is on. If you do not have a battery-operated clock (which stays on when the computer is turned off), you have the option to enter the current date and time when you boot up the computer. Nevertheless, there is an internal clock that keeps time and date information. You can have the WordPerfect program insert the current date (as kept by the internal clock) into the document.

- With the cursor anywhere in Doc 2, enter **SHIFT/F5**.

  > The following message appears on the status line:

  `Date: 1 Insert Text; 2 Format; 3 Insert Function: 0`

When you insert the current date by using option 1, the text of the current date becomes a part of the document. It is never updated. If you use option 3, Insert Function, however, the date displayed is updated to the current date each time you retrieve or print the file.

- Type **1** (do not press ENTER).

  > The current date is inserted at the cursor position.

PRACTICE TIME

1. Clear Doc 2 (**F7,N,N**).
2. Enter the partial letter given below. The address and date are to be entered flush right.

   1728 Forest Road
   Takoma Park, Maryland
   <current date function>

   Mr. Gary Bradshaw
   Computer Parts Shop
   1234 Byte Street
   Golden, Colorado 81234

   Dear Mr. Bradshaw:

   Please accept my orders for the following items:

3. Save the text as LETTER1.

TAB ALIGNMENT

In the letter you started to enter in the previous PRACTICE TIME, the next step was to specify the items you want to order, quantity, and price, as shown below:

50	boxes of diskettes @14.75	$737.50
5	printer ribbons @11.95	59.75
1	diskette container @9.95	9.95

The first column is typed flush right (at a specific position—19 in this case), the second column is typed left justified (at another specific position—24 in this case), and the third column needs to be aligned at the decimal point (at position 60 in this case). You can set the tabs so that this type of data entry is simple.

- Make sure that the cursor is at the bottom of the letter, LETTER1. (There should be at least one blank line after the end of the text.)
- Enter the tab set screen by entering **SHIFT/F8**, then 1.
- Clear all tabs by entering **CTRL/END**.

You will set tabs at 19, 24, and 60. However, at 19, you want to specify that the entries are to be made flush right; at 24, left justified; and at 60, decimal aligned. You indicate these by using R, L, and D, respectively.

- Move the cursor to column 19, then type R.
- Move the cursor to column 24, then type L.
- Move the cursor to column 60, then type D. Your screen should look like the one in Screen Display 3-2.

```
                                                 1728 Forest Road
                                             Takoma Park, Maryland
                                                       May 1, 1989

Mr. Gary Bradshaw
Computer Parts Shop
1234 Byte Street
Golden, Colorado 81234

Dear Mr. Bradshaw:

Please accept my orders for the following items:







.........R....L...................................D............................
0123456789012345678901234567890123456789012345678901234567890123456789012345678
          20        30        40        50        60        70        80
Delete EOL (clear tabs); Enter number (set tab); Del (clear tab);
Left; Center; Right; Decimal; .= Dot leader; Press EXIT when done.
```

Screen Display 3-2

- Return to the text of LETTER1.
- Press **TAB**.

  > The cursor jumps to column 19.
- Type **50**.

  > The entry is made flush right at column 19.
- Press **TAB**.

  > The cursor jumps to column 24.
- Type **boxes of diskettes @14.75**

  > The entry is made left justified at column 24.
- Press **TAB**.

  > The cursor jumps to column 60.
- Type **$737.50**

  > The entry is made with the decimal point at column 60.
- Press **ENTER**.

PRACTICE TIME

1. Type in the next two items.
2. Insert a blank line after the third item.
3. Reset the tabs so that they appear every 5 positions. (*HINT*: At the tab set screen clear all tabs, then type **5,5** and press **ENTER**.)
4. Enter the rest of the letter.

   My check for $807.20 is enclosed.

   Yours very truly,

   <your name>

   Enclosure
5. Exit Doc 2 by using **F7**. In doing so, save the text again, as LETTER1.

CREATING A FORM

In an office environment there are documents that have standard formats. An example is a memorandum, which usually includes a date (DATE:), the name of the person to whom the memo is being sent (TO:), the name of the person sending the memo (FROM:), and a brief description of the subject being discussed (SUBJECT:). You can have these category names already entered and saved on a disk as a memo file. All you have to do each time you need to write a memo, then, is to retrieve the memo file and supply the missing information. You can then print the memo or save it under another name. The original memo file can be used over and over again, thus retaining consistency in your memo format.

Assume that you want your memo to have the following format (notice that the colons are aligned):

MEMORANDUM

```
           DATE:  <current date>
             TO:
           FROM:
        SUBJECT:
```

Tab Align

In the previous section you did the decimal alignment. You can align on any character at a tab set. You just need to tell WordPerfect what character you want to align on. You want to align on the colon (:).

- Switch to Doc 2.
- Clear all tab settings, then set a tab at column 24 with a **D**.

Now you will specify what character you want to align on.

- Enter **SHIFT/F8**.
- Type **6** (do not press ENTER) to select Align Char.
  > The following prompt appears on the status line:

  ```
  Align Char = .
  ```

The Align Character is currently set to a decimal point (.). You will change it to a colon (:).

- Type **:** (colon; do not press ENTER).
  > The blank screen returns.

You are now ready to enter various headings for the memorandum. The word MEMORANDUM is entered in a normal way.

- Type MEMORANDUM and press **ENTER** three times to insert two blank lines.

  > Press **TAB**.

  > The cursor jumps to column 24.

- Type DATE (do not press ENTER).

  > The characters appear flush right, starting at column 24.

- Type : (colon) and press **SPACE BAR** twice to insert two blank spaces.

  > The colon appears on column 24 and the cursor moves to the right.

- Insert the date function for printing the current date.

- Press **ENTER** twice to insert a blank line.

This works the same as decimal alignment.

PRACTICE TIME

1. Enter **TO:**, **FROM:**, and **SUBJECT:** with colon alignment on column 24. Be sure to enter two blank spaces after the colon.
2. Save the text as MEMO.
3. Clear Doc 2.

FINDING TEXT

There are times when you need to move the cursor to a specific word that you know is somewhere in the document. WordPerfect has a command to help you do just that.

- Switch to Doc 1, MYFILE.

Pretend that this is a long document on record management, and you need to find the word "cuneiform" because you have additional information you want to insert.

NOTE ■ There are two search commands: F2 and SHIFT/F2. F2 is a forward search. It is displayed as **->Search** on the function key template. That means the text is searched from the cursor forward. SHIFT/F2, on the other hand, is a backward search, shown as **<-Search** on the template.

- Place the cursor at the beginning of the document since you will do a forward search.

- Enter the **Search** command, **F2**.

  > The following message appears at the bottom of the screen.

  `->Srch:`

WordPerfect is waiting for you to enter the text you want to find. If the text you enter is in lowercase, the search is not case sensitive. That is, the text is matched with both upper- and lowercase occurrences within the document. The characters you enter in uppercase, however, are subject to a case-sensitive search. WordPerfect looks for an exact match.

NOTE ■ The text to be sought can be a code that is embedded in the document as well. For example, if you are searching for an occurrence of the Bold command, you press F6 when prompted to enter the search text.

- Type cuneiform (do not press ENTER).
- To begin the search, enter **F2**.

  > The cursor stops at the first occurrence of the word "cuneiform."

If you want to find the next occurrence, you need only press F2 twice. A * **Not Found** * message is displayed when there are no more occurrences of the search text.

PRACTICE TIME

Find all occurrences of the word **productivity** in MYFILE.

NOTE ■ When you press F2, the word "cuneiform" still appears as the text to be searched. Just type **productivity**. It will replace the previous entry.

REPLACING WORDS

In the course of editing a document, sometimes you are looking for a particular word that needs to be replaced. For example, you had written a rather lengthy report on a client only to find out that there has been a change in the client's company name. Rather than searching through the entire document visually, looking for the occurrence of the company name and replacing the name, you'd like the WordPerfect program to find and replace it for you.

PRACTICE TIME

1. Switch to Doc 2.
2. Enter the following text, then save (using F10) as the file LETTER2.

November 30, 1989

Mr. Smith
Personnel Office
Republic Engineering
3570 Fruitland Avenue
Maywood, OR 97119

Dear Mr. Smith:

I am applying for the draftsperson position advertised by Republic Engineering. My resume is enclosed. As you will notice, my background includes drafting, presentation graphics, photography, and computer-assisted drawing. My experience is similar to the background stated in the advertisement.

I have also served as the supervisor of three draftspersons during the past two years. Our department was awarded a divisional citation for productivity. While I cannot take all the credit for the achievement, I am proud of our department's teamwork.

I hope to hear from you concerning an interview date and time. In the meanwhile, could you ask somebody to provide me with some information concerning the computer systems used for drafting at Republic Engineering?

Sincerely,

Michael Gregory

Encl.

You just found out that Mr. Smith is no longer with Republic Engineering. The letter has to be sent to Ms. Matthews.

- Place the cursor at the beginning of the letter.
- Enter the replace command, **ALT/F2**.

  > The message

  `w/Confirm? (Y/N)`

  appears at the bottom of the screen.

You can have WordPerfect prompt you for each occurrence of "Mr. Smith" whether you want to replace it with "Ms. Matthews" or not (reply Y), or you can have all occurrence of "Mr. Smith" replaced with "Ms. Matthews" without asking you (reply N).

- Type Y (do not press ENTER).

  > The message ->**Srch:productivity** appears at the bottom of the screen.

The word "productivity" is still left over from the previous search.

- Type Mr. Smith (do not press ENTER).

  HINT: If an ENTER is pressed when typing the search phrase, the program assumes it to be a part of the search phrase and a [HRt] symbol appears.

- Press the **F2** function key.

  > The message at the bottom changes to

  `Replace with:`

- Type Ms. Matthews then press **F2** to start the search.

  > The first occurrence of "Mr. Smith" is found.

  > The message at the bottom asks

  `Confirm? (Y/N) No.`

- Type Y.

  > "Mr. Smith" is replaced with "Ms. Matthews."

  > The next occurrence of "Mr. Smith" is found.

- Keep on confirming the replacement until all occurrences of "Mr. Smith" have been replaced by "Ms. Matthews." You will know that it is complete when neither message (*** Wait *** or **Confirm? (Y/N) No**) appears on the screen.

PRACTICE TIME

1. Replace all occurrences of "Republic Engineering" with "Conway Architects" without confirming.
2. Save the letter as LETTER3.
3. Clear both Doc 1 and Doc 2.

NOTE ■ Replacing text without confirming can cause problems at times. The replace command replaces a "phrase" with another "phrase," not necessarily "words" with "words." You might have been replacing the last name Thorn with Smith. What if there was a Thornapple mentioned in the document as well? It will become Smithapple.

When you want to replace a *word* rather than the phrase, insert blank spaces before and after the phrase (" thorn ").

MAIL MERGE

In Chapter 7 of *Business Computer Systems* you learned about mail merge, used for sending the same letter to different persons whose names and addresses are stored in a file. Review that chapter now if you need to. WordPerfect includes a mail merge function—merging a letter on a file, called the *primary file,* with mailing information on another file, called the *secondary file.*

You will have to create the primary and secondary files in order to use the merge feature. The primary file, also called a *template file,* contains the form letter. It also contains special codes that tell what information needs to be merged, or brought in. The secondary file is a data file that contains the information needed to fill the blanks in the primary file. The files can be created in whatever order you want. It is essential that the order in which data appears in the secondary file matches up with the codes in the primary file.

Here is the personalized form letter you want to send out:

July 20, 1989

Sam Sherman
3983 West Blvd.
Los Angeles, CA 90016

Dear **Sam**:

If you need $2000 worth of equipment right away, it's a serious matter. And borrowing money to make the purchase is not always easy. But because you, **Sam**, have a good credit rating with us, you are now preapproved for a $2000 credit limit.

If you are interested, give us a call and one of our sales people will visit you in your fair city of **Los Angeles** right away. Also, if you need more than $2000 credit limit, **Sam**, please let us know. We'll go out of our way to help you any way we can.

Sincerely,

In the letter above, all text displayed in bold characters is *personalizing information*. Within the form letter, you need to specify where to insert the first name, address, city, and so forth.

All information related to a person is referred as a *record*. Each record contains *fields*: a field that contains first name, a field that contains last name, a field that contains street address, and so on. All records in a secondary file must contain the same fields, listed in the same order.

The fields that are needed for this specific example are as follows:

Field 1	First name
Field 2	Last name
Field 3	Company
Field 4	Street address
Field 5	City
Field 6	State
Field 7	Zip code

Secondary File

When you are entering information for the secondary file, you must press **F9** at the end of each field entry and **SHIFT/F9** at the end of each record. The first record contains **Nancy Gunther** of **Buttons & Banners**. The address is **P.O. Box 2110, Incline Village, NV 89450**.

- Switch to Doc 1, and make sure that it is cleared.
- Type the first field of the first record. That is, type Nancy and press **F9**.

  > The text on the screen appears as follows:

  ```
  Nancy^R
  ```

  ^**R** indicates the end of a field.
- Type the second field, Gunther, and press **F9**.

  > The screen now shows

  ```
  Nancy^R
  Gunther^R
  ```
- Enter the other five fields. Make sure to press F9 after each. Also, do not enter the comma (,) after city.

> Your screen should display the following:

```
Nancy^R
Gunther^R
Buttons & Banners^R
P.O. Box 2110^R
Incline Village^R
NV^R
89450^R
```

Now you need to tell WordPerfect that this is the end of a record.

- Enter the **Merge Codes** command, **SHIFT/F9**.

> An ^**E** appears on the screen.

PRACTICE TIME

1. Enter the information on four other customers. If a field does not contain information (such as no company name given), just press F9.

   Sandra Davalos
   Language Technologies
   2451 Vegas Valley Drive
   Las Vegas, NV 89121

   Bob Newell
   Casino Computers
   1255 W. Second Street
   Reno, NV 89502

   David Small
   Heritage Products
   P.O. Box 320
   Minden, NV 89423

   Christy Juhl

   3000 S. State St.
   Ukiah, CA 95482

2. Save the text as MM1.SCD on the data disk.

NOTE ■ The extension SCD is used here to identify a secondary file.

Primary File

You are now ready to create a form letter.

- Switch to Doc 2.
- Enter the date code for the current date, flush right.
- Press the **ENTER** key four times to insert three blank lines.

Since it is hard to remember which field (first, second, third, etc.) contains what data, you will split the window and display the secondary file as well.

- Split the window. You want Doc 2 to take up 15 lines.

  > Doc 2 appears at the bottom.

- Switch to Doc 1 and scroll the screen so that you can see one complete record.

- Switch back to Doc 2.

The next thing you need to type is the name (First name and Last name) of the person you are writing to, followed by the Company name one line down, Street address, then City/State/Zip on the next line down. This information has to come from the secondary file.

- Enter the **Merge Codes** command, **ALT/F9**.

  > The following appears at the bottom:

  ```
  ^C; ^D; ^F; ^G; ^N; ^O; ^P; ^Q; ^S; ^T; ^U; ^V:
  ```

These letters stands for different codes. For example, pressing D inserts a date function in the document. These codes are not explained in this manual. Right now, you want to press F to indicate that you are inserting a field number.

- Type F (do not press ENTER) to indicate that you are specifying a field.

The First name is the first field.

- Type 1 and press **ENTER.**

  > The screen shows ^**F1**^.

When entering field codes into a document, these codes are treated as if they were actual words or blocks of text. Any spacing or punctuation you would normally place in the text should be inserted around the code. Here, for example, you want a blank space between the First name and the Last name. Hence you need to place a space between the two codes.

- Press the **SPACE BAR**.

- Enter **ALT/F9**, followed by F, then 2 (to indicate Last name), then **ENTER**.

- Press **ENTER** to go to the next line.

The second line is to print the Company name, which constitutes the third field. This field may be blank, however. As you recall, the fifth record, one on Christy Juhl, did not contain the Company name. All you need to do is reply **3?** when asked for a field number. When a question mark is included after the field number, the blank line is eliminated.

- Enter **ALT/F9**, F, 3?, then press **ENTER**.
- Press **ENTER** to go to the next line.
- Similarly, enter Street address on the next line down; and City, State and Zip code on the one after. Remember to insert a comma after City.

  > The screen should look as follows:

```
^F1^ ^F2^
^F3?^
^F4^
^F5^, ^F6^ ^F7^
```

Next you need to insert a blank line; then the salutation should be entered.

- Press the **ENTER** key twice.
- Type **Dear** then press the SPACE BAR, but do not press ENTER.

To make the letter personal, you will insert the customer's First name here.

- Enter the merge code for First name field, followed by a colon (:).
- Enter the following text. Insert the proper merge code wherever you see <FIRST NAME> or <CITY>.

If you need $2000 worth of equipment right away, it's a serious matter. And borrowing money to make the purchase is not always easy. But because you, <FIRST NAME>, have a good credit rating with us, you are now preapproved for a $2000 credit limit.

If you are interested, give us a call and one of our sales people will visit you in your fair city of <CITY> right away. Also, if you need more than $2000 credit limit, <FIRST NAME>, please let us know. We'll go out of our way to help you any way we can.

Sincerely,

- Save the file (using F10) as MM1.PRM.

NOTE ■ The extension PRM is used here to identify it as a primary file.

MERGING

You can now begin the merging procedure. This is where the information from the secondary file is merged into the letter on the primary file. WordPerfect will create five letters (since there are five records in the secondary file).

- Return the screen to one window.
- Switch to Doc 1.
- Clear Doc 1.
- Enter the **Merge/Sort** command, **CTRL/F9**.
  > The following options are displayed:

  ```
  1 Merge; 2 Sort; 3 Sorting Sequence: 0
  ```
- Type 1 for Merge.
  > WordPerfect asks for the name of the primary file.
- Type MM1.PRM and press **ENTER**.
  > WordPerfect asks for the name of the secondary file.
- Type MM1.SCD and press **ENTER**.
  > The message * **Merging** * is displayed.

  > After a while, a document of the merged letters appears on the screen.

Scroll through the letters. Notice the fifth letter, to Christy Juhl. The blank line (for company name) is eliminated.

You can print these five letters or save the letters as a file. As you can imagine, the information you can merge in a letter is not limited to mailing information. You can include account balance, due dates, or any other information that needs to be personalized. To include such information, make sure that it appears on the secondary file.

END OF LESSON 3

- Exit from Doc 1 and Doc 2 (using F7) without saving the files.
- When you see the DOS prompt, remove the disks from the disk drives.
- Turn OFF both the monitor and the computer.

SUMMARY

In this lesson many of the terms and concepts that are necessary to use a word processor effectively are introduced.

- By splitting the window (screen), both Doc 1 and Doc 2 can be viewed at the same time.
- Copying a block of text from one file to another uses the same procedure as copying a block of text within a file.
- Text can be entered flush right, left justified, or decimal/character aligned at each tab set.
- Mail Merge requires two files. The first, the primary file, contains the form letter, along with all codes necessary to tell WordPerfect what information is to be merged. The second file, a secondary file, contains records of data that are to be merged into the primary file.
- The following commands are presented:

CTRL/F3,1,UP ARROW	Split the window
ALT/F6	Flush right
SHIFT/F5,1	Insert the current date as text
SHIFT/F5,3	Insert the date code for the current date
SHIFT/F8,6	Change the character used for decimal/character align
F2	Forward search
SHIFT/F2	Backward search
ALT/F2	Search and replace
F9	Insert a code indicating the end of a field (Mail Merge)
SHIFT/F9	Insert a code indicating the end of a record (Mail Merge)
ALT/F9,F,number	Insert into the primary file, a code indicating the field (number) to be merged (Mail Merge)
CTRL/F9,1	Start merge

REVIEW QUESTIONS

1. What is the difference between the Copy and Cut commands? ______

2. What does "flush right" mean? How do you enter text flush right? ______

3. What does "decimal align" mean? How do you enter numbers with decimal align? ______

4. What happens if you enter a forward search with the cursor at the end of the text? ______

5. What is the purpose of splitting a window? ______

6. What is the difference between entering **date text** and **date function**? ______

7. In a search, what is the difference between entering the search text in lowercase and uppercase? ______

8. In Replace, what is the difference between answering Yes and No to Confirm? ______

9. In Mail Merge, how do you automatically eliminate blank lines for a field that is empty? ____
____

10. What are the two files needed in Mail Merge? Define each file. ______
____
____
____

EXERCISES

Exercise 1

1. Retrieve the file MEMO.
2. Enter the following memo. This exercise also requires you to copy information from the file WP2EX2.
3. Check the spelling.
4. Save the file on the disk as file WP3EX1.
5. Print the letter.

MEMORANDUM

DATE: <current date>

TO: All Employees

FROM: Jill Johnson

SUBJECT: Recipe Contest Winner

Jackie Copeland, of the Finance Office, was selected the winner of the food contest held at our annual fall picnic. The following spaghetti recipe won first prize of $25.

****** Copy the recipe from file WP2EX2 here.

***** Add to ingredients:
½ cup diced celery
Parmesan cheese

Exercise 2

1. Retrieve the file MEMO.
2. Enter the following memo. This exercise also requires you to copy information from the file WP1EX3 to paste into this document.

3. Check the spelling.
4. Save the file on the disk as WP3EX2.
5. Print the memo.

MEMORANDUM

DATE: <current date>

TO: Market Analysis Department

FROM: Dallas Irving, President

SUBJECT: Water Saddle

Al Jenkins of Research has come up with a water saddle which shows some promise.

> ***** Copy text from WP1EX3, beginning with "Recently, our department . . ." and ending with " . . . causing chafing." Indent it 5 spaces.

Please look into the dude ranch market and provide an estimate for product orders over each of the next five years.

Exercise 3

1. Create the following report.
2. Check the spelling.
3. Save as WP3EX3.
4. Print the report.

CHILD-WATCH SERVICES COMPANY
TRIAL BALANCE
<current date>

Cash (111)	$ 1,780.00	
Accounts Receivable (112)	1,600.00	
Equipment (141)	990.00	
Buses (143)	7,400.00	
Notes Payable (211)		$7,000.00
Accounts Payable (212)		1,470.00
Janet Escamilla, Capital (311)		3,300.00
	$11,770.00	$11,770.00

Projects

PROJECT 1

By this time in the tutorial, you have learned how to use an electronic spreadsheet program, a personal data management program, and a word processor. Each of the products you learned to use is produced by a different vendor; the obvious drawback has been that the user interface varies from one product to another. For example, to retrieve a spreadsheet file—say INVENTRY—in VP Planner, you type /FR INVENTRY. To retrieve a database file in dBASE III Plus, you type USE INVENTRY.DBF (or highlight various options with ASSIST). And to retrieve a text document in WordPerfect, you type F10 INVENTRY.TXT.

Using WordPerfect, write a four-page commentary on the software packages you have learned, comparing and contrasting the strengths and weaknesses of their user interfaces. Conclude by describing your personal requirements for a user interface—what you would do if you could redesign all the products.

Format your report as follows:

- Name, class, teacher, and date appear at the top of page 1; only your name appears at the top of page 2.
- Number the pages in the upper right corner.
- Top and bottom margins are 1 inch.
- Left margin is 1½ inch, right margin 1 inch.
- Use underlining or boldface only where it serves a legitimate purpose, for example, for emphasis. Otherwise, it is distracting to the reader.
- Indent the first line of each paragraph.
- Spelling, punctuation, and proper grammar count. This report is a reflection of your thoughts and your opinions. Be clear and concise.

PROJECT 2

For this project you will write a resume and cover letter for a job you would like to get. Keep in mind that the purpose of a resume (or curriculum vitae, if you are entering academia) is to inform a prospective employer that you are interested in that organization, and to prevent the employer from rejecting you out of hand as an applicant. A resume will not get you a job. The most you can hope for is that it will not wind up in a wastebasket along with dozens (sometimes hundreds) of others.

The purpose of a cover letter is to get an interview. Almost no one is hired without at least one face-to-face interview. The interview is your chance to sell yourself. But first you need to get your foot in the door with your resume and cover letter.

In preparation for this project, visit your library, career counseling center, or alumni/ae office, and study resumes. Several dozen books have been written on this subject. Many resume formats are used—there is no single "correct" one. You need to select one that is right for you. A word of caution: In a resume, you are entitled to (in fact, expected to) blow your own horn. By all means, put your best foot forward, but be truthful and concise.

Address your cover letter to a person likely to interview you (or to a particular personnel officer in a large company). Be sure you have an addressee's name and title. Sending a letter to Whom it May Concern is not as effective as to Mr. Sanchez or Mrs. Chu. Use generally accepted business letter format for the cover letter. (If you do not know what that means, do some research.)

Prepare your cover letter as the primary document for a mail merge function. The secondary file must contain at least five addressees to whom you will send your resume. By all means, personalize your cover letter. But be careful to keep it professional and businesslike—do not make it cute or folksy.

Print five (or more) cover letters and resumes.

PROJECT 3

Enter the following text, get a printout, and save it as WPPROJ1.

MEMORANDUM

DATE: December 16, 1989

TO: Dallas Irving, President

FROM: Keiko Pitter

SUBJECT: Water Saddle Market Evaluation

Our recent survey of market prospects for water saddle yielded the following conclusions.

1. The projected sales for five years should be about 1600 saddles.
2. The dude ranch market is but one of three viable markets. Private owners and horseback riding stables are other strong markets.

3. It is important to get in first with a quality product. Potential buyers are very conservative. If our initial product has serious flaws, all our subsequent products will not sell.
4. Cowpokes, Inc., is currently well positioned to enter this market.

Some details of our findings include the following items.

Breakdown by Market and Year

YEAR	MARKET			
	Dude Ranches	Private Owners	Horse Rides	Total
1	50	100	50	200
2	100	100	50	250
3	150	100	50	300
4	200	100	100	400
5	250	100	100	450
Total	750	500	350	1600

Consumer Concerns about a New Product

* Is it produced by a company that can be relied upon?
* Does it represent an improvement, not just a trendy twist?
* Is it reasonably priced?
* Is it durable?

Consumer Suggestions for Product

1. Exhibit at shows. This idea seems so different, people may not realize its value without trying it out.
2. Custom designs. Some interviewees suggested that water saddles might be useful for parades. If they could special order saddles to match their existing tack, this would create another viable market.

PROJECT 4

1. Enter the following document that will be used as the primary file in a merge. The following fields are needed:

Field 1	Borrower
Field 2	Lender
Field 3	Principal

Field 4	Payment
Field 5	Date
Field 6	Rate
Field 7	City
Field 8	State
Field 9	Day
Field 10	Month
Field 11	Year

Promissory Note

<BORROWER> agrees to pay <LENDER> the principal sum of <PRINCIPAL>. By this note, <BORROWER> agrees to make monthly installments in the sum of <PAYMENT> or more, until said obligation is paid in full. The first payment is due on or before <DATE>, and all successive payments are due on the first day of each succeeding month thereafter until paid in full.

This obligation shall bear interest on the declining principal balance at a rate of <RATE> per annum. In the event the undersigned fails to make a required payment within thirty days when due, then the remaining balance of the obligation shall become due and payable in full. Furthermore, if <BORROWER> is more than 30 days late on a required payment, <LENDER> can elect to recover the collateral securing this obligation, as described below, and dispose of same in any commercially reasonable manner, applying the proceeds of such sale toward the balance remaining hereon.

Additional payments or prepayment in full may be paid by <BORROWER> without penalty.

No delay on the part of <LENDER> in the exercise of any right or remedy shall operate as a waiver thereof, and no single partial exercise by the same of any right or remedy shall preclude further exercise of any right or remedy.

The obligation evidenced hereby has been made in <CITY>, <STATE>, and shall be governed by the laws of the State of <STATE>.

Dated this <DAY> day of <MONTH>, <YEAR>.

____

<BORROWER>, borrower

____

<LENDER>, lender

2. Save it as WPPROJ2.PRM.
3. Create a secondary file.

Field 1	Marty Python
Field 2	Bank of Arizona
Field 3	$100,000
Field 4	$1,300
Field 5	December 11, 1989
Field 6	10%
Field 7	Phoenix
Field 8	Arizona
Field 9	11
Field 10	November
Field 11	1989
Field 1	Roni Andrews
Field 2	Bank of Nevada
Field 3	$67,000
Field 4	$612.88
Field 5	October 14, 1989
Field 6	10.5%
Field 7	Reno
Field 8	Nevada
Field 9	14
Field 10	September
Field 11	1989

4. Save the file as WPRPOJ2.SCD.
5. Merge the files and get a printout.

Command Summary

This section is a quick reference for WordPerfect commands covered in this manual. This is not a complete list of all WordPerfect commands. However, some commands that were not covered in the lessons are listed here for your convenience. Try them on your own.

Commands	**Key(s)**
Block	ALT/F4
Bold	F6
Center	SHIFT/F6
Cancel	F1
Delete (ch to left)	BACKSPACE
Delete (ch cursor is on)	DEL
Delete (wd cursor is on)	CTRL/BACKSPACE
Delete EOF	CTRL/END
Exit	F7
Format - Line	SHIFT/F8
Page	ALT/F8
Print	CTRL/F8
Help	F3
Indent	F4
Justification	CTRL/F8, 3 or 4
List Files	F5
Margin	SHIFT/F8,3
Margin Release	SHIFT/TAB
Move cursor	arrow keys
a word at a time	CTRL/RIGHT or LEFT ARROW
to beg of doc	HOME,HOME,UP ARROW
to end of doc	HOME,HOME,DOWN ARROW
Move text	CTRL/F4
Print	SHIFT/F7

Retrieve doc from disk	SHIFT/F10
also use	F5, highlight, 1
Retrieve deleted text	F1
Reveal Codes	ALT/F3
Save	F10
also use	F7
Screen	CTRL/F3
Spacing	SHIFT/F8,4
Spell	CTRL/F2
Switch	SHIFT/F3
Tab (set/rel)	SHIFT/F8,1
Tab Ruler Line	CTRL/F3,1,UP ARROW
Thesaurus	ALT/F1
Typeover (toggle)	INS
Underline	F8

Index

NOTE: IBM = IBM PC; DOS = Disk Operating System; VP = VP-Planner Plus; dB = dBASE III PLUS; WP = WordPerfect 4.2